CAPTIVE
RUMANIA

a decade of soviet

CONTRIBUTORS:

Romulus Boila
Aristide Burillianu
Mircea Carp
Emil Ciurea
G. Ionescu
Mircea Ionnitziu
Radu Plessia
Basil Ratziu
Virgil Veniamin
Constantin Visoianu

CAPTIVE RUMANIA

rule

EDITED BY *Alexandre Cretzianu*

RAEGER · NEW YORK

The present work attempts to give as thorough and faithful a picture as possible of the impact of communism on Rumania during the last decade. The collaborators have endeavored to show what happens when a handful of communists, imposed and maintained in power by the Soviet armed forces and police, undertake to "revolutionize" a country's constitutional and administrative organization, justice, education and cultural life, religion, economy, armed forces, and labor.

The book is the work of a panel of persons who, for the last several years, have dedicated themselves to reading, studying, analyzing, and evaluating all available information about Rumania. Particular attention has been given to official statements by members of the government of the so-called Rumanian People's Republic and officials of the local Communist party; decrees, laws, and administrative measures introduced by the government and offshoots thereof; Communist newspapers and publications; and radio broadcasts. Most of the members of the panel are writers or editors of *La Nation Roumaine,* a newspaper that has been appearing in Paris for the last eight years. The material was originally prepared in the form of specia studies. Editorial changes have been kept at a minimum, but in certain cases the material has been rearranged or condensed.

contents

introduction

The case of Rumania is undoubtedly one of the most instructive illustrations in contemporary history of the methods employed by Soviet Russia to subjugate an independent non-communist country. It also exemplifies the illusions and weaknesses of a democratic power challenged by the Soviet will to expand.

Rumania's case shows how Soviet Russia violates its most solemn international undertakings; it shows the manner in which Soviet Russia interprets such pledges. Rumania's independence and security were guaranteed through formal pacts and solemn statements. Each and every one of these was set at nought by Soviet Russia.

Rumania's case demonstrates how a non-communist country, once subjugated, is forcibly transformed into a communist society by the brutal destruction of its traditional institutions, the suppression of public liberties and human rights, and the prohibition of dissent.

It shows how any attempt at cooperation or coexistence is used by Soviet Russia as a step toward total domination. It shows how any friendly overture is made use of by Soviet Russia as a bridgehead for subsequent advances. It shows the fate of private organizations that allow themselves to be seduced by communist appeals, in the sincere belief that in so doing they serve the cause of understanding or of peace.

Rumania's case shows how the vocabulary and ideas of Western civilization are utilized and corrupted by communist propaganda, their power of attraction and persuasion used deliberately to destroy their content.

It demonstrates how a country, once subjugated, is exploited, its material resources and manpower absorbed into Soviet Russia's economy to increase her military and political might. At the present time, when the Soviet government is waging a full-scale campaign of "anti-colonialism," it is practicing, to the detriment of nine formerly independent European countries, a policy of oppression and exploitation that goes far beyond any known form of colonialism.

The case of Rumania, finally, demonstrates how the process of Sovietization goes hand in hand with a process of Russification. The latter is particularly evident in Rumania, by comparison with the rest of the subjugated countries, because of the Latin background of the Rumanian people. It thus provides the best proof of a feature of Soviet policy—underscored by many analysts—namely, the combination of Imperial Russian Messianism and communist will to dominate.

It is our belief that in presenting the most salient of these lessons to the Western readers, we are contributing to an understanding of Soviet policies and perhaps helping to stimulate the defensive reflexes of the countries that are still free.

In these studies we have sought to provide exact documentation of the facts set forth. The facts themselves are in general clear and brutal. They hardly require commentaries. However, we realize how difficult it is for the Western reader, who has had no personal experience of such things, firmly to grasp the facts. On the one hand there is the oblique use of the accepted Western vocabulary by the communists, and on the other hand there is the essential difference, under a communist regime, between legal provisions and their implementation. A striking instance of this is provided by the Constitution of the so-called Rumanian People's Republic. That Constitution unambiguously proclaims almost all the essential principles of political liberty, and the guarantees of individual security, to be found in the most advanced Western Constitutions. In practice, however, not one of these liberties is available to the people; not one of these guarantees protects the citizen.

Communists explain such contradictions by pointing out that the liberties and guarantees provided in the Constitution must necessarily be contingent upon the interests and security of the state. The judge may not interpret them, and the authorities may not implement them, except in so far as doing so is wholly congruent with the interests of the state, as formulated by the leadership of the Communist party.

Here, therefore, we have a fundamental difficulty that must be overcome in order to appreciate conditions in a communist-ruled country.

Very many travelers and investigators of Western background and up-bringing have been unable to overcome this difficulty. In the existing legal texts, they saw practical rules for the organization and functioning of communist societies. Coming to communist countries with the standards of their own homelands, they could not grasp that a constitution was no more than a propaganda instrument, or that a judge was simply a party functionary.

Under a communist dictatorship, laws set forth obligations for the citizen; they provide for no restraints upon the absolute liberty of action of the state, which is the supreme goal. This basic conception must at all times be borne in mind by the reader, in order to grasp the full import of our studies.

The other difficulty stems from the misuse of the Western political vocabulary by the communists. Such terms as *liberty, democracy, law, right, security*, when used by communists, acquire a meaning wholly at variance with their proper definition. In most cases, they become utterly void of content. Such terms then become mere propaganda expressions, empty appeals to the hesitant conscience of the Westerner. They are used because they are attractive to a citizen of the free world, lulling him into a feeling of security and lowering his resistance to the seductions of communist propaganda.

Thus under communism "liberty" is assured to the individual precisely when he is being subjected to the most ruthless terror—the explanation provided being that he has indeed been set free from capitalist exploitation. And a nation is said to be "liberated" when it has been subjugated by Soviet Russia—with the additional explanation that it has been set free from the exploitation of the great capitalist powers. A country has its "security" guaranteed only when it is protected by the might of the Soviet Union, the Soviet Union which has subjugated it. Other instances abound, but these should suffice. Familiar though this procedure is, it is still a trap that continues to snare the unwary, and its victims continue to multiply even at this late date.

In Rumania, such victims—few in number—were found particularly among intellectuals, a handful of scientists, artists, and writers. The subtle and complex minds of these people were initially impressed by communist propaganda, which, indeed, singled them out for seduction and pressure. Some of these people had in the past collaborated with one or another of the forms of dictatorship, either domestic or foreign, and were subjected by the communists to the torture of making the choice between capitulation and imprisonment. Toward the others, the more attractive means of flattery, material advantages, high formal positions, and the like, were used.

Intellectuals are often subject to a sense of frustration. They may feel that they contribute to a certain extent to the elaboration of spiritual values. Yet, though they may belong to select associations and noble institutions, they lack the feeling of wielding a corresponding influence on political decisions. In this respect, the communists are prepared to give them certain factitious satisfactions. Such people have in the beginning received appointments of a political nature, in parliament and in other political bodies. They have been sought out to participate in various ceremonies. Some have been placed at the head of propaganda movements. But nowhere have these people been allowed to play any truly effective role. Everywhere the ultimate decisions have been taken by some mysterious party member.

On the other hand, the minds of such intellectuals are directed toward abstractions. Their reasoning ranges freely in fields untroubled by the trivial relativities of every-day life. This perhaps explains why so many are surprised to find that politics has a different character from their usual pursuits; they are alien to the usual brutalities and to the cynical and corrupt reasoning involved. Seeking to give a measure of nobility to political thinking, such people fall victim to the most ruthless of ideologies. In the belief that they advance fascinating ideas, they help to destroy societies.

Yet under a communist regime it is assuredly the intellectuals who suffer most. Having a greater craving for freedom, they feel its loss more deeply. Sought out by the regime for its own propaganda purposes, they become its most exposed and most vulnerable functionaries. What scientists, writers, and artists are required to say and write in today's Rumania must fill the heart of any honest man with shame and pain. Under a communist regime none may stay silent. Anyone refusing to speak and write, in defiance of the party's orders, is simply turned out of the "field of labor" and left without a livelihood.

As a whole, the people of Rumania have stoutly resisted the seductions of communist propaganda, as they have resisted the pressures of the communist police. The communists cannot point to a single thing they have achieved with the free cooperation of the people. Everything they have been able to do has been done forcibly, under duress, with the protection of the Soviet forces which occupy the country to this day.

Of all the countries subjugated by Soviet Russia, it is Rumania that is subjected to the heaviest pressure, it is Rumania that is most ruthlessly exploited. All foreign visitors unanimously agree on this point.

The explanation must be sought in a combination of circumstances. The Rumanian people are of Latin origin, and Soviet Russia is only too well aware of the deep resistance stemming from this. The Rumanians have always looked toward the West, and have always shown resistance to suggestions coming from the East. The Rumanians are predominantly peasant individualists strongly attached to their own plot of land. The Rumanians are a deeply religious people, and, throughout the vicissitudes of their long history, their patriotic hopes and endeavors have always been supported by their faith in God.

A Communist party did not really exist in Rumania; there was but a mere handful of communists, who now owe their position solely to the force of Soviet Russian arms, and who maintain that position only by virtue of total submission to the orders of Moscow. They have at no time displayed any original thinking or, indeed, any personal competence.

Yet, powerful as the weight of Soviet subjugation assuredly is, the resistance thereto in the conscience and will of the Rumanian people is equally powerful.

The studies collected in the present volume show that the resistance of the peasantry was so telling in its effects that land collectivization had to be halted before it could be carried out to any significant extent.

At the latest congress of the Communist party of Rumania, held late in December, 1955, public statements by the party's secretary-general revealed that resistance is also great in the ranks of the industrial workers. The secretary-general's report disclosed that less than 10 per cent of Rumania's workers are members of the so-called Workers' Party, and that the proportion of workers within that party is barely 40 per cent of the total membership.

The country's prisons are full of political prisoners: of intellectuals, of members of the clergy of various faiths, of peasants, workers, and students, whose sole crime is resistance to the regime.

The radical changes in the administration and public institutions have been achieved by force, but the minds and souls of the people remain intact. However, continuing pressure and the mounting successes of Soviet Russia throughout the world make the future appear gloomy indeed.

Throughout the centuries, the Rumanian people have struggled for unity and national independence. Yet, while fighting for their own integrity, they have never lost consciousness of belonging to Europe. Aware that their country was on the eastern marches, they have always felt their struggle to be also on behalf of the other European nations. Invasions have invariably come from the east. Against them the Rumanians have always been disposed to fight. The people of Rumania feel justified therefore in their belief that, alongside the other nations now enslaved by Soviet Russia, they have made important contributions to the security and quiet of Western Europe, thus enabling that West to develop the high forms of its own civilization.

The authors of the individual studies have, by and large, direct and personal knowledge of the things and events they describe. This has assuredly helped them to understand them. We trust that this circumstance will contribute, in the minds of our readers, to adding authenticity to this volume.

There are some who feel that personal experience of the things described, or the fact that the writer has personally witnessed the events discussed, throws a suspicion of bias upon the author. A writer, in other words, is suspect precisely because he has too great and too close a knowledge of his subject. For our part, we feel that ignorance is not a guarantee of objectivity.

1

the background

Within its natural borders, as they were established following World War I, Rumania, with an area of 113,998 square miles, was a country comparable in size to Italy or the United Kingdom. At the time of the 1930 census it had a population in excess of 18 millions. Roughly elliptic in outline, bounded by the Black Sea and the Danube, Tisa, and Dniester rivers, it stretched between latitudes 43' 38" and 48' 20" north, and longitude 20' 30" and 30' 30" east. From the three ranges of the Rumanian Carpathian Mountains—the Eastern, Southern, and Western, whose highest peaks exceed 7,500 feet and which enclose the Transylvanian plateau—the land drops gradually downward to the plains of the girdling rivers. Viewed on a relief map, Rumania is strikingly reminiscent of a moated citadel, whose ramparts face respectively toward the center of Europe, toward the Danubian and Balkan regions, and toward the eastern reaches of the continent. This treble exposure accounts in part for the complex synthesis of three widely differing civilizations, which is the main trait of Rumanian culture. The country lies indeed at an immemorial crossroads of Europe's North and South, between the Occident and the incipient Orient.

The significance of Rumania's geographical position is enhanced by the riches of its soil and subsoil. While it is rightly considered a predominantly agricultural country, with more than three-quarters of its people engaged in farming, its varied natural resources—petroleum, methane gas, coal, iron, manganese, copper, lead, bauxite, zinc, gold, silver, salt—are of vital significance to any appraisal of Rumania's economic potential. In the mid-nineteen-thirties, with some 28.5 million acres under grain cultivation, yielding almost five million metric tons of wheat, considerably more than this quantity of corn, almost half a million metric tons of oats, and more than 800,000 metric tons of barley, Rumania also produced in excess of 8.5 million tons of petroleum annually. With coal reserves estimated at approximately 2,792,000,000 tons, with an increasingly impressive production of natural gas, and with a vast hydroelectric potential, the country can assuredly be said to possess the requisite bases for an extensive industrialization.

The remotest forefathers of the Rumanian people recorded by history were the Daco-Getae, a major branch of the ancient Thracians, who in the second millennium before Christ ranged over the vast territories stretching from the shores of the Aegean and Adriatic to the western shores of Asia Minor and far up into the Pripet Marshes, to the Bug River and into the very heart of the European stronghold of Bohemia. Settling early in the region roughly bounded by the western shores of the Black Sea, the Danube, the Dniester, and the Tisa, the Daco-Getae came in close contact with the Scythian, Celtic, and Hellenic civilizations. Long before the Romans arrived on the scene, the ancient Greeks had established prosperous trading centers on the Dacian shores of the Black Sea.

Though exposed to the ever shifting stresses and influences of neighboring peoples, the Daco-Getae succeeded in setting up a succession of territorial organizations, headed by powerful kings. The last of these, the Dacian kingdom of King Decebal, was conquered early in the second century A.D. by the legions of Emperor Trajan, and the land became a Roman province. Strongly colonized and organized, the prosperous province soon became known as Dacia felix. The Roman influence, already felt before the conquest, stamped what was to be the Rumanian people with its Latin character, although the province had to be officially abandoned by the third quarter of the next century, before the ceaseless onslaught of the barbarians. The withdrawal of the Roman administration did not mean the evacuation of Dacia, and the manifold ties between Rome and the abandoned province continued through the centuries that passed until the seat of the Empire moved to Constantinople. Indeed it was by Latin missionaries coming from the south across the Danube that Christianity was brought to the people of Rumania in the fourth and fifth centuries.

During the thousand years that followed the abandonment of Dacia, however, the land was to be traversed by various barbaric tribes and peoples, Germanic, Slavic, and Asiatic, in their migratory movements. The Slavs, arriving in the seventh century for a prolonged stay, left deep influences upon the inhabitants. So too did the Hungarians, who came during the ninth century to the lowlands of the Danube and Tisa rivers, and settled in Transylvania, which had been the cradle and center of the Dacian kingdom. Finally, the dark ages were marked by the Tartar invasion of the mid-thirteenth century, that was to have deep repercussions throughout South-Eastern Europe as well as upon the historic developments of the Rumanian lands.

About the middle of the thirteenth century documents begin to mention the Rumanian political formations set up between the Carpathians and the Danube. These may be presumed to have been in existence for some time. The fourteenth century, which saw profound changes in neighboring Hungary and Bulgaria, was particularly favorable to the establishment of the Wallachian principality as an autonomous state. Similar factors favored the emergence of a strong and independent Moldavia soon thereafter, notably the need to secure the existing trade routes, which was to give that principality its military character.

A precarious equilibrium that ensued was soon to be upset by the arrival of the conquering Ottoman Turks in South Eastern Europe. In the prolonged and desperate struggles against these invaders, two Rumanian princes notable for their long and eventful reigns—Mircea the Old of Wallachia (1386-1418) and Stefan the Great of Moldavia (1457-1504)—gained the respect of the Christian world. Stefan, indeed, whose statesmanlike endeavors to rally the forces of Europe against the Moslems came to nought and whose Rumanian armies had to bear the brunt of battle time and again, in the course of the years scoring some astounding military victories against great odds, was titled The Athlete of Christ by Pope Sixtus IV. With Wallachia already fallen into a state of quasi-vassality before the advancing Turks, Stefan's Moldavia was to be the last obstacle to bar the way into the heart of Europe. Thereafter, once Constantinople fell, once the Turks established themselves along the Danube, and once the battle of Mohacs was fought and lost, the Christian world was to suffer successive defeats, the Crescent advancing up to the very walls of Vienna by 1683.

Several of the successive princes of both Moldavia and Wallachia were to inflict temporary setbacks on the Turks in the century that followed the reign of Stefan. The Wallachian prince, Mihai the Brave (1593-1601), succeeded even in uniting, for a short while, Wallachia, Moldavia, and Transylvania, this remaining in the memory of later generations as the embodiment of Rumanian aspirations. Perhaps even more noteworthy than such sporadic military achievements was the efflorescence of culture that marked the 17th century throughout the Rumanian lands. Under enlightened princes, the Church flourished, and learning, printing, architecture, and the arts made great and lasting progress.

The 18th century, which saw the emergence of Russia as a great power, and renewed enterprise on the part of the Habsburg Empire, led the Porte to secure its dominance in the Rumanian principalities by placing on their thrones men of trust and devotion.* The fortunes of war favoring the Turks, there followed a succession of princes, both in Moldavia and in Wallachia, selected by the Porte from among its Greek dignitaries. This is known in Rumania's history as the Phanariot epoch, because most of the notable Greek families that were to furnish the rulers of the two Rumanian principalities resided in the Phanar (Fener) quarter of Constantinople.

The Phanariot century was one of political decay for the principalities, whose autonomy was lessened and whose territories suffered corresponding losses, notably Bukovina to Austria in 1775 and Bessarabia to Russia in 1812. An armed revolt of Tudor Vladimirescu in Wallachia, even though ultimately repressed, brought to a close these troubled times. Rumanian princes once again came to the thrones of Moldavia and Wallachia with the assent of the Porte, and the Peace of Adrianople (1829) between the Sultan and the Tsar established, among other things, freedom of navigation in the Black Sea and along the Danube. The harbors of Braila and Giurgiu, held by the Turks up till then, were given back to Wallachia. After almost four centuries of virtual isolation, the Rumanian principalities once again came in direct commercial contact with the West, and could undertake their own sorely needed reorganization and modernization.

Unfortunately, the decades that followed were marked by an accentuation of the Muscovite drive toward the Balkans, and both Moldavia and Wallachia were subjected to long periods of Russian military and administrative occupation (1828-1834, 1848-1851, and 1853-1854). Yet there was steady progress of Western liberal ideas. Revolutionary movements, indeed, appeared in 1848, not only in Moldavia and Wallachia, but also in Tran-

---

* Demetrius Cantemir, the learned historiographer, who became Prince of Moldavia in 1711, was instrumental in tying the fortunes of that country to those of Peter the Great. His purpose in so doing was to try to regain from the Turks that part of Bessarabia, and hence of Moldavia, known as the Budjak.

sylvania. In the latter province, the Rumanians, who were the majority population, rose against Magyar rule and claimed the rights that had been denied them. The revolts were suppressed, but they served at least to arouse interest in the Danubian principalities in the West.

The Congress of Paris (1856) brought to a close the Crimean war and marked the restoration to Moldavia of three districts of Southern Bessarabia, securing to the Rumanian principalities a role in controlling the mouth of the Danube. Finally in 1859, with a signal support from Napoleon III, Moldavia and Wallachia were united *de facto* by the election of Alexander Ion Cuza to the throne of both principalities. The union was recognized *de jure* in 1862, and in 1866 a foreign prince, Carol, of the German house of Hohenzollern-Sigmaringen, was elevated to the throne.

The long and beneficent reign of Carol I (1866-1914) saw Rumania achieve independence on the battlefield, the country's armies playing a notable part as Russia's ally in the war against Turkey (1877). The Kingdom of Rumania, proclaimed in 1881, was founded on the constitutional and democratic bases of a modern state. Thereafter the country progressed at a remarkable rate, politically, socially, and economically, and its administration, judiciary, and legislature were constantly improved, while corresponding progress was made in education, military organization, and standard of living.

Under King Ferdinand I, Rumania fought alongside the Entente in World War I in response to the strong current of public opinion, and made signal contributions to the final victory of the Allies. Following the war, in response to the freely expressed will of the popular assemblies that met in Chishinau, Cernautzi, and Alba-Iulia, the provinces of Bessarabia, Bucovina, and Transylvania were at long last united with the mother country. Rumania's ethnical borders were confirmed by the peace treaties of 1919–1920. The mere statement of the facts, indeed, as the noted British historian R. W. Seton-Watson observed, "suffices to show that it was the peoples themselves who were responsible for establishing the new order of things." (*Treaty Revision and the Hungarian Frontiers.* London, 1934.) As to the treaty confirmation of Rumania's new borders, Seton-Watson has this to say: "There never was a treaty in modern times upon which so much expert knowledge and minute preliminary study was expended by the picked representatives of many nations."

The international guarantee was confirmed in the Pact of the League of

Nations, Article 10 of which provided that "The Members of the League undertake to respect and preserve as against external aggression the territorial integrity and existing political independence of all Members of the League." Article 16 set forth the means of translating into deeds, when necessary, these obligations.*

The initial weakening of the general system of reciprocal guarantees came when the United States Senate refused to ratify the Versailles Treaty in November 1919. It was to become definite when one year later the Republicans came to power on an isolationist platform overwhelmingly accepted by the American electorate. The course of international events thereafter made it increasingly evident that the guarantee mechanism provided by the League of Nations Pact had become uncertain and inadequate, and that major improvements were called for.

Though Rumania emerged victorious and unified from the war, the country, which had suffered extremely severe losses, both military and civilian, was faced with complex problems both domestic and international. At home its manpower was sadly depleted and its economy was thoroughly crippled. The administration had to cope with the bold democratic reforms that had been promised the embattled people while the war was still in progress. Universal suffrage and the sweeping agrarian reform were introduced.†

The land reform involved the expropriation of large estates and the distribution of land to the peasantry. Some 14 million acres were shared out to 1,393,353 persons. Coming at a moment of deep economic depression, this extensive reform resulted initially in an aggravation of the country's situation. Production, hence availabilities for export, fell steeply. Later, when production rose again, the corresponding betterment of the peas-

---

* To this general guarantee we may add the joint pledge of the allied Great Powers. It will be recalled that President Wilson stated at the Peace Conference, on May 31, 1919: ". . . And yet there underlies all of these transactions the expectation on the part, for example, of Rumania, of Czechoslovakia, and of Serbia, that if any covenants of this settlement are not observed, the United States will send her armies and her navies to see that they are observed. Under those circumstances, is it unreasonable that the United States should insist upon being satisfied that the settlements are correct?"
† Following the peasant revolts of 1907, Ion I. C. Bratianu had as early as 1913 announced that he intended to introduce the two general reforms. (His father, Ion Bratianu, had been one of the leaders of the 1848 revolution, and one of the men who had shaped modern Rumania.) As head of the Liberal Party, he was instrumental in 1914 in convening the Constituent Assembly which adopted the requisite constitutional principles.

antry's living standards still kept the export surplus down. Nor were the general world conditions any too favorable. Domestic recovery came slowly and at great cost.

The sincere and wholehearted support which the League of Nations and the idea of collective security commanded from all of Rumania's democratic parties was not merely idealistic. It had an obvious logic. In order to preserve her territorial gains, and to achieve social and political consolidation, Rumania had necessarily to seek peace and security on the international plane.

To meet the challenge of the revisionist powers, Rumania naturally had to tackle the special problem of consolidating peace and order in Central and South-Eastern Europe. The 1921 treaties of alliance with Czechoslovakia and Yugoslavia led to the establishment of the Little Entente, and this system of reciprocal guarantees was completed by the treaty of alliance with Poland that same year. It must be stressed that these agreements were of a purely defensive nature, and that, furthermore, the participants made every effort to establish normal relations with all her neighbors. Already, on March 3, 1920 the Rumanian Prime Minister, Vaida-Voevod, had defined the country's attitude, in a message addressed to the Soviet Commissar for Foreign Affairs: "Rumania desires to set the bases of her future economic and political development upon a foundation of democracy, at peace and in friendly relations with her neighbors. As for the events and struggles within Russia, Rumania has persisted and will continue to persist in maintaining the principle of abstaining from any interference in the domestic affairs of neighboring countries."

So long as it was isolated, the Soviet Union had given certain indications that it might be prepared to accede juridically to the acquisition of Bessarabia by Rumania. But after the Rapallo treaty with Germany, and, especially, after it had gained recognition by Great Britain, France, and Italy, the Kremlin changed its tune. By the time of the Soviet-Rumanian talks of 1924, it was asking for a plebiscite in Bessarabia. On the other hand, Great Britain, France, Italy, and Japan had recognized that Bessarabia was Rumanian by the treaty of October 28, 1920. With her position thus strengthened, Rumania continued to make every effort to come to an understanding with the Soviet Union. The one condition insisted upon was that the Soviet government abstain from making any formal reservations concerning Bessarabia. On the general international plane too, Rumania contributed in every possible way to such projects as the draft treaty for mutual assistance in the event of aggression, and the draft agreement for the peaceful settlement of international disputes, which for one reason or another other countries failed to support.

Welcoming every move to translate the general principles of collective security into practice, Rumania adhered to the Briand-Kellogg Pact of August 22, 1928, and accepted at the same time the Litvinov proposal for an anticipative application of the agreement as between the Soviet Union and its Western neighbors. The so-called Litvinov Protocol was signed in Moscow on February 7, 1929, with Rumania asking for the insertion of the words, "in order to contribute to the maintenance of the peace existing among them (i.e.: the contracting parties)," so that all confusion be avoided and that the relations among the signatories might be determined as precisely as possible. On that occasion, the Rumanian parliament, in which the National Peasant Party, headed by the great Transylvanian statesman Iuliu Maniu, had the majority, unanimously expressed its desire to live in peace and good neighborly relations with the Soviet Union.

Unfortunately, the Briand-Kellogg Pact came at a time when international harmony and optimism were ebbing, when the preliminary discussion of disarmament (1926–1929) showed increasing divergencies among the great powers. In 1929 the Dawes Plan was replaced by the Young Plan, but the issue of war debts still embittered the international climate. Then two major events occurred: the world economic crisis and the rise of the Nazis in Germany.

In the meantime Rumania strengthened her ties with her partners of the Little Entente by concluding in quick succession the General Act of Counciliation, Arbitration, and Juridical Settlement (1929), and the complementary agreement to the Treaty of Friendship and Alliance, also known as the Statute of the Little Entente (1930). The latter provided for an incipient common executive organ, in the sense that, under certain conditions, one of the three Ministers of Foreign Affairs became the spokesman for the Little Entente as a whole. A joint Secretariat was likewise established.

But while such moves were being made in South-Eastern Europe, France and Britain were acceding to Mussolini's proposal for the creation of a four-power directorate that included the Third Reich. The main purpose of this was to grant progressive rearmament rights to Germany, Austria, Hungary, and Bulgaria, and thus to lead up to a revision of the peace treaties. Hitler's Third Reich was already emerging as the new dynamic power in Europe. Spurred by the energetic reaction of the Little Entente and of Poland, France ultimately backed out, and the Four-Power Pact, initialled on June 7, 1933, was not ratified. Five years later at Munich, Germany and Italy were to revive the idea of the Four-Power Directorate at the expense of Czechoslovakia. They carried the day with catastrophic ultimate results.

Hitler's rise to power had its effects on Soviet policy also. The USSR, initially hostile to the League of Nations, now began to approach the Western democracies and their East-European allies. In 1932 the Kremlin signed non-aggression treaties with Finland, France, Poland, Latvia, and Estonia; but negotiations with Rumania came to nothing because the Soviet government insisted on the insertion of a formal reservation concerning Bessarabia or, at minimum, the recognition of a dispute unresolved by agreement. In 1933, however, the Soviet Union signed the London conventions with its European and Asiatic neighbors, for the definition of aggression. The following formula was adopted: "The act of invading the territory of a state constitutes essentially an act of aggression, independently of any declaration of war. *Territory* must be understood here to mean the territory over which a state exercises its authority in fact."

As a consequence of this agreement, normal relations were established between the Soviet Union and Rumania, as well as diplomatic relations. The exchange of letters between Rumania's Foreign Minister Titulescu and Litvinov on June 1934 that constituted the reciprocal *de jure* recognition, stated: "The governments of our countries mutually pledge one another full and entire respect for the sovereignty of each of our states." It should be stressed that the Soviet government made no kind of reservations in connection with Bessarabia, either on the occasion of this exchange of letters or on that of the signature of the Convention for the Definition of the Aggressor. This implied at least the tacit acceptance of the Rumanian point of view. In recognition of this, Rumania gave her active support and vote to the Soviet Union, when that country was admitted to the League of Nations in September, 1934.

The very next year the dangerous precedent of unilateral denunciation of international agreements was to be set by Hitler's Germany, when, on March 16, 1935, the Third Reich reintroduced compulsory military training. Austria, Bulgaria, and Hungary then sought the abrogation of the military clauses that concerned them in the peace treaties of 1919-1920.

The Great Powers, whose representatives met at Stresa, showed themselves not unfavorably disposed. They agreed, in fact, to recommend to the "other states concerned" to "examine this question with a view to its settlement by mutual agreement within the framework of general and regional guarantees of security." The dismay produced by this resolution, especially in the countries of the Little Entente, was not diminished by the British-German naval agreement of June 18, 1935 which, by permitting the Third Reich's naval rearmament, amply demonstrated the lack of firmness and solidarity of the Stresa powers.

The next international test came when the Italian-Ethiopian conflict broke out. In spite of every inducement and notwithstanding the grave disadvantages involved, Rumania voted in favor of sanctions against Italy. This attitude was to be recalled by Mussolini in 1940, when the Axis imposed heavy territorial concessions to Hungary upon Rumania.*

In the meantime Hitler denounced the Locarno treaty on March 7, 1936, and remilitarized the Rhineland, thus striking yet another blow at France's system of alliances in Europe, hence further threatening Rumania's security. Meeting in extraordinary session, the Council of the League of Nations failed to authorize military action as provided in the Locarno Treaty. Reporting on this, The *New York Times* of March 19, 1936, said: "The strongest denunciation of Germany of the whole day came from N. Titulescu . . . who declared, 'The safety of France is closely connected with our own.' 'If the unilateral repudiation of treaties is to be accepted,' he said, 'it will be the end of international agreement. It will replace the strength of right by the strength of force.'" The failure of Great Britain and France to react by the use of force marked a decisive turning point. From then on the balance of power increasingly favored Hitler. Jungle law prevailed in Europe. The Anschluss, Munich, and the fall of Czechoslovakia were but the unavoidable consequences of Franco-British defaults in 1936. Having failed to stand up on behalf of their own interests on the Rhine, France and Great Britain were in no position to defend Austria and Czechoslovakia.

In Rumania, too, the effects were soon to be felt. King Carol II, with the help of a few unprincipled and compliant politicians, gradually estab-

---

* Titulescu, Rumania's Foreign Minister, had taken an active part in the technical organization of the sanctions. He was fully aware that the defense of Ethiopia's independence was of great interest to Rumania, who might herself one day become the victim of aggression by a Great Power.

lished his personal dictatorship. An authoritative constitution was introduced on February 27, 1938, and on March 30 the political parties were formally abolished by decree to be replaced on December 15 by the Front of National Rebirth.

King Carol had forced Titulescu to resign in 1936, as though he had been responsible for the failures of the League of Nations and collective security. Though Carol announced then that Rumania's foreign policies would remain unchanged, the country's position became increasingly precarious, as did that of all the small countries, whose independence could endure only so long as there was a favorable balance of power in Europe.

To the threats from without, the internal actions of the Iron Guard were now added. This extreme rightist party was attached to Hitler's Nazi movement both ideologically and materially. As Hitler's power grew, the Iron Guard became increasingly menacing, resorting to terrorism and even to assassination. Its propaganda among the peasants took the form of a most outrageous demagogy. To weaken the democratic political parties, King Carol at first showed himself favorable to the Iron Guard. His ultimate aim was to establish a personal dictatorship, however. When he saw how threatening the Guard had become, he had recourse to violent means, but was unable to liquidate it.

Developments in Europe—the German threat against Poland and the Italian conquest of Albania—finally brought a change in the attitudes of Great Britain and France. In a belated attempt to forestall further aggression, the British and French governments extended a joint guarantee to Greece and Rumania on April 13, 1939, and Great Britain concluded a treaty of mutual assistance with Poland. Negotiations with the Soviet government also got under way. The issue of the passage of Soviet troops over Polish and Rumanian territories made those negotiations drag on until late in the summer. Then, on August 23, 1939, it was learned that the Kremlin had signed an agreement, not with France and Britain, but with the Third Reich. With Stalin's complicity in a third partitioning of Poland assured, Hitler unleashed World War II.

The months preceding the outbreak of war had been critical for Rumania. In March, following the liquidation of Czechoslovakia, there had been Hungarian troop movements on Rumania's borders, while on the Hungarian frontiers an estimated 25 divisions of the Wehrmacht stood poised for action. The Rumanian army had been partially mobilized to meet the emergency. But presently, on March 23, 1939, a trade agreement was concluded with the Third Reich, which could be interpreted as a relaxation of the tension that had arisen when the head of the Hitlerite Iron Guard had been executed the previous autumn, shortly after King Carol's return from a visit to Berchtesgaden. Without actually establishing a monopoly in favor of Germany, the trade treaty did set up a plan for economic collaboration, including German deliveries of war materiel, and the creation of joint German-Rumanian oil companies. It was clear that it was Hitler's deliberate intention to dominate Rumania both economically and politically.

When the secret clauses of the Ribbentrop-Molotov agreement were finally published, it was learned that Article 3 of the secret protocol read as follows: "With regard to South-Eastern Europe, attention is called by the Soviet side to its interest in Bessarabia. The German side declares its complete political disinterestedness in these areas." And certainly, throughout the period of close cooperation between Berlin and Moscow, the Soviet Union played the effective role of an ultimate, deadly threat that was used by the Third Reich in its progressive coercion of Rumania.

In dealing with Rumania, the Kremlin intervened diplomatically with hostile intent, employed threatening troop movements, and seized territory by ultimatum. When the Polish chief of state, the government, and part of the Polish army took refuge on Rumanian soil, Molotov raged bitterly at Rumania, and troop demonstrations along the border backed his words. The Turkish government was openly sounded as to its attitude in the event of an overt Soviet move against Rumania, in the full knowledge that this would be duly reported to Bucarest. In the course of a speech on foreign policy on March 29, 1940, Molotov underlined the existence of a dispute with Rumania over Bessarabia. He also said that the Soviet government had entered into no agreement of non-aggression with Rumania because of that fact. In so doing, Molotov chose deliberately to ignore the Briand-Kellogg Pact and the Convention for the Definition of the Aggressor, both of which had been signed by Rumania as well as by the Soviet Union. Soon thereafter, Molotov called the attention of the Rumanian Minister in Moscow to certain alleged border incidents, which he said had been provoked by Rumanian troops. In the most threatening tone, he hinted that serious consequences would follow a repetition of such incidents.

This situation was aggravated by the uncertainty that surrounded the support from abroad on which Rumania might count. On December 14, 1939, the Rumanian government had received a statement from the British and French governments to the effect that the existing guarantees would go into effect *vis-à-vis* the Soviet Union only in the event that Turkey would immediately come to Rumania's assistance, and then only if no opposition should come from Italy. When Italy entered the war against France and Great Britain, one of these conditions automatically lapsed, but soon the military defeats in the West made the guarantees as such inoperative in any case. Once the French armistice was concluded, Rumania found herself alone and isolated.

On the night of June 26, 1940, Molotov handed the Rumanian Minister in Moscow a 24-hour ultimatum, demanding immediate cession to the Soviet Union of Bessarabia, Bucovina, and the Hertza district. Hungary and Bulgaria made unmistakably warlike moves on the country's frontiers. Danger threatened on every side. The Balkan allies held out no hope of relief. Germany and Italy urged compliance with the Kremlin's demands. A desperate last-minute attempt to negotiate met with a second ultimatum from the Soviets. There was no way out.

On the morning of June 28 the Rumanian reply was sent to Moscow: "The Rumanian government, *in order to avoid the grave consequences of a recourse to force, and the opening of hostilities in this part of Europe,* is constrained to accept evacuation conditions specified in the note of the Soviet government." The Bucarest government thus stressed that it had yielded to force, and avoided any direct and explicit acceptance of the cession. Though the Rumanian authorities and troops scrupulously observed the rigorous conditions imposed, the Red army overstepped every limit with deliberate brutality and unwarranted lawlessness. Retreating Rumanian units were captured, disarmed, and even fired upon by the advancing Soviet armies.

With full encouragement from an openly hostile Axis, Hungary and Bulgaria moved in for their share of dismembered Rumania. By the Vienna award, Ribbentrop and Ciano gave Hungary a large part of North-Eastern Transylvania—well over 16,000 square miles with more than two and a half million inhabitants, of whom fully one-half were Rumanians and only one-third Magyars. Bulgaria obtained Southern Dobrudja. Thus in the course of less than three months Rumania was forced to yield practically one-third of her territory, together with a corresponding proportion of her population.

It is interesting to note here, concerning the Vienna *Diktat*, that the British government issued a strong statement of disapproval. Speaking before the House of Lords on September 5, 1940, Lord Halifax declared indeed that his government was "unable to accept the settlement now announced of the Hungarian-Rumanian dispute over Transylvania, since that settlement is the result of dictation by the Axis powers, imposed on Rumania under duress . . . We do not propose to recognize any territorial changes which take place during the war, unless they take place with the free consent and good will of the parties concerned."

On the other hand, the Soviet Union took an active part in the intimidation of Rumania throughout that period and subsequently, thus foreshadowing further and more far-reaching plans of conquest. The first objective was the mouths of the Danube with the consequent control over Danubian navigation, a long-standing aim of Russian expansionism. This had to await the Belgrade conference of 1948.

Rumania's dismemberment led to the overthrow of King Carol's dictatorship. The 1938 Constitution was abrogated. The King abdicated. On September 6, with General Ion Antonescu as "leader" of the state, King Mihai came to the throne. The new government, formed by General Antonescu, whose extensive powers—granted by Carol prior to his abdication—infringed even the traditional royal prerogatives, included some of the top men of the notorious Iron Guard. Horia Sima, the commander of that Nazi-type organization, became vice-president of the council of ministers. Not many months later, the deep-seated conflict between Antonescu and the Iron Guard came to a head, the latter staging an armed rebellion in an attempt to gain sole power. The revolt was put down in January 1941, Antonescu gained control, and the leaders of the Iron Guard fled to Germany, where Hitler sheltered them and held them in reserve as a means of putting pressure on Antonescu. Mihai Antonescu became Vice-Premier and interim Minister of Foreign Affairs, while General Ion Antonescu remained titular head of the government.

The Soviet seizure of the Rumanian provinces had had a deep effect on public opinion and when Hitler attacked the USSR on June 22, 1941, Rumanian troops joined in the attack and crossed the Pruth with understandable enthusiasm, bent on liberating their forcibly enslaved fellow-countrymen. As proclaimed in General Antonescu's order of the day, the reason for entering the war was the liberation of Rumania's lost provinces.

The move against the Soviet Union did not entail any thought of hostility toward Great Britain or the Dominions, which in fact were in no way allied with the USSR at that time. The British government knew the true sentiments of the Rumanian people. When urged to declare war on Finland, Rumania, and Hungary, Winston Churchill stated on November 4, 1941: "My judgment is against it, because . . . Rumania and Hungary . . . are full of our friends; they have been overpowered by Hitler and used as a cat's-paw, but if fortune turns against that ruffian they might easily come back to our side." It is a matter of record that throughout the war, the Antonescu regime constantly made a distinction between the Eastern campaign and Rumania's attitude toward the Western democracies. It is sufficient to recall here the friendly treatment accorded to all British and American fliers shot down and taken prisoners.

When the troops were pushed far into Soviet territory beyond Rumania's border, feelings changed. Since a large part of Transylvania was in Hungarian hands as the result of the Vienna *Diktat*, the absurdity of continuing the immensely costly war effort alongside the Axis became increasingly evident. In a letter they jointly addressed to General Antonescu in January, 1942, Iuliu Maniu and Constantin Bratianu, the heads of the National Peasant and Liberal parties, urged that Rumanian troops be withdrawn from Russia, pointing out that the country was being exposed to ultimate disaster otherwise. The battle for Stalingrad, in which Rumanian casualties were exceptionally heavy, came to shake the confidence of the Antonescus in a German victory. By 1943, the Bucarest government was trying to contact the Western Allies through Ankara, Lisbon, Madrid, the Vatican, and even the Soviet government in Stockholm, with a view to withdrawal from the war. The Antonescu government sought to come to an understanding with the Western democracies only. This however, especially following the conferences of Quebec, Moscow, and Teheran, which all stressed the solidarity among the Allies, was an increasingly obvious impossibility.

THE ARMISTICE NEGOTIATIONS

Appalled by the heavy responsibility weighing upon him, General Antonescu decided to allow a spokesman of the opposition parties to contact the three principal Allies on neutral ground. Prince Barbu Stirbey, a former Prime Minister, left for Istanbul and from there went on to Cairo. On March 17, 1944, he opened negotiations with the British, American, and Soviet representatives in Cairo. Toward the end of May he was joined by a second emissary of the opposition, Constantin Visoianu, former Rumanian Minister to The Hague and Warsaw.

Barbu Stirbey had from the very beginning requested that the Allies give precise assurances with regard to Rumania's independence and territorial rights. Soon thereafter, on April 2, Molotov issued a public statement. "The Soviet government," he told a press conference, "declares that it does not pursue the aim of acquiring any part of Rumanian territory or of changing the existing social order in Rumania. It equally declares that the entry into Rumania of Soviet troops is solely the consequence of military necessities and of the continuation of resistance by the enemy forces." The Soviet Foreign Minister stressed that his statement was being made with the assent of the British and American governments, and this was subsequently confirmed officially by Prime Minister Winston Churchill and Secretary of State Cordell Hull.

Ten days after the Molotov statement, Soviet Ambassador Novikov handed Prince Stirbey what he described as the "minimum conditions of an armistice with Rumania," to be communicated both to the Antonescu government and to Maniu and the opposition. The stipulations contained in this document had been endorsed by the Western Allies and were of three kinds: conditions exacted by the Soviet Union from Rumania, guarantees extended to Rumania, and points of a technical nature. Under the first heading came the demand that Rumania break with the Axis and co-operate with the Allies, reaffirmation of the transfer of Bessarabia and Northern Bucovina to Russia, reparations, and the return of Allied prisoners of war and internees. The second category comprised a Soviet declaration to the effect that Rumanian territory would not be occupied for the duration of the armistice, and requiring the free movement of Allied troops in view of military operations. The Moscow government further stated it considered the Vienna award to be unjust, and was prepared to cooperate with Rumanian troops in the recovery of Northern Transylvania. The technical provisions concerned the establishment of contact between Rumania and the Soviets.

On June 10, the Rumanian representatives in Cairo made known the formal and definite acceptance of the Soviet armistice terms on behalf of King Mihai and the leaders of the democratic political parties. They further informed the Allied representatives that a plan had been drawn up for the cessation of hostilities. An Allied reply, however, failed to materialize. The explanation for this came to light much later, the agreement of the "Big Three" that for a period of three months Rumanian affairs were to be left exclusively to the Soviets while matters affecting Greece were left solely to the British. This arrangement had been approved by President Roosevelt on June 12, 1944, acting independently of his Secretary of State, Cordell Hull. The Russians chose to prolong the Rumanian negotiations in the expectation that military successes would lead to a forcible solution.

Aware of the impending Soviet offensive, Maniu telegraphed to Cairo that the opposition was ready to go into action. On August 23, King Mihai asked General Antonescu to conclude an armistice and, when the latter replied that he would have to give prior notice to the Germans, the King gave the signal for a *coup d'état*. The two Antonescus were placed under arrest and a new government, headed by General Sanatescu, was formed. The government included the heads of the democratic parties—Iuliu Maniu, Constantin Bratianu, and C. Titel Petrescu, as well as a representative of the Communist party, L. Patraschanu. The Minister of Foreign Affairs was a career diplomat, Grigore Niculescu-Buzesti. That evening, after the new government had been sworn in, the King broadcast a message announcing the cessation of hostilities against the Allies and the acceptance of armistice conditions by Rumania. Constitutional liberties were re-established. Prince Stirbey and Mr. C. Visoianu were instructed to sign the armistice.

The new Rumanian government had requested that the Soviet government allow fifteen days to the German troops to withdraw from Rumanian soil. But on the following day, August 24, the Germans attacked Bucarest in force. Military steps were then taken to clear the country of German forces. This effectively brought Rumania into the war on the Allied side.

The armistice convention was finally signed in Moscow on September 12, 1944. From the point of view of international law, it differed considerably from the conventional conventions of the past, both as to the complexity of its provisions and the nature of those provisions. The military clauses were unilateral obligations assumed by Rumania. The clauses of a political and economic nature were unusual, designed to make the Soviet Union the exclusive beneficiary of a far-reaching exploitation of Rumania. The Soviet occupation authorities were subsequently to carry this out without effective opposition from the Western Allies.

Articles 11 and 12 provided for reparations to the amount of 300 million dollars, with the additional obligation of restoring everything of value that might have been taken from Soviet territory during hostilities. The political clauses covered the Soviet annexation of Bessarabia and Northern Bucovina, but they annulled the Vienna *Diktat*. On the other hand they established a Soviet military control over Rumania of an exorbitantly severe character. The armistice convention amounted to a comprehensive peace treaty in miniature. It was a perversion of the original Soviet armistice conditions, a perversion that was to continue as the ever-increasingly harsh Soviet interpretations of the terms came to light.

Russia's unilateral action in Rumania was soon rendered all the easier by the verbal agreement concerning the division of zones that was reached between Churchill and Stalin in Moscow in October. It gave the Soviet Union a 90 per cent "predominance" in Rumania, and while Churchill's understanding was that this should apply only for the duration of the actual hostilities, the Soviets acted on the assumption that it was final.

With Rumania back in the camp of her traditional allies, the main task on the home front was to restore democracy to Rumania. Theoretically this was to have been carried out under the supervision of the three principal Allies. In practice, however, only one—the Soviet Union—exercised control.

In order to convey a clear picture of what faced the new administration, we must recall a number of salient facts: the presence of large Soviet forces in the country hampered and in certain cases, as in Moldavia, actually cut communications with local authorities. In the liberated parts of Transylvania the administration was absolutely forbidden to function at all. The state of war against Germany and Hungary added immeasurably to the difficulties encountered. Lastly there were the heavy burdens imposed by the armistice convention.

Rumania's contribution to the Allied war effort against the European Axis has been examined in the appropriate chapter of the present work. Here we shall only recall that this campaign cost the country 168,591 casualties.

As for the deliveries exacted by Soviet Russia in the guise of reparations and maintenance of its occupation troops, they are dealt with in the chapter on the economic field. They disrupted Rumania's economy for years. In the late summer of 1944, realization of the Kremlin's ruthlessly predatory intentions was only beginning to dawn on the people.

On August 25 Molotov had seen fit to renew the assurances the Soviet government had voiced some months earlier, to the effect that "the USSR has no intention of acquiring any part of Rumanian territory or to change the existing social order there." Indeed, he declared, "The Soviet govern-

ment considers it imperative to restore Rumania's independence, together
with the Rumanians liberating the country from the fascist yoke." Two
days later a *Pravda* editorial stated: "The importance of Rumania's quit-
ting the Axis goes beyond mere Rumanian affairs . . . it signifies the
crumbling up of the entire German system of defense in the Balkans. . . .
It would be difficult to overestimate the importance of this blow." The
new Minister of Foreign Affairs, Grigore Niculescu-Buzesti, felt justified
under the circumstances to declare that "the Rumanian government is
profoundly persuaded that everything agreed upon with the Soviet Union
would be fully respected." Unfortunately events were soon to show that
Soviet Russia's guarantees were worthless and that the Kremlin had quite
different intentions.

Meantime the new administration tackled its most urgent business with
commendable zeal. A decree was issued on August 31 broadly reinstating
the constitution of 1923. Before that, however, two steps were taken to
clear the way for the re-establishment of the country's political life: as
early as August 23—the very day of the *coup d'état*—all concentration
camps were abolished, and an extensive amnesty was granted to political
prisoners. The old democratic parties set about reorganizing themselves.
Party and independent newspapers reappeared. People once again breathed
freely. But this was not to last.

The Soviet occupation authorities, working hand in glove with the Communist party, immediately set about harassing and hampering the free
press. Presently the communists went a step beyond merely seeking to suppress the free press which, after all, was but a manifestation of public opinion. Their objective became to create artificially a state of anarchy, thus
undermining the authority of the government of which they themselves
were a part. By direct verbal attacks from within, and by violent demonstrations by "goon squads," they strove to justify the Soviet contention that
was not long in coming, namely that the administration was unable to
maintain order. The government, so the Soviet-sponsored slogan ran, was
opposed by the "people." It was, in other words, anti-democratic. The
government must go!

The communists, of course, were fully aware that the overwhelming
majority was utterly hostile to them. They knew—who better?—that they
themselves were but a tiny minority group. Had not Ana Pauker herself
publicly stated that prior to the entry of the Red army, Rumania's communists numbered barely one thousand members? The press of the West

reported this statement, notably the New York *Herald Tribune* of November 15, 1946. The thing to do, therefore, was to set up one of those spurious "democratic fronts" to give weight and ostensible support to the Communist party line.

A so-called National Democratic Front appeared. It comprised a number of groups, like the Plowmen's Front, and splinter factions of the existing parties, none of which had any real following in the country. It also attracted various second-rate politicians, some of whom had been staunch supporters of Carol's dictatorship of a few years before. This "bloc" was later to be of great use in manipulating the elections. For the time being its role was to demand as noisily as it could that the government be replaced.

Radio Moscow, with the stage thus set, now took up the outcry. By the beginning of November, 1944, the Soviet propaganda machine was clamoring for a change of government in Rumania.

On November 4 General Sanatescu formed a new government. Maniu, Bratianu, and Titel Petrescu were no longer members, but the National Peasant, National Liberal, and Social Democratic parties were duly represented in the cabinet. Petre Groza, the head of the Plowmen's Front, became Vice-President of the Council of Ministers; the "National Democratic Front" was represented by no less than six other members holding portfolios in the government. The communist leader Gheorghiu-Dej was given the Department of Communications. The Soviet government expressed satisfaction. Vishinsky, who had arrived in Bucarest, attended a party on November 14, and proposed a toast "to the health of the new democratic government of Rumania, which thus enters the great family of democratic countries of the world."

One might have thought this was nothing short of an official endorsement by the Kremlin. But words mean one thing to communists and another thing to non-communists. Right away the new government was subjected to even more violent forms of sabotage than its predecessor. With the connivance of the Soviet occupation authorities, the communist-dominated FND (National Democratic Front) started a new series of lawless acts. In various parts of the country its partisan groups seized the buildings of the local authorities by force; street riots were staged in Bucarest and in other large cities; vociferous dissensions arose within the government itself, with the communists clamoring for yet another change.

The Sanatescu government was forced to resign. It was replaced by one headed by the Chief of Staff, General Radescu. By the beginning of 1945 this government too was in the throes of communist-created difficulties. Gheorghiu-Dej had visited Moscow in the meantime and had come back with precise instructions. This time there were no half measures: the communist attack was of unprecedented violence; a radical solution was now called for; in the guise of a demand by the FND, the communists proposed their own governmental program. Interestingly enough, it was a relatively moderate one. The important thing was that it had to be put into effect by one agency and one agency only: the FND itself.

The main line of attack against the Radescu government was provided by the issue of land reform, which the administration proposed to postpone because any wholesale expropriations would necessarily have resulted in a decrease of farm production, and this could not be tolerated at a time when Soviet demands on Rumania were already far too heavy a burden on the country's economy. Furthermore, it would obviously have been highly improper to introduce any sweeping agrarian reform at a moment when so many Rumanian soldiers were fighting a major war outside the country's frontiers. But none of these points mattered to the communists. They were out to anarchize the country by hook or by crook. They clamored— still in their guise as the National Democratic Front—for immediate land expropriation and distribution. More, they incited the peasantry to seize the land. At the same time, violence broke out at the major industrial plants throughout the country, to show that the workers were in full sympathy with the peasants—and solidly against the government. This carefully staged action was led, under the patronage of the Soviet occupation command, by communist members of the government, notably the Under-Secretary of the Ministry of the Interior, Teohari Georgescu. Other luminaries of the Communist party of Rumania, such as Gheorghe Apostol and Gheorghiu-Dej himself, actually led the rioting at Bucarest's large industrial establishments. Indeed, in the course of one such affray, Gheorghiu-Dej accidentally shot and wounded Apostol. This happened at the Malaxa Plant on February 20, 1945, as the communists were demonstrating against the election of a trade union committee in which the National Peasant candidates had polled a great majority of votes.

A great communist rally was staged on February 24th in Bucarest. Shots were fired and some people were fatally wounded. The communists declared the Radescu administration was responsible, but everyone knew that the victims had been mowed down deliberately by the communists themselves in an effort to force Radescu's removal. Autopsies revealed that the fatal bullets were of Soviet manufacture, of a type neither the Rumanian army nor the police possessed.

As early as February 26, telegrams from Moscow to the *New York Times* reported the replacement of Radescu by an FND administration. The FND thereupon called for a mass meeting on March 8. Meanwhile a communist front organization known as *Apararea Patriotica*, the Patriotic Defense, feverishly distributed arms among such workers as could be found who sympathized with the communists. The Soviet occupation command took care to empty the capital of Rumanian armed forces.

The stage thus set, Vishinsky arrived in Bucarest. There followed the well-known scene: the Kremlin's emissary raved and ranted, he pounded the King's table with his fist, he slammed the door of the audience room. When the King suggested that Barbu Stirbey try to form a government, Vishinsky was adamant: none other would do but Petre Groza. With Soviet tanks ostentatiously brought out to parade the streets, there was no choice. On March 6, 1945, Groza formed a government which proved to be a milestone in Rumania's history.

Vishinsky's spectacular intervention, which resulted in the advent of the Groza government as a puppet regime imposed on Rumania by the Soviet occupier, subsequently made the headlines in the Western press. It came to be regarded as the outstanding illustration of what the Kremlin meant by a "friendly" government in a neighboring country. Its significance, from the point of view of this study, is twofold: for Rumania, it heralded the opening of a new chapter in the country's tormented history: a dark era that is still in progress. On the international scene it marked a turning point in the relations of West and East.

Barely three weeks before, a policy of close cooperation between the Big Three had been jointly and solemnly announced at Yalta: ". . . the three Governments will jointly assist the people in any European liberated state or former Axis satellite, where in their judgment conditions require, . . . c) to form interim governments, broadly representative of all democratic elements in the population, and pledged to the earliest possible establishment, through free elections, of governments responsive to the will of the people; and d) to facilitate where necessary the holding of such elections."

In vain the American government called to the Kremlin's attention that the Soviet procedure violated the spirit of the Yalta agreements. Two

American Notes, dated March 5 and 6, 1945, remained without results. Then, once the Groza government was set up, Washington asked that a tripartite commission be constituted in Rumania to ensure the application of the principles enunciated in the Declaration on Liberated Europe. The proposal was rejected by Molotov on March 17, according to former Secretary of State James F. Byrnes (*Speaking Frankly*).

As far as Rumania was concerned, Vishinsky's initiative came as an unmistakable warning: this was how the Soviet government meant to orient the country's public life; such were the methods to be expected henceforth. Would the Western Allies allow such things to go on? More important still, could the Western Allies do anything about the situation? The next two years were to bring the answers. The gloomiest Cassandra peering into the future during those early autumn days of 1945 could scarcely have foretold a more dismal outcome.

In order to get a clear picture, it should be recalled that the armistice convention had given the "Big Three"—and particularly the Soviet Union —far-reaching rights of control and intervention in Rumania's domestic affairs. The Yalta agreements had raised these stipulations to the rank of principles of policy toward the "liberated" countries of Central and Eastern Europe.

As constituted on March 6, 1945, the Groza government appeared to be the outcome of a broad coalition of political groups forming the so-called Democratic Front. But the reality could not escape either the people of Rumania or competent foreign observers. The government was simply a communist-led conglomerate of front organizations. A segment of the Social-Democrat party, not including its leader, C. Titel-Petrescu, was drawn in by the classic lure of "unity of action." Such strictly local groups as the so-called Plowmen's Front, which could not poll a majority even within the district where its wealthy landowning head, Petre Groza, was boss, became political parties overnight. There was the communist-front organization that called itself the Patriotic Union; there were dissident splinters of the National Peasant and National Liberal parties; there was, of course, the Communist party itself—barely one thousand strong the year before, and now the self-appointed and Russian-supported paragon of democracy.

The government set up by this hodge-podge of utterly unrepresentative minorities was equally "democratic" in composition. The vice-premier, who was also Foreign Minister, was none other than George Tatarescu, who had headed Carol's dictatorial governments a few years before.* The Minister of Culture was the former Iron Guard priest, Burducea. As for the communists, they held the key positions, the Ministries of the Interior and Justice. The head of the Communist party, Gheorghe Gheorghiu-Dej, was Minister of Public Works and Communications. From the very beginning, this administration became the obedient tool of the Soviet occupying authorities. The latter no longer had to intervene directly to foster the process of disruption and gradual communization. Their work was greatly facilitated through the cat's-paw initiatives of the compliant puppet regime. All the Russians had to do now was to maintain this unlawful administration in power, in defiance of Rumania's truly representative and constitutional forces, and of the Western representatives on the "joint" Allied Control Commission.

The people of Rumania were, of course, bitterly opposed to this government. Their opposition and hopes centered about the two great parties, the National Peasant and the Liberal, whose heads, Iuliu Maniu and Constantin Bratianu, were now looked up to more than ever before. These two Grand Old Men of Rumania's political life now stood up against the communist-dominated regime with the same fearless patriotism with which they had in the past so resolutely opposed all other undemocratic and dictatorial governments.

As was but to be expected, the Groza administration's first concern, on a par with the agrarian reform, was the introduction of politics into the state control and security apparatus. This entailed the appointment of communists or at least communist sympathizers as heads of district administrations (prefects), and the thorough reorganization of the police force, which was merged with the communist security formations and placed under the direct orders of the local prefects. The gendarmerie was likewise "reformed". The armed forces were subjected to repeated mass purges.

Presently, wave after wave of mass arrests struck the political opposition. Not only prominent members of the democratic parties, but the rank and file, and indeed, the citizenry as a whole, were soon to become familiar with the inside of prisons and concentration camps. Even the staunchest anti-communist might well quail at the thought of the consequences of active opposition. The press was systematically gagged by censorship.

* Professor Mihai Ralea, who had likewise belonged to Carol's dictatorial government, was given an important cabinet post.

Martial law was introduced. Impartial foreign observers were either expelled or refused entry into Rumania as all civic liberties and basic human rights were gradually suppressed. Well might Churchill observe to Stalin at the Potsdam conference that "an iron fence had come down around" the unfortunate country—such was thenceforth to be the climate prevailing in Rumania.

Repeated protests from the Western Allies came to nought. Like Rumania, the two neighboring countries of Bulgaria and Hungary were also gradually becoming "integrated" to the communist colonial empire. The problem of peace treaties with the three regimes came to the fore, but the Western Allies could hardly consider these regimes to be representative. They had no hesitation in so saying. On his return from Potsdam, President Truman told the American people on August 9, 1945: "At Yalta it was agreed, you will recall, that the three governments would assume a common responsibility in helping to re-establish in the liberated and satellite nations of Europe, governments broadly representative of democratic elements in the population. That responsibility still stands. We will recognize it as a joint responsibility of the three governments. It was re-affirmed in the Potsdam declarations on Rumania, Bulgaria, and Hungary. These nations are not to be the sphere of influence of any one Power."

The British Foreign Secretary was even more emphatic. On August 20 he told the House of Commons: "The governments which have been set up in Bulgaria, Rumania, and Hungary do not, in the view of the British Government, represent a majority of the people. The impression I got from recent developments was that one kind of totalitarianism was being replaced by another . . . The form of government being set does not impress me as being sufficiently representative to meet the requirements of diplomatic relations."

In sharp contrast, the Soviet government formally recognized the Groza regime at the beginning of August 1945. The American and British Representatives in Rumania informed the King that their government could not consider the Groza government representative in the sense of the Yalta agreement. Faced with this situation, on August 21 the King asked Groza to resign. Strong in the Kremlin's support, Groza refused. There was, under the circumstances, no other solution left to the King than to refuse any further sanction for the acts of the administration, and to address himself to the Three Great Powers for a way out of this unprecedented deadlock. As the dramatic crisis developed, the hopes of the Rumanian people turned toward the United States and Great Britain. But all Western intercessions remained unavailing against the inflexible stand of the Kremlin.

At the beginning of September, Groza visited Moscow together with some prominent members of his cabinet, notably Tatarescu. Before leaving he issued a public statement to the effect that he was resolved "to continue the fight to the end against the actions of anti-democratic elements . . . and to remain at the post." This piece of defiance was promptly echoed and enforced by *Izvestia*, which on September 7 stated editorially that the situation that had developed in Rumania was the result of British and American intrigues and pressure.

The deadlock brought no letup on the domestic scene. On the contrary, the opposition press was effectively suppressed, arbitrary arrests mounted in number, new prisons and concentration camps were set up. A spontaneous public demonstration honoring the King on the day of his patron saint, November 8, resulted in the police and the Tudor Vladimirescu division (recruited in Russian P.O.W. camp) shooting up the huge crowds that had assembled in front of the palace. This was followed by another series of mass arrests.

Such were the circumstances under which the foreign ministers of the three Allies met in Moscow between December 16 and 26, 1945, to consider, among other matters, the problem of recognizing the Rumanian government. Hopes rose anew. The final communique included two conditions required by the United States and British governments for recognition: that the government include a representative of each of the two major parties, the National Peasant and the National Liberal; and that the government thus completed assume the obligation ". . . that free and unfettered elections will be held as soon as possible, on the basis of universal and secret ballot." Furthermore, "all democratic and anti-fascist parties should have the right to put forward candidates", and "the reorganized government should give assurances concerning the grant of freedom of the press, speech, religion, and association."

A special supervisory commission, made up of Vishinsky, Ambassador Averell Harriman, and Ambassador Sir Archibald Clark-Kerr, was sent to Bucarest. Groza gave the required assurances both verbally and in writing, and the British and American governments granted him recognition respectively on February 4 and 5, 1946.

However, it was clear to the opposition from the very beginning that all was far from well, notwithstanding the decisions taken in Moscow. In a statement issued on December 10, 1946, Iuliu Maniu, as the best qualified exponent of his country's public opinion, was to say: "Rumanian public opinion received with joy the decisions of Yalta and Potsdam. Not so did it receive the decisions of Moscow. And this, not because the contents of these decisions were displeasing to Rumanians, but because not the slightest guarantee was given that the government would truly carry out its promises. I have declared to the Ambassadors who were in Bucarest at that time that it is my absolute conviction that the government would fail to fulfil the obligations it assumed. I am all too well aware that this government has no scruples whatever, and that its aim is solely to continue in power, which could not come about, were the freedoms stipulated by the representatives of the three Great Powers meeting in Moscow, to be truly granted to us."

The Elder Statesman was only too right. The lawlessness of the Groza regime was in no way hampered by the Moscow conference decisions. The year 1946 was almost wholly dominated by the matter of the promised elections. In note after note the American and British governments called upon the Groza administration to proceed with the elections. Finally two decrees were passed on July 15. The first abolished the Senate. The second was the electoral law. So flagrantly did it violate the principles proclaimed in Moscow by the three Great Powers that the representatives of the two principal opposition parties, whose objections had been completely disregarded, withdrew from the Council of Ministers that approved the two texts.

Plans to falsify the will of the electorate were carefully laid. The judiciary, which might have frustrated the fraudulent intentions of the regime, had already been thoroughly purged on the strength of two laws ostensibly "reorganizing" that body, passed on January 17 and June 27 of the previous year. And, while setting up the legal framework for the impending elections, the administration set about boosting a number of alleged mass organizations under its control, such as the General Confederation of Labor, the Union of Democratic Women, and the Progressive Youth organization. Minority groups of ethnical origin were also set up. Each and every one, under the high-sounding labels adopted, was dominated by, and utterly subservient to the Communist party. The Social-Democratic party was effectively broken up. The final result was that, through the use of fraud, threats, and outright violence, the communists set up a so-called Bloc of the Democratic Parties on May 17, 1946, to face the elections jointly with a single list of candidates. This bloc included, in addition to the Communist party itself, its satellites the Plowmen's Front, the National-Popular Party, Tatarescu's group, and the turncoat splinter of the Socialist party. Subsequently the official textbooks, as, for instance, the 1952 *High-School Textbook of the History of the R.P.R.*, by Academician Mihail Roller, were to state openly that this coalition was in fact a creation of the Communist party, which had at the time already secured the leadership of the bloc.

The democratic parties themselves were subjected to every conceivable form of intimidation and outright terrorism. As for the press, the radio, and other facilities, perhaps as good a description as any of the situation that prevailed at the time of the election campaign was that given in an official United States press release, dated June 7, 1946: ". . . It was noted that out of a total of twenty-six papers published in Bucarest, the traditional parties, the National Peasant and National Liberal parties, have been able to publish only one daily each, and neither of these two opposition parties has been able to publish dailies in the provinces. By contrast, the government has at its disposal ten daily papers and nine weekly or bi-monthly papers in Bucarest alone. In addition, there are six more or less independent papers. The Rumanian government chooses to regard the organs of the dissident offshoots from the historical parties, subservient to the National Democratic Front, among the publications of the traditional parties themselves. Statements by the United States President and by leading United States officials like Senator Vandenberg are systematically censored, with all passages which might offend the Soviet Union deleted, whereas Mr. Stalin's or Molotov's statements are highly publicized in full."

As a matter of fact, the two opposition papers allowed to appear, *Dreptatea* (National Peasant Party) and *Liberalul* (National Liberal Party), were increasingly restricted and persecuted. Newsprint allocations were cut down to a minimum, the communist-dominated labor unions sabotaged them in every way, and the government censors seized upon every pretext to curtail and suppress. A succession of British and American protest notes went unheeded.

Here are two excerpts concerning the radio facilities: "Access to state broadcasting facilities . . . remains the monopoly of certain parties within the government, contrary to the government's commitments under the

Moscow decisions." (United States note of May 27, 1946) "The participating parties outside the governmental electoral bloc have been wholly denied the use of broadcasting facilities, although they were promised equitable use of such facilities to present their views, and although they are subjected to constant attack by the bloc parties through that medium." (United States note of October 28, 1946).

Freedom of assembly and every other means of directly reaching the electorate had been similarly set at nought. The communique issued by the Permanent Delegation of the National Peasant Party on August 24, 1946, put the matter squarely: "Meetings are not free. With the knowledge and tolerance of the government, notably of the Ministry of the Interior, armed bands have been organized. These bands attack public meetings and the heads of the opposition parties. They kill, maim and manhandle the adversaries of the regime. They make use of iron bars, knives, and clubs. They are paid to do so, and most of the participants are convicted criminals. They not only enjoy immunity for any brutalities they commit, including even murder, but they act under protection from the police and gendarmerie." All these facts were duly confirmed in official United States notes, notably those dated May 27, 1946, and October 28, 1946.

Yet even this campaign of ruthless terrorism could not bring the desired results. The government had to resort to frauds and abuses in the elections themselves. The official statement issued by the U.S. Department of State on November 26, 1946, is on record: "The Department of State has now received extensive reports concerning the conduct of those elections, and the information contained therein makes it abundantly clear that, as a result of manipulations of the electoral registers, the procedures followed in conducting the balloting, and the counting of votes, as well as by intimidation through terrorism of large democratic elements of the electorate, the franchise was on that occasion effectively denied to important sections of the population. Consequently, the United States Government cannot regard those elections as a compliance by the Rumanian government with the assurances it gave to the United States, United Kingdom, and Union of Soviet Socialist Republics Governments in implementation of the Moscow decision."

No less emphatic was the statement made by the British Under-Secretary of State for Foreign Affairs in the House of Commons on December 2, 1946: "The information at the disposal of His Majesty's Government leaves me no alternative but to agree . . . that the elections were neither free nor fair. During the election campaign, parties other than those comprising the government bloc did not enjoy full freedom of speech or association. The arrangements on polling day itself were, moreover, such as to permit wholesale falsification of the results, and full advantage was taken of this by the government authorities. In these circumstances, His Majesty's Government consider that the results of the Rumanian elections do not truly represent the opinion of the Rumanian people."

Nonetheless, the general impression inside Rumania immediately following the actual elections was that the government bloc had been decisively defeated. Opposition estimates placed the National Peasant Party well ahead with a total of about 70 per cent of the votes. The elections were held on November 19, and the machinery set by the administration could easily have made the final results available on the morrow. Yet it was only on November 22 that they were announced. The country learned then that the Bloc of Democratic Parties had secured 349 mandates out of a total of 414. According to the official version, the National Peasant Party obtained but 32 mandates, and the National Liberal barely 2.

We might note in passing that even this falsification is no longer considered compatible in retrospect with pride in "party achievements". In the new official textbooks of Rumanian history, such as that by Academician Mihail Roller mentioned above, we now find that the government bloc gained no less than 384 mandates out of the 414. Who knows what the figures will be ten years from now?

Faced with such results, the two principal opposition parties had no choice left. They both withdrew their representatives from the government, and abstained from participating in the work of the newly elected parliament which met on December 1. The government was reshuffled on November 30. A new phase began. Thereafter, the victorious communists proceeded methodically with the preliminaries designed to lead ultimately to the sovietization of the country.

The first step was to liquidate the opposition. In July 1947, the heads of the National Peasant Party, including Iuliu Maniu and Ion Mihalache, were arrested. A wave of arrests rounded up their partisans throughout the country. Two mass trials were rigged late that fall, and Maniu and Mihalache were sentenced, together with other prominent politicians and diplomats, to life terms of hard labor, subsequently commuted to life imprisonment. In the meantime, the National Peasant

Party was abolished by a special law, and the mandates of its parliamentary representatives were formally annulled by the National Assembly. Yet another series of British and American protest notes came to swell the record of the misdeeds of the Bucarest administration. They came, but went unheeded.

The ruthless drive against the democratic opposition was but part of the over-all sharpening of government action aimed at the suppression of all individual liberties. And all this, let it be noted, went on even before the peace treaty was actually put into effect and, as we have just pointed out, in utter disregard of the stream of British and American protests.

This development, as a matter of fact, was not limited to Rumania alone. The year 1947 saw a general break between East and West. In July the Soviet Union and its satellite regimes had rejected the Marshall Plan. In September the Cominform was set up. Concomitantly, in each of the subjugated countries the opposition was being systematically crushed, notably the agrarian parties. In Hungary, Prime Minister Nagy resigned at the end of May. In Bulgaria, Petkov was arrested and his trial began the following August, culminating with his execution on September 23. In Poland, Mikolajczyk was forced to flee abroad the following month.

In Rumania, the government turned to economic concerns. With Gheorghiu-Dej now heading the Ministry of Industry and Commerce, the National Bank was taken over by the state pursuant to a law passed on December 28, 1946. By June 14, 1947, the future Prime Minister could put through a communist program for the thorough reorganization, economic and financial, of the country. The first important application of this program was to be the currency reform of August 15, 1947, which struck a crippling blow at both the farmers and private commercial enterprises.

As the disruption of the existing order progressed collaboration with the political groups of bourgeois background became increasingly difficult. Speaking on the thirtieth anniversary of the Communist party of Rumania, Gheorghiu-Dej saw fit to explain the position: ". . . We had for a certain time to maintain collaboration with part of the bourgeoisie, directing our main fire against the basic coalition forces of the bourgeoisie and land-owning class, represented by the parties of Maniu and Bratianu." (*Viata Sindicala*, May 11, 1951.) It is not without interest to note, however, that the communists employed the services of other satellite splinter groups in liquidating the collaborationist formations mentioned above, notably that headed by the former Prime Minister of King Carol, Tatarescu. This was to be but an intermediate stop before the Communist party itself finally took over all of the country's public life.

In December 1947, three other communist leaders, Ana Pauker, Vasile Luca and Emil Bodnarash, became members of the government, as Ministers for Foreign Affairs, Finance, and National Defense respectively.

On December 30, 1947, Petre Groza and Gheorghiu-Dej, threatening to "plunge Rumania in a blood bath," forced King Mihai to sign his abdication. The so-called National Assembly proclaimed the Republic. The Constitution was abrogated. The Kingdom of Rumania became formally the Rumanian People's Republic (R.P.R.). King Mihai, upon reaching Paris, declared that his signature had been obtained under duress and that he considered his abdication null and void.

On February 24, 1948 the National Assembly was dissolved and new elections were carried out. Previously, on January 21, a special electoral law had been passed, which deprived certain categories of citizens of the franchise. Under the law, those who had displayed an "anti-democratic attitude" (the nature of this was left carefully undefined) were simply deprived of the vote.

The elections, held on March 28, 1948, were to be the first in Rumania in which the electorate had no alternatives. It was to inaugurate the communist-style "manifestations of unanimity" characteristic of the "Marxist democracies". The so-called Front of Popular Democracy emerged victorious, with the Communist party in control.

In the meantime, on February 23, came a bombshell announcement that Patrashcanu, the Minister of Justice, had been ousted on accusation of "nationalism". He was tried and sentenced to death on April 18, 1954, according to the official version, after having sunk completely out of sight during the intervening years.

The newly elected National Assembly met on April 6, 1948. On April 13 it voted the new constitution introducing Stalinist constitutional principles and formally confirming the nature of the Rumanian People's Democracy. There is no need to examine at length this transitional charter. It was replaced by the constitution of September 24, 1952, which is analyzed in another chapter of the present volume.

With this radical change, the role played up till then by the front and satellite parties was taken over by the so-called mass organizations. The thorough control by the P.M.R. (*Partidul Muncitoresc Roman*)—

that is the Communist party—was openly proclaimed in a resolution passed by the Central Committee plenary in December 1948: "The comrades who are active in mass organizations or in democratic committees of the nationalities must consider themselves activists of the party within those organizations and committees. They must guide the latter with determination, under the leadership of the party, in the spirit of class warfare."

This in turn called for a thorough review of the party membership. The operation began in November 1948. The result was that almost 200,000 members were expelled, and rules for new admissions were tightened considerably. It was only in 1952 that new "militants" began to be admitted again into the party.

A new party statute was likewise adopted by the congress of February 1948, closely following the pattern set by the bolshevik party of the Soviet Union. The upheavals that marked the death of Stalin were to have far-reaching effects in the Rumanian Communist Party also.

The year 1948 was marked by the launching of sweeping reforms designed to provide the bases of the future socialist state. The most obvious of these changes was embodied in the law of June 11, 1948 nationalizing all the principal industrial, mining, banking, insurance, and transportation enterprises. The state took over the greater part of the means of production. The administration, the armed forces, and the judiciary had not been neglected in the meantime. The transformations introduced in each of these sectors will be found discussed at length in later chapters of this volume, as well as in the fields of education and of religion.

The mounting terror that was to provide the background for these manifold changes remains to be mentioned. In an official statement, published by Scanteia on January 13, 1949, the R.P.R. administration proclaimed:

> The state is nothing but the machinery of oppression of one class by another. Our regime of popular democracy is a form of the dictatorship of the proletariat. It is successfully carrying out the task of liquidating the economic positions of the exploiting classes, of stifling all attempts to restore the old order, of training the masses of the workers in the construction of socialism under the leadership of the proletariat . . . We, the state of the workers, come and say so openly: Yes, the dictatorship of the proletariat against the landowners and capitalists who are drones living off the toilers, who plan their evil plots against the peaceful work of our people, who scheme in the dark against the Popular Republic, who

betray the fatherland and the people, in the pay of the imperialists, those foes of freedom and independence.

This was no idle boast. To the waves of arrests were added such large-scale persecutions as the mass evacuations carried out on the night of March 1, 1949, on the occasion of the new expropriation. The forcible dissolution of the Uniate Church, described in another chaper of this work, was a further step in the ruthless intimidation of certain categories of citizens.

On April 2, 1949, the Western signatories of the peace treaty of February 10, 1947, the United States, Great Britain, Canada, Australia, and New Zealand, lodged formal protests in Bucarest against the manifest infringements of the human rights expressly stipulated in the treaty. British and American attempts to set in motion the procedure provided in the treaty for such an event were fruitless in face of the opposition of the Soviet Union.

Meanwhile the death penalty, not traditional in Rumania, was introduced by the law of January 13, 1949, and the R.P.R. government proceeded unchecked with what was officially described as the "building of the socialist state."

The old economic order once destroyed, and the means of coercion firmly in hand, the administration embarked on its policy of planning. The Grand National Assembly passed the first of the state plans on December 27, 1948. The main objective of the 1949 Plan was the socialization of agriculture. The decree of March 2, 1949, enacted a new expropriation of farm properties. Carried out with exceptional brutality and thoroughness on the previous night, it consisted simply of the expulsion of all former landowners from their remaining properties. The unfortunates involved were then assigned compulsory residence and thus at one stroke liquidated as a class.

The Central Committee Plenary Meeting of March 3–5, adopting the report submitted by Gheorghiu-Dej, traced the new party line and outlined the means of enforcing it.

It introduced a "class fiscal policy" designed to liquidate the so-called kulaks (the Rumanian word designating a kulak, which was to become a term of opprobrium synonymous with "class enemy", is *chiabur*). In 1949 the first collective farms were set up throughout the country. The "socialist revolution in the villages" had begun in earnest.

Stepped-up industrialization and farm collectivization were the major aims of the 1950 State Plan. The tenacious resistance of the peasantry resulted in increased terrorism. The notorious Danube-Black Sea Canal was begun in 1949. It was to provide a vast scope for the use of slave labor for some years, until it was finally abandoned as an impractical project.

In July 1950, the Central Committee carried out administrative reform. This introduced the Soviet-type territorial divisions, the "region" and the "raion". On December 3 of that year elections for the newly instituted people's councils (i.e. soviets) were held. The administration was able to boast of unprecedented successes, with the alleged participation of no less than 95.27 per cent of the qualified voters endorsing the single lists of candidates submitted solely by the communists themselves.

Two more notable events marked the year 1950. In October the country-wide electrification plan was launched. In December the first R.P.R. Five-Year Plan was initiated. The megalomaniac projects thus inaugurated in complete disregard of the immense difficulties involved resulted in a serious crisis that developed in 1951. The fall of that year saw a slowing down of the forced collectivization policy. The previous summer had witnessed mass evacuations and forced mass migrations of the peasantry. While the ultimate objective was in no way renounced, temporary relief came in the form of a stress laid on the agricultural associations patterned on the Soviet TOZ, wherein the associated farmers kept the nominal ownership of their properties. A very severe food shortage developed. It struck the urban and industrial centers with particular force during the winter of 1951–52.

Then came the currency reform of January 27, 1952. The grave disturbances that ensued led the communist administration to take a truly spectacular step. On March 6, 1952, a communiqué of the Council of Ministers made known that the entire higher hierarchy of the Ministry of Finance and of the State Bank had been dismissed for "serious offenses against the laws and the decisions of the government prior to the currency reform". The most prominent communist dignitary involved was Vasile Luca, who was dismissed from the post of Minister of Finance three days later. To this day it is impossible to make a satisfactory appraisal of what really happened within the party leadership of the P.M.R. The seriousness of the crisis, at any rate, can be gauged at least by the fact that three of the highest ranking communists, Ana Pauker, Vasile Luca, and Teohari

Georgescu, fell from grace as the result, together with a multitude of lesser luminaries.

On March 26, the Grand National Assembly, in disregard of the new constitutional provisions, decided to postpone the forthcoming elections, scheduled for March 28, suitably changing the constitution for the purpose. The reason given was "the country's economic interests." Two months later, on May 26 and 27, the plenary of the Central Committee met and passed a resolution condemning what was described as the "rightist opportunism" of Vasile Luca, who was accused of having grievously deviated from the party line. Teohari Georgescu was likewise denounced for rightist deviationism, lack of revolutionary vigilance, and a "conciliatory attitude." Both were ousted from the party secretariat and central committee. An extensive reshuffling of the government was put into effect.*

On June 2, 1952, the Grand National Assembly met. It passed in short order a number of laws reorganizing the judiciary to bring it closer to the Soviet model. It also elected Petre Groza President of the Assembly's Presidium, and appointed Gheorghiu-Dej Prime Minister in his stead. The very next day, *Scanteia* revealed that Ana Pauker had been formally accused by the Central Committee plenary of serious deviations, together with Teohari Georgescu and Vasile Luca. She was subsequently to be accused of both rightist and leftist deviations in connection with the party's agrarian policies.

With Gheorghiu-Dej now in command, "verification" of alleged deviationists was stepped up. Purges were carried out not only within the Communist party itself, but also within the U.T.M. (the Union of Working Youth) and other mass organizations. It may be taken for granted that these changes were dictated by the Kremlin itself, though, as we have already pointed out, it is impossible to determine the exact causes. An added indication may be found in the similar changes that occurred in Hungary about the middle of August that same year.

Presently the R.P.R. administration began to stage the so-called public debates in view of the introduction of a new constitution. An alleged political coalition dubbed the Front of Popular Democracy was set up to conduct the proceedings. The draft constitution was widely publicized and strenuously advocated. It was voted with commendable unanimity by the Grand National Assembly on September 24, 1952, without having

* Vasile Luca was tried and sentenced to death, but his sentence was subsequently commuted to life imprisonment.

been changed in any essential respect. With the electoral law once again duly changed, the new elections were announced for November 30.

The elections of November 30, 1952, provided yet another "success" for the regime. It was officially announced that fully 97 per cent of those permitted to vote had cast their ballots, and that 98 per cent of these had voted for the lists of the Front of Popular Democracy. There were no opposing candidates. According to official statements, in Bucarest alone 33,000 agitators had taken part in the election campaign.

The results of these "elections" were to provide a further indication that the purges had been even more extensive at the top levels than had previously appeared. Only 93 out of 414 members of the preceding Grand National Assembly came up for reelection. The resulting assembly had a membership of 423. Going back somewhat farther, it was found that only 24 of the 70 communist candidates elected to the 1946 assembly reappeared in the 1952 Grand National Assembly.

The regime became increasingly similar to the model that inspired it from the outset, the Soviet regime itself. During the year 1953 this was to be seen in the increasing centralization and specialization that resulted from the various mergers and reshufflings of government agencies of ministerial rank. Thus the Ministry of the Interior was merged with State Security; Higher Education was absorbed by the Ministry of Education; various special state committees were set up (arts, radio, cultural establishments) and grouped under the Ministry of Culture; the Ministry of Agriculture absorbed Forestry and the hitherto separate department of State Farms. On the Soviet model, two categories of vice-presidents of the council of ministers were introduced.

The changes that occurred in the Soviet Union following the death of Stalin had repercussions in the R.P.R. The note was set by the enlarged plenary of the Central Committee of the Communist party, held on August 19–20, 1953. It was then that two important decisions were taken, one relating to "the tasks of the party in the domain of the development of national economy and of the constant raising of material and cultural standards of the workers," the second "concerning the betterment of party work in strengthening the ties of the party with the masses."

It was hardly a coincidence that the R.P.R. administration came to the sudden decision that the pace of forced industrialization, and notably the disproportionate efforts directed toward heavy industry, seriously affected the production of consumer goods. The Malenkov government had come

to the same decision in regard to Soviet production shortly before. It was
decided therefore to step up the production of consumer goods during
the years 1954 and 1955. Special attention was to be given to agriculture.
The gigantic project of the Danube-Black Sea canal was abandoned. Likewise renounced were certain other equally impractical projects like the
Bucarest subway system and the creation of the "Danube harbor of
Bucarest". Hitherto the blueprints of these grandiose projects had been
officially publicized and sung in prose and verse by the regime's scribes,
as magnificent examples of socialist construction. Now, suddenly,
silence descended upon them. The backhanded but none the less eloquent confession of failure was lost on no one in the country.

A determined effort was also made to achieve the newly fashionable
"collective leadership" of the party. A directive was issued in August 1953,
requiring "all party committees to respect most strictly the supreme
principle of party leadership." It proclaimed that "any tendency to infringe this principle must be combated with severity." The prime objective
was defined as a drive against the "cult of personalities". Gheorghiu-Dej,
who up till then had invariably been officially described as "the best son
of the people," announced sternly, "we must say with full determination
that we shall fight against any manifestation of the personality cult, from
whatever quarter it might come, and in whatever field it might occur."

Yet another development was that the party tended to strengthen its
control over the activities, especially the economic activities, of all
state organs and of the various mass organizations. For this purpose, a
party "active" was to be instituted. This was to include 80–100,000
"militants" who, together with party leadership organs, would represent
the core of future activities. Party organizations were thus placed under
the obligation to ensure the proper conduct of all activities of trade union
organizations, and of such bodies as the U.T.M. (the Union of Working
Youth, the R.P.R. version of the Soviet Union's Komsomol), where certain weaknesses had become apparent. All party members belonging to
various institutions and enterprises were to set up separate party organizations for the special purpose of checking the activities of their respective
establishments.

A new party line was to be solemnly proclaimed on the occasion of the
second congress of the Communist party, scheduled for March 1954. A
draft statute was submitted to the country at large for the now customary
—though nonetheless meaningless—"public debate" that must precede

the enactment of all most important changes. On April 19 however, the plenary of the P.M.R. Central Committee decided to call the congress on October 30, 1954, instead of at the time previously set. At the same time a number of decisions were adopted with regard to the inner organization of the party leadership.

It was decided that the secretariat would be composed of four members instead of five, and that its members should no longer also hold government posts. As proposed by Gheorghiu Dej, it was decided that the Secretary General of the Central Committee be replaced with a "First Secretary". A number of former members of the government had thus to renounce their offices, and the top party men were suitably reshuffled. The most notable move was the withdrawal of Gheorghe Apostol from the government and his appointment of First Secretary.

Though even the details of the agenda had all been decided by the Central Committee on August 2, and the draft statute had been extensively "discussed", a communique was issued without prior warning on October 28—barely two days before the congress was scheduled to meet —stating that the congress was again being postponed. No plausible reasons were vouchsafed.

The plenary meeting of the Communist party Central Committee, that was convened between September 30 and October 1, 1955, "unanimously" elected Gheorghiu-Dej First Secretary of the Central Committee, displacing Gheorghe Apostol.

On October 3, 1955, the Grand National Assembly met and took cognizance of a letter in which Gheorghiu-Dej asked to be relieved of his duties as Prime Minister, and to be replaced by Chivu Stoica. The avowed purpose of this change was given as "the consolidation of the leadership" of the Communist party.

The Second Congress of the Communist party finally opened on December 23, 1955. It is known that such congresses are regarded by the communists as "balance sheets of the struggles and victories of the party." At this congress, the "balance sheet" was submitted in the form of a political report from Gheorghiu-Dej. He listed among the party's "struggles and victories" such events as the resumption of normal relations with Tito. (It must be recalled that, following the rupture that intervened in 1948, Gheorghiu-Dej had been vociferous in denouncing Tito as a "spy," an "assassin," and "libertine.") Gheorghiu-Dej also listed some of the "realizations" of the R.P.R. regime during the eight years that had intervened since the last congress. Industry and foreign trade, he said, had shown gains of 100 per cent, transportation 90 per cent, and domestic trade 80 per cent. As for investments made, Gheorghiu-Dej admitted that 67 per cent went to industry, notably to the steel industry, while the food industries accounted for only 33 per cent. Agriculture, Rumania's most important economic sector, was vaguely stated to have achieved "a constant increase," but no figures were given. However, the "socialization of agriculture" (the communist euphemism meaning forcible collectivization) had been dealt with by Gheorghiu-Dej earlier that year. On the occasion of the country-wide agricultural conference of March, 1955, he disclosed, among other things, that "between 1948 and 1953, the area of corn (maize) cultivation has been reduced by some three and a half million hectares." Shortly before, on February 24th 1955, *Scanteia* gave an authoritative list of the things the Rumanian consumer can occasionally find in his daily bread. These included such oddments as "a piece of wire, a bit of rag, and a shoe patch."

The sequence of events briefly outlined above shows that the R.P.R. communists, self-described as the Rumanian Workers' Party, are but the agents of the Soviet government carrying out as best they can the integration of Rumania into the Soviet system. The ups and downs of individual luminaries, and even the wide swings of the party line, are of no great significance in themselves. They simply reflect the changes within the Kremlin itself. Brought to power and maintained in power by Soviet force alone, their fortunes are separate from those of the Rumanian people. For the latter, and from the point of view of Rumanian history, the political developments of the last decade have marked but the successive stages of enslavement. The government should, therefore, be regarded as alien to both the will and the requirements of the people. The people of Rumania have had no direct say in their own government since 1945.

2

the economic field

The period between the time when the communists were forcibly installed and the end of the first Five-Year Plan stands out, from an economic point of view, as an incoherent succession of confusing moves and no less confusing countermoves. Before attempting to present an intelligible chronicle of events, we must therefore stress the element that provides the recognizable constant throughout this period. That constant is *Sovietization*.

The term Sovietization must be understood to have a double meaning. Its first and obvious meaning is the subjection of Rumania's economy to the Soviet economy. In this sense, it may be said that Sovietization began from the very moment the Soviet occupation authorities took over, following the armistice of August 23, 1944. It continues to this day. The second meaning is the actual adaptation of Rumania's traditional economic structure to the economic pattern obtaining in the Soviet Union itself or, at least, to that variant of Soviet economy prescribed by the Kremlin's experts for second-rate communist regimes like the so-called people's democracies of South-Eastern Europe.

In other words, in the first sense we must study Sovietization as a process of outright seizure; in the second, we must consider the effects of progressive communization. And here a preliminary remark is in order: the simple action of intensive exploitation undertaken by the Soviet Union has been infinitely more successful than that of communization. The latter, indeed, has so far been carried out with far less coherence and determination. It also began considerably later than the other, being initiated in earnest only in 1949, to be, ostensibly at least, interrupted in 1953. This does not mean that the ideological objectives have ever been repudiated. It means simply that the communist government of Rumania has had time and again, manifestly on orders from Moscow, to resort to non-Marxist solutions and formulas, thus contradicting its own program. This had had to be done in order to cope with serious crises, and does not preclude the official hope that the ideological aims may ultimately be attained.

There can be no doubt, moreover, that communization has time and again suffered serious setbacks from the very fact that undisputed priority had at all times to be given to the process of exploitation by the foreign power. It has become amply clear that communist economic formulas are wholly unsuitable to Rumania's traditional economic structure and utterly unacceptable to the Rumanian people. Another and no less obvious reason for the resounding failure of these alien forms is that so disproportionally large a share of the country's output has been from the outset appropriated, without any compensation, by the Soviet Union. The communist "plan" to break up the traditional framework of Rumania's economy simply lacked the requisite means because of Soviet Russia's insatiable demands. It could therefore be applied only in such sectors of the national economy where Soviet exploitation was least intensive. The conflict between these two contradictory trends will form a principal line of study in the present chapter.

Another line of observation will be the resistance of Rumania's traditional economic institutions to the twofold trend of Sovietization; the resistance by the people of Rumania to alien encroachments. Resistance must be understood to have been primarily passive. Yet, as is shown throughout this book, it is certainly proper to say that the country's productive elements, notably the peasantry, have constantly opposed a mute though wholly open-eyed resistance both to communization and to Soviet exploitation, wherever and whenever such resistance was at all possible. And resistance continues to this day.

It may be objected that a decade is too short a time to enable us to appraise objectively the extent to which the structure of a society has changed, economically or socially, under pressure from a totalitarian ideology. We feel however that there is sufficient information available even at this early stage, to indicate the true state of affairs. We shall try to bring before the reader the incontrovertible evidence of communism's failures, under the prevailing quasi-occupational regime. We shall attempt, too, as dispassionately as possible, to show the economic evolution of an agrarian country under Marxist-Leninist rule.

Before this, however, we must present a brief outline of Rumania's pre-communist economy and its specific problems, in order to permit the reader to draw his own conclusions.

RUMANIA'S PRE-COMMUNIST ECONOMY

Even before World War II, Rumania's economy was faced with major problems whose solution called for important structural adjustments.

The weightiest of these problems was agricultural over-population. This, of course, was general in that part of Europe. According to Wilbert E. Moore's authoritative *Economic Demography of Eastern and Southern Europe* (Geneva, 1945), Rumania's excess farming population about the year 1930 was of 51.4 per cent. The figures given by Moore for neighboring countries were: Yugoslavia 61.5, Bulgaria 53, Poland 51.3, and Hungary 22.4 per cent. Of course, methods of computing agricultural over-population are controversial. But in 1930, whereas Rumania's farmers represented 72 per cent of the total population, the country's farm production accounted for but 50 per cent of the total national income. On the other hand, the noted Rumanian economist Virgil Madgearu estimated the annual contingent of surplus farm workers to have been approximately 150,000. Clearly enough, this called both for an intensification of agricultural production and for the absorption of the surplus farm workers into other fields of production, notably manufacturing.

The three major political parties, the Liberal, the National Peasant, and the Social Democratic, fully agreed that changes were necessary. (Virgil Madgearu's works had a great influence in this.) They differed only in the methods and programs advocated to bring about the changes. But any far-reaching changes required favorable political conditions. And general political conditions throughout Europe, and notably in Rumania, hard hit by the 1929–1932 slump, were far from favorable as Hitler came to power in 1933. The needed economic reforms would have required not only peace on the international scene, but also the progress of democracy on the domestic. Unfortunately democracy, which had made such important gains in Rumania following the establishment of the Kingdom, and particularly during the first decade that followed World War I, was destined to suffer repeated setbacks under the influence of spreading fascist totalitarianism. The international scene, too, grew ever more threatening. Under such conditions, it is hardly surprising that economic progress and economic reforms became increasingly difficult.

The three major tasks that faced Rumania's economy before the outbreak of the second world war were: to raise agricultural productivity, to foster industrialization, and to increase foreign trade. We shall take them in order.

Rumania stood low in the scale of farm production. Taking 100 as the average for Europe, the Rumanian farmer had a per capita index of 48, and the index per hectare was 69. Denmark's figures were 354 and 256 respectively, those of Czechoslovakia were 105 and 129, and those for Yugoslavia 38 and 69.

This poor showing was due to two main causes. The first was of lesser gravity. It was that average properties following the extensive land reforms of 1919-1921 were too small to be really productive. The distribution of (arable) land for 1927 was as follows:

Acreage	Number of Owners	Per Cent	Total Hectares	Per Cent of Total Area
Under 5 hectares *	3,231,463	84.54	6,280,944	47.29
5–10 ha.	435,715	11.06	2,919,853	18.77
10–50	148,860	3.96	2,392,691	16.26
50–250	18,122	0.39	1,505,259	10.46
over 250	2,597	0.05	1,305,672	7.22
TOTAL:	3,836,757	100	14,404,469	100

* 1 hectare: about 2½ acres.

The plots of less than 5 hectares could not feed even the farm family that worked them. For Rumania, in fact, it was estimated that only properties in excess of 7 hectares could be accounted productive. In the twenty years that intervened until 1941, that is just prior to Rumania's entry into World War II, the picture changed considerably. The statistics of land ownership for that year are as follows (we give only the percentage figures, because the country had suffered extensive territorial amputations by then, as may be seen in our introductory chapter, and thus the other figures would be meaningless in this context):

Properties	per cent of total number	area percentage
under 5 hectares	76.8	33.3
5–10 hectares	16.9	26.0
10–50 ha. in	5.9	21.4
excess of 50 ha.	0.4	19.3

That is to say, medium-sized and larger peasant holdings had grown in number relative to the very small plots, thus correcting in part the excesses of the post-World War I land reforms, which had set Rumania in the forefront of Eastern European countries from the purely social point of view, to the detriment of the economic.

The second, and more important, cause of the country's low agricultural output must be sought in the poor supply of farm equipment and investment. The census of farm equipment for 1941 shows the following figures:

Category	Total number units	Number of units per 100 holdings	Number of units per 100 ha.
Ploughs	1,083,018	48.0	14.5
Harrows	752,063	33.3	10.0
Seed drills	58,589	2.6	0.8
Reapers	29,345	1.7	0.5
Tractors	8,416	0.4	0.1
Carts	1,191,254	58.7	15.7

Compared to the majority of European countries, this was certainly extremely unsatisfactory. Madgearu calculated the following comparative figures:

Country	Value of agricultural inventory (in Lei) per hectare	Average production of wheat per hectare in kilograms
Rumania	1,000	860
Bulgaria	2,000	1,320
Poland	3,000	1,440
Germany	15,000	2,070

Manifestly the most urgent need was to mechanize farm production and build up farm inventories, as well as to intensify the use of chemical fertilizers and the like. This, however, immediately raised the problems of providing the requisite investment and facilities for buying the needed commodities abroad. Successive governments of the democratic parties made great efforts, between 1920 and 1935, to supply credit to the country's agricultural producers and to direct foreign trade toward the industrial countries of the West.

This brings us to the crucial problem of industrialization. In the first place, what sort of industrialization could be envisaged at the time?

Between 1926 and 1938 Rumania made great progress in the field of industrial production. According to figures issued by the League of Nations, the index for manufactured production rose almost 80 per cent in this period. But the greatest rise occurred in the industries handling the country's raw products, such as petroleum and lumber, and in those producing consumer goods, such as the food industries, textiles, and so forth. It was only after 1936 that greater progress was registered in heavy industry. This is to be explained once again by the prevailing conditions in Europe, which throughout the continent promoted autarchy to the detriment of trade, and fostered an excessive, unnatural protectionist trend favoring national industries.

Starting about 1935, the general armament race contributed to the development of the metallurgical industries. This growth, however, was clearly artificial and parasitical. The products of the domestic heavy industries were more expensive than similar or better products that could be purchased abroad. The state was the principal buyer (in 1938, for instance, the Rumanian state was the direct purchaser of fully 70 per cent of the country's metallurgical output). This resulted, as might have been expected, in a severe burden on all other economic activities.

Under such circumstances, the first condition for a healthy development of industrialization would have been to favor those branches of manufacture that used the raw materials to be found in abundance locally. This would have been of benefit both to domestic consumption and to foreign trade. As it was, with the accent placed on the development of the metallurgical industries, the cost of living could not but rise, and the general financial situation suffered accordingly.

A second condition would have been to make available increasing quantities of manufactured goods to the farmers. However, the actual results of industrialization from this point of view were far from encouraging, as can be seen from the following table:

Year	Price index of agricultural products	Price index of industrial products used by farmers
	(1929 : 100)	
1930	68.2	98
1932	47.7	80.9
1934	44.1	82.6
1936	54	95.4
1938	64.6	101.8
1939	72.7	112.5

The "scissors" effect resulting from this situation, severely heightened by aftermath of the 1929-1932 slump, could not be offset by the rapid growth in the production of the metallurgical industries that marked the years 1935–1939, though in the meantime the prices of farm products improved somewhat.

Finally, the third condition called for in a healthy process of industrialization, to wit an increase of the national income resulting therefrom, could be but partially attained in Rumania. Certain industries, working with foreign capital, produced primarily for export (notably the oil industry, where Rumanian capital was only 27 per cent of the whole, while the rest was British, American, French, Dutch, Belgian, or German). Since petroleum products accounted for fully 33 per cent of the country's exports, the fact that the oil industry operated mostly with foreign capital, the profit accruing to Rumania therefrom was disproportionately small. In the words of an American author, Prof. Henry L. Roberts: "A large part of the industry was owned by foreigners, and a considerable proportion of the proceeds from exports did not reach the country in terms of foreign exchange. Moreover, the petroleum industry, being something of a lucky windfall and detached from the rest of the Rumanian economy, did not greatly influence the pattern of exports, though it added to their total value." (Roberts, Henry L.: *Rumania, Political Problems of an Agrarian State.* Yale, 1951.)

Under these circumstances, industrialization could not be satisfactorily carried out. The outbreak of World War II, the concomitant penetration of monopolist German capital, and the excessive encouragement of protective tariffs, further hampered a healthy industrialization. When, following the end of the war, the communist government of Rumania tackled the problem, it did so disastrously. This will be found described in detail later in this chapter.

For now we turn to foreign trade. To Rumania foreign trade is of paramount importance. Indeed it is inconceivable ever to industrialize such a country along healthy lines without intense and well-directed foreign exchanges. In the interwar years such a policy of foreign trade was carried through with persistence. Statistics for the years 1930–1938, for instance, show that exports exceeded imports, that exports went by preference to the industrialized capitalist countries of the West, and that imports were mainly finished products (fully 75 per cent of the total), of which the greater part comprised industrial plant and equipment, machinery, and the like. In 1937, one of the last years that it might be considered "normal", Rumania's foreign trade was as follows:

Imports: $143,550,000   Exports: $210,456,000
Value per ton: $19.80   Value per ton: $21.80
Per capita — $7.20   Per capita — $10.80

Three quarters of this foreign trade went to Western Europe and the United States; the countries of Southern and Eastern Europe accounted for the remaining quarter; while the Soviet Union appeared with less than 1 per cent in the table of imports, and with zero in that of exports.

The outbreak of the war in Europe marked the end of Rumania's long-standing trade with the Western countries. From 1940 to 1944 most of the foreign trade had to go to Germany, without profit to Rumania. At the end of the war another great totalitarian and imperialist power found itself in full control of the country's entire economy.

THE SOVIET SECTOR OF RUMANIA'S ECONOMY

With the Soviet seizure of Rumania, the paramount feature of the country's economy became what we may refer to as the Soviet "free zone" of the national economy and income. Quite apart from all other economic servitude imposed by the Kremlin, which we shall deal with in the sections on agriculture, industry, and foreign trade, the Soviet Union maintains a kind of extra-territorial right in virtue of which the riches of the country are either taken outright or exploited directly. This situation was imposed upon Rumania from the very outset of the Soviet occupation, and has been elaborated since then to suit the interests of Soviet Russia. Forced deliveries of goods to the occupation troops, additional massive deliveries on the basis of the armistice agreement, and the establishment of the so-called *Sovrom* joint companies marked the main phases of this process.

Two issues were raised at the very outset of the "collaboration" between Rumania and the Soviet Union, that of direct seizures and goods deliveries, and the question of German-owned property. The latter was subsequently to provide the basis for the formation of the Sovroms.

It is common knowledge that Rumania broke with the Third Reich on August 23, 1944, and from then on made considerable contributions in men and materials to the Allied war effort. This was confirmed in the terms of the armistice convention formally signed in Moscow on September 12, 1944, which even set down the precise hour of the day when the event occurred: 4 o'clock. However, the peace treaty, signed in Paris on February 10, 1947, mentions that Rumania took active part in the war against Germany only "following the conclusion of the armistice, on September 12, 1944." This discrepancy might appear slight and of no further significance. It was, however, no slip on the part of the Soviets. (The story is completely told in E. Ciurea: *Le traité de paix avec la Roumanie du 20 Février 1947*, Paris, 1954.) The latter, indeed, used it to justify the massive seizures effected by their armies as "war booty," taken between August 24 and September 12. This was a severe blow to Rumania's economy. In the first place, it served as a pretext for the seizure of the country's entire war fleet and of the major part of its merchant fleet, the latter comprising more than 700 ships, tugs, and barges. The seizure of huge quantities of oil equipment, representing fully one and a half times the amount of the technical material imported by Rumanian petroleum companies annually before the war, was similarly justified. So was the seizure of some 50 per cent of the available railway rolling stock and of all automobiles.

The effect of this wholesale looting was an immediate drop in national production. Oil production, for instance, dropped fully one-third in the year 1944. The country's entire economy, already suffering from the effects of the war, was disorganized at one stroke. The Soviet "experts" obviously preferred to resort to direct seizures, instead of seeking to maintain Rumania's economy for the sake of greater subsequent advantages to the Soviet Union. This utter disregard for Rumania's long-range economic interests, in favor of some immediate Soviet requirement, was to become the most notable feature of the occupying Power's attitude thereafter.

Under the economic clauses of the armistice convention Rumania had undertaken to pay the Soviet Union $300,000,000 in goods (oil products, lumber, grain, and so forth). But all prices of such deliveries were interpreted by the Soviets to be the prevailing world prices of 1938. Hence, for instance, the 1,700,000 tons of oil to be delivered in the course of six years were simply doubled in reality, because the price per ton had risen from $15 in 1938 to $30 by 1945. The total value of goods and services appropriated by the Soviets, both directly and in virtue of the armistice convention, between September, 1944, and June, 1948, reached (according to Mr. Willard Thorp, U.S. delegate at the Paris Conference) the vast sum of $1,785,000,000.

At the same time, of course, the country's production as a whole dropped. During the first two years of this "collaboration" it went down to barely

45 per cent of the figure for 1938. The national income dropped by fully one-half. The cost of living went up 25,000 per cent. The inflationary spiral gathered momentum, and led to two successive currency reforms, that had the main purpose of taking off the market the vast quantities of paper money issued to finance the Soviet exactions. The droughts of 1946 and 1947 were disastrous to agriculture; added to the large-scale deprivations resulting from the currency reforms, they brought the people of Rumania to such straits of want and starvation as had never been known before.

Soon after coming to power, the communist-dominated Groza government proceeded to conclude a far-reaching economic agreement with the Soviet Union. The convention, dated May 8, 1945, consisted of four separate texts that together organized future economic relations between Rumania and the USSR. Protocol No. 4 covered the establishment in Rumania of a number of so-called joint companies. Sovrompetrol was brought into existence by a convention signed on July 17, 1945. It was followed by Sovromtransport on July 19, Sovrombank on August 14, Sovromlemn on March 20, 1946, and Sovromgaz, Sovromasigurare, Sovromchim, Sovromconstructie, Sovrommetal, and Sovromtractor were set up in turn between March and August, 1949 following the introduction of the first one-year economic plan. Other such companies continued to be formed up to 1952. Interestingly enough, the formation of the secret Sovromquartz, which handles and controls uranium production, was never announced. Nor is the name of this concern listed among those alleged to be currently in the process of liquidation.

In principle, these companies were supposed to be set up with equal contributions by the two partners, the Soviet and the Rumanian states. However, in practice, the Rumanian share consisted of real estate, general production rights, and the necessary technical and financial capital, while the Soviet contribution consisted of what were referred to as "former German and Italian properties" in Rumania. Great Britain and the United States had renounced reparation rights relating to German and Italian properties in Eastern Europe in favor of Soviet Russia, in the Potsdam agreement of August 2, 1945. By a strained interpretation of this agreement, the Soviets ceased making any distinction between truly German and Italian-owned properties in Rumania, and the former French, Dutch, and Belgian properties there that had been fraudulently acquired by the Third Reich during the war. So what the Soviet state did in most cases was simply to contribute, aside from the shares in such companies as they had taken over, some of the installations and industrial equipment the Red armies had seized in that country during 1944. The "Soviet" materiel thus "contributed" to Sovrompetrol and Sovromtransport, for instance, was almost exclusively Rumanian in origin.

The privileges granted these Sovroms amounted to a species of extraterritoriality. So far-reaching were these privileges, that special provisions of the 1947 Law on Nationalization (Article 5) exempted from expropriation the properties "of a member state of the United Nations, which has acquired such properties as a result of the fulfilment of the peace treaty or of war reparations." This oblique provision, which could designate only the Soviet Union, made the Soviet government in effect the sole large capitalist owner in Rumania.

To round off the sorry tale of these Sovroms, we shall dwell on two outstanding examples, Sovromlemn and Sovrompetrol, the first being characteristic of the ones that failed, the second the only known instance of a prosperous Sovrom.

To Sovromlemn, the communists of Rumania brought as their initial contribution all timber land belonging to the State, to the Church, and to private owners—all of Rumania's forests. The Soviet contribution was to consist of plant, equipment, machinery, and rolling stock. Though the communist press of Rumania makes a point of playing up any materiel sent in from the Soviet Union, there has been significantly little said concerning lumbering equipment. There is ample evidence indeed that the Soviet "contribution" to Sovromlemn has been very small. Yet between 1946 and 1951, by official admission, lumbering operations on an unusually large scale took place, while published statistics revealed that lumber exports to the Soviet Union soared. In 1952 the R.P.R. government came out with a vast program of reforestation. By then it was clear that the country's timber lands had been markedly diminished. It can be inferred from official texts, issued in 1954 and 1955, that the entire burden of the reforestation program must now be borne by the R.P.R. administration. Sovromlemn had been played out—at least the Soviet obligations toward it.

Not so is the case of Sovrompetrol. When the convention setting it up was signed, it provided that each of the partners would contribute 2,500,000,000 lei. The Rumanian share consisted of the assets of two local companies, "Creditul Minier" and "Redeventa," and of various further oilfields that were not publicly identified, as well as 75 per cent of the

Rumanian State's share in the country's entire oil production. Prices were calculated at the 1938 levels, which meant that deliveries to Sovrompetrol on account of the last-named item were at one stroke doubled. The Soviet contribution consisted of plant and materiel, and of five former German companies, of which two had belonged to French, Dutch, and Belgian shareholders before the war. The general manager of Sovrompetrol was, of course, a Soviet citizen. So were the financial manager, the geological director, and two other directors out of a total of six.

Up to the passage of the Law on Nationalization (June 11, 1948), Sovrompetrol accounted for 34 per cent of Rumania's output of crude oil. Nonetheless throughout this time it was paid compensation by the R.P.R. government, "for the low prices paid by the government of Rumania for petroleum products delivered as part of the reparations." On just one occasion, in June, 1947, Sovrompetrol was thus paid a lump sum of $400,000,-000 in this guise.

For three years Rumania had delivered to Soviet Russia a total of some 1,700,000 tons of oil, at $15 per ton. As a consequence, all existing oil companies, which had in turn to make these huge deliveries to the Rumanian State at such low prices, were ruined. But Sovrompetrol, being partly owned by the Soviet Union, had to continue to be compensated by the Rumanian State for the losses inflicted by that same Soviet Union on Rumania. (*The Rumanian Oil Industry*, a most authoritative book on the subject, by Constantin Iordan, New York University Press, 1955, provides a complete account of these developments.)

In 1948 all other oil companies were nationalized, and two large state companies, "Muntenia" and "Moldova," were set up. These were to produce 66 per cent of all the country's oil. This created an interesting situation. It would have been natural for the R.P.R. administration to favor its own state enterprises; the success of these enterprises might have been expected to be of primary interest to the regime. There was no evidence of any such thing. The two "socialist" state-owned companies were mercilessly subjected to competition by the "capitalist-style" Sovrom, with the result that they both had to be liquidated on September 1, 1950, and soon thereafter absorbed by Sovrompetrol. No precise details have come to light regarding this weird and paradoxical conflict. But one thing might be noted: forced oil deliveries to the Soviet Union ceased at about the same time that "Muntenia" and "Moldova" were scrapped.

The communist propaganda apparatus was reticent throughout; not a word was said for several months. Finally, vague and utterly uninformative references were made by the R.P.R. press to the "former" state companies, a backhanded confirmation of their mysterious demise.

The main conclusion to be drawn from the above is that the Soviet Union has indeed operated a monopoly in Rumania's economy, at least between 1944 and 1955, with every evidence of extra-territorial privileges. This confirms the existence of a quasi-occupational regime that endures to this day. In other words, the Soviet Union has thorough control of the country's economy from the inside.

A joint Soviet-R.P.R. communique issued on September 25, 1954 stated that twelve Sovroms had been bought back by the Bucarest government and that this had been arranged through two conventions signed respectively on March 31 and September 18. Significantly enough, nothing was said either about the price to be paid by Rumania or about the date upon which the "sale" had been effected. Indeed, there was no change in the administration of the companies as late as the autumn of 1955. Two of the original sixteen, Sovromfilm and Sovromasigurare, had been repurchased by the R.P.R. some time in 1954, according to official reports.

THE AGRICULTURAL MUDDLE

The agrarian policy of the R.P.R. government has been exceedingly confused and contradictory throughout. Orders and counterorders, programs and counterprograms have come and gone, some intended for propaganda purposes, others dictated by the very real difficulties encountered. Two major contradictions are discernible as the main causes of these waverings. The first is the inevitable discrepancy between the ultimate aims of the communists and the "dialectic phases" they must accept as the means for attaining those aims. During these phases, principles and theses opposed to the averred purposes must temporarily prevail for demagogic reasons, and such members of the party and government as cling, either truly or allegedly, to the ultimate doctrines are necessarily denounced and "purged." The second contradiction stems from the sudden and imperative changes thrust by the Kremlin's planners and experts upon the local puppets, upsetting "plans" and "party lines." There is every evidence that the sinuosities of the R.P.R. government's attitude toward the social and economic problem of the peasantry are in reality but reflections of the orders received from Moscow, hinging primarily on the immediate needs of the communist-dominated bloc now directed by the Council for Mutual Economic Assistance.

It must be admitted that in Rumania, where the peasantry as a whole has throughout offered an extremely dogged resistance to the communist regime, the task of the communists has not been easy. Contradictions have time and again occasioned the most humiliating self-denunciations and self-accusations in the highest quarters, alternating with upsurges of ruthlessly brutal attempts to solve the difficulties by "direct action." All in all, the latter have failed even more resoundingly than the former. It is no accident that as these lines are being written, the R.P.R. communists find themselves once again attempting to coax the recalcitrant peasantry by a show of friendliness, as they did at the outset, after repeatedly failing to compel compliance by force and terror.

Almost immediately after it was brought to power, the communist-dominated Groza government proceeded to introduce a so-called land reform, based on a law passed on March 23, 1945. It expropriated all farm properties of those who had collaborated with the Germans, of "war criminals," and of those who had not worked their own properties in excess of 10 hectares during the previous seven years. It also expropriated all other properties of over 50 hectares. Thenceforth privately owned land was strictly limited to 50 hectares. This sweeping confiscatory measure resulted in the expropriation of 143,219 individual holdings, totalling 1,143,-911 hectares. A total of 1,057,674 hectares were distributed among 796,129 individuals, and the State kept for itself 37,565 hectares. The individual beneficiaries received on an average a plot of some three acres. Compare this with the land reforms of 1919-1921, when 4,312,920 hectares were distributed to 1,036,367 landless peasants, each getting approximately 4 hectares, under a "capitalist-bourgeois-landowners' regime."

It will be recalled that more or less similar land reforms were carried out in the other "liberated" countries of South-Eastern Europe during the years 1944-1946. In many cases all basic conditions of a social and economic nature were simply ignored. This was notably so in Rumania, where, after the reforms that followed World War I, a new land distribution could lead but to a further fragmentation of holdings that was economically unsound. R.P.R. statistics published in *Probleme Economice* (September-October, 1948) give the following figures:

Size of Individual Holdings	Per Cent of Total Area in 1941	Per Cent of Total Area in 1948
Less than 1 hectare	1.9	7.1
1– 3 hectares	14.2	26.2
3– 5 hectares	16.7	24.4
5–10 hectares	30.1	23.0
10–20 hectares	14.6	10.6
20–50 hectares	6.9	5.7
Over 50 hectares	15.6	3.0
	100.00	100.00

This means that the only category of holdings that benefited from the expropriation was that of less than 5 hectares, which, as we have already pointed out earlier in this chapter, are economically unproductive. The plots comprising between 5 and 10 hectares and those ranging from 10 to 20 hectares, which had tended to be consolidated between 1921 and 1941, decreased in number once again. The communist-enacted land reform, by fostering the splinter-holdings, necessarily resulted in a general decline of farm production.

The reason why Rumania's communists took this step in 1945, in such flagrant contradiction to their doctrine of collectivization is complex. In the first place came perhaps the compliance to the Kremlin's directives. Then came the notion that by thus "handing over the land to those who work it" popularity might accrue to the regime among the peasantry. This, of course, in view of what had been done along these lines a quarter of a century before, was an illusion. Lastly, the purpose may very well have been to demonstrate precisely that individual small-holdings are impracticable, and thus provide an argument for collectivization. This is supported by the official attitude that endures to this day toward the peasant owners of larger farms, who are at every turn denounced as *chiabur*, or kulaks.

Less than four years had to elapse before the communists revealed themselves in their true colors as the enemy of every basic belief and tradition of the Rumanian farmer. The Resolution of March 3-5, 1949, of the Plenary of the Rumanian Workers' Party Central Committee provided this confirmation. Though subsequently obscured for tactical reasons, the Resolution remains the main text of communist agricultural doctrine. It stated unambiguously that the ultimate aim of the party's "general agrarian line" was total collectivization. It announced that, "in order to free the masses from darkness and want, socialism will be built up in the villages: in other words, the villages will have to become collective farms." This, of course, meant the expropriation of individual holdings. The model adopted was that of the *Artel*, as prescribed by Stalin 1930, when the struggle for collectivization was at its height in the Soviet Union itself. The model statute for collective farms provided that members must pool their entire land, equipment, and livestock, being permitted to retain property rights only in regard to small vegetable plots, implements, and livestock. Ownership of everything else had already been expressly repudiated in the Cominform Resolution of June 28, 1948, directed against the Yugoslav communist party: "It is impossible to solve this task so long as individual peasant economy predominates in the country, inevitably breeding capitalism." In an article in the Cominform paper for August, 1949, Vasile Luca, who was subsequently purged but who at the time was highly authoritative, stated flatly that "the working peasantry of the R.P.R. is even more resolutely following the way charted by the Party—the way of the socialist reorganization of agriculture. In his article on Co-operation, Lenin wrote, 'Under our system, co-operative enterprises differ from capitalist enterprises because they are collective enterprises, but they do not differ from Socialist enterprises if the land on which they are situated and the means of production belong to the State, i.e., to the working class. Only such producer co-operatives together with State farms are a socialist type of farming.'" But the Rumanian farmers, while not opposed to a cooperative system in principle, resolutely rejected the "way" so glibly announced by the communists. Barely 55 collective farms were set up during the year 1949. The administration thereupon dropped the pretense of "persuasion." A bitter campaign began in the winter of 1949 against the embattled farmers. But this provoked a series of uprisings throughout the country and their bloody suppression. The death penalty was reintroduced at the time and terror reached new heights. Later, by February, 1950, the regime resorted to its usual method in such cases: a Resolution was made public, criticizing the local authorities of the regions where repression had been most violent, for "failing to apply the methods recommended by the Party for the enactment of collectivization," and promising that pressure would henceforth be eschewed.

One year later the administration had to admit that neither persuasion nor terror would achieve the speedy collectivization they wanted. In the entire country only 1070 collective farms had been set up by the summer of 1951, comprising barely 300,000 hectares—one-thirtieth of the total arable area, and one-seventy-third of all farm land.

On September 18, 1951, a sweeping Decision was issued regarding the "organization of work in the sector of collective farms and of agricultural associations (i.e., farming associations of the Soviet TOZ-type)." This was an admission of failure and a partial capitulation before the peasantry's stubborn resistance. The Decision while denouncing "serious deviations from the Party line," also introduced to Rumania the TOZ-type association of individual farmers, in the hope that it might prove less unpalatable to the country's farmers than the true collective farm, since it was of a temporary nature and allowed the retention of property rights, thus coming close to the producers' cooperatives familiar in Rumania since before the war. Of course, the Decision stressed that this was an "inferior form"; but it was already a far cry from the previous shrill denunciations of anything remotely resembling true cooperatives.

Obviously, the communists realized by then that the expropriation of the land was the one thing which would be opposed by the Rumanian (and Eastern European) peasants with violent determination; and at the same time, the situation of these countries differed from that of Russia in that they did not have the huge reserves of virgin land which Stalin found in 1929–1930 (and Krushchev in 1954–1955) in the Asiatic regions of Russia. Mass deportation of the peasant cultivators to those untilled lands, and their replacement on their own private land by collective brigades is not possible in small countries where the last patch of earth is worked by the industrious peasants.

A subsequent outcome of this first tactical change was the massive purge of the "scapegoats," carried out in the spring of 1952. Ana Pauker, while holding down the job of Foreign Minister, was made responsible for mistakes in the agricultural field and accused of "rightist and leftist deviations" (brutal collectivization and purchasing from the kulaks), fell from grace. Soon thereafter, Vasile Vaida who had been Minister of Agriculture, was likewise purged, and replaced by Gheorghe Apostol. The latter immediately reverted to the coaxing tactics that had in the past so dismally failed. However, by the summer of 1953, what was to be described as a "new look" was introduced in the entire field of agriculture, ostensibly replacing administrative persecution with outright assistance. The farmers were required to deliver increasing quantities of produce to the state. The effects of this "new look" will be discussed later in this chapter. By official count there were 1,980 collective farms in existence in Rumania in August, 1953, accounting for a total of 732,000 hectares, or almost double the number set up by 1951. But the TOZ-type agricultural associations, introduced in 1951, numbered 2,000 and accounted for a total area of 250,000 hectares. Thus the number of TOZ associations had grown at a greater pace than that of true collective farms. In August, 1954 there were 2,048 kolkhozes in the country, as against 2,410 agricultural associations.

The change in agrarian policy or the "new look" was officially announced by Gheorghiu-Dej on August 23, 1954, when he publicly admitted that "serious economic errors" had been made by the regime, not only in the field of agriculture, but also in industry, trade, technical education, and so forth. The communist Prime Minister admitted notably that the general objectives set by the Five-Year Plan had proved to be beyond the economic possibilities of Rumania, and that the living standards of the "workers" had not shown "sufficient improvement." From then on, he announced, the immediate task of the administration was *to reach and to surpass the pre-war level of agricultural production.*

At one stroke the communist boss of Rumania thus set at nought all the triumphant statistics of "progress" and "success" issued by his regime up to that time. The country's principal industry, farming, had, under communist rule, actually fallen far below the level attained under the much-decried "bourgeois-landowning" regime.

There had, of course, been incredible incompetence and gross negligence. There had been wholly insufficient farm machinery. There had been looting by the local communists themselves, added to the looting by the Soviet occupation armies. There had, too, been stubborn opposition from the peasantry. In agriculture, the notion had been that production per hectare could somehow be increased by decreasing the areas sown, provided mechanization was intensified. Collectivization had resulted mainly in pauperizing the peasantry. But the greatest single reason for failure was the communist plans themselves. Investments in agriculture had been withheld, all efforts being directed to the factory industries, notably that woeful Moloch, heavy industry.

The Five-Year Plan allowed but 10 per cent of total investment to agriculture. Indeed the plan for 1949 provided but 9.4 per cent, and that for 1950 a bare 6.6 per cent. Moreover, this very small percentage of the investments in agriculture has been further reduced *pro rata* by the non-fulfilment of the entire program of investments in all branches of production. According to United Nations' statistics, the entire investment plan of Rumania has been under-fulfilled by 13 per cent. It is obvious that, under such conditions, the agricultural sector suffered most—the communists considered it the least important. Thus, what happened in Bulgaria, Czechoslovakia and Hungary (which, unlike Rumania, did release some statistics) and where the UN (Economic Survey of Europe 1948) detected a "negative result" in the estimated net investment in fixed capital in agriculture, happened also in Rumania.

Let us, for instance, look into the situation with regard to tractors in 1953. In 1941 there had been some 12,000 tractors in Rumania. Many were lost as the result of war operations and Soviet looting. But in August, 1953, Gheorghiu-Dej announced with pride that there were 14,080 farm tractors in operation in the country—this after eight years of communist rule and allegedly increased industrial production! And even the absurdly low figure given by the communist Prime Minister can hardly pass muster, for in 1949 he had announced that there were 8,500 tractors in the whole country, and, if we add the avowed yearly production of some 1,500 tractors to this, we still get a total of only about 13,000 for 1953. There have, moreover, been official statements to the effect that in 1953 between 40 and 50 per cent of the tractors of the S.M.T.'s (the State Tractor Stations that operate the overwhelming number of the country's farm machinery) were out of commission for one reason or another. Let it be borne in mind, too, that the S.M.T.'s were under orders then to work only land belonging to collective farms and agricultural associations, and that individual farmers simply had to make out as best they could.

As to the livestock position, in 1938, in the territory that is today's Rumania, there were well in excess of one and a half million horses. In 1949 there were less than one million. The Five-Year Plan provided that by the end of 1955 there should be 1,200,000 farm horses—almost half a million less than there were in 1938. Much the same thing had happened in regard to oxen and other livestock. Hence the individual farmers could do little to keep up production on the land.

The more general aspects of the "new course" will be discussed in the part of this survey dealing with industry. Here we must try to answer two questions relevant to the agricultural sector. First, from an economic point of view, did agricultural production receive the help and investment which were promised in the preliminary propaganda? Secondly, from a social point of view, were the private cultivators less persecuted, and indeed encouraged, as the communist government pledged?

Investment, according to the changes in the Five-Year Plan in 1953, was to be differently allocated. Heavy industry, which in the original Plan had been assigned 44.1 per cent of the total, was to get only 34.1; the production of consumer goods would get 14.1 instead of the original 9.3 per cent; agriculture was allocated 13.1, instead of the original 10 per cent.

Between the percentages there could be detected a supplementary fund of 5 billion leis (the total investment forecast at the beginning of the Five-Year Plan was 66.5 billion leis). These 5 billions were divided as follows: 3 billions for consumer goods industry, shoes, textiles, etc.; and 2 billions for agriculture, out of which 650 millions were allocated to the kolkhozes and sodhozes, and 1 billion 350 millions for the endowments and maintenance of the machines and tractor stations and for the improvement of the livestock.

Great plans were set afoot by the "Directives" of August 27, 1954: the total area sown to cereals in 1955 was set at 7,220,000 hectares; in 1956 the area would be 7,360,000 hectares (in 1938 there were well over 8,000,000 hectares under grain cultivation). "During the next two or three years that follow," it was promised that the total output of cereal would reach 10,500,000 tons, with all sorts of improvements in the offing, like greater use of fertilizers and "new" agro-technical methods.

So far as can be determined from communist statistics, the announced investments for the mechanization of agriculture had reached 1,800,000,000 lei by 1954. The R.P.R. administration states that 5,820 tractors were made available during the years 1953 and 1954. This, however, comes altogether too close to the figure officially stated to be the total number of tractors produced in that time (some 6,500), of which, likewise by official boast, 1,800 were exported in 1954 alone. Also, it must be noted, the tractors currently made and given to agriculture at this time are mostly 15-horsepower machines, "conventional tractors." And even if we accept the R.P.R. figures, we must still observe that the Five-Year Plan provides at least 10,000 more tractors to be made available than the announced number. The same may be said for other farm machinery, of which the distribution of 1,780 threshers, 615 combines, and 2,777 reapers has been officially announced.

As for the results of agricultural production as a whole, official figures set the total cereal production for 1954 at 9 million tons (the goal for 1955 was 10 million tons).

The current official insistence on corn production is significant. It is, of course, the direct reflection of the "Krushchev policy." Alleged improvements in this field were stated to have resulted in a total of 6 million tons in 1954, an average of "almost 2,000 kilograms to the hectare," according to the boasts of Radio Bucarest. It was similarly boasted that the wheat yield averaged about 1,100 kilograms to the hectare (in 1938 the average was 1,300 kilograms to the hectare); but it is amply evident that wheat is currently of far less interest to the communist bosses of the R.P.R. To be sure, the increase of corn production is intended to improve the livestock position, and ultimately to supply more meat (it is not clear whether for the internal market of Rumania or for export to Soviet Russia). But the fact that Rumanian peasants are obliged now to cultivate less wheat than corn will have a melancholy effect. For generations Rumanian peasants have striven to eat more bread than "mamaliga," or corn-mash. The situation has steadily improved over the last fifty years. Consumption of bread rose simultaneously with the increase of wheat production. By reducing the production of wheat, the communists bring back the villagers to the elementary standard of life of fifty years ago.

Generally speaking, the conclusion which might be drawn at the end of the first "two years of new course" is this: mechanization, and investments for the mechanization, of agricultural production are lower, at the end of this effort, than in the initial Five-Year Plan; the total quantity of arable land has been enlarged by 300,000 hectares; the productivity per hectare of corn, and especially of wheat, was lower than the pre-war one; the expenses of state controlled agricultural production were considerably raised by the creation of administrative teams, destined only to "organise, control and stimulate" the work of the peasants whose salaries created a very heavy burden on the general cost of agricultural production.

What of the "new course" from the social point of view, the attitude toward the peasants themselves? According to communist reckoning, there were in 1944 the following categories of agriculturists: 1.1 per cent classed as landlords, 11.8 per cent *chiabur* (kulaks), 44.7 per cent "middling" peasants, 19.1 per cent "poor" peasants, 15.8 per cent farm workers, and 7.5 "others." If we take into account that 83 per cent of all the cultivated land was effectively worked by purely family concerns (Roberts:

Rumania, Political Problems of an Agrarian State), these percentages confirm the patriarchal social character of the Rumanian countryside. However, the communists took the line of discriminating among the various
categories they distinguished, and of seeking to split them into antagonistic groups. The party line was one of "containment" toward the
chiabur, with liquidation as the ultimate goal. The "middling peasant"
had to be won over—first to separate him from the *chiabur* and second
to seek to persuade him to enter the collective farms. The "poor peasant"
was considered the "natural ally" of the regime for what seemed to be
self-evident reasons.

Discrimination worked in two main ways: technical facilities and
credits were extended to collective farms and to poor peasants, while disproportionately high taxes were imposed on self-supporting households.
Delivery quotas were scaled so as to add to the burdens of the latter. In
1949 the "poor" peasant was required to deliver 20 per cent of what he
produced, while the "rich" had to give up some 60 per cent. Official prices
for all deliveries were absurdly low: 5.60 lei for a kilogram of grain, as
against 30 lei, the price on the free market. In 1951 a system of fixed
quota deliveries was introduced, under which "poor" peasants had to deliver 70 to 250 kilograms per hectare, "middling" peasants 300 to 350
kilograms per hectare, and "rich" peasants between 590 and 825 kilograms
to the hectare. Collective farms in contrast were held to deliver only 200
kilograms per hectare, though they were favored by being provided with
farm machinery, fertilizers, and other facilities. Similar discriminations
existed in the matter of taxation: in 1950, 1,100,000 "poor" peasants paid
no taxes at all, 1,850,000 "middling" peasants accounted for 55 per cent
of all agricultural taxes, and 150,000 kulaks made up the balance of 45 per
cent.

The pressures put on the persecuted categories had a double purpose,
to squeeze as much as possible from the proceeds of their labor, and to
force them in sheer desperation to join collective or state farms. But the
results were otherwise. An attitude of hostile passivity became general
among the peasants, and farm production dipped sharply to the barest
subsistence level.

Under such circumstances, it was hardly surprising to see the communists, after four fruitless years, changing the line of approach. In his address
of August 23, 1953, Gheorghiu-Dej announced among other things: "The

State will help small and middling peasant households with farm machinery, provide cheap credit . . . help them to obtain chemical fertilizers, building material, and so forth." On the following November 6, in an article in the Cominform Journal, he remarked: "It is necessary in the interests of the national economy to ensure that kulak farms turn out a considerable proportion of agricultural production. Whilst pursuing the consistent policy of restricting the kulaks, . . . it is necessary at the same time to enable them to take part in agricultural production and commodity exchanges."

In reality this new official attitude meant simply that thenceforth all categories of farmers were placed under the obligation to make increasing deliveries of produce in proportion to their output. For this, all categories had to be provided with a minimum of facilities, notably farm machinery from the machine-and-tractor-stations (SMT).

A word must be said here about the way in which the SMT-stations work. Here, too, fixed quotas were introduced which must be paid either in goods or cash by the peasant who hires machines and tractors. In August 1955 these quotas were as follows:

Kind of work	Tariff of payment per hectare in kg.				
	ZONE I	II	III	IV	V
Ploughing for autumn sowing	96	86	79	71	56
Preparation for autumn sowing	157	142	179	118	94
Sowing	32	29	26	22	17
Reaping and binding	74	67	61	56	44

This means that, for instance, a wheat-producer, who produces an average of 1000 kgr. per hectare must pay for the hiring of machines between 241 and 369 kgr.—that is to say between a quarter and a third of the production. (Agricultural association (TOZ) benefits form a reduction of 10% and kolkhozes of 20%.) If one adds to that the forcible deliveries-quota which represent a scale of between 20–60% per hectare, one might easily see how little is left to the farmer.

The concessions made by the administration immediately following the introduction of the "new look" proved to be inadequate. Debts and undelivered quotas of the preceding year were cancelled. Certain taxes and such delivery quotas as those for milk, meat and wool were reduced. A new system of advance sales for cattle and animal produce, for industrial raw materials, fruits, and vegetables was instituted. Lastly the taxes on the sales of surplus farm produce (that is, of such com-modities as the farmer had left after delivery of his quotas to the state) were halved, on condition that such sales be made on the official market. Thus, by hook or by crook, the communists sought to secure a monopoly of all farm produce, no matter who the producer might be. This official anxiety was shown by the fact that prices paid for grain by the state were, as often as not, higher than they had been before.

Though there have been some signs of improvement as the result of all these conciliatory measures, there is no evidence that the peasantry has been won over by the regime. One thing cannot be denied, and that is the utter failure of the "ideological policies" of the communists. Col-lectivization has resulted in nothing more impressive than accounting for a bare 12 per cent of farm production. The policy that was launched in 1953 is a simple one of state monopoly. It remains to be seen how it will fare in the long run, and what changes will be made as future necessity or orders from Moscow require. It would seem that the current Regional Plan obligates Rumania to improve its farm production for at least the next five years. So long as this is true, the present attitude of duplicity toward the peasantry may be expected to continue.

This is not an altogether unprecedented situation. Much the same de-velopments have been noted in Tito's Yugoslavia, and have attracted bitter criticism from the Cominform. Conditions in Rumania and in the other countries of South-Eastern Europe are not the same as in the Soviet Union, and the resistance of the local peasantry must be expected to be more difficult to overcome. In none of these small countries is there any scope for mass deportations as there is in the Soviet Union, but it is not out of the question that their recalcitrant rural populations may yet be forcibly uprooted and moved bodily to the still available wastes of the USSR. An experiment along these lines was made in Bessarabia in 1954–1955. But such measures would involve the communists in almost in-superable difficulties, so that it seems likely that the R.P.R. government will have to continue along its current line for some time to come at least—for its own good, if not for the good of Rumania's peasantry itself.

THE PRICE OF INDUSTRIALIZATION

The industrialization program initiated by the communists in 1948 and carried through to the year 1952–1953 appears to have had some success.

This may be said even in the case of Rumania, where that drive started later and made slower headway than, for instance, in Poland and Bulgaria. It was in fact shown once again that much can be done in this field in the countries of Eastern Europe, and that, had circumstances been favorable, these countries might have become active competitors of the industrialized countries of Western Europe, where both their resources of raw materials and their manpower potential are still under-estimated. There can be no doubt that in time, if the pace is not forced and if all local conditions are carefully taken into account, the so-called satellite countries can indeed become predominantly industrial. The coal of Poland and Czechoslovakia, Rumania's petroleum, and the vast available electric energy that can be harnessed in these countries are sufficient for the needs of that region. Let us note in passing that by the end of 1953 the per capita output of fuel and energy of Eastern Europe was almost equal to that of the Soviet Union.

Why, then, were the communists forced in 1953 to stop—be it even provisionally—this obviously promising process? The answer to this query is threefold.

In the first place, the goals set were unattainable. They were in the main both too high and disproportionate to the natural production of raw materials in the individual countries. Furthermore, these goals, especially after 1951, were primarily military rather than truly economic. The second cause must be sought in the ruthlessness of the methods adopted. The communists made the fullest use of every conceivable means to force the pace, ranging from the constant increase of "production norms" to the use of forced labor on a large scale. The result was that resistance increased throughout the field of production, and disorganization set in and presently became general. The third reason is the one we have already touched upon in our introductory remarks, the impossibility of building up adequate technical capital in an under-capitalized country without suitable trade exchanges with other countries, notably with industrialized countries that are able to export capital goods. The "satellite" economies were forced into an unprofitable "collaboration" with the Soviet Union.

Let us now see how these adverse conditions worked in the case of Rumania: how, in other words, the communist regime bungled the country's industrialization in practice.

Rumania's industry showed the following distribution as of 1938 (industrial concerns with more than 20 employees)*:

	Number	Personnel	Value of output (1000 lei)
Food	974	38,376	15,577,444
Textile	640	74,077	14,691,948
Chemical	397	28,298	14,154,605
Metallurgic	366	54,321	11,362,803
Wood	713	43,376	3,583,563
Leather	158	13,366	3,437,533
Paper	157	15,222	3,088,518
Electrotechnic	31	2,684	674,620
Glass	39	5,691	527,135
Ceramic	34	1,652	148,948
TOTAL:	3,767	289,117	69,206,738

The oil industry suffered heavy damage during the war years, first from the intense exploitation introduced by the Germans, then from Allied aerial bombardment. The rest of the country's industries had also suffered from depreciation and obsolescence in that period. But, by and large, it can be said that Rumanian industry was in working order at the time it was taken over by the communists.

On July 11, 1948, all industrial enterprises were nationalized. Meanwhile the Soviet occupation authorities had caused production to drop considerably through forced deliveries, dismantling and removal of plants, and disorders systematically provoked among the workers against the "capitalist" owners. Thus oil production dwindled from the 6,610,000 tons reached in 1938 to 3,804,000 tons in 1947, paper from 70,000 tons (as of 1931) to 47,000 tons in 1947, coal from 299,000 to 170,000, electric energy from 1,148,000 kw (1938) to 700,000 in 1946–1947, chemical fertilizers from 2,500,000 tons (1938) to 1,330,000 in 1948, and so forth.

Immediately following nationalization, as early as 1949, when the first one-year plan was put into effect, production began to rise. The fact that the State, and, notably, the Sovroms had become the "capitalist bosses," made the attitude of both the administration and the Soviet occupation authorities favorable to industry. An iron hand was clamped down on the industrial workers. Following two "general rehearsals" in the form of two

* Source: V. Madgearu, Evolutia Economiei Romanesti Dupa Rasboiul Mondial (Bucarest, 1940).

successive one-year plans, the first five-year plan was announced on December 16, 1950. It was designed to run from 1951 to 1955. Article 2 of the plan stated that investments to the total of 1,330 billion lei (at prices calculated for 1950) would be made. They were to be allocated as follows:

Industry	51.4%
of which	
Capital goods	(42.1%)
Consumer goods	(9.3%)
Agriculture and forestry	10%
Transportation	16.2%
Building industry	2%
Social and cultural projects	13.4%
Government administration	2%
Scientific and geological research	2.8%

The plan also provided that the productivity of labor would be raised by 57%. The summary of planned production for 1955 was laid down as follows:

Coal	8,533,000 m tons
Crude oil	10,000,000 m tons
Methane gas	3,900,000 cubic meters
Coal, metallurgical	200,000 m tons
Pig iron	800,000 m tons
Steel	1,252,000 m tons
Electric motors	433,000 m
Tractors	5,000 pieces
Tractor ploughs	6,250 pieces
Reapers, binders	2,500 pieces
Cement	2,855,000 m tons
Lumber	3,500,000 cubic meters
Soda ash	51,000 m tons
Soda, caustic	52,000 m tons
Sulfuric acid	143,000 m tons
Cotton and vigogne	266,500,000 square meters
Flax and hemp fabrics	40,300,000 square meters
Wool cloth	39,400,000 square meters
Silk fabrics	41,800,000 square meters
Footwear	20,700,000 pairs
Rubber footwear	2,700,000 pairs
Bread	1,240,000 m tons
Sugar	278,000 m tons
Electrical energy	4,700,000,000 kw/hrs

"Installed" electric power was to be in excess of 1,700,000 kw in 1955. The machine-building industry, "the pivot of industrial development of the national economy . . . which will produce the necessary equipment for the oil and mining industries, the tractors and agricultural machinery, etc." was stressed in particular. It was also announced that the living standards of the "working masses" would constantly improve, so that by 1955 they would be "80 per cent higher than in 1950."

Additionally it was stated that there would be approximately 3,000,000 workers, technicians, and office workers in the "national economy" by 1955, representing an increase of 38 per cent over 1950. The "working class" itself was expected to increase by 570,000 men and women. In 1955 the population would receive, through state trade and cooperatives, 1,235 tons of bread, 165,000 tons of sugar, 271,000,000 square meters of cotton fabric, 27,000,000 square meters of woolen fabric, and 20,700,000 pairs of shoes of various sorts. We reproduce these figures mainly for the purpose of comparison with the actual production figures given above.

The critique of the five-year plan and of the production plan in particular will be found in the introduction to this chapter. Here we shall simply note that because of the discrimination in investments production dropped steeply both in agriculture and consumer goods, and that living standards fell correspondingly from even the very low level of 1950.

What, now, of those branches of industry where successes were truly attained, at least during the initial stages of the plan?

Good results were unquestionably registered, for instance, in oil production. While, of course, the percentage figures of which the communists are so fond cannot provide much information, a noted refugee Rumanian economist, C. N. Iordan, has gone to great pains in his book, *The Rumanian Oil Industry*, to establish the real state of oil output from 1949 on. He gives the following estimates: Production for 1949 was probably about 4,530,000 tons, that is, 9.4 per cent higher than in 1948 (estimated by international circles at 4,300,000 tons). In 1950, notwithstanding the sanguine predictions and the triumphant official statistics published at the end of the year, production fell to a total of 4,052,000 tons (we shall presently discuss the causes for this severe drop). In 1951 production rose again to 4,988,000 tons. This remarkable recovery is to be explained by the complete monopoly gained by Sovrompetrol under the circumstances described earlier. In 1952 a new gain was registered, the impressive total of 6,430,000 tons being attained. Finally in 1953 the communist authorities announced that the production plan for petroleum was realized only to the extent of 96.7 per cent, which would mean approximately nine million tons. This is certainly an exaggeration, and the best available estimates place the true figure at about 7,500,000 tons, still an increase.

It must be borne in mind that (although a certain school of thought among geologists considers that Rumania's general reserves of oil are declining) the drop in production between the years 1938 and 1945 is to be explained mainly by the conditions of war, and by the excessive exploitation operating under German domination. From 1945 to 1948 the further decline was due to the mindless dismantling of plants carried out by the Soviet occupation authorities, and, as we have pointed out already, to the measures enacted against the petroleum companies as such.

Under the Sovrom regime, from 1950 on, special efforts came into play. In the first place, though shortages still persisted, there was marked improvement in technical equipment. Rumanian metallurgical production increased, while Soviet-made equipment also began to be made available. The quality of equipment is still far from satisfactory, but certainly great efforts are being made to better it. Then, too, much was done in the field of prospecting and exploration, with Soviet technical assistance quite lavishly provided. Yet in spite of all this, and the efforts of Sovrompetrol notwithstanding, there is much evidence that incompetent management, poor materiel, and especially poor maintenance are still responsible for production lags. Official admissions abound, and there is much talk of "sabotage." Special punishments for carelessness have been set up by law in the field of oil production, stressing this official concern.

It must be noted, too, that sheer quantity of production means little by itself, and that production costs are more surely indicative of true successes. In the R.P.R., the entire price structure is arbitrary and artificial. Though under current circumstances it is virtually impossible to establish any precise figures or even proportions, a careful evaluation made by Mr. Iordan shows beyond a shadow of doubt that costs far exceed the prices paid by the Soviet Union for deliveries of petroleum products. In the past, when the Rumanian oil industry operated under normal conditions, marketing its products abroad at the prevailing world prices, it accounted for fully one quarter of the state revenue. Today, in contrast, it is the state revenue and budget that must contribute to meet the Soviet Union's vast demands in this field.

Though labor is extremely cheap in the R.P.R. oil industry, owing to the system of high norms, the cost of production is manifestly disproportionately high. There are a number of causes for this, that have recently come into play. We may list the following: costly investments made in highly priced materiel supplied by the Soviet Union; uneconomical exploitation of oil wells, entailing, for instance, the abandonment of wells of lower yield; and the profits demanded by Sovrompetrol (analogous to an unprofitable burden of dividends in a capitalist system). In view of the fact that, working under such conditions, Rumania's oil industry sells almost exclusively for export, at low prices set by the Soviet Union, it is immediately apparent why this industry is not only unprofitable to the country's economy, but an outright burden.

Two conclusions follow. First, the Rumanian oil industry, which always in the past was open to the criticism that its profits did not go to increase the national income to any equitable extent, has become a losing concern under the communist regime because of the monopoly position of Sovrompetrol up to the end of 1955. The second is that, if even under the very unfavorable conditions we have outlined above, quantitative production of petroleum has increased, it would have assuredly done immeasurably better had the oil industry had the advantage of truly modern improvements, as the oil industries of the free world have had in the course of the last ten years.

Let us now turn to another field where some success has been registered: electric energy. Here we have two plans working in combination. The first, the ten-year plan for electrification, introduced on November 15, 1950, which is itself divided into two five-year phases. This provides the following:

	1950	1955	1960
Installed Power	740,000 kw.	1,700,000 kw.	2,600,000 kw.
Available Power	600,000 kw.	1,660,000 kw.	2,500,000 kw.
of which			
Thermic	550,000 kw.	1,370,000 kw.	1,665,000 kw.
Hydraulic	50,000 kw.	290,000 kw.	835,000 kw.
Power per sq. km.	2.53 kw/sq.km.	7.0 kw/sq.km.	10.6 kw/sq.m.
Power per head	37.5 w/head	105 w/head	150 w/head

The second plan, the five-year plan itself, makes much the same provisions, setting production for 1955 at 4,700,000 kilowatt-hours. The largest hydroelectric plants were to be built at Bistritza-Stejar and Moroeni, and the important thermoelectric installations at Ovidiu (on the planned but uncompleted Danube-Black Sea Canal) and at Doicesti (now called Gheorghiu-Dej).

Careful evaluations and calculations show the country's electric energy production to have grown as follows:

1950 — 2,000 million kw/hours
1951 — 2,470 " "
1952 — 2,900 " "
1953 — 3,290 " "

The progress is indubitable, but it is no less indubitable that it falls far short of the plan's provisions. The goal set for 1955—4,700,000 kw/hours became in fact increasingly unlikely as the years went by. In the speech on the slowing down and reduction of the Plan, Gheorghiu-Dej showed that as far back as 1953 that "installed power" was to be reduced from 1,700,000 kw/hours to 1,380,000 kw/hours. Hence, though Gheorghiu-Dej did not say in so many words, we may presume that production too was meant to be reduced to a total of 3,700,000 to 3,800,000 kw/hours.

In this field too all communist-issued figures are utterly unreliable, and blatant discrepancies have been discerned in them by Mr. and Mrs. Bunescu, two experts in this field. For instance, the figure given by the R.P.R. Ministry of Electric Energy for 1954 production, namely 1,000,000 kilowatts, is grossly in excess of the true figure, which is some 822,000 kilowatts according to the most painstaking calculations. Another official assertion, that the production for 1954 represented 3,658,600,000 kilowatt-hours, must likewise be rejected, since the total number of hours set down in the plan is 2,765, which even multiplied by the boasted million kilowatts, does not amount to more than 2,765,000,000 kw/hours, which is almost exactly the figure given by the regime for 1952 and falls short by 1,100,000,000 kw/hours of the figure announced officially for 1954.

The greater part by far of all the electric energy that is being produced goes, by official admission, to industry, notably to the mining and petroleum industries. Domestic consumption was greatly reduced as far back as 1950 by rationing in the cities and by the outright prohibition of the use of electricity for cooking or heating purposes in rural areas. As for the number of villages—400—stated by the administration to have been electrified since 1950, it should be pointed out that the greater part are in or close to the large industrial centers, and in them, the major part of the available electric current is consumed in factories and offices.

Finally, a word is in order concerning the agreement for the export of electric current to Bulgaria, signed in 1947 and put into effect in 1949. The exact amount of power thus drained from the country cannot be ascertained, of course, such a matter being of the nature of a state secret under a communist regime. What is known, however, is that, whereas Bulgaria pays at the rate of o.o6 Swiss francs per kilowatt-hour, the private citizen in Rumania pays three and a half times this price for domestic consumption. There is much reason to believe, moreover, that it is in fact the Soviet army and navy that use the greater part of the electric energy supplied to Bulgaria. As is the case with most of the power supplied by the two plants Ovidiu I and Ovidiu II, the ultimate beneficiaries are the large Soviet naval bases set up on the Rumanian and Bulgarian coast of the Black Sea.

What of the production of coal? Here increases are much more questionable. A large coke plant has been constructed in Hunedoara, but its output is as yet unascertained, though communist sources place it at 700,000 tons. Total coal production figures are approximately as follows:

1938	2,396,000 tons
1946	2,012,000 "
1947	2,268,000 "
1948	2,400,000 "
1949	2,750,000 "
1951	3,600,000 "
1952	4,000,000 "
1953	4,300,000 "

To foster this increase, the sum of 25,900,000,000 lei was earmarked in the plan as investment scheduled to be made up to the year 1955. The real investments, however, would appear to exceed this sum, seeing that equipment was imported from the Soviet Union by Sovromcarbune and by Sovrommetal. The latter company has brought in plant for the processing of lignite by chemical means. It is known that most of the coal produced in Rumania is immature lignite of low caloric content, that it is unusable in its natural state for the manufacture of metallurgical coke. This means, among other things, that the production price of the coke used in industry is excessively high. Yet even this costly increased production falls short of domestic requirements and of the initial targets. This is shown by the fact that the R.P.R. continues to import coal from the Soviet Union, Poland and Czechoslovakia. Moreover, at the Second Congress of the Rumanian Workers' Party in December 1955, the R.P.R. government confessed that coal production had fallen short by two million tons of the Five-Year Plan target. This was the most resounding failure recognized by the government in its report.

In metallurgy, too, advances have been registered. In an official publication of the British Iron and Steel Federation, *Steel Developments in Rumania* (Vol. 27, No. 2, February, 1952) we find the following note: "Before nationalization in June 1948 there were three main plants, together with a number of smaller iron and steel works in Rumania. Their relative importance is shown by the following table of capacities, as they stood just before transfer of ownership.

Capacity of Rumanian Iron and Steel Plants *

	Resita	Hunedoara	Titan Nadrag-Calan	Others	Total
Iron ore (own mines)	45,000	120,000	80,000	15,000	260,000
Coke	90,000†	Nil	Nil	Nil	90,000
Charcoal (output)	Nil	20,000	22,000	6,000	48,000
Pig iron	120,000	150,000	25,000	3,000	298,000
Open hearth steel	240,000	100,000	75,000	10,000	425,000
Electric steel	10,000	8,000	Nil	12,000	30,000
Rolled products	220,000	100,000	105,000	110,000	535,000‡
Tubes	Nil	Nil	Nil	35,000	35,000

* First half of 1948.
† Since doubled.
‡ Including 120,000 tons of plates.

However, the British publication points out, the greatly increased capacity achieved in 1949 and 1950 does not correspond to the reserves of raw materials: "Iron ore is also close at hand, but despite expansion of local mining, ore output is insufficient to cover Reshitza's [Resita] requirements. Since Hunedoara supplies are also tight, considerable quantities have to be obtained abroad, and in 1947 imports were exclusively from the USSR. The 600-mile rail/water journey from the Ukraine naturally results in greatly increased costs." Indeed it is this discrepancy between increased capacity and lack of sufficient raw material that determined the line of production. International data show this line to have been as follows:

Year	Iron minerals	Pig iron	Steel	Metallurgical products
		(in 1,000 tons)		
1948	209	191	341	306
1949	324	275	458	349
1950	395	335	556	387
1951	477	350	643	442
1952	653	390	694	512
1953	653	456	750	512

In 1953, according to official statements, pig iron production dropped by about 20 per cent below plan provisions for that year. This is not due to the industrial plants themselves, which continue to have a capacity in excess of available raw materials. The activity of Rumania's metallurgical industry as a whole after 1950 has been in direct relation to the imports of ores. An acute shortage of raw materials became evident in 1951, when an intensive campaign for the collection of scrap metal was initiated. In 1950 Rumania imported approximately 250,000 tons of ores, mostly from Krivoy Rog, and in 1951 some 300,000 tons. By 1953 stagnation was even more manifest. The United Nations *Economic Bulletin for Europe* for May, 1955, states: "The steel industries of the smaller producing countries, Hungary and Rumania, both handicapped by their dependence on distant sources for their ores, were to stabilize their output in the knowledge that it would be factors other than steel supplies which would limit the output in their engineering industries."

Thus the metallurgical industry, the key of heavy industry in communist economic plans, reached a deadlock in Rumania in the year 1953.

The grandiose industrialization plans, even had they not been endangered by the major domestic causes which we shall presently examine, had to be slowed down, owing to the insufficient supply of raw materials and to the refusal of Soviet Russia to increase its exports to Rumania in proportion to the requirements of the Plan. The return to agriculture also implied the abandonment to a great extent both of the initial plan and of the pace of the industrialization plan.

In 1950 the Kremlin decided to impose a new rearmament program on the satellite states. According to a study titled "Rumania in 1952" (in *World Today*, London, July, 1952), the satellite countries "were to be forced to take a greater share in the renewed effort of Soviet Russia whose main aim was to maintain the margin of superiority in fighting potential which she had achieved since 1945 and which would be endangered were the West to implement its own new armament programme. The satellite armament and heavy industries were to be increased, standardized and kept up to the mark. Rumania's army, restricted by the Peace Treaty to 200,000 men exceeded its limits by the addition of a further 100,000 men. The speed of this reform was astounding, and it also brought with it immediate economic changes. The industries of the satellite countries, as well as fulfilling their own military programmes, had to be integrated within the Eastern bloc's programme of armament production. Such an effort would not be produced without straining to the utmost the already meagre and exhausted resources of the countries and imposing new sacrifices upon the population. The United Nations *Economic Survey of Europe in 1951* noticed that 'In all the Cominform countries output plans were revised upwards with an increased emphasis on heavy industry, and one of the reasons given for the revisions was the need to secure much larger armaments production and the maintenance of larger forces.' The same survey also reported a further lowering in the average standard of living of the industrial workers of those countries 'accentuated by the diversion of a greater share of the industrial effort towards the defense programme. Inflation and a shortage of consumer goods followed, while a higher output was demanded and disciplinary measures were taken in the factories.' "

This threefold effort of continuing deliveries to the Soviet Union, while carrying forward the industrialization plan, and at the same time taking part in this regional rearmament program inevitably led to three main results. An appalling inflation was followed by the almost complete disappearance of consumer goods, whereupon working conditions became increasingly stringent, with the introduction of stepped-up norms and harshly punitive disciplinary regulations. In turn this brought about a proliferation of forced labor camps.

The inflationary spiral, which in spite of such measures as the so-called currency reform of 1947 continued to mount, reached unprecedented heights during 1950 and 1951. A new currency reform was carried out in January, 1952, which struck particularly hard at the peasantry and at the highly specialized workers and stakhanovites in the industries who had been able to save something of their earnings. It will be found discussed at some length in another section of this work.

The endemic shortage of consumer goods and food reached a new low during the years 1951–1952. Long lines waited from dawn to dusk for a little bread, a handful of beans, or a cupful of watered milk, and many returned home empty-handed, day after day. On the other hand, the possibility of buying from the so-called free market was remote, as its prices, already high, became, after the currency-reform, totally inaccessible to the working people. Moreover, the administration, striving to attain the "planned objectives," decided at the same time that productivity must be increased. Production norms were raised anew. Piece-work was generally imposed. Sanctions and disciplinary measures were sharpened. This provoked further discontent in the working-class. "Absenteeism," which is a form of mute strike in communist countries, spread irresistibly. Workers who did not come to work, and those who did not fulfil the often unattainable norms of production, were considered "saboteurs." Once condemned, they immediately joined the dark contingents of laborers in forced-labor camps.

Indeed, the miserable ranks of slave labor swelled considerably as the result of the circumstances just described. Surely the notorious Danube-Black Sea Canal project will stand out in the record of communist inhumanity to man. It was unquestionably one of the most ambitious slave-labor projects of Eastern Europe, comprising as it did at least eight separate labor camps with an excess of 40,000 prisoners, to which we must add another 20,000 so-called free workers brought in as skilled labor once the initial excavation work was well advanced. The dreadful living and working conditions have already been described in detail for Western readers, notably in the Report of the United Nations Ad-Hoc Committee, published in June, 1953. There is no need to repeat these horrors here. We must point out some notable aspects of this slave-labor project. First, that it was without doubt an economic undertaking, and its main purpose was not "re-education" as the communists pretended, but simply to carry out a Pharaonic scheme as cheaply as possible. The project stemmed from the COMECON (Council for Mutual Economic Assistance) which was set up in 1949 as a device for coordinating the efforts of the satellite countries. It was not even mentioned in the R.P.R. plan for that year, but a few weeks after the 1949 plan was made known it was announced as one of the greatest economic projects "undertaken on the initiative of the Council for Mutual Assistance," and described as a gigantic "mobilization of human endeavor." In point of fact, the Canal was a project related to Soviet Russia's economic and military schemes, and as such was given top priority by the R.P.R. administration. The official version stated that it would reduce the cost of transportation between the People's Democracies of the Danubian Basin and the Soviet Union.

Then, it should also be recalled that the vast slave labor force brought to toil on this gigantic project was made up of political prisoners and of people officially branded as "vagabonds and beggars" who in reality were unfortunates deliberately deprived by the regime of the right to seek

gainful employment, in other words of various social categories considered
to be enemies of the communist regime. It was then the policy of the
R.P.R. administration to add such pariahs to the annual contingents of
50,000 to 55,000 youngsters recruited in the labor corps, to set up a constantly available "pool" of cheap labor, operating under the Directorate
of Labor-Reserves which became afterwards the General Directorate of
the Labor Service.

By 1952 this had become one of the most salient characteristics of the
R.P.R. regime, and huge labor camps had sprung up all over Rumania.
The use of forced labor was by then an official system, not so much of
"re-education" for socially undesirable elements, but of "socialist construction." The hydroelectric installations at Stejar-Bicaz, for instance,
were constructed mostly by the use of such slave labor. By then, too,
the camps of Galatzi, Craiova, Vlahitza, and Ialomitza had become by-
words among the people of Rumania.

But presently owing to the pressure of world public opinion, alerted by
the United Nations' revelations of conditions in the satellite states, con-
current with the change in political and economic circumstances that
came to be known as the "new look," the use of slave labor fell into dis-
repute throughout the Soviet empire. By 1954 work on the Canal was
"suspended," and a number of labor camps were closed down. Though
there is ample evidence that the use of slave labor continues in the R.P.R.
at this time, and though there is no reason to believe its use on a large scale
will not again prevail, given the appropriate circumstances, it is nonetheless a fact that the part played by slave labor in the general economic
activities of the country diminished considerably during the years 1953–
1955.

We have already examined the meaning of the "new look" in agriculture. Let us now see its workings in the field of industry. By the spring
of 1953, the policy of industrialization and rearmament resulted in unmistakable signs of exhaustion in all of the satellite states of Eastern
Europe. In each, production was in a decline. Though each was being
mulcted as mercilessly as ever by Soviet demands, all suffered from the
lack of raw materials and plant equipment which the Soviet Union
should have supplied but did not. Everywhere the disgruntled workers
showed their discontent by absenteeism, deliberate slow-down strikes, and
even outright protests. The revolts staged by the workers of East Germany

in the early summer of 1953 were the most resounding instances of this. The outside world was not slow in learning that similar demonstrations had been staged in Czechoslovakia, Poland, Rumania, and Hungary.

Following the first official intimation of alarm, which came in July, 1953, in the form of a speech by Hungary's communist Prime Minister Nagy, which was rightly considered to be the manifesto of the "new look" for the European satellite regimes, Gheorghiu-Dej spoke on August 23, 1953. He admitted in so many words that serious mistakes had been made in the policy of industrialization.

"In the first place," announced Gheorghiu-Dej, "the pace of industrialization has been forced, especially as regards heavy industry. This led to the attribution of too large a volume of capital investment by comparison with the national income, exceeding even the provisions of the Five-Year Plan." Inadequate prior study had resulted in the attempt to carry out the five-year plan in four years, which did not correspond to the true prospects of the national economy. A glaring disproportion had resulted between the accumulative fund, which includes capital investments, State reserves, and the funds allotted to socialist enterprises, and the consumption fund, which must cover the material and cultural needs of the working people. The result was that living standards had not kept pace with the general development of the national economy. Investments in heavy industry and in certain construction projects had cut down investments in agriculture and in the production of consumer goods. The latter were both badly lagging as a consequence: there was, in other words, not enough food, clothing, and other basic goods available.

The open confession of failure fell far short of the truth. The initial targets of industrialization could not be attained; agricultural and consumer goods production had fallen and the country's general living standards had indeed fallen to a new low, and the regime had little or nothing to show in exchange.

The remedies proposed by Gheorghiu-Dej may be summed up as follows. The accumulation fund would be reduced to represent only 27.8 per cent of the national income, while the consumption fund would be brought up to the balance of 72.2 per cent. Five billion lei would be transferred from the funds allocated to heavy industry and construction to the production of consumer goods and to agriculture. Capital investments for the latter would be increased in 1955 to double the amount of 1953. Industrialization and industrial production would be slowed down in proportion with the requirements of the national economy as a whole. In heavy industry attention would be concentrated upon the branches that had sufficient domestic reserves of raw materials.

Before attempting to evaluate the effects of this alleged "new look," we must remark that it was no more than a transitional policy, which, from the point of view of the satellite states, ended in 1955, when they were all integrated militarily by the Warsaw treaty, and economically through the new regional five-year plan, all under the closest Soviet co-ordination. Bearing this in mind, the effects of the changes announced by the R.P.R. Prime Minister in August, 1953, may be summed up, so far as they can be appraised at the end of 1955, as follows:

The goals set in the original five-year plan for heavy industry have been maintained practically in their entirety. The exceptions are that the output of steel and electric energy was lowered, while the production of petroleum was raised somewhat.

Here is the "before and after" table of production goals:

	Oil (tons)	Pig iron (tons)	Steel (tons)	Electric power (kwts)	Cement (tons)
Original	10,000,000	800,000	1,252,000	1,700,000	2,855,000
Revised	11,000,000	800,000	1,000,000	1,380,000	2,700,000

The implication is obvious: though investments were to be reduced, production was to be maintained at practically the same level. In the steel industry, the drop was allowed simply because Soviet Russia refused to provide Rumania with the requisite raw material. In the oil industry, Soviet Russia's need for petroleum products coupled with the fact that, through Sovrompetrol, it kept an absolute control of a monopoly in the field, explain the increased goals. As for the production of consumer goods, the goals indicated by Gheorghiu-Dej in August, 1953, far from being maintained, were considerably lowered:

	Cotton textiles (million sq. meters)	Woolen textiles (million sq. meters)	Silk (million sq. meters)	Leather shoes (million pairs)
Original	766.5	39.4	41.8	20.7
Revised	250.0	32.5	19.0	10.0

The only explanation one can offer for this paradoxical situation is that, had the additional effort been made, the production of consumer goods in the last phase of the five-year plan would have been little short of disastrous.

The situation as a whole could hardly have been remedied by the changes introduced. Additional investments in the textile industry and the leather (footwear) industry did not amount to more than 1,200,000,000 lei, and the rest of the consumer goods industries together were to get but an additional 1,800,000 to cover raw materials and plant repair costs. These amounts, equal if not inferior to the investments provided for in the original five-year plan, could not conceivably affect an output that fell short of even the goals set in the original plan.

We must conclude from the above, first, that while throwing dust in the eyes of the workers by pretending to make a shift in favor of the production of consumer goods, the regime was in fact doing nothing more than confessing its inability to meet its initial program. What happened was that the goals in both heavy industry and the consumer goods industries had to be lowered on account of the lack of investments and lowered productivity.

Secondly, it will be noted that there is a great difference between the production figures and the quantities of consumer goods promised for distribution. As has been already pointed out, a great part of the "increased" production of consumer goods of the years 1953-1955 went directly to the Soviet Union. Like the rest of the "satellites," Rumania must actively contribute to the provisioning of Soviet Russia's domestic markets, to make good the promises of Malenkov to the Soviet people. On the authority of Mikoyan, more than half the supplementary funds earmarked for the import of consumer goods during the years 1953-1955 were to be spent by Soviet Russia in the countries of Eastern Europe. An article in *Pravda* of February 4, 1954 (which was not reproduced by the Rumanian press) further revealed that Soviet Russia had purchased during 1953 and 1954 "large quantities of furniture, leather footwear, and other products for wide popular consumption" from Rumania. So it is not very surprising that during the years of the "new look" the R.P.R. sales cooperatives were unable to offer much to the domestic market of Rumania.

The much-trumpeted lifting of rationing at the end of 1954 provides yet another instance of the difficulties of provisioning the population with staples through state cooperatives. The move was in reality a subterfuge for bringing a number of products on the market in the guise of unrationed goods but at prices far higher than those fixed under the old rationing system.

It is true that workers' salaries had been revised on November 27, 1953.

The higher categories of skilled workers got increases ranging from 22 to 30 lei monthly. But in January, 1954, wages were changed anew, and monthly earnings were more stringently tied to daily norms than before, with norms to be revised twice a year in proportion with the "level of technical development" of the respective enterprise. This new system, while improving the salaries of technicians and highly skilled workers (a feature to be observed under all communist regimes), considerably worsened the lot of the working class as a whole. The average worker saw his take-home pay constantly diminish as a consequence.

As a matter of fact, the problem of "true wages" is currently one of the main preoccupations of the R.P.R. economists. That is, the concern consists in trying to explain to the workers that only a proportional decrease in both wages and the price of consumer goods is apt to result in improving living standards. They insist that "the lower the prices, the higher the real wages. But then, in order to reduce the production cost, a just relation must be established between productivity and wages." This theory is undoubtedly true, and, as a matter of fact, it belongs to the arsenal of the capitalist economic theory. But with its help we might try to find out here, on the one hand, whether the Rumanian workers are now, in the "new course" better off than they were in the first years of the communist regime; and, on the other, whether they are working under better conditions than those characteristic under pre-war regimes. By analyzing the purchasing power of foodstuffs in Rumania at various stages, this is what a group of British economists discovered:

PURCHASING POWER OF FOODSTUFFS IN RUMANIA*

Foodstuffs	Prewar	1951 †	1954 †
		(in minutes of work)	
Bread kg.	34	23	37
Flour kg.	57	64	65
Potatoes kg.	23	22	14
Sugar kg.	183	172	160
Beef kg.	131	163	148
Milk litre	42	58‡	68‡
Eggs each	15	33‡	34‡
Butter kg.	578	1.222‡	1.111‡
Other fats	289	954‡	686‡

* Based on official sources.
† Includes 70% rationed foods, 30% free market.
‡ Free market prices, not obtainable on rations.

COST OF WEEKLY FOOD BASKET*

(Which includes Bread 4 kg., Flour 1 kg., Potatoes 1 kg., Sugar 0.10 kg., Beef 0.40 kg., Milk 2 litres, Eggs 2, Butter 0.05 kg., Fats 0.10 kg.)

	Prewar	1951	1954
Working time required (in hours)	7.70	10.05	10.50

REAL WAGES

	Prewar	1954
Nominal wages	100	17
Cost of living (based on cost of food only)	100	23
Real wages	100	74

* Rumanian economists in exile have asserted, on the basis of a calculation made on essential food items, that the purchasing power of the wages of a skilled worker was 2.8 times higher in 1938 than in 1956 (see *România*, No. 3, 1956).

But in spite of lower real wages and living standards production costs in industry went up. It is, as has repeatedly been pointed out, impossible to find any satisfactory bases for calculating production costs from communist statistics. However, we find in *Lupta de Clasa* (No. 6, June, 1955) how serious the situation is. In 1954, this communist magazine states, production costs in certain branches of industry, for instance, the textile and the clothing industry, were considerably reduced, but the production costs in general were not lowered as planned. Some even rose above the cost of production of 1953, notably in non-ferrous metallurgy, in the coal industry, in the machine industry, in the lumber industry, in the chemical industry, and in the light and food industries, or in all important industries!

Finally, we find in the same article an important revelation about what is, in reality, a main cause of the rise of cost of production, and generally speaking, of economic maladjustment in communist economies. This is unnatural size of the administrative apparatus. The article quotes frequent cases of factories and industrial concerns which employ one clerk, or office worker, for every four and even for every three plant workers. This is a startling confession, but it explains much about the way in which communists carry on their economic activities.

Returning now to the main issue of industrialization, we see that certain progress was made in precisely those fields of production in which the Soviet Union was vitally interested—either interested in a permanent manner, as in the case of petroleum, or else in a temporarily acute sense, as in the case of metallurgical production during the years 1949-1953. Such progress, as we have seen, corresponded to the actual investments made; and this progress is only relative. The fact is that the *absolute* growth of industry in Rumania during the last ten years has been considerably slower than that of the majority of free countries, which, starting out initially from a considerably higher level than, say Rumania, show statistically a relatively lower rate of growth.

There can be no doubt that industrial progress in Rumania, had that country been free to make the fullest and most advantageous use of its national income, as well as the possibilities of foreign trade, would have been very much more impressive, both relatively and absolutely than is the case under prevailing conditions.

As it is, industrialization has been carried out under the most disastrous circumstances imaginable. Such successes as have unquestionably been achieved were attained at the price of ruining agriculture and lowering the country's living standards to the barest subsistence level, and this, too, only with the introduction of higher norms of production and, at times, of slave labor on a large scale.

Under such conditions, the resort to the "new look" was hardly a surprise. It was the necessary confession of failure. The first two years of the "new look" did not make any real improvements in the general conditions of Rumania's economy. With Rumania's integration into the new five-year regional plan, a new period begins.

FOREIGN TRADE

To complete the picture of Rumania's economy between 1945-1955, we must look at foreign trade. It is, of course, a truism that foreign trade is a vital factor for a predominantly agrarian country in the process of industrialization. As we have shown, Rumania had followed a foreign trade policy prior to the advent of the communist regime that favored industrialization. In spite of the depression years and even of the disruptive circumstances of war, this was by and large successful. Of the total volume of foreign trade, Western Europe and the United States accounted for approximately three-quarters, and the countries of Eastern Europe (Czechoslovakia, Hungary, Poland, and Turkey notably) for the remaining quarter. As for the Soviet Union, the year 1938 showed imports therefrom to amount to less than one per cent of the total, while exports stood at precisely nil.

On May 8, 1945, a trade agreement and an economic treaty were signed

with the Soviet Union. The former included the list of goods to be exchanged; it was renewable every year in January or February. The result
was that in two years Rumania's foreign trade was completely changed.
Official statistics for the year 1947 show the following situation:

	Per cent of total imports	Exports (per cent)
Soviet Union	48.8	50.1
Czechoslovakia	10.1	16.9
Hungary	5.3	9.7
Bulgaria	3.6	10.9
Yugoslavia	1.3	1.6
Poland	1.1	1.6
Eastern bloc as a whole:	70.2	90.8

It should be made clear that exports to the Soviet Union did not include
what came under the heading of war reparations. This explains why the
total amount of Rumania's foreign trade suddenly fell to very low figures. A comparison between two typical years will show what is meant:

	1938	1947
Exports	$153,000,000	$34,000,000
Imports	$133,000,000	$61,000,000
Balance	plus $ 20,000,000	minus $27,000,000

If we add to the total exports the "reparations" deliveries to Soviet Russia,
which, as we have seen amounted to 100-130 million dollars yearly, we
get approximately the pre-war figure for Rumania's normal exports, the
difference being accounted for by the disruption of industrial production
and by the lower agricultural production (aggravated in 1947 by the
catastrophic droughts). Even under such circumstances, the Soviet Union
forced Rumania to deliver additional quantities of the products considered to be reparations. This was, let us note, what the R.P.R. propaganda
machine described at the time as the "unstinting and brotherly assistance
received from the Soviet Union by Rumania."

In 1947 Rumania's main exports were as follows:

Petroleum and petroleum products	$ 8,974,000	26% of total
Lumber and lumber products	$ 8,435,000	24.5% "
Grain, etc.	$ 1,983,000	5.8% "
Chemical products	$ 2,760,000	8% "
Sundry	$12,148,000	35.7% "
TOTAL:	$34,300,000	100% of total

During the following years the total volume of foreign trade rose again: on July 1, 1948, the Soviet government graciously permitted a 50 per cent reduction of the remaining reparations due. As a result, the general situation evolved as follows:

Year	Exports	Imports	Total	Western total	Balance
1949	$159,000,000	$181,000,000	$340,000,000	$74,000,000	—$22,000,000
1951	$211,000,000	$252,000,000	$463,000,000	$79,000,000	—$41,000,000

(The Western total refers to trade with countries of the free world.)

From the above we note in the first place that the balance of foreign trade remained deficient; in the second place that the percentage of trade with non-communist countries declined from 33 per cent in 1949 to 20 per cent in 1951; and finally that of the 80 per cent that went to the communist-dominated bloc, 60 percent represented trade with the Soviet Union itself.

A more detailed analysis of Rumania's foreign trade with non-communist countries for the year 1951 reads as follows (in million dollars):

	Import	Export
Great Britain	6.8	5.2
Holland	0.9	0.6
Belgium-Luxembourg	2.7	0.2
France	2.5	0.1
Norway	0.0	0.0
Sweden	0.0	2.4
Finland	0.9	6.2
Denmark	0.4	0.3
West Germany	4.7	0.3
Austria	3.9	3.6
Switzerland	6.7	0.3
Italy	3.6	2.9
Greece	0.0	0.0
Israel	0.3	1.8
Turkey	0.4	0.0
Egypt	9.9	9.0
United States	0.3	0.3
TOTAL:	43.5	33.2

From this it follows that from each of the free countries Rumania imported more than she could export there. These imports were, of course, mostly machinery and equipment, while exports consisted of petroleum and raw materials. Had Rumania been free to sell more than she did to these countries, it is obvious she could have purchased more from each.

Rumanian imports from Soviet Russia consisted mainly of coke, steel, coal, and iron ores, with cotton and wool sent in for processing and re-exported to the USSR. The latter operation resulted in plant deterioration with no compensation to the country's economy.

According to official statements, the total volume of trade with the Soviet Union grew fully 250 per cent between the years 1948 and 1949. This was the period when, turning down the Marshall Plan, the Kremlin closed down satellite trade with the West, and forced the enslaved countries to trade exclusively within the communist bloc, under strict supervision by Moscow.

Czechoslovakia thus had the first place in inter-satellite exchanges. The total volume of trade between the R.P.R. and that country rose from 12 million dollars in 1947 to 53 million in 1948, and reached 75 million dollars in 1949. Rumania imports mostly Czechoslovak plant installations, steel rails, and tubing, and exports petroleum, grain, chemical products, zinc, manganese, lumber, and so forth in exchange.

The second place is now taken by East Germany, with whom the total volume of trade rose from 1.5 million dollars in 1949 to 16 million in 1951, reaching almost 50 million in 1952. The goods exchanged are much the same as those mentioned in the case of Czechoslovakia.

Trade with Hungary consists of Rumanian raw materials (oil, lumber, and chemical products) and Hungarian agricultural machinery, locomotives, and buses. With Poland, the main exchanges are coal against petroleum, with Polish steel, iron, and sugar covering Rumanian deliveries of fruit, grain, and lumber in addition.

To Albania and Bulgaria, it is Rumania which exports finished products and semi-manufactured goods (electric energy to Bulgaria, as noted earlier in this chapter), in exchange for tobacco, iron ores, seeds, and fertilizers.

On August 24, 1951, it was officially announced that total exchanges with the Soviet Union during 1952–1955 would be 50 per cent higher than during the years 1948–1951. The most reliable calculations on available data lead us to conclude that the total volume in 1952 was approximately $250,000,000, or fully 60 per cent of Rumania's foreign trade. By 1953 a probable total volume was $330,000,000, or three-quarters of all foreign trade.

It should be noted that the currency reform of 1952 revalued the R.P.R. currency at 2.80 lei to the ruble, tying the lei to the ruble obligatorily. To this we must add the fact that prices in trade agreements between the

R.P.R. and the Soviet Union are in all cases fixed arbitrarily by the latter, with Rumanian export prices bearing no relation whatsoever to prevailing prices on the world markets. Furthermore, most of Rumania's production, notably oil production, is still under rigid Soviet control. Finally, under the regional coordination of the Comecon, the Soviet Union is now in a position to act as a clearinghouse, intervening in triangular arrangements of compensation (as in the case of Finland). In other words, the Soviet monopoly of Rumania's foreign trade, set up in 1949–1953, continues to this day to be a constant heavy drain on the country's economy.

The changes introduced in industry and agriculture in 1953 had certain effects on Rumania's foreign trade too. The beginning of 1954 saw the communist propaganda machine making much of the "intensification of East-West trade relations." In May of that year, the R.P.R. Foreign Trade Chamber officially announced that Rumania's exchanges with the countries of Western Europe had been increased by 50 per cent, and that new trade connections had been set up with seven more "capitalist" countries.

This trend was first manifest at the economic conference held in Moscow in the spring of 1953, where, like the rest of the satellites, the R.P.R. administration had offered to increase trade relations with the non-communist countries. The R.P.R. delegation offered to purchase between 1953 and 1955 goods to the amount of approximately one and a half million Swiss francs on Western markets—notably iron and steel, textiles and textile raw materials to the amount of 200 million Swiss francs, machines and industrial plants to the amount of 400–500 million Swiss francs, and chemical products to the amount of 150–200 million Swiss francs. It offered in exchange to the Western world cereals to the amount of 1–2 million Swiss francs, lumber and lumber products to the amount of 1 million, petroleum and notably petroleum products to the amount of 500 million, and food products (eggs, meat, and so forth) worth some 50 million Swiss francs.

This proposal was repeated in practically identical terms by the R.P.R. delegation at the Geneva conference on East-West trade, held under the auspices of the United Nations Economic Commission for Europe. Whereas the Moscow proposals were ignored by the West, the Western governments made counterproposals at Geneva. The satellite governments were requested in the first place to reduce the prices they asked for the goods they offered for export, which were much higher than prevailing world prices. They were also asked to offer other products than those listed by them. Finally the satellite governments were insistently asked to pay at least part of their debts to the Western countries (which resulted from their failure to carry out former trade agreements, and, especially, from the expropriation of industries), of which the Rumanian oil industry was an outstanding example. The Western governments went to the length of proposing that the Soviet Union assume the payment of these satellite debts, and that a common organ for foreign trade be set up to apportion the satellite debts among the Eastern bloc. These proposals were, of course, rejected by the Soviet government, notwithstanding the known fact that it wholly controls the satellites' entire economies and, hence, their foreign trade. In view of the flat refusal of the communist bloc to contribute to any real improvement of East-West trade relations, all that resulted was that certain limited trade agreements were concluded—some amounting to little more than "compensation" arrangements—between some of the communist regimes and certain Western governments or special trade organizations.

Here is a list of such agreements concluded by the R.P.R. government:

On December 24, 1954, a trade agreement was signed with France, to cover three years, beginning January 1, 1955. The total annual sum of exchanges is about 27 million dollars. French exports, to the value of 14 million dollars, are listed as pharmaceutical products, textiles, steel and steel products, machinery, utensils and tools, electric apparatus, etc. Rumanian exports are aviation gasoline, gasoline and petroleum products, lampblack, and agricultural produce.

On December 4, 1954, a one-year agreement was signed with the special trade organization of the Bonn (West German) Republic (with which at that time the R.P.R. had no diplomatic relations). The total volume of exchanges is set at 30 million dollars. The German exports are listed as plant installations and technical equipment, optical goods, clothing and textile products, and, notably, iron and steel to the amount of almost one-half of the total. The Rumanian list includes raw materials, cereals, petroleum and lumber products, pharmaceutical raw materials, etc., totaling 7½ million dollars.

The trade agreement with Italy, signed on November 25, 1950, was to extend to the end of 1955. The exchange of goods has been particularly brisk, and it must be noted that, with the Italian foreign trade organizations that work with the satellite countries under the control of the Italian Communist party, a specialty of smuggling prohibited merchandise has been established.

The one-year trade agreement signed with Norway on May 18, 1954, established the value of exchanges at $5,600,000 with Norway getting Rumanian grains and petroleum products in exchange for margarine, fats, iron alloys, and so forth.

The trade agreement with Finland, signed on October 24, 1954, provides for Finnish exports to Rumania to the amount of $5,600,000 and for Rumanian exports totaling almost $10,000,000, with the balance to be paid to Rumania by the Soviet Union. This is a typical instance of the triangular arrangements we have mentioned above, which result in the satellite countries paying for Finnish exports to Soviet Russia with their own exports. In this case, Rumania exports gasoline, kerosene, bitumen, petroleum products, chemical products, dyes, and so forth, importing in exchange paper, cellulose, machinery and light industrial equipment from Finland.

On April 19, 1955, a trade agreement was signed with Austria. Its duration was one year, and the total amount involved was set at $28,000,000. Austria was to sell machines and equipment, electrical and technical equipment, and agricultural machinery, in exchange for Rumanian agricultural products, pharmaceutical herbs, lampblack, and so forth.

The trade agreement signed with Denmark on April 1, 1954, with a one-year duration, set a volume of trade amounting to approximately $5,800,000. With Greece, an agreement was signed on May 19, 1954, with the volume of exchanges set at three million dollars. With Turkey one was signed on April 7, 1954, with exchanges valued at some 20 million dollars (Rumanian imports set at 12 million). And that with Egypt, signed on March 11, 1954, shows a total value of exchanges of 9 million dollars.

It would seem from the above that Rumania will be increasingly active in trade with the free world. If all the recent agreements are carried out, and the amounts set therein actually attained, this would represent some $200,000,000 devoted to trade with the non-communist world, which is still but one-half of the trade with the Soviet Union, and barely one-third of Rumania's entire foreign trade potential.

But, in truth, this apparent change conceals three secondary considerations. In the first place, the R.P.R. administration is now concentrating its efforts on increasing agricultural and petroleum production; hence it will be in a position to offer increasing quantities of such goods on the foreign market. In the second place, the production plans of the satellite administrations being now geared to those of the Soviet Union for 1956–1961, and because of the activity of the Soviet Union in triangular and even, in some cases, in four-sided arrangements, it is no longer possible to determine the extent to which any of the satellite countries really benefit from foreign trade. Indeed, it is no longer possible to say for sure what goods any given member of the Council for Mutual Assistance actually exports or imports itself. And, finally, we must observe that provisions on paper tend to differ widely from actual results of foreign trade agreements. It appears that the R.P.R. has succeeded in gaining a particularly poor reputation abroad for the negligence and carelessness with which it carries out its trade agreements. Indeed, the propaganda requirements of the current "coexistence line" has led the R.P.R. government to assume obligations abroad that it is far from certain it can carry out. The increase in Rumania's trade with the non-communist countries may be gauged by the following table:

Country	Imports (in million dollars)			Exports (in million dollars)		
	1951	1953	1954	1951	1953	1954
Austria	6.7	7.1	5.7	3.6	8.3	2.5
Belgium-Luxembourg	2.7	11.2	1.5	0.2	0.7	1.9
Denmark	0.4	0.4	0.7	0.3	0.6	0.7
Finland	0.9	0.7	2.3	6.2	20.2	26.5
France	2.5	8.6	1.0	0.1	1.7	4.2
West Germany	4.7	9.8	11.8	0.3	1.7	10.6
Italy	3.6	3.8	3.7	2.9	4.1	6.1
Netherlands	0.9	1.7	3.8	0.6	0.2	0.3
Norway	0.0	1.5	1.5	0.0	1.5	2.1
Sweden	0.0	0.1	0.0	2.4	2.5	1.6
Switzerland	6.7	4.8	2.4	0.3	2.7	3.4
United Kingdom	6.8	7.8	7.3	5.2	4.0	6.1
	35.9	57.5	41.7	22.1	48.2	66.0

This table suggests the following conclusions: First, while exports have grown uniformly and impressively, imports have not increased proportionally—they even fell in 1954 by comparison with 1953, the last year under the old policy. The country's substance is still being funnelled abroad. Secondly, it is significant to note that the increased exports go mostly to Finland (from 6.2 to 26.5). Finland is a country to which

Soviet Russia is in debt. Thus, the so-called increased trade between Rumania and Finland is in reality a triangular operation through which Rumania is exporting more of its merchandise to Finland, but does not receive Finnish goods in exchange (Rumanian imports from Finland have risen only from 0.9 to 2.3). The difference is being swallowed by Russia, who continues to import from Finland, while Rumania is paying her debts. The same triangular arrangements have been made also between Egypt–R.P.R.–U.S.S.R. They represent, that is, a further dead loss to Rumania's economy.

Of course, the figures for 1954 are still too insignificant to permit categorical inferences to be made. They do allow at least the general statement that the ultimate outcome of an increased trade with the free world is that, as long as she is politically subjugated, Rumania will be increasingly exploited by the Soviet Union. The much trumpeted "new look" cannot be expected to mean anything else, under the conditions we have described in this section.

THE SECOND FIVE-YEAR PLAN

The second Five-Year Plan presented at the Second Congress of the Rumanian Workers' Party at the end of December, 1955 is a section of the regional plan, 1955–1961, drafted by the Council for Mutual Economic Aid. It shows clearly that in the future industrial development will be based largely upon local resources, the electrical industry on increased use of water power, on the development of local solid fuels and of uranium, particularly on the expansion of the chemical industry by using oil, methane gas, coal, salt and other local raw materials.

Two points may be noted. First, it looks as if the uranium recently discovered in Rumania is of real interest both to the Russians and the Rumanians. As far as the Russians are concerned, this is clear from the fact that they have retained their share in Sovromquartz (the most recent and least known of the joint industrial concerns), while selling back their holdings in all the others, including Sovrompetrol. It is likely that this decision was taken because Sovromquartz is working only on Soviet Army requirements; but also it may mean that of all the Sovroms, this is the one which may yield the best results with the least investment. The Rumanians, on the other hand, have formed a commission for nuclear energy and Gaston Gheorghe Marin, the president, reported to the congress that once nuclear energy was developed in Rumania, the country's economy would be able to dispense with the greater part of the hydro-electric power from the Transylvanian alps.

The second point which must be stressed is that in the new Plan the chemical industry seems to be the main target. It is to be developed according to special provisions over ten or more years. Its production will increase in the period 1956–1961 by two and a half to three times, the largest gain in the whole new Plan. Other industries, particularly coal and iron, seem to be destined in the long run simply to serve the more specialized chemical industry. Undoubtedly, the oil industry will continue to produce as much as possible, especially for export. It is very probable that the heavy price to be paid for the repurchasing of Sovrom petrol will be paid, as in the years of the Armistice Convention, by direct deliveries of oil and oil products to Soviet Russia at below production cost.

The two industries which seem to be in a critical situation are coal, which was officially recognized as having fallen short by two million tons of the target set by the first five-year plan; and the metal industry, about which Gheorghiu-Dej said that "our own production of coke and iron-ore does not meet the needs of our heavy industry by 50%, which means that it leads to an insufficient use of the capacities of our furnaces and of the steel works and also that it badly obstructs our balance of trade." This is a clear reference to Rumania's difficulties in importing iron ore from Krivoi-Rog. It is evident that the U.S.S.R. does not intend to export such raw materials in sufficient quantities to Rumania. It explains also the switching of the Rumanian plan from the rapid development of heavy industry to increased production in the chemical field.

The shortage of capital for investment is acute. The sum of 100–110 billion lei for the second plan is, at what the congress called "comparable prices," very small. Inflation is rampant again in Rumania and it is likely that a new currency reform will have to be undertaken. Reference to the "great monetary gains" of the peasants in contrast to the real purchasing power of the workers, punctuated the speeches. This is another way of saying that the money spent in the two years of the new course on purchasing cereals from the peasant must be recaptured. Nevertheless, even the relatively limited capital available will not be allocated at once. The directives make that clear: "In the first part of the five year plan the efforts for investment will be directed especially towards the completion and bringing into function of the units (or plants) still uncompleted. The growth of the production capacity will be obtained primarily through the

working units already in existence . . . through the development and repair of some factories and the construction of new units will begin only
when the increased capacity thus obtained will have become insufficient."

From this two conclusions may be drawn. One is that Soviet capital is
becoming even scarcer in Rumania since (and because of) the withdrawal
of the Russians from the Sovroms. The other is that the failures in fulfilling the first five-year plan must be greater than are already known (coal,
electricity and consumer goods); and that to a very large extent the second
plan includes many of the old targets not reached by the first.

The key to the new plan is to be found in the two major slogans: raise
productivity and lower production costs. Productivity, according to the
directives, will rise by 45–50% in industry and 50–55% in construction.
The growth of industrial production on the basis of increased productivity,
will be in the nature of 78–80%, from which can be deduced the insignificant percentage of additional productivity expected from direct investment. One means of raising productivity will be through changes in the
labor norms; that the adjustment of these will be frequent was indicated
by Chivu Stoica. This has a sinister connotation for the workers. In 1952,
at the height of the stalinist sharpening of norms, there was a noticeable
increase in absenteeism. According to the figures given during the congress, it accounted for the loss of 9,000,000 working days. What is more,
the rise in productivity thus defined is to be accompanied by a lowering of
the costs of production by 15–20% in industry as a whole. The theory
of the "real wage", that is to say the reward for work in terms of purchasing power, is now enjoying great popularity in the People's Democracies.
An essential point of this is to stress that wages will not be increased but
even reduced if possible. Thus if the situation is properly analyzed the Rumanian worker is invited to work harder, earn less, and with his scanty
earnings to have greater difficulty in buying consumer goods!

The New Course is indeed dead and buried. The new investment plan
shows that outlay will be as follows: industry, 56%—of which 50% is for
heavy industry and 6% is for consumer goods; construction, 2.5%; agriculture and forestry, 12.5%; transport and communications, 11.5%; social
and cultural activities, together with certain small items, 17.5%.

The new agricultural policy is less easy to define. The future development of socialist agriculture is predicted again and again, but the expressions used are ambiguous. According to the directives, "the principal task
in agriculture is the continuous development and strengthening of the

socialist sector by organizing new collective farms and other forms of co-operation in work". The socialist "sector will have to develop so that by the end of the second five year plan it will provide 60–70% of the entire agricultural production of merchandise". The slogan is to increase the production of the socialist sector; but there is no direct reference to the amount of land to be collectivized. The major and immediate concern is to increase agricultural production and to lower purchasing costs for the State; hence the need for socialist agriculture. Moghioros said: "For the solution of the problem of increasing agricultural production . . . there is only one way: the freely consented association of the individual holdings into large units based on common cultivation of the land and use of agricultural machinery." The economic balance of the communist state requires that more than half of the total agricultural production should come from the socialist sector.

What is meant today by the words "socialist sector?" From statistics re-leased by Gheorghiu-Dej in the report of the Central Committee, arable land is now divided as follows: the socialist sector represents 26.5% of the total, of which the state sector (Sovhozes) accounts for 13.7%; collective farms (kolkhozes) 8.3%; agricultural associations of the Toz-type, introduced into Rumania in 1951 after the failure of the first brutal attempt to collectivize by direct expropriation 4.1%, and simple types of cooperation 0.4%. Privately owned holdings account for 73.5%.

In all the major pronouncements of the congress there is not a hint that collectivization by expropriation is to be intensified. On the contrary, in the report of the Central Committee there is an unexpected statement about the recent changes in the social structure of the countryside: "changes of its class structure, which we must of necessity bear in mind when we apply our agricultural policy. According to official statistics, the present social structure of our villages is as follows: members of collective farms, 5.5%; members of agricultural associations, 5.8%; agricultural workers less than 1%; working peasants with small holdings, 45.2%; working peasants with medium holdings, 40.5%; kulaks, 2%. Thus while the percentage of small holdings has decreased from 57% as it was in 1948 to 45.2%, the percentage of the middle peasants has risen from 34% to 35%. This shows that the middle peasant has become more and more the pivot of the village and that his importance as a producer of agricultural merchandise is growing." It should be remembered that small holdings are those of under five hectares; medium holdings are those between five and twenty hectares. That farmers were able to purchase land under a communist regime may be explained partly through the migration of some elements to the towns, partly by the fact that other peasants prefer to sell their plots to their neighbors. It is also remarkable that the latter had money to buy them.

This being so, it seems that the main plank in the agricultural program for the next few years will be to try to increase production by bringing the farmers into any form of joint association. "We must strengthen our lines to the middle peasant in order to help him overcome his hesitations and attract him into cooperatives." The word "cooperatives" appears often, notably in the essential text of such a congress, the final telegram to Khrushchev in which, while no mention is made of collectivization, it is said: "Our Party will follow unabatedly the way of socialist transformation of agriculture on the basis of cooperativization of the agriculture of Rumania."

While the final aim is undoubtedly total collectivization on the Soviet model, the target of the second five-year plan is rather the formation of big productive units, as envisaged by Khrushchev, on a cooperative basis. This shows that because of the stubborn resistance of the Rumanian peasant the social and economic structure of the Rumanian countryside has been very little altered in the last ten years despite the most strenuous efforts.

CONCLUSIONS

We have seen that Soviet Russia has set up for itself an extra-territorial occupation sector within Rumania's economy, which represents, with certain variations and oscillations, between one-third and one-half of the country's national income. This heavy mortgage on an economy that was already too weak to produce alone the financial and technical capital requisite to industrialization and successful progress, has upset the equilibrium of that economy. It is clear that Rumania cannot restore that equilibrium so long as this mortgage weighs it down.

We have seen how agriculture, Rumania's principal production, has been persecuted by the communist administration; how, owing to the lack of foresight and concern, agricultural production fell far below pre-war levels, which were themselves inadequate to the full employment of those engaged in agriculture. Collectivization, which remains the principal objective of the communists in this sector, has not succeeded—in ten years;

it has not been extended to any substantial area, and does not provide a determining part of agricultural production. The resistance of the peasantry against this alien means of production has been constant. More than that, from the moment when Moscow made known to the R.P.R. government in 1954 the order to concentrate thenceforth on agricultural production, the government has had to rely on individual producers, land-owning farmers, working with the help of the state.

In industry the first years of communist planning brought progress in increasing the potential and production of heavy industry. But this was achieved at such heavy cost and sacrifice to the entire economy and to the people as a whole, including the working class, that in 1953 the government had to proclaim a slow-down. Also significant is the fact that Soviet Russia refused to assume any additional undertakings to export either the plant or raw materials necessary to Rumania's industrialization. In the new "regional" Five-Year Plan Rumania is not authorized to continue a policy of intense industrialization, her role in the regional organization being that of a producer of raw materials, of electric power, and, especially, of cereals.

As to foreign trade we have seen that this is wholly directed by Soviet Russia. On the one hand, Rumania has no interests "complementary" to those of Soviet Russia, the latter country being itself—on a gigantic scale —in the process of industrialization, as well as an agricultural producer. On the other hand, Soviet Russia is depriving Rumania, through the arbitrary prices and conditions it imposes on exchanges, of any profits, and of the possibility of importing massively from other markets, the capital and industrial installations she so badly needs. The improvements allegedly made since 1953, through the intensification of trade with other countries, are, so far as can be judged up till now, insufficient. Also, the most disturbing fact from this point of view remains that Soviet Russia, directly and through the Council for Mutual Economic Assistance, controls from the inside, more firmly than ever, all of Rumania's exchanges with the free countries and turns them to its own benefit. Under these conditions, it is very doubtful that Rumania herself benefits from any intensification of the East-West trade.

Lastly, we have seen that the second five-year plan acknowledges that both in industry and in agriculture the doctrine of the Party has to be played down.

Thus, if we look at the aspect of sovietization described as "communization"—and ask ourselves in what measure governmental action has succeeded in transforming the economic structure of the country from the ideological point of view, impressing upon it the economic and social pattern of a Marxist-Leninist state, the answer is that Rumania's old economic-social structure is still in being. Industrialization and collectivization have both been slowed down. Agricultural production has come back to the important position it traditionally had, and in its framework the production of landowning farmers has again been accepted as the determining factor. Assuredly the future, if we can possibly imagine that the communist regime of Rumania will long survive, may show that in both directions—in that of industrialization and in that of collectivization—the communists will make a "forward leap" whenever they can do so. But, so far, it can be asserted, the communizing of Rumania's economy has encountered far greater difficulties than those who advocated it anticipated. It can also be asserted that the country's traditional social structure has resisted the pressures to which it has been subjected.

The only new phenomenon, from this point of view, produced by these ten years of communist administration is, on the demographic plane, the growth of the urban population in relation to the rural. This might be an extremely interesting development. In the course of a natural and harmonious industrialization, it might signify the attainment of one of the major objectives, to wit, the absorption of surplus agricultural population into industrial production. Unfortunately, such is not the real meaning of the increase shown in the statistics published by the R.P.R. government. For it to be so, two other phenomena would have to be confirmed by these statistics. In the first place, agricultural production should also have increased proportionally. For, with an equal or, worse, a lowered or limited agricultural production, this population shift means that the contingents of "agricultural over-population" continue to be produced by the discrepancy between production and available agricultural labor. In the second place it would have to be confirmed that the intensification of industrial production, as it was observed between 1950 and 1953, is a sure and continuous factor for the future. Only in this way could the increasing integration of the agricultural over-population into the new ranks of labor be assured. We know, however, that industrialization has been slowed down. And it is very probable that the reduction of Rumania's industrial production, ordered by the new regional Five-Year Plan, will create unemployment within the present class of industrial workers. What, then, does the "increase of the urban population" of the R.P.R. mean? According to the statistics published by the R.P.R. administration, the number of salaried workers has grown between 1948 and 1954 as follows:

1948 — 1,700,000	1952 — 2,600,000
1949 — 1,740,000	1953 — 2,700,000
1950 — 2,170,000	1954 — 2,850,000
1951 — 2,460,000	

On the other hand, the difference between the urban and the rural population was reduced during this time as follows:

	1948	1953
Urban	3,713,139 (23.4%)	5,700,000 (34.8%)
Rural	12,159,485 (76.6%)	10,675,000 (65.2%)

Which means that, while between 1948 and 1953 the number of salaried workers grew by one million, the number of urban dwellers grew by some two million.

This can be explained by the fact that half the new town dwellers are not industrial wage-earners, that is, workers in an expanded industry. Indeed, as can be seen in our chapter concerning the state administration, the number of functionaries and office clerks needed by this dictatorial state is almost one million. In this connection we must recall that Article 33 of the Five-Year Plan, which is the article dealing with the increase of the number of workers, and with the absorption of the agricultural surplus population through the intensification of industrial production, stated that: "In 1955 the number of *workers, technicians, and office workers* in the national economy will be approximately 3,000,000." It was likewise estimated that, of this yet unattained figure of 3,000,000, only 1,800,000 would be true industrial workers. However, while the recruitment of industrial workers has not brought the expected results, but, on the contrary, was forcibly slowed down after 1953, what did continue to increase was the number of office workers and functionaries in industrial and agricultural enterprises, needed in the centralist and totalitarian control and direction of this sort of a regime. From a study in the official communist magazine *Lupta de Clasa*, previously quoted, we have seen that industrial enterprises sometimes employ as many as one functionary for every four or even three workers. If to these employees we add the enormous number of "aparatchiki"—the Party functionaries—who have direct economic functions, we can see what proportions this unnatural growth of the parasitical bureaucracy has attained. (In the report on the 1956 budget the Minister of Finance recognized that administrative expenses had become one of the great burdens on the State budget. He quoted especially the expenses of the State-apparat, the personnel employed for agricultural purchases and collections, and the personnel of the local councils).

Urban agglomeration is, therefore in good part, a symptom of the growth of the communist-created white-collar class. The abnormal development of the class of technicians, bureaucrats, Party functionaries and civil servants (those defined in one sense as "holders of posts of responsibility" and in another, more general sense by the Russian word "intelligentsia") is the basic phenomenon, both political and economic, of the development of totalitarian dictatorship, both in the life of the state and in the economic life.

Thus the final conclusion we reach is that, instead of a modified demographic and social structure, we still have the old structure persisting almost identically. Its basic problems have not been solved. The economy, which was already fragile, has been smothered under the monstrous weight, on the one hand, of the Soviet occupation apparatus, occupying a privileged sector, and, on the other, of the apparatus of political and economic dictatorship required by the communist state.

3

financial policy

A study of the financial policies pursued by the R.P.R. administration from the time it was forcibly installed in power cannot be confined to investigating merely whether the public moneys have been used in the best interests of the nation. It must primarily examine the endeavors of the communist regime to further its basic aim—the "class struggle"—through the wholesale proletarization of the population, both rural and urban, by means of fiscal and monetary policies.

It will be seen, indeed, that the publication of every budget, the introduction of every statute of a fiscal character, and the enactment of each of the successive currency manipulations, have been but so many instances of the persistent efforts to confiscate all individual wealth, and thereby to deprive the citizenry of every free activity. Far from dissembling this purpose, the heads of the communist administration have publicly stressed it on every occasion. Official speeches and writings, as well as the overt motivations given in the form of preambles to decrees and laws, have always underscored that the main reason for introducing any new measure was "a redistribution of the national income," or the seizure of "moneys accumulated by the bourgeoisie and the kulaks," or even the "liquidation of the enemies of the people," and ever and again presented such enactments as "aimed at ensuring success in the class struggle."

It will be seen, on the other hand, that a number of measures have been introduced solely in order to provide the Soviet Union with the necessary legal means to appropriate Rumania's substance in one guise or another, under the best possible conditions. Such, for instance, was the currency manipulation that occurred in January 1954, whereby the value of the Rumanian leu was doubled in relation to the Soviet ruble.

The salient financial enactments that have marked the past ten years of Soviet occupation are all, as we have pointed out, part of an over-all policy; often, as we shall see, they are but successive complementary steps. For the sake of a clearer understanding, we propose however to examine these measures under three separate headings:

    a—currency manipulations of a confiscatory nature;

    b—budgetary policies in pursuit of an uneconomic industrialization to the detriment of agriculture;

    c—persecution through fiscal policy.

A few brief data on the situation prior to the arrival of the Soviet armies, and on the immediate consequences of the Soviet occupation are in order.

Rumania's estimated national income for 1938—within its borders as of that time—was $1,650,000,000. Calculated within the borders as of 1945, this figure must be placed at $1,339,000,000. Taking into account the rise in world prices, that followed the end of the war, the national income might have been expected to be at least 25 per cent higher by the end of the hostilities. Unfortunately, with the country's economy disrupted by the war, and, notably after August 1944, by the Soviet occupation, the estimated national income by 1946 had fallen to but $537,000,000.

The overwhelming proportion of this striking decline must be attributed to the huge seizures effected by the Soviet armies. The effects of the Soviet occupation upon the country's financial and monetary situation, hence upon the national income, can be shown also from the following sets of figures. The figures for the total monetary circulation evolved as follows:

> End of 1938: 34.9 billion lei
> June, 1944: 211.8 billion lei
> End of 1946: 6,099.3 billion lei
> August 14, 1947: 48,451 billion lei.

The disastrous consequences of the Soviet occupation are obvious. This runaway inflation meant, of course, a staggering rise in prices, which is best shown by the concomitant evolution of the cost-of-living index:

> August, 1939:   100
> August, 1944:   944
> April,   1947: 440,869 (official figures, given in Argus, May 16, 1947)

The leu, which stood at 150 to the dollar in 1938, had fallen to 4,200,000 to the dollar by the beginning of August, 1947.

The disastrous inflationary trend that had been set off by the Soviet occupation had to be brought to an end. This meant, of course, not only a currency reform but, especially, the suppression of the causes of inflation. In the first place it should have entailed the cessation of the huge exactions of the Soviets. The aim of the currency reform introduced on August 15, 1947, however, was not the creation of a new, healthy currency through the elimination of the causes of the mounting inflation. Indeed, the reform proved to be planned so as to result in a sweeping change of the country's social structure. In other words, the communists meant to use the device of currency reform solely in order to strike a telling blow at the bourgeoisie and at the individual farmers. The operation was neither planned nor controlled by Rumanian economists; it was the brainchild of the Soviet economist Varga.

The reform was prepared in the greatest secrecy, and came as the most stunning surprise to the entire people. It had, however, been preceded by a series of preliminary measures, though it would have taken unusual discernment at the time to recognize in these preparatory steps the over-all plan, and to foresee that it was aimed at nothing short of the wholesale pauperization and proletarization of the Rumanian people. In the months that preceded the reform, the administration studiously displayed an openhandedness amounting almost to generosity. The entire public debt (which, by then, had been whittled by the inflation to a quite insignificant amount) was paid off. The state purchased—for cash—the entire cereal crop of that year, though this entailed collecting the crops before they could reach the village, under pressure and control by the gendarmerie. Then a decree was issued, forcibly confiscating all merchandise stocks on hand, the merchants and industrialists having to content themselves with the prices paid to their accounts in exchange for the seized commodities. Finally another measure was taken: the wholesale dismissal of fully 30 per cent of all employees, not only from every administrative office and state enterprise, but also from all private concerns (private enterprises had at that time not yet been "nationalized"). This sweeping "compression" of personnel was not, of course, left to the discretion of the respective managements, but was carried out through the communist-dominated trade unions. The latter naturally proceeded in most cases to dismiss, in the first place, not only the managerial staff, but also all employees considered to be opposed to the regime.

Incidentally, the communists chose the very eve of the currency reform to effect the arrest of Iuliu Maniu and of the other leaders of the National Peasant Party. We shall have more to say on this event presently; for the time being we need merely note the timing of the move.

Having thus generously transformed the bulk of privately held wealth into money, the communist administration sprang the trap on the evening of August 15, 1947. It was announced that a new leu had been put in circulation, the value of the new unit fixed at the exchange parity obtaining in 1938. The new leu, that is, was worth 6.60 milligrams gold at nine-tenths purity, at 150 lei to the dollar. At the same time it was announced that the old currency would be exchanged at the rate of 20,000 old lei for one new leu.

With the old lei withdrawn from circulation, the public was invited to deposit their entire cash holdings at certain public counters, beginning on the morning of August 16, over a period of three days. However, they would not receive in exchange the value of such deposits in the new currency, but only a tiny proportion; the rest would remain "frozen." In other words, the bulk of private cash holdings were confiscated by the state.

Even the small sums paid out in the new currency varied according to the category of the depositors. Farmers were favored; they were issued 250 new lei each ($1.66). Bearing in mind that the administration had forcibly "bought" their entire grain production only a month before, not, however, including corn, which had not been harvested then, and paid them off in old lei, this meant that each farmer had in effect sold his year's output for $1.66.

Next came the salaried workers, who were issued 150 new lei each ($1.00) in exchange for their cash deposits. The rest of the citizenry, that is, the members of the families of the above two categories, as well as all those who had been forcibly reduced to unemployment by the communist regime, were granted only 75 new lei ($0.50) each. In this manner, all those whom the administration considered to be opposed to it (and whose remaining real estate, industrial property, or commercial holdings would soon be wholly expropriated), those who were refused ration cards and who had therefore to provision themselves on the hugely expensive "free" market, all those unfortunates of whom there were hundreds of thousands in the country, were at one stroke robbed of their cash holdings and left in exchange with the equivalent of fifty cents.

Commercial and industrial enterprises were given the right to change their cash balances on hand as of August 15—ten days after the currency reform came into effect. They were, however, required in the meantime to continue to pay the wages of their employees regularly. Now, it was evident, that, under the inflationary conditions that had for so long preceded the currency reform, no enterprise kept more than an absolute minimum of cash on hand. Almost all were caught by the enactment with no cash available to meet their obligations under the reform. But the communists, ignoring this obvious reality, proceeded to organize violent demonstrations against these enterprises that faced bankruptcy through no fault of their own. The "capitalists" were forced to liquidate everything they possessed; personal holdings, gold, foreign currencies, even furniture and personal effects had to be sold in a hurry. With no ready cash available anywhere, it is not difficult to imagine what losses were incurred.

But influential communists (as well as the members of the Soviet occupation forces, who were privileged to exchange immediately the equivalent of two months' pay each) were permitted to change large sums of money. So it was hardly surprising to see the "unofficial" rate of exchange in private deals rising to 40,000 old lei for one new leu, and many were the Kremlin's favorites who reaped huge gains.

On the other hand, the communist banks, that is to say, those that had already been "nationalized", were moved to issue private loans in the new currency, at rates that amounted to 10 per cent per month. Most private enterprises had to resort to such loans in order to meet their current obligations—under the added pressure of communist-staged demonstrations already mentioned—with the consequences to be anticipated.

Bank accounts as well as savings accounts were frozen; they were not changed into the new currency, seeing that the maximum sums that could be exchanged as shown above included all holdings, cash and accounts, for each individual. It was only about a year after the currency reform that some of these accounts were unfrozen, and credit balances transformed into the new currency. But this, too, was limited to but small sums. Of course, as might have been expected under the catastrophic conditions of the preceding inflation, it was very rare for anyone to keep important sums immobilized in bank or savings accounts, so that the sum total of such accounts amounted to relatively little.

The wholesale impoverishment that marked the currency reform may be judged by the fact that, of the 48,500 billion old lei that were in circulation on August 14, 1947, only 27,500 billion were exchanged. But the extent of this spoliation becomes apparent only when it is recalled that the latter sum included the total of fiduciary money held, not only by the government itself, but also by the Soviet authorities. It included, too, the important amounts exchanged by the members of the Soviet occupation forces and by the high-ranking communists. So that, deducting these huge sums from the total, it will be realized that the part exchanged by the Rumanian people themselves in this operation came to but a most insignificant proportion of the 27,500 billion lei. To all intents and purposes, the operation amounted to the confiscation of practically all the money available in the country. Indeed, the communist leaders had no scruples in publicly asserting afterwards that the currency reform had been dictated by the need "to put an end to inflation and *to recuperate the money accumulated by the bourgeoisie and by the kulaks.*"

The currency reform had other aspects too. All holders of gold and foreign currencies were ordered—under penalty of imprisonment—to bring whatever gold, minted or otherwise, and foreign currency they had in their possession, within a maximum of ten days, to the public counters designated for this purpose. Subsequently this delay was extended to 18 days. Deponents were given in exchange new lei, but at a most disadvantageous rate. For one dollar, for instance, which had been worth 4,200,000 old lei, they got but 150 new lei, instead of the 210 they might have been entitled to expect at the announced rate of 20,000 old lei for one new leu.

Now, the amount of foreign currencies and of minted gold in circulation throughout Rumania at the moment of the currency reform was very large indeed, as might have been expected in the inflationary conditions described above, in which everyone sought to invest in some stable and sure value. The communists therefore had high hopes of laying their hands on a large stock of readily negotiable wealth. They counted, not only on the threat of legal penalties involved in withholding the desirable commodities, but also on the urgency of the need that would be felt by everyone to get some ready cash just to stay alive. However the people displayed no confidence in the new currency, and moreover there was no sign of a letup in the matter of Soviet exigencies, which, after all, were the real crux of the inflation. And so, to the deception of official expectations, the amount of gold and of foreign currency thus squeezed from the embattled citizenry turned out to be small.

But the communist administration had other tricks up its sleeve. The police were ordered to act on the strength of denunciations. Denunciations were officially solicited, in accordance with the "most advanced police techniques", and a special corps of controllers was set up and instructed in the enforcement of the law on foreign currencies. A special decree was issued providing that homes would be searched pursuant to denunciations received. Of whatever valuables were thus collected, the State Bank was to set aside 25 per cent, to cover investigation expenditures; 10 per cent went to the successful denouncer, and another 10 per cent went to those who effected the seizure, that is to the police.

Though the penalties involved in being caught in illegal possession of gold or foreign moneys were up to ten years of hard labor, even this drastic method failed to yield the desired and expected results. As late as August 20, 1948, another decree had to be issued, extending a further delay for the holders of gold or foreign currency to declare and bring in their holdings. The decree—issued, as we have just said, more than one year after the reform—now promised that people taking the required action need no longer fear the rigors of the law originally prescribed. No identity papers were required of depositors, nor was there need to present evidence of the provenance of holdings thus deposited with the state. But, by 1948, the citizenry had become so thoroughly familiar with the methods and nature of the communist administration that even this tardy show of leniency failed to bring much to the regime's coffers.

Not content to despoil the people by confiscating almost the whole of privately held money, the communist administration resorted to a variety of complementary measures aimed at further pauperizing the population.

A most striking instance is provided by the manner in which taxes were calculated for the budget year in progress at the moment of the currency reform. Every taxpayer had been obliged to pay some part of the taxes assessed for the current year by August 15. That part varied between one-third and one-half of the total due. But when the currency reform went into effect, the administration did not proceed—as would have been normal—to deduct from the total taxes due the part proportional to the sum already paid out in old lei, leaving the rest to be paid in new lei. A person, for instance, assessed to pay a total of 100,000,000 old lei for the budget year 1947–1948 and having already paid 50,000,000 in old lei, might reasonably have expected still to pay the full equivalent of the remaining 50,000,000 old lei, that is, 2,500 in new lei. But this was not the view of the administration. What was done was that the taxes due for the year 1947–1948 were recalculated at different rates. The rate was 4,500 old lei for 1 new leu for the purpose of tax assessments on agricultural incomes; 3,000 for 1 for commercial incomes; and 2,500 for 1 for the incomes of members of the liberal professions and others, with the sole exception of incomes from wages. In other words, for tax purposes, the rate of exchange was set so as to result in staggering increases that went from four and a half to eight times the original assessment. Furthermore this applied retroactively, since it applied to the entire tax assessed originally, and since the part already paid was converted, not at the rates mentioned above, but at 20,000 old lei for 1 new leu. Thus, in the instance just given, if a physician, say, had already paid 50 per cent of his taxes (originally set at 100,000,000 old lei), he found that the whole tax he was expected to pay for the year amounted to 20,000 new lei, but that he had paid, not 50 per cent thereof, but only 6.25 per cent, and he still had to pay the remaining 93.75 per cent in new lei.

And, while income taxes were thus raised up to eightfold their original assessment, rents were raised, too, by 100 to 200 per cent. But it was not the owner who received the differences: landlords were only allowed to collect an increase of 16 to 25 per cent. The state took the rest. This, too, was but a beginning, for less than a year later, by the simple expedient of expropriating all urban real estate (without any payment whatsoever to the owners), the state took over all rents.

At the same time, prices went up on all public services. Railroad fares were raised to no less than forty times the former rates; telephone services went up eightfold; street cars and buses cost twelve times more. Prices of commodities soared too. The new meat prices were set at 2.6 times the former rates, milk was raised 100 per cent, clothing materials 160 per cent, and gasoline 2,400 per cent. Subsequently it was found necessary to reduce the fares on railroad trips of less than 150 kilometers, in order to permit the peasants to come to the nearest cities to sell their produce. This was dictated, not by any official regard for the farmers, but by the fact that the towns could no longer be provisioned while the peasants, unable to pay the exorbitant fares, stayed away from the markets. The over-all rise in prices for staple commodities during this period was set at approximately 100 per cent over those obtaining in 1938.

It is true that workers' wages were also raised about 100 per cent (compared with the rates of 1938). After all, a regime calling itself a working class democracy had to make some concessions to placate the class it allegedly represented. The wages of office workers were set somewhat below those of industrial workers. The rest of the people—that is, about 85 per cent of the entire population—simply made out as best they could; the administration made no provisions to lighten their lot once it had so effectively impoverished them by the currency reform.

For the overwhelming majority of the citizenry merely to keep body and soul together became a major and all-absorbing problem. In place of their cash savings each was left with just enough of the new money to tide him over a couple of days. But food and lodging had to be provided for in this new currency. There was no way out but to seek credit. And there was very little of the new money available anywhere. Yet such indispensable things as tomorrow's meal for the children and carfare to go to work simply had to be forthcoming. These daily problems became an obsession.

It was precisely the atmosphere best suited for the next step planned by the communist administration. With the attention of the people focused on the urgency of essentials, this was the time to act in another direction, striking yet another blow at the fundamental liberties. It will be recalled that it was right at the time of the currency reform that the administration arrested Iuliu Maniu and the other leaders of the National Peasant Party, the country's most popular party and the most obvious rallying-point of opposition to the communist regime. So now came a time for mopping up operations. Arrests multiplied; everyone who had ever been prominent in politics and public life was threatened; the prisons were soon filled to overflowing. The slightest hint of public opposition or reaction was put down in the most ruthless manner. Terror was intensified. Thousands upon thousands who might give trouble were taken into custody. Where no charges of a political nature could be placed against them, new offenses were invented, notably "economic sabotage." In very many cases no charges at all were forthcoming: the suspect was simply seized and kept under arrest without ever being told what there was against him.

The country's economy continued to go from bad to worse, following the currency reform of 1947. But the regime, which in the meantime entrenched itself in power, continued for years to refer to the operation as a "notable achievement of the working class." In its propaganda, both at home and abroad, it never ceased pointing out that it had given the country "a stable and healthy currency, without any assistance from the capitalist exploiters," whose evil works it had indeed set at nought.

Yet notwithstanding the boasts of the communist administration, the new leu had begun to depreciate almost from the moment of its introduction. Month after month and year after year, prices continued to rise, while living standards declined. Wages remained at subsistence level; commodities disappeared from the market. Between 1947 and the end of 1951 staple foods had gone up threefold, while wages increased by barely 50 per cent. There was, of course, no reason to expect a cessation of this constant inflation, since the true cause had not been removed: Soviet plundering of the country's dwindling resources continued unabated.

When finally, on January 28, 1952, the communist administration sprang a second currency reform on the people of Rumania, it was obvious that it was the people who would once again have to take the consequences. A new monetary unit was created—it was still called a leu, only it was henceforth tied to the Soviet ruble. "It was no longer possible," claimed the regime's propaganda, "to align the leu with the U.S. dollar, whose value is unstable and whose purchasing power shows a constant decline." Hence the Soviet ruble, "the stablest currency in the world," was chosen as the standard for Rumania's leu. Such was the new line trumpeted to domestic and foreign listeners—the insinuation being, of course, that Rumania's monetary plight was due to the "systematic depreciation" of the dollar.

The decree issued on January 28, 1952, fixed the leu's new parity at 2.80 to the Soviet ruble; twenty of the now old lei represented one unit of the new. At the then official rate, which was 4 rubles to $1.00, one U.S. dollar stood officially at 11.20 new lei. At this rate, the old lei, which in 1947 had officially been 150 to the dollar, should in reality really have been worth, not 20 to 1 new leu, but 13.20. This simple calculation is sufficient to show up the realities behind the ceaseless propaganda of the Bucarest regime, for it clearly indicates that the old leu of 1947 had depreciated by fully one-third by 1952—by official admission.

Such trifles however were ignored by the R.P.R. propaganda machine. There was the new conversion to carry through. Here is how it was done. Depositors of sums in old lei were given in exchange 1 new leu for every

100 old lei, for the first 1,000 lei brought in; 1 new leu for every 200 old, for the next 2,000; and, finally, 1 new leu for 400 old, for the remainder turned in.

Savings accounts were similarly recalculated at variable rates, but slightly less disadvantageously than cash holdings. The administration went through the motions of sugaring this bitter pill: a concomitant lowering of prices for a number of commodities was announced. Prices, however, instead of going down, continued their upward trend. In other words, once again the communist administration, under the guise of a currency reconversion, contrived to confiscate the money accumulated by the citizenry during the preceding lean years. Significantly enough, this time no discrimination was made among the various categories or professions. All cash holdings were legally plundered. The theft amounted to 80–90 per cent for the small initial sums turned in (ranging from $6.60 to $13.30), and to fully 95 per cent on the remainder.

There was no attempt to conceal the political purpose of the reconversion. On the contrary, the R.P.R. administration's spokesmen asserted repeatedly that the currency reform of January 28, 1952 was motivated by the need to set an end to the inflation, and to recuperate the moneys accumulated by the bourgeoisie. Radio Bucarest put it this way: "The purpose of the reconversion was to restore the nation's finances by striking at the capitalist speculators who, through the funds they had accumulated, had become a menace to the social order established in Rumania."

It is hardly necessary to point out the absurdity of the notion that a wealthy class of citizens had arisen in Rumania by 1952, who could indulge in speculations with the means they had succeeded in accumulating since the 1947 currency reform had been enacted. The truth is that, as can well be imagined under the circumstances already described, the overwhelming majority of the "bourgeoisie" had been reduced to the most miserable subsistence level, and was barely managing to stay alive through the sale of its last remaining resources. The bourgeois, indeed, by 1952 had already sold whatever valuables they had left: household furnishings, carpets, jewelry, tableware, clothing had all been long since bought up by the favored few—prominent communists and members of the Soviet occupation forces and administration. And, as we have pointed out above, since 1947 a number of laws had intervened, "nationalizing" without any compensation whatsoever all industrial and commercial properties, all urban real estate, and all rural land holdings which did not belong to peasants.

Far from representing anything remotely resembling "accumulations made through the exploitation of the workers", such money as still remained in the hands of the bourgeoisie was in fact but the last resource of a class of people already thoroughly impoverished, deprived of the right to regular employment, and came from the sale of the last remaining personal effects. In the case of moneys held by the peasantry, the available cash represented the proceeds of the forcible sale to the administration of crops forcibly collected for the state. The communist authorities had hastened to make cash payments for agricultural produce thus collected, and now once again the farmers lost the proceeds of an entire year's labor through the confiscation of their cash.

One immediate result came in the form of a wave of suicides. Thousands upon thousands of unfortunates, driven to despair by the loss of their last remaining resources, took their own lives.

The aim of proletarizing the people of the cities, and of forcing the peasantry into collectivization was—and is—but part of the purpose of the R.P.R. regime. The principal purpose, which is more far-reaching, is to serve the purposes and interests of the Kremlin in every way. In pursuit of this, and carrying out the orders of the practitioners of the "most advanced economic science in the world" the Bucarest administration proceeded with the next step.

The third currency reform, introduced on January 31, 1954, represented a further manipulation of the leu. For purposes of foreign exchange, the decree enacting the change doubled the value of the leu: from 2.80 to the Soviet ruble, it was set now at 1.50 to the ruble. It was announced at the same time that, instead of the previous gold content of 0.079346 grams, the foreign exchange leu would have a gold content of 0.148112 grams.

This mention of a gold content came as a surprise. It was recalled that a great case had been made officially, on the occasion of the 1952 currency reform, of the abandonment of the dollar and gold standard in favor of the Soviet ruble, that sole stable value. But the greatest surprise was occasioned by the fact that no concomitant changes were brought to the domestic value of the leu. Surely, doubling the foreign exchange of a currency involved considerably more than minor adjustments of a domestic nature. It would normally be expected to entail thoroughgoing deflationary measures on the home market, or else a radical change of the currency itself—an operation which, as we have seen, in no way deterred the communist planners. Yet no major change took place inside Rumania; neither were prices reset nor was a new currency introduced.

Many were the foreign observers who were at a loss to account for the seemingly mysterious currency manipulation carried out by the R.P.R. administration in January 1954. Many sought an adequate explanation in vain. But the explanation existed. And it was an obvious one. Obvious, that is, if one kept in mind that the interests involved were those of the Soviet Union.

The currency reform of 1954 was not aimed at once again despoiling the people of Rumania as individuals, as the previous two had been. Its purpose was the spoliation of the country as a whole, for the benefit of the Soviet Union.

It had been decided in Moscow to retransfer from Rumania the Soviet capital holdings in the Sovroms. As has been pointed out elsewhere, there had never been any actual Soviet investments involved, the contribution of the Soviet Union having been simply self-attributed. Doubling the exchange value of the leu now meant doubling at one stroke the value of these so-called capital holdings in terms of rubles.

Bearing in mind further that prices of Rumanian merchandise exported to the Soviet Union are billed in rubles, and take no account whatsoever of cost prices inside Rumania, the vastness of the organized plundering of Rumania's substance realized through the 1954 revaluation of the foreign exchange leu will become apparent. Considering also the immense amounts of Soviet capital to be transferred to the USSR at double their original bookkeeping value, it becomes obvious that for many years to come Rumania will have to send the greater part of its exports to the Soviet Union without getting anything whatsoever in exchange. Surely, whatever else one might say of this operation, it may be asserted that never has any "bourgeois capitalist imperialist exploiter" hit on a more masterly scheme than this instance of "the most advanced economic science in the world."

The full magnitude of the deal was to be revealed only after many months had gone by. It was only on September 24, 1954, that a joint communique was issued in Moscow, stating the decision of the Soviet Union to "sell and deliver" to the R.P.R. the Soviet parts in the Sovroms. The Bucarest propaganda machine greeted the event with a paeon of praise for the Soviet Union. Not only did it describe the Sovroms as outstanding contributions to the country's economy, but it presented the "cession" of the Soviet participation as a supreme instance of the "multilateral and unstinting brotherly assistance afforded by the great Soviet Union."

It is clear from all the above that, far from benefiting Rumania's economy and contributing to the welfare of the Rumanian people, each of the successive currency manipulations carried out between 1947 and 1954 have had the exactly opposite effect. It is obvious, too, that this was done deliberately, and that, in the field of finances as in every other field, the determining factor is what the communists themselves refer to as the "class struggle", behind which again stand the interests of the Kremlin.

Most salient aspects of a country's economic life can normally be accounted for by a perusal of its budget. One might reasonably expect, therefore, that under a regime of state socialism, when a country's entire economic activity is taken over by the administration itself, leaving no room for private initiative and enterprise, the budget would be a comprehensive accounting of the use of public funds. Such however is not the view countenanced by the Kremlin. Nor can the henchmen of the Kremlin acting as the R.P.R. administration hold such notions. And so, if the accompanying propaganda exposé is not taken into account, the yearly budgets hitherto published by the R.P.R. government have been singularly uninformative and brief.

Here, for instance, is the budget for 1954 as it was presented for the rubberstamp approval of the Grand National Assembly (on April 20, 1954, when it was already obvious that no changes could be made, and when, at the same time, the final budget for 1952 and the provisional one for 1953 were likewise submitted):

Revenues (in million lei)

State budget	36,487
Local budgets	2,768.5
Social insurances	1,582.5
TOTAL:	40,838.0

Expenditures (in million lei)

State budget	32,694.1
Local budgets	5,061.4
Social insurances	1,582.5
TOTAL:	39,338.0

A more laconic accounting can hardly be imagined in a report to the nation. But the report with which the Minister of Finance accompanied the budget was a long-winded political tirade, in which a great many other figures were cited, none helpful in obtaining an over-all view of the country's economic life or of any sector thereof.

But occasionally even the propaganda dressing that is officially supplied in this way can be informative. It is a peculiarity of the communists to assume a conveniently short memory in their audiences, being themselves so prone to discard and ignore yesteryear's loudly advocated views when today's party line happens to have taken a new twist. Thus, for instance, alert observers learned from the official comments that accompanied the presentation of the R.P.R. budget on January 24, 1953, that there had been budget deficiencies in 1951, whereas earlier it had been no less officially stated that the 1951 budget had been balanced with an important credit margin. It is true that in the meantime the former Minister of Finance, Vasile Luca, had been branded an "anti-revolutionary anti-state criminal", and his trial was impending.

As we have already seen, similar discrepancies have been evinced in relation to the successive currency reforms. It is, in fact, a constant feature of propaganda in the "people's democracies" that the "resounding success" and "notable victory" of today are but the forerunners of tomorrow's "necessary change", itself predicated on admitted "failures and deficiencies" of the past.

Under such circumstances, one must accept any figures issued by a communist regime with at least a grain of salt. In relation to the R.P.R. budget, incidentally, we should note that successive mutually contradictory official statements indicate that no control whatsoever exists in the matter of applying budget provisions. Nonetheless an examination of the general lines of a budget can provide at least an indication of the current orientation sought by the regime for the country's economy.

For instance, the allocation of expenditures points up the government's over-all policy. Here, then, expressed in percentages, are the main budgetary expenditures for the past few years, as issued by the R.P.R. administration:

	1954	1951	1949
Financing the national economy	61%	56%	41%
Social and cultural works	. .	24%	20.3%
Administration maintenance	. .	7.2%	12.1%
National defense	11%	16.6%	8%
International obligations (i.e.: payments to the Soviet Union)	. .	3.8%	7.4%

These figures are given in percentages, seeing that the successive currency manipulations make the absolute figures expressed in lei meaningless

We note from the above that the principal segment of expenditures is the financing of the national economy, which is but to be expected under a regime of "socialist collectivization." The importance given by the communists to such investments is obvious. Let us note further that during 1954, for instance, investments financed by the various enterprises themselves amounted to a total almost as large as that provided for in the state budget. There can be no doubt therefore that the moneys devoted to such capital investments are wholly out of proportion to the country's revenues. Such excessive efforts, of course, can be made only at the expense of the people's living standard. In other words, the output of consumer goods is compressed to the absolute limits of subsistence, to compensate for the ambitious plans of the administration.

More serious still is the fact that, throughout the period of 1948–1953, these excessive investments were not even aimed at a normal and healthy development of the national economy. The communist administration had steadfastly and deliberately withheld investments, not only from the industries producing consumer goods, but also from agriculture. Such investments would have permitted a rise in living standards. They would also have fostered a far greater and more rapid turnover. An equal investment allocated to the production of agricultural and consumer goods would have resulted in swifter and more frequent "production circuits," than are conceivably possible from investments in heavy industry. The accumulation of capital itself would have been accelerated, seeing that each "circuit" would have a normal margin for reinvestment. But instead, the communist administration chose the way of the most excessive efforts in seeking to develop heavy industry, whose "circuit" from investment to the circulation of goods produced is considerably slower. It is hardly surprising therefore that the country's economic development had been so slow.

Certainly the forced development of heavy industry may be necessary, and may even be dictated by existing conditions, in a country that is rich in deposits of iron and of industrial coal. In such cases, too, foreign capital is also available. This, however, is far from being the situation of Rumania. Hence, unfortunately, the excessive investments pumped into heavy industry are made to the detriment of the people and for the purpose of complying with the exigencies of the Kremlin, which in turn is concerned with its own strategic requirements. The interests of the Rumanian people are neglected. Thus, for instance, the budget for 1951 allocated nothing whatever to the consumer goods industries, and set aside for agriculture (jointly with forestry) a maximum of 10 per cent of total investments provided. For 1950, the entire allocation for agricultural investments was less than the sums set aside for the construction of the Danube-Black Sea canal (which, as is told elsewhere in this work, was abandoned after three years of intense efforts).

This policy, so disastrous for the people's well-being, was nevertheless pursued by the communist regime with the utmost ruthlessness year after year. Suddenly, following the death of Stalin, it was publicly repudiated. On August 28, 1953, Gheorghiu-Dej, in a widely publicized speech, severely condemned the excessive investments that his own administration had up till that time forced into heavy industry. He promised that things would change from then on, and that agriculture and the production of consumer goods would be afforded the government support wrongly withheld so far. In the very middle of what the R.P.R. propaganda machine had been assiduously describing as the crucial year of the then current five-year plan, the acknowledged head of the communist regime announced, in other words, that the regime meant to bring the most radical changes in its economic and financial policy, ushering in a new era of increased well-being for the "workers".

Though the need for such a change had long been evident, its announcement was received with skepticism by informed observers even as it was made. This disbelief was soon to be proven justified. The radical changes turned out to amount to very little. True enough, the budget for 1954 allocated 60 per cent more than that of the preceding year for agriculture. But 60 per cent more than the inadequate allocation for 1953 still amounted to little. The same held good for the allocations made to the consumer goods industries. And heavy industry continued to get the lion's share. Though the 1954 budget provided for investments in heavy industry that represented but 26.6 per cent of the total expenditures, whereas the budget for 1953 made provisions that amounted to 36.9 of total expenditures, the investments financed by the enterprises themselves during the 1954 budget year were far higher than previously. In this guise, total investment in heavy industries were actually double that provided for in the budget. It is safe to assert therefore that there is no evidence of any sweeping changes in the R.P.R. administration's economic policies.

It must be noted further that while investments represent the greater part of expenditures made for the "financing of the national economy," important sums are devoted to covering the deficits of badly managed enterprises and of the many enterprises that sell their products below cost price. This is a current practice in all communist-ruled economies, where production prices are not necessarily taken into account in establishing sale prices. Let us point out that this is particularly true in the instance of Rumanian goods exported to the Soviet Union, the prices for which are invariably set arbitrarily by the Soviet authorities, and bear no relation whatsoever either to the cost of production or to sale prices inside Rumania.

Expenditures of a military nature might be expected to represent but an insignificant portion of the R.P.R. budgets, in view of the strict limitations imposed on Rumania by the peace treaty provisions. However, the Kremlin's decision to arm the countries under its domination has resulted in a disproportionate increase of the budget allocations to the Defense Ministry. These represented 8 per cent of the total expenditures in the 1949 budget, rose to 13.6 per cent in 1950, and reached 18 per cent in 1953. They represented 11 per cent of total budgetary expenditures for 1954. We shall have more to say on these figures presently.

The R.P.R. propaganda machine also has much to say about these military allocations. They compare these figures with the military expenditures of the Western countries, and point out that in the "warlike budgets" of the United States, for instance, they amount to 70 per cent of the total expenditures, while in those of France they account for 40 per cent. The much smaller percentages shown in the R.P.R. budgets, they say, clearly stress the peace-loving nature of that people's democracy, in sharp contrast to the aggressive character of the "imperialist countries." The bad faith of this propaganda line is obvious enough. In the first place, it is impossible to compare the budget of a Western country, which comprises but a limited proportion of the accounts of the country's entire economy, with the budget of a collectivized regime, where private enterprises have been wholly suppressed, which therefore necessarily reflects the country's economic accounting. Should, that is, Rumania's military expenditures be calculated on the basis of a budget resembling that of the Western countries, they would assuredly be found to attain at least 30 if not 40 per cent of the total expenditures.

It must be noted that there are certain military expenditures that are not shown under "national defense," but are concealed under other rubrics. We must not forget the expenditures allocated to the Ministry of Domestic Affairs, providing for the equipment and maintenance of the security troops and of the militia, which constitute together a very powerful paramilitary force, fully armed and well equipped. In addition to the above, every budget of a communist regime sets aside a sum representing 5 to 10 per cent of the total provided and leaves it "at the disposal of the Council of Ministers." There is no reason to suppose that part of this does not go to maintain and equip the secret police force belonging to the Ministry of Defense. Lastly, it must be noted that the section titled "financing the national economy" includes important allocations to enterprises that work wholly or to a large extent for the armed forces, such as munitions plants and certain construction enterprises. Under these circumstances, it is easy to see that military expenditures play a far greater part in the R.P.R. budgets than might be supposed from the figures actually given out by the communist administration.

Let us now look into the expenditures allocated to so-called social and cultural activities. Much stress is being laid on these activities by the R.P.R. propaganda machine, which on occasion has boasted that moneys spent on such activities represent fully 20 per cent of total budget expenditures in 1949, 24.3 per cent in 1951, and 14.3 per cent in 1953. Now, as is shown elsewhere in this book, almost everything that the communists lump together under the heading of cultural activities is in fact nothing but propaganda in one or another form.

In this connection we must note incidentally the official assertion made on the occasion of the presentation of the 1953 budget, to the effect that, whereas the allocations made in the budget of the United States for public education amount to only 0.50 per cent of the entire budget, those provided for in Rumania represent 7.50 per cent of the total. This deliberate falsehood is aggravated by the fact that most of what the communists describe as education is but the forcible indoctrination administered to each and every category and all age groups in the country. Under this heading, too, come such projects as the construction of the *Casa Scanteiei*, that huge and complex publishing concern, into which vast allocations have been poured under the pretext that it represents an extraordinary "cultural achievement" for the benefit of the people.

In contrast to the above, the one issue that most precisely reveals the nature of a regime's social policies, to wit the wage level, is consistently treated with the utmost disregard, indeed with cynical contempt, by the successive R.P.R. Ministers of Finance in their comments on the budget. When he presented the 1951 budget, Vasile Luca thundered against the alleged fact that certain enterprises had raised wages without concomitantly increasing production. "It is intolerable," said Luca, "that salary funds be increased more than production!" Luca was purged not long thereafter, but his successor, in presenting the budget for 1954, did not hesitate to take up the "anti-state anti-revolutionary" deviationist's theme. He too loudly denounced certain wage increases, which, he claimed, had raised wages up to 12 per cent above the previous level in industry, and had far outstripped any production increase. He was particularly bitter in his denunciation of the enterprises under the General Directorate of Industrial Equipment, where there had been average wage increases representing 5.1 per cent in excess of the plan, whereas productivity had lagged 2.3 below plan provisions.

It is evident that the communist administration has no intention of allowing industrial wages to increase above subsistence level, even though it claims the utmost concern for the welfare of the "workers". And it is no less evident that the usual propaganda falsehoods cannot be resorted to in this field, for even the communists cannot hope to convince the workers that they are enjoying higher wage rates when the workers know only too well that such is not the truth. So by indirection the Rumanian workers must be persuaded that, though their own wages do not improve, their lot is nonetheless infinitely better than that of the workers under capitalist regimes. Thus, in the official comments on the 1953 budget pointed out that there were "more than 13 million unemployed" in the United States, and that the "true wages" of French and Italian workers in 1952 represented less than one half of their pre-war wages. It was further pointed out that capitalist countries are in the throes of a constant inflation, and that, in the United States for instance, the cost of living in 1953 was three times what it had been in 1939. In making these assertions, the R.P.R. administration was conveniently ignoring, and apparently hoping the workers would also ignore, the catastrophic inflation it had itself brought upon Rumania.

We shall now briefly glance at the final heading, that of "international obligations." This, as we have already said, means payments made to the Soviet Union pursuant to the provisions of the peace treaty. As such, they have appeared regularly in R.P.R. budgets up to the year 1952, representing 7.4 per cent of total expenditures for 1949, 4.6 per cent for 1950, and 3.8 per cent for 1951.

We shall remark in the first place that, notwithstanding the above percentage figures, the actual sum in lei has invariably throughout these years been approximately 17 billion annually. With the official exchange rate of the leu at 150 to the dollar, as it was throughout this period, this means that Rumania has paid to the Soviet Union an annual amount of some $110,000,000, or more than two and a half times the payment set in the peace treaty's Article 22. Yet the official comments on the 1949 budget stressed that the Soviet Union had "most generously" consented to halve Rumania's obligations beginning July 1, 1948. The manifest discrepancy between the officially acknowledged Soviet "generosity" and the true figures can be explained in but one way: the prices at which the Soviet Union rates the goods received from Rumania are truly ruinous for the latter country's economy.

Turning to the revenues, we note that there are three broad categories of income under the present system—taxes on the circulation of products, enterprise profits, and income taxes. Their importance in relation to the total revenues varies slightly from year to year, but their relative order of size remains more or less constant.

The largest of the three, taxes on the circulation of products, represents between 42.7 and 50.7 of the total yearly revenues. The importance of these consumer taxes, which are added to cost prices, might lead one to expect that they are a determining element in the establishment of price levels. This is however not entirely so, because under the communist regime prices are set arbitrarily, as we have already pointed out, often without reference to cost prices. A striking instance was provided in the official comments on the 1951 budget where it was stated that the cost (or production) price of one egg at state farms was double the sale price of eggs on the so-called free market.

With all enterprises operated by the administration and belonging to the State, it is but normal that revenues from profit-making enterprises be prominent among listed state resources. Well, in R.P.R. budgets, profits from enterprises represent about 10 per cent of total income on an average. And let us hasten to add that this figure does not stand for the net total balance of all enterprises, but only the sum of the revenues of such enterprises as show profit. The financial assistance that the state must grant to enterprises working at a loss comes under the expenditures heading financing the national economy, which we have just examined above.

Lastly, taxes on individual incomes represents but a relatively small and constantly shrinking part of total state revenues. Income taxes accounted for 11.5 per cent of total revenues for 1949; they were only 7.7 per cent of the total in 1954. Obviously this decline is due to the increased rate of collectivization—or "socialization"—that has resulted in an almost total proletarization of the population. Income taxes, moreover, are set and collected on the basis of the "class struggle" which is aimed at the total pauperization of the people. For to the communist regime it is more important to level down the people to the point where no vestige of personal independence is left to the individual than to collect a larger proportion of taxes from a prosperous citizenry.

We have noted, in discussing the currency reform of 1947, that the R.P.R. regime saw fit to raise income taxes considerably at the very time it proceeded to confiscate practically all the money in circulation. We have further noted that, according to official statements, the purpose of that currency reform was, not only to establish a new and healthy currency, but also to effect a new distribution of the national income. Yet we learn from an official report issued by the R.P.R. Higher Economic Council on April 1, 1948, that the index for tax collections (calculated on the basis of 100 for 1938) reached 344.1 as early as December 1947, and went up to 414 by January 1948. Since the currency had been "revalued" in 1947 to the exchange rate of 1938, it follows from the above that Rumanians were paying on an average more than four times higher income taxes than they had paid prior to the outbreak of World War II.

However, the rise in income taxes is far from uniform, but strikes far harder at those whom the communists are particularly anxious to do away with. Here is how the index of taxes for 1948 stood in relation to that for 1938—no longer on an average but by professions—according to the official report cited above:

Agricultural income taxes	500
Taxes on commercial incomes	793
Taxes on wages	94
Taxes on professional incomes	350

These figures show that wage-earners clearly appear to be deliberately favored by the regime—at least by comparison with the "undesirable" categories. But, by thus maintaining the workers' wage level at that of 1938—the wage level under the now so bitterly denounced capitalist regime—the communist administration did not stand to lose anything essential. All wage earners permitted to hold regular employment are, as we know, under the strictest control of the authorities, through the all-powerful and all-pervading trade unions. As a matter of fact, this favored position of the workers was short-lived. Soon after 1948, income taxes were raised once again, not only introducing new discriminatory persecution by fiscality, but also increasing the tax rates for the workers themselves.

By the beginning of 1949 income taxes in Rumania were, on the average, six times higher than those in France. Comparing the situation in these two countries at that time, the excessive fiscality practiced by the R.P.R. regime becomes apparent in other ways too. For instance if we compare the total of taxes collected in relation to the total currency in circulation, we find that, according to the figures published officially for August, 1948, taxes collected in France during that month amounted to 65.2 billion francs, for a total fiduciary circulation of 850 billion francs, which means that monthly tax collections represented 7.1 per cent of the money in circulation. In Rumania, during the month of December, 1947, and the first five months of 1948, monthly tax collections varied between 9.8 and 11.8 billion lei, for a total fiduciary circulation of approximately 25 billion lei. That is to say, monthly tax collections in Rumania represented 40 to 47 per cent of the money in circulation. (The relationship during 1938 had been 8.5 per cent on an average.) Of course, in order to make an exact comparison between the two countries from this point of view, the relative "speed" of currency circulation should be established precisely. This is a practical impossibility; hence it is by assuming this rate of turnover to have been equal in the two countries, that we arrive at the conclusion that Rumanians were paying about six times more income tax than Frenchmen prior to the beginning of 1952.

The decree of January 11, 1952 introduced the following income tax rates:

Monthly wages in 1947 lei	Expressed in U.S. dollars	Tax rates
Up to 2,500	16.60	0
Up to 4,000	26.60	5%
Up to 6,000	40.00	8%
Up to 10,000	66.60	12%
Up to 15,000	100.00	17%
Up to 30,000	200.00	23%
Up to 50,000	333.00	30%
Over 50,000	333.00 plus	35%

For the professions considered "independent," the decree set the following income tax rates:

Annual income in 1947 lei	In U.S. dollars	Physicians	Artisans	Industrialists, merchants, and artisans employing salaried workers
Up to 30,000	200	20%	25%	40%
Up to 48,000	320	25%	28%	43%
Up to 360,000	2,400	55%	60%	70%

We may note in the first place the very high rate of taxation even for incomes of the lowest brackets. A wage earner making 6,000 lei ($40.00) monthly, for instance, paid 8 per cent of it in income tax. Knowing further that such salaries were then wholly inadequate to meet living expenses (at that time, butter sold on the "free" market for 1,300 lei —$8.60—a kilogram), we realize what hardship this entailed. In the case of an artisan managing to make a scant $26.60 a month ($320 a year!), the income tax amounted to more than one quarter (28 per cent) of his earnings. If he made more than $200 a month, they took 60 to 70 per cent from him. And it should not be imagined that there can be any question of tax evasion. Then, as at the present time, even inadvertent tax evasion was punished with imprisonment, in addition to fines ranging from 10 to 30 per cent of the sums due. Time and time again the official *Scanteia* published long lists of "economic saboteurs" who had been brought before the criminal courts for non-payment of income taxes. We must recall that this fiscal inquisition went to the length of requiring every merchant, artisan, or state enterprise—even for retail sales of a minimal nature—to make out bills of sale bearing the name of the buyer, and to furnish tax collection offices with full lists of all suppliers and clients, with full details of goods delivered. This rule, introduced by a Decision of the R.P.R. Ministry of Finance on April 20, 1948, is still in effect at the present time.

This was no mere temporary party line. The preamble to the 1954 budget, which was supposed to bring in a new policy less disadvantageous to individual farmers, still mentions the "need to make the kulaks pay."

We may take it for granted that it is a permanent concern of the R.P.R. regime to pauperize the individual peasants, not only in the latter's capacity as known foes of the regime, but in their capacity as independent farmers, and that everything has been and still is being done to force them into the collective farms. This deliberate policy became particularly evi-

dent on the occasion of the second currency reform, when the administration first bought up forcibly the entire harvest, and then proceeded
to confiscate the paper money distributed in exchange. Yet on that occasion all farmers, moneyless though they had become, were compelled
by a special decree to pay in advance 50 per cent of their income taxes,
in two instalments, one set for February 25 and the second for March 25,
1952. The currency reform, it will be recalled, had been put into effect
on January 28 of that year. In view of the quasi-impossibility for the individual farmer to procure the necessary money for his taxes between January and February 25, what other explanation can there be for this draconic
measure than that the administration meant to force the peasants to abandon their land and form collective farms?

It is, we believe, the deliberate and constant aim of the communists
to pauperize both city dwellers and peasants, in order to secure themselves
in power over an urban and rural proletariat denuded of the last vestiges
of independence.

To these excessive taxes and exaggerated fiscality, we must add the other
impositions of the R.P.R. financial administration, which further diminish
the incomes of all, no matter what their profession may be. We must cite,
in the first place, the enormous increase of rents—300 per cent—for all who
occupy more than the individual allocation of 8 square meters. All rents,
as has already been pointed out, are collected by the state, and it is only
high communist officials who are exempt from the general rule. We should
also mention the so-called "tax on transportation" instituted by a decree
published in the Official Gazette of January 18, 1952. This tax is set at
500 lei yearly for owners of a bicycle, and at 3,000 yearly for owners of
a motorcycle.

Income taxes for agriculture were fixed by a law submitted to the Grand
National Assembly on July 7, 1949, as follows:

Income in lei (yearly)	Tax in lei	Per cent
Up to 12,000	none	. .
15,000	1,020	6.8
20,000	1,670	8.3
30,000	3,370	11.2
50,000	7,770	15.5
100,000	21,770	21.8
200,000	56,770	28.4
300,000	99,770	33.3
400,000	149,770	37.4

In addition to these high rates, a special tax increase applies to those who are considered to be kulaks, hence "enemies of the regime." The law provides that "income taxes on kulak exploitations shall be increased by 20 to 50 per cent, upon proposal by the respective people's council." In other words, we have here a tax increase of a purely arbitrary, political nature, since it hinges, not on higher incomes (it is clear from the table given above, that taxes are already progressive in this respect), but on the identity of the taxpayer against whom it discriminates. Indeed, in his comments on the agricultural income tax law, Vasile Luca, then Minister of Finance, made this quite clear. "In closing this introduction," he stated, "I want to underscore the class struggle character of this law."

cultural life

For a brief time following the coup of August 23, 1944, the illusion prevailed that Rumania's cultural life would once again enter a period of liberty. Books and periodicals from the West were on sale again. Publishing houses began issuing works by Rumanian writers, as well as translations from the writers of the West. A number of new editions came out, but a still larger number were destined to be pulped, for it was not long before the freedom of the press was disregarded. Soviet censorship, operating through the so-called Allied Control Commission saw to that.

At first the censorship affected only such texts as might be interpreted as anti-Soviet. Military security, too, was interpreted in increasingly broad terms. Soon, with the forcible installation of the Groza government on March 6, 1945, censorship became an administrative concern and, wielded by the dominant communist element, increased in severity. A decree issued on May 4, 1945 listed a long series of works published between 1917 and 1944, and banned them as "harmful." Subsequent lists of prohibited books were issued each successive quarter, until they came to include the majority of editions of Rumanian authors published prior to 1945. By 1949, the list of banned works had become a sizable tome, covering no less than 8,000 titles.

A decree published in the R.P.R. Official Bulletin No. 11 of January 14, 1949, set forth the manner in which authors could henceforth have their works published. Article 10 provided that "publishing enterprises are required to forward to the Ministry of Arts and Information duplicate copies of every individual contract concerning literary works, for approval."

The communists, however, did not rest there. As early as 1945 they began to set up a "socialist type of culture" in Rumania, devoted exclusively to the "interests of the working class." In order to be allowed to make a living, writers, musicians, artists, and scientists were gradually forced to contribute to what was officially described as "progressive culture," serving the "construction of socialism." Soon the only acceptable patterns of this "new" culture, in every field of endeavor, were those set by "the most advanced culture in the world," that evolved in the Soviet Union.

It soon became apparent, in Rumania as in all the other countries of popular democracy, that any kind of activity is regarded from the social angle and must be made to contribute to "socialist construction." Under such regimes, that are totalitarian to the fullest meaning of the term, culture must necessarily lose all freedom, becoming but another medium of governmental propaganda.

From 1944 to 1948, the Communist party of Rumania did its utmost to attract as many intellectuals as possible to this task of setting up the new culture that was to become official once the "People's Democratic Republic" itself came into being.

The two most prominent writers to join in these endeavors from the very beginning were George Calinescu, university professor, critic, and novelist, author of the monumental *History of Rumanian Literature*, and Mihail Sadoveanu, a very talented writer, rightly considered to be the greatest living Rumanian novelist. Because of the exceptional significance of their cases, we shall briefly outline the development of their activities in the service of the communist dispensation.

Calinescu, who headed a typical middle-class publication, *Natiunea*, initiated by the communists themselves shortly after the coup of August 23, 1944, launched an appeal to all Rumanian writers: "The fact that the contemporary artist is also a citizen implies, from the social point of view, adherence to work discipline. The artist is a highly skilled worker; it is his duty to produce. Collective happiness requires not only bread, men also have an intellectual hunger. Nowadays, alongside economic sabotage, there is such a thing as artistic sabotage, to wit, a certain reluctance among those who write for publication, apparently suggesting difficulties of work that in reality do not exist."

Having thus taken a theoretical stand, Calinescu went on to provide an enlightening example himself. In 1946, he published a slim volume titled "Three Tales" with subjects calculated to meet with the approval of the regime—the revolutions of 1848 and 1907. However, he met with a two-fold failure. For non-communist readers, the book has no literary value whatsoever and is of a rare intellectual baseness. Communist critics, on the other hand, lashed out at the author, denouncing him as a petty bourgeois and a decadent. The fact is that Calinescu remains to this day the type of intellectual who, notwithstanding all efforts to the contrary, is unable to adapt himself to the new circumstances.

His novel, *Poor Ioanide*, published in 1953, was coldly received. "In closing this book," one critic remarked dourly, "you remain with the impression that you have read a novel written prior to August 23, 1944 by a writer devoid of the notions of the materialist interpretation of history." Nonetheless, in spite of repeated official rebuffs, Calinescu, whose literary and academic standing had already won wide recognition before the outbreak of the second world war, continues to labor strenuously in the alien vineyard of the new culture.

Entirely different is the success of Mihail Sadoveanu in this field of endeavor. Astute and with a long experience in making himself agreeable to every successive regime, he is, as one communist critic put it, "still among us, in full creative swing, actively participating in the great revolutionary transformations through which we are passing, he, too, transforming himself the while, under the influence of the century lit up by the genial ideas of Lenin and Stalin." True enough, Sadoveanu has been "transforming himself" constantly during the last half-century. After having held high posts under the former regime, including that of President of the Senate in the years 1930–1931, he has come to be considered not only the greatest writer of the R.P.R., but also to fill the position of Vice-President of the Grand National Assembly.

Adapting himself to changed conditions as early as 1944, Sadoveanu started out somewhat cautiously. Asked in the course of an interview that appeared in *Gazeta Literara* of August 19, 1954, what he now thought of the assertion he had made ten years before to the effect that "light comes from the East," Sadoveanu replied: "In the first place, let me make a minor point, which is, if you like, one of literary history. Ten years ago I gave a lecture titled *The Light from the East*. This lecture subsequently came out in pamphlet form, and was titled *The Light Comes from the East*." This is indeed an interesting and significant point. Whereas the initial title implies simply that "the light from the east" is not necessarily more than one light among other possible ones, the title of the printed work is peremptory: all light comes from the east.

This detail is particularly noteworthy in that it is characteristic of the manner in which the communists proceeded in 1944, when they had barely begun to taste the fruits of power. It illustrates the manner in which texts wheedled at the time from prominent personalities in the fields of literature, arts, or science appeared in communist publications with clever changes that fostered the belief that the author was wholly in agreement with the communist creed, though the author himself had no idea of thus committing himself. And once the harm was done, the writers could be counted upon in the great majority of cases to hesitate to set the record straight.

Sadoveanu himself, however, had thrown all prudence to the winds during the intervening years, as the regime consolidated itself in power. A few years after the incident of the "minor point" occurred, we find him writing in no less an authoritative journal than the Soviet *Literaturnaya Gazeta*: "Literary concerns become an integrant and organized part of the party's work. . . . The new country needs militant writers who work in behalf of constant progress."

Other writers, the majority perhaps, held back at first. Many preferred to give up writing altogether, rather than become paid propagandists for a party they detested. This constituted the "artistic sabotage" of which Calinescu wrote, in the quotation given above. It gave rise to much alarm at the time. As another of the regime's scribes put it later, it was "a sorry attempt to determine a strike of silence in the ranks of the writers."

But, impressed on the one hand with the fate of certain writers like Serban Cioculescu, Radu Gyr, Vladimir Streinul, Romulus Dianu, etc., who were thrown into jail or concentration camps, and, on the other hand, scared by the prospect of the dire consequences of unemployment, not a few writers have accepted work under and for the communist regime. Starvation is not a pleasant thing to contemplate, especially when one has a family. And, anyway, by 1949 the status of writers had sunk low indeed, for we find in the newspapers of that year announcements like the following: "The Provincial Committee of Bucarest brings to the attention of all pensioners, service personnel (i.e., servants and the like), writers, composers, and artists . . . that the distribution of food ration books will begin . . ." By then, too, as such announcements make clear, artists and writers could no longer obtain ration privileges unless they were members of trade unions. Unless they worked for the administration, as ordered, they went hungry; for only members of trade unions were by then eligible for ration privileges.

"The writers, in the mass," wrote L. Rautu in No. 8 (1954) of the Cominform magazine *For a Lasting Peace, for a Popular Democracy,* "answered the call of the party." As early as 1948 there could no longer be any idea of literary activity aside from that under party control. In many cases, these literary hacks had to produce works specifically ordered by the authorities. *Flacara* of July 30, 1949 made no bones about their situation: "As we fight to get out more coal, more iron, and more bread, we must fight to bring out more novels, short stories, poems, and plays. Writers must follow the example of their comrades in the mine pits and at the metal lathes. In this effort of theirs, the literary works commissioned by the Ministry of Arts constitute a good support, destined to give the fruits so anxiously awaited by millions of men now clinched in the heroic struggle for creating a happy life."

Not only is literature wholly subject to the party, but the party must become the center of concern for the writer in his creative work. In speaking of what it described as "the invincible force of the working class party," *Gazeta Literara* of September 30, 1954, said: "It is but natural that this transforming force, which is stronger than the might of everything that for so many centuries seems petrified in backwardness and adversity, should constitute the principal hero of our present-day literature. . . . For the writer who, in depicting the current life of our society, relies upon a deep knowledge of reality, in its revolutionary development, the reflection of the party's organizational force is not only natural, but also compulsory."

In the meantime, the party is also busily "reconsidering" the literary works of the past. As we have said above, long lists of classical writers whose works are banned have been published officially. This, however, should not be taken to mean that these classical writers have actually been "purged." It is merely the older editions of their works that are banned. For it is only under the present regime, the communists proclaim, that the classics can be presented in their "true light."

Writing in *Gazeta Literara* of August 19, 1954, Camil Petrescu, one of the better-known novelists of pre-communist vintage, states flatly: "It is thus that the working class rediscovers itself and recognizes itself anew in what was best in the forerunning writers, and embraces it with love. This cultural process, which was advocated in so lively a manner by Lenin, whereby the literary creations and traditions of the past must be assimilated by the working class, constitutes at the same time a proof of the vitality of that class."

However, the works of writers of the past must be "purged" in such a way that nothing is reprinted that might contradict the current party line. "The classics of Marxism-Leninism," said Academician Professor Cherestesiu, in an address before the R.P.R. Academy, reproduced in the magazine *Studii* for January-March, 1954, "teach us to appreciate the values of the past, and to know how to evaluate *in a critical* manner everything good of the past." The phrase "in a critical manner" is italicized in the article.

Pursuant to this new approach, it is hardly surprising to find, for instance, the works of Rumania's greatest poet, Mihail Eminescu, "cleansed" of a number of poems considered to be too "reactionary" by the present literary pontiffs. Among these are some of his best-known Doine, the pride of Rumanian literature. Like Eminescu, the other writers and artists of the past are now presented as "progressives" primarily engaged in struggling against the "reactionary forces" of their times. This is so, not only in school manuals for the young, but also in what pass for serious critical studies nowadays.

As for the artists and writers of the current regime, the doctrine that must dominate and direct their every creative endeavor is that of "socialist realism." One of the most prominent exponents of this official view, H. Wald, put it as follows, in *Gazeta Literara* of May 6, 1954: "The history of art itself presents us with a multitude of artistic currents which, in the last analysis, are but diverse forms of manifestations of the same two essential lines of all history of art: realism and anti-realism. Artists can but give a personal form to the conception of art of one of these two essential orientations of the history of art: realism and anti-realism."

Socialist realism, therefore, means that the artist must be imbued with historical materialism in order to be able to describe society appropriately. The photographic description of reality, however, is what the communists call "naturalism." It is not acceptable. Nor is it proper to depart from reality. This constitutes the deviation the communists describe as "idealism." And there are, in addition, several other deviations, all considered to be characteristic of "bourgeois" art, like "formalism," "decadentism," and so forth, which the "socialist" writer must know how to avoid in order not to get in serious trouble with the regime's literary watchdogs.

Mihai Beniuc, currently one of the most appreciated poets of the R.P.R., in the authoritative collective volume titled *Problems of the New Literature*, prescribes the duties of poets—and, indeed, of artists in general—under the tenets of the socialist-realist method: "The works of the poets are called upon to contribute to increasing the love of our people for the achievements of the workers in the construction of socialism, and to arouse an ever growing bitter hatred against the enemies at home and abroad of our fatherland, against the enemies of peace among the peoples, the British and American imperialists." And, in order the better to deepen their knowledge of realist-socialist principles, Beniuc goes on to recommend that poets should achieve "an increasingly lively contact with Soviet literature, from which the poets can, to an ever greater extent, acquire the method of socialist realism."

To these basic principles that must guide all poetic endeavors in the Rumanian People's Republic, another should be added: a slavish admiration for everything pertaining to Soviet Russia. Thus formulated, we have the basic principles that govern, not only the arts, but all cultural activities in the R.P.R., including all branches of science, technique, and education. It is these principles, too, that rule every aspect of what is officially included under the heading of cultural activity throughout the land.

Within the framework of this militant conception of literature, it behooves the poet to step carefully when he dallies with muses. Whenever he strays from the earnest task of celebrating the "new life," the regime's critics stand ready to pounce on him. Here is one recent instance of such a call to order, from *Scanteia*, the official organ of the communist party's central committee, of May 14, 1954. Taking to task the magazine *Tanarul Scriitor* (The Young Writer) for having printed two poems of a non-political character, the editors of *Scanteia* said: ". . . Poems like the two mentioned above resemble the patterns of evasionist, puny, bourgeois poetry, alien to the life of the people." The party demands quite another kind of poetry from the R.P.R. bards. L. Rautu, in the article already quoted above, published in *For a Lasting Peace, for a People's Democracy* makes it clear what is expected of them: "There have been epic poems written with talent, setting forth the toil and heroic struggle of our country's workers, and lyric poems whose hero lives the life of his contemporaries, sharing their joys and sorrows. . . . Many prominent works by our poets are dedicated to the peoples' fight for peace, to unmasking the hideous face of American imperialism, to stressing the international solidarity of the workers, and to showing feelings of lively gratitude to the Soviet people."

And so, today's poets must glorify the Communist party:

We, whom the Party from the mud did raise,
Build with the Party the great Feast of Peace,
That happy songs among the people may increase,
To cheer the unborn babes of future days.

(Victor Tulbure: *Contemporanul*, December 31, 1954)

For the party is ubiquitous, and its slogans grace the screens of village cinematographs:

The hall is full. The screen is white.
The slogans red go up in light.
And watchful on guard is the Central Committee
As are all party comrades in village and city.

(From *Flacara* of July 30, 1949)

One old "progressive" poet, who died in 1954, A. Toma, who, though completely unknown before the advent of the communist regime, is now celebrated as a great artist, commemorated the party line as follows:

Neither magic to soothe, nor witchcraft to fool,
Oh, Party, thou wieldest invincible rule!
The slogans of Lenin and Stalin and Marx
Like the forces of fate to fulfilment is sparks.

(*Viata Romaneasca* No. 8/1954)

It is open to the poet to seek inspiration from the most prosaic things. For instance:

Your own voter's certificate? Why, yes,
It truly stands for nothing less
Than the new Presence in all men's concerns
(Your own life now importance earns,
To which before no heed was paid,
But now can no more be gainsaid),
Concerns of all who now are well aware—
As in the past they never were—
Of the small things that form the flow of life,
Deeds and endeavors, wants and sins and strife,
But are no less aware of all the implications
Of A. Vishinsky's fight before the United Nations.

(Cited by Mihai Beniuc in *Problems of the New Literature*)

Fullest poetic license of the most fanciful nature is permitted when it comes to embroidering official themes. Here, for instance, is the Anthem of the Rumanian People's Republic (text by Eugen Frunza and Dan Desliu). It has three verses; the chorus goes:

> Powerful, free,
> Master of fate,
> Long live the Rumanian People's Republic!

The second verse runs:

> A brother our people shall be evermore
> To the Soviet People, the liberator.
> Leninism is our guiding light,
> Our inspiration and our might.
> Led by the dauntless Party, trusting we toil
> And construct socialism on our own soil.

Returning to more workaday subjects, here is a piece dedicated to a collective farm by the poet Iosif Negrea, in the pseudo-traditional style of the old folk ballads:

> Green leaf of the clover,
> Comrades all, come over!
> Green leaf of the rose,
> Come, join the kolkhoz!
> Let us through our joint endeavor
> Poverty escape forever.

And here is how the poet Petre Sascu treats a political meeting:

> A large crowd that Sunday at the Cultural Center:
> The peasants are listening, all who could enter.
> The chairman reads out, just received from the city,
> The latest Decision of the Central Committee.

Young love, too, may be sung by the poet, provided there is also an inspirational angle included. Ecaterina Mihaescu sees an amorous tête-à-tête thus:

To her sweetheart, Ion, a stakhanovite miner,
Said Nora, our spinning mill's party front-liner:
Though the frost may burn like live ember,
To me it is May in December.
For with my shock brigade this very day
I started work on quotas for next May.
Oh, Ion, my joy is more than I alone can bear.
Come, let's my joy in socialist competition share!

Topical events come in for their share of poetic magnification. In celebration of the World Youth Congress and Festival, staged in Bucarest in the early autumn of 1953, an impressive number of songs won recognition. Here are a few of the titles: *Song for the Youth of Korea* (N. Radu), *The Song of the Young Constructors* (Montia), *The Romance of Bucarest* (Virgil Teodorescu), *Song Dedicated to the Soviet Youth* (V. Iosif), *Under the Banner of Peace* (Ion Firescu), *Song Saluting the Guests* (A. Mendelssohn), *Song About the Five-Year Plan* (M. Chiriac). All had music specially composed for them.

Even construction projects of the future, such as Bucarest's ambitiously planned but soon abandoned subway, provide themes for poetic flights of fantasy:

. . . . . .
See how the Kremlin's ruby rays
Within the marbled concourse rest
To guide the subterranean ways
Of our own Metro-Bucarest.
Beauty is here that shall not wilt.
Yearnings are here transposed in fact:
By teeming, toiling thousands built,
The people's wondrous artifact.
Yes, there is deathless beauty here,
Invincible, the future's beam.
My warmly beating heart speaks clear:
This is no idle fancy's dream.
Thus shall it be, the time is near—
Unfaltering our way is lit—
When we shall live, my comrades dear,
This wondrous poem yet unwrit.
. . . . . .   (*Scanteia*, November 30, 1952)

Well, the poet's heart did not speak quite so clearly, and the whole thing was destined to be an idle fancy's dream. Projects of socialist construction, like power stations, new railroad lines, and even the notorious Danube-Black Sea canal, where countless thousands lost their lives before it was abandoned, have been sung by the regime's bards in their time.

It is the poet's duty, among other things, to fight against the enemy from within and from without. "We poets," writes Mihai Beniuc, who is not only an established poet himself, but also secretary of the R.P.R. Writers' Union, "must cultivate in the souls of men hatred for the enemies of the people, the sacred hatred against that bitterest foe of ours, imperialism, and in particular American imperialism. In the field of anti-imperialist poetry, we have obtained signal successes." A recent instance of such signal successes was provided by Beniuc himself when, writing in *Gazeta Literara* of May 27, 1954, on the occasion of the Geneva Conference, he expressed himself in the following manner:

> It seems that Mr. Dulles is afire
> And wildly bites his lips in ire:
> He smells agreement among nations
> When he himself desires abominations—
> The smell of gunpowder and chains,
> Of fettered peoples as all freedom wanes,
> A world enslaved to Yankee gains.

The domestic enemy, too, comes in for his share of poetic treatment. Beniuc again provides the example, in "The Golden Apple," published by *ESPLA* (Bucarest) in 1954:

> Impale me without mercy on the highest spire
> And let me perish in the hottest fire
> If I should ever fail to see
> And let my enemy go free!

Nor are the political exiles spared or overlooked:

> But if longing suffocates you
> And for your return you sigh,
> Come, the country all awaits you
> For you left without goodbye.
>   (Mihu Dragomir, in *Contemporanul* of November 12, 1954)

At all times, the Soviet Union and all things Russian provide poetic inspiration. Again we turn to Mihai Beniuc, this time grappling with his feelings as he leaves the Stalingrad railroad station:

> But when you get your ticket at the stand,
> You don't feel you're just visiting some land,
> Intent on business or tourism;
> You feel you've truly entered communism.
>
> (*Contemporanul*, October 8, 1954)

The Soviet Union is, of course, also the great liberator.

> Flower of the linden tree,
> Oh, that August twenty-three,
> Happy day for our country,
> When the Soviet people came,
> Brought the help that is their fame,
> Made us of the fascists free
>
> . . . . .
> Now, free of that horrid band,
> We are masters in our land.
>
> (*Universul*, October 20, 1951)

The reference is to August 23, 1944, and the "horrid band" is not the Soviet people but the fascists. This adulation can fringe the psychopathic realms of fetishism occasionally. But that, too, is acceptable to the R.P.R. literary authorities. The poet N. Tautu describes his return from Moscow, in *Contemporanul* of October 15, 1954, as follows:

> Asked my wife: "And in your pack,
> From Moscow what did you bring back?"
> "From the banks of the great Don,
> The finest accordion.
> Hear it play but once, my dove,
> You'll know the meaning of love."

Beniuc, too, was deeply impressed with Moscow. He reported—as quoted by *Scanteia* of June 14, 1951—in awed doggerel that,

> Many a fair place and town,
> Many cities of renown,
> Grace the earth and nations crown,

> Yet, though you walk iron-shod
> The whole world to roam and plod,
> None with Moscow can compare,
> None so beautiful and fair.

But, from time to time, poems of a non-political slant still appear. Again and again the fellows of the erring poet gang up to denounce him. Writing in *Gazeta Literara* of November 25, 1954, Maria Banush approvingly quoted an article by Mihu Dragomir, in which the latter, "Rightly asks himself . . . why do non-political poems, poems in which the pulse of our times is not felt to beat, still appear? Poems in which the soul of a lyrical hero, identified with the people and with his times, poems that are not written from revolutionary positions, poems in which still can be sensed alien influences inimical to our conception of the world and of art?" Yet Maria Banush herself had declared openly her adherence to a creed that is the exact opposite of this view. In a poem titled "No, Never!" published in *Viata Romaneasca* No. 5/1951—barely four years before—she had sounded a note of revolt against the official art of the R.P.R.:

> "No, never shall I forbear to sing
> Of the lightning, the sun, and young love on the wing!"

So flagrant was her spirited deviation that *Scanteia* itself intervened to bring her to her senses. In the issue of June 29, 1951, a long article was devoted to scoring the "ideological confusions" of Maria Banush. How could she criticize so harshly the whole poetic output of the country? Had she forgotten the existence of such commendable pieces as "Comrade Matei Has Been Awarded the Order of Labor" by Veronica Porumbacu, and "Song for Gheorghiu-Dej" by Mihai Beniuc? As for her own poem "No, Never!" *Scanteia* declared: "The mistake of Comrade Maria Banush is that, in speaking of nature and of love as subjects dear to her . . . she is isolating herself from the entirety of other themes proper to a literature that places in the center of its preoccupations *man*—the advanced man of our days."

Following this rebuke, Maria Banush suffered a temporary eclipse. It was only at the price of prolonged and excessive penance that she was readmitted to the official R.P.R. poets' roster. She won grace with her long poem "About the Land" which came out in 1954, and of which *Contemporanul* of November 25, 1954, consented to report that "It reflects the growth of patriotic consciousness of the working peasantry, and its struggle to translate into reality the Decision of the Rumanian Workers' Party plenary Central Committee of August, 1953." The poetess herself, turning her back on "the lightning, the sun, and young love on the wing," told how she came to get the necessary inspiration for her redeeming poem. Writing in *Gazeta Literara* of November 25, 1954, she stated: "It was necessary for me to be present there, at the Presidency of the Council of Ministers, in the midst of the heroes, to live through every pore, and to imbue myself wholly with the full beauty and grandeur of that spectacle."

But it is not only the administration as such that makes use of poets for propaganda purposes. Individual institutions, too, have their official bards. There is, for instance, a publishing concern that is run by the C.E.C., the Savings Bank, which puts out collections of verses, plays, and stories, designed to promote deposits. The quality of this output may be gauged from this little ditty:

> I feel like jumping straight in the sea,
> I haven't saved a penny with the C.E.C.

which appeared in *Informatia Bucurestiului* of April 7, 1954.

As we have shown already, there is a determined attempt to create a new folklore, one that conforms to Marxist-Leninist theory. The old traditional forms of popular ballads are simulated, the contents being furnished by approved topical themes. This has led to the creation of the R.P.R. Folklore Institute in 1949. By 1954, its researchers had managed to collect no less than 60,000 pieces of alleged folklore, according to *Contemporanul* of December 10, 1954, which stressed that the researchers are required to have a solid ideological training. Approving the work done so far, the newspaper adds, "The essential merit of these researchers is that they have demonstrated concretely and extensively that the new creation of popular songs is characterized by specific stylistic traits, and that these traits are connected closely with the new psychic qualities of our people as a socialist nation in the process of formation."

It is obvious that the task of the researchers consists in twisting and distorting and inventing texts in compliance with the current ideological requirements. Here are a couple of instances, selected from a long article in *Universul* of October 20, 1951:

> Flower of the blood-red rose,
> Up on high great Stalin goes.

How to thank him no one knows,
For he freed us of our woes;
On life gave us a new lease,
Brought us freedom, bread, and peace.

Green leaf of the hickory,
Let me of great Stalin sing.
Red flower of the chicory (*sic*),
Let me my love to him bring.
From our village on the fill
To his distant window-sill
May our love o'er mounts and vales
Sing a song of nightingales.

These pieces and others in the same vein came to light, of course, at the time when Stalinolatry was at a peak. The epoch was to come to an end with the beloved and genial leader's death, an event that was itself still marked by elegiac efforts like the poem titled "At His Monument" by Eugen Frunza, which saw the light of day in *Romania Libera* of March 10, 1953, in which the poet sadly says,

We shall return to work without a song today.
Goodbye, our Loved One, I whisper filing by.
But, heartened, on we go upon our way
To fight for victory: the banners fly.

With the dawning of the post-Stalinist era, the glamor of exalted personalities had perforce to yield the way to the more pedestrian themes of collective anonymity. More taxing though this may be for the popular democratic muses, it has at least the advantage of obviating the heart-breaking pursuit of finding appropriate rhymes for Khrushchev—a task the fabricators of spurious folklore have for the time being been spared.

The novelists, short story writers, and playwrights of the Rumanian People's Republic are free to select their subjects either from the past or from the present-day life. In writing of more distant times, they must portray life in accordance with materialist dialectics, stressing the historic class struggle, the struggle of progressive characters of the past against their contemporary reactionary elements, in other words, the conflict between the "old" and the "new." Of course, heroes of bygone days had to do without benefit of Marxist-Leninist-Stalinist doctrine. Their great deeds were inspired solely by their own revolutionary consciences. Nonetheless, literary works portraying the past must always insist upon the rapacity of the exploiting classes, and upon the bitter lot of the workers. This is a minimum requirement. If the subject chosen is placed at any time after, say, the middle of the last century, then the corruption of the bourgeois-landowning regime must be played up for all it is worth.

Currently considered officially as one of the most successful novels is *A Man Among Men*, by Camil Petrescu, a writer well known long before the advent of the communist regime. This novel purports to portray the life of Nicolae Balcescu, the Rumanian historian and revolutionary (1819–1852), whom the communists see as one of the most prominent forerunners of their regime. It grossly misrepresents the hero, and conveniently overlooks his truly libertarian views. This, being wholly congruent with the views of the present-day critics, is considered most acceptable.

A number of recent novels describe events situated between the two world wars. In them the stress is laid on the Communist party's struggle as an illegal underground movement. The bourgeois society is savagely caricatured, and the hero is almost invariably armed, not only with wholesome militant zeal, but also with the elements of Marxism-Leninism, in his upward progress. No good whatsoever is admitted to have existed in the prevailing regime, but the "men of the future" are not only full of every virtue but comely and in every way lovable.

Such works are seriously discussed by the critics as though they were valid books of history. The vanishing margin between fiction and reality may best be gauged by the following extract from an article in *Scanteia* of January 26, 1952:

"Experience has proven that literature is a particularly precious asset in the study of the history of the workers' movement. Hence it is proper to advise students of certain chapters of the *Short Course of the History of the Communist Party of the Soviet Union* to read works that tally with these chapters. Among these there is, for instance, *Tilled Land* by Sholokhov, or the wonderful novels created by Soviet writers in the period of the Great War for the defense of the Fatherland, and those describing the work of the Bolshevik party after the war, in behalf of the construction of communism . . . For the history of the workers' movement in our own country, literary creations like *The Dawn of the Slaves* by V. Em. Galan, *Sparks of Darkness* by A. G. Vaida, *The End of Petitions* by Al. Jar, etc., are of use."

Before going on to the more recent novels, we shall examine the novel which is considered to be the greatest literary masterpiece of the present regime, *Mitrea Cocor* by Mihail Sadoveanu, which came out in 1949. The action takes place in recent times and goes on to the year 1945, the year when the communists were brought to power. The hero, Mitrea Cocor, is a poor peasant. His brother, a miller, had made money and become a kulak. The two brothers—their very family names are different—symbolize the Rumanian peasantry divided into poor working peasants and kulaks. The landowner in their village, Cristea, is rich; he is a large fat man. Ghitza Lungu, the brother of Mitrea Cocor, is also a fat man, only he is short. But "Three-Noses," as Cristea the landlord is nicknamed, and Ghitza Lungu are much alike; they might well have been brothers, "Three-Noses" the elder, and Ghitza Lungu the younger. Here, too, we find the obvious kind of symbolism that, to a reader unused to socialist realism, seems rather contrived: the similarity between the kulak and the landowner exploiter. Ugly as sin, Cristea is portrayed by the author as having every conceivable vice. Ghitza the miller comes a close second to him in villainy. In this way, Sadoveanu complies with one of the basic canons of his trade: "The fundamental principles of realist art demand that the writer show the enemy in his true abject light, in all his nakedness, tearing all masks from his face," as prescribed in the magazine *For a Lasting Peace, for a People's Democracy*, No. 8, 1954.

As for the hero, Mitrea Cocor, his first encounter with militant communists comes while he is in the army. Later he takes part in the Russian campaign. The author stresses the inhuman ways of officers and noncommissioned officers of the Rumanian army and, of course, the outright bestiality of the Germans. By contrast, the Russians are nothing less than angelic. Mitrea Cocor is taken prisoner. The Soviet soldier who gives him his first orders as a POW is a veritable choirboy. Here is the scene, as the author describes it through the unlikely medium of a letter written by Mitrea Cocor to his beloved: "One of them (the Soviet soldiers), who had gray hair and whitish eyebrows, and whose eyes were like blue beads, patted me on the back and smiled as he gave the order to line up with the rest."

In line with the doctrine of socialist realism which demands that everything pertaining to the Soviet Union be praised without reservations, the Soviet army must at all times be described as an angelic host. The lengths to which this can go are almost incredible. Here, for instance, is what the poetess Veronica Porumbacu finds to say, in a poem titled "In a Railroad Station," in which she describes a group of Soviet soldiers:

'Tis here we see the secret of the daintiness
With which the Russian soldier so surprised us.

Let the reader note that the Rumanian word "gingasie" used by Veronica Porumbacu is the exact equivalent of "daintiness," a word aptly to be used to describe, say, a flower or a maiden; but applied to a soldier, even a Soviet one, it is simply grotesque.

Sadoveanu, too, goes overboard in vicariously admiring everything his hero sees in the Soviet Union. In his enthusiasm, Mitrea Cocor joins the Tudor Vladimirescu Division, which the Russians formed of Rumanian prisoners of war, and which was later to be officially referred to as "the initial elements of the R.P.R. armed forces."

In addition to all these conformist features, the novel abounds in socialist realist elements. Thus it has "positive characters" and "negative characters," with the most notable of the former category appearing in the closing chapters: Voicu Cernetz, a militant communist, who wears a leather jacket, whose eyes are "guarded by bushy eyebrows . . . and whose face is clean-cut and seems carved in stone." This Voicu Cernetz seems to emanate an almost superhuman force: when he enters some peasant's yard, the dogs do not bark at him.

We have insisted at some length upon this novel, because it remains acknowledged officially as the most successful novel to appear in the R.P.R. *Mitrea Cocor* has been awarded the 1950 gold medal by the World Peace Congress. It has been translated into Russian and into many other languages. It has been made into a film. The great talent of its author raises it above a mere propaganda piece, it must be admitted. It is indeed a remarkable novel.

The same, however, cannot be said of the overwhelming mass of literary production under the communist regime. Novels and short stories dealing with current aspects of life have a bleak sameness; their plots are drearily similar. As summarized by one prominent critic, O. S. Crohmalniceanu, the successful novel *Steel and Bread* by Ion Calugaru, "portrays the struggle of the new manager, the worker Pavel Ilie, of the activists sent to Hunedoara by the Central Committee, and of the conscientious workers, against the machinations of the bourgeois and former landowners who have managed to infiltrate the labor union and the command posts of the plants, and who from their concealment are carrying out their destructive activities unhampered. The novel tells how Pavel Ilie succeeds in paralyzing and crushing the plans of the class enemy, how the high furnaces come to life, how the shops of the plant begin to hum, and how the entire surroundings pulse with the rhythm of socialist competition."

Such, indeed, with a few changes of locale, is the tenor of practically all novels dealing with present-day life in the R.P.R. Whether they take place on a collective farm or on the construction site of a new electric station, there are invariably the "positive" and the "negative" characters in conflict, like some ever-present latter day embodiments of good and evil, with the good triumphing in the end, to the advantage of the commonweal and of production. It also behooves the authors to develop such secondary themes as the "non-political attitude" (the non-political but otherwise decent character is ultimately won over by the "positive hero"), "bureaucracy" (the bureaucrat is always ousted in the end), "careerism" (the character who is indifferent to the class struggle and cares only for his own advancement), and, wherever it can be brought in, the praise of the Soviet Union.

It is hardly surprising that, with such material to work on, it is only very rarely that anything of true literary value emerges from the boring monotony of the current literary production. Again and again certain writers have tried to escape this stultifying restraint, seeking a modicum of liberty in bygone settings. But again and again the regime's literary watchdogs have brought them to order in no uncertain terms. For instance, Zaharia Stancu, writing in *Gazeta Literara* of May 20, 1954, scolded "the increasing number of writers who take refuge in an ever more distant past, shrugging off what is perhaps their most difficult task, but also the greatest honor: the task of selecting themes from the life lived this day by our working people." The critic further pointed out that this issue has often been raised in the Writers' Union of the R.P.R., though he conveniently ignored the unpleasant fact that both the novels he himself has published under the present regime have subjects drawn from the past.

The "positive character" we have already mentioned poses one of the most important problems of socialist realist literature. The manner in which this hero is apt to be treated has been wittily satirized in a well-known Soviet cartoon: a little boy is offered an apple by a little girl. "No," says he, "I am a positive hero: I take only cod liver oil." And certainly it must be a difficult thing to make the reader, be he child or adult, stomach a hero who has only exalted virtues and no human failings. Small wonder, then, that we find a young writer, Petre Luscalov, complaining (in *Contemporanul* of October 8, 1954) that, "our literature, notwithstanding the remarkable successes registered of late, has not yet succeeded —aside from a few exceptions—in creating on a high artistic level, the figure of the positive hero, the advanced man of our epoch." Luscalov goes on to show how the positive hero is usually contrived, "starting off with a pre-established list of traits frequently found in the positive character, like, for instance, aggressiveness, heroism, vigilance, spirit of sacrifice, and so forth. Thus the positive character becomes the embodiment of a list of qualities of an obviously dogmatic nature." It is only occasionally that the positive character is hampered with some weakness, like, for instance, a serious illness, or, as in the case of the positive heroine in the play *The Lovers*, by Maria Banush, the fact of being in love.

Under such circumstances, there is some justification in the criticism voiced by L. Rautu, in the article already quoted above, from the magazine *For a Lasting Peace, for a People's Democracy*, to the effect that, "in many novels, short stories, and plays, the positive hero is but a wan apparition, a scheme bereft of life, speaking in cliches, and having nothing in common with the real heroes of the new life."

Yet none dares to come out into the open and pose the question whether perchance the difficulty of transposing into literary form this notion of the "positive hero" arises from the very fact that this character does not exist in reality, but is only a figment of doctrinaire theory. Notwithstanding the plentiful evidence available, this would mean tampering with the holy of holies.

In addition to such difficulties, aside from deviations ascribed to hidden influences of bourgeois art, realist-socialist literature can give rise to various other sins specific to itself. The principal ones are "schematism" and "idylism." When, for instance, the critic Rautu writes, "Our writers often limit themselves to reflect in their works well known phenomena . . . the same conflict, the same formal manifestations of the class struggle, similar characters," he refers to "schematism." But the fact is that the party constrains the writer to work according to pattern, though at the same time it requires him to avoid the pitfall of schematism. "Idylism" consists of presenting the realities in rosy hues, in implying, for instance, that the class struggle is ended, that the enemy has at last been routed. This leads to a feeling of "self-appeasement" apt to lull the readers' combativeness and vigilance.

As for the influence of bourgeois literature, the R.P.R. critics never cease to deplore that it is found even in the young writers. This is all the more deplorable seeing that the younger writers are not supposed to know anything of bourgeois letters. Worse still, the young writers show weakness in satire. As *Scanteia* of March 13, 1954, stated, "they attack with none too much spirit the class enemy." Hence, as *Scanteia* puts it, "The horrid figure of the warmongers who aspire to world domination, that of the American imperialists primarily, has not been unmasked with sufficient vigor."

But even literary criticism is not exempt from risks under a people's democracy. The critic, not knowing what the ultimate official reaction might be, has to step with the utmost caution when he is not quite sure of his ground. He may, for instance, deal harshly with a work that subsequently is awarded a state prize. Or he may praise another that *Scanteia* is about to rake over the coals. *Scanteia* itself has more than once demolished the critic of some other publication. In the issue for November 3, 1954, for instance, it scolded those who "wait for other reviews to come out first, in order to orient themselves." And in the issue for November 5, 1954, the newspaper *Contemporanul*, obviously emboldened by this, proceeded to accuse critics in general for "the rather strange habit that has become rooted in this country, to wit, regarding newcomers in the field of letters in a troubled and shy, noncommittal way."

Yet there have been critics who have tried to deal with problems of literary values in conformity with party directives. Thus, for instance, Crohmalniceanu committed himself in two articles that appeared in *Contemporanul* as far back as 1949. What happened was that he got a blistering rebuke from *Scanteia* (issue for August 2, 1949): "The negative examples selected . . . are taken almost exclusively from works that deal with the struggle of the working class and of the working peasantry. . . . Cosmopolitanism is manifest in the lack of love for the fatherland's productions, in the 'contempt argument' of cosmopolites without a fatherland." *Scanteia* then went on to lay down the law once and for all: "Together with literature, literary criticism forms an integral part of the general cause of the proletariat." The criteria for judging a literary work under a people's democracy were set down as follows: "The form of a literary work is the more beautiful and the more perfect, the more the writer shows insight into the essence of life and of men, the better he succeds in seeing sharply their problems, and discovers more of the numberless aspects of the struggle of men for progress and for happiness."

The dramatic arts are beset with even more complex problems than the rest of the literary field, involving as they do, not only a greater outlay and more responsibilities, but also a more direct and far-reaching contact with the general public. A play or a film without an adequate ideological content is inconceivable. As early as 1947, the 45 conditions that a play must fulfil were officially prescribed in an article, titled "Directives for dramatic production," that appeared in *Semnalul* of September 2, 1947. These "democratic" conditions include the stressing of class warfare, socialist vigilance, friendship with the peoples of the Soviet Union and of the people's republics, the struggle for peace, anti-Western propaganda, and the like.

Faced with such tricky requirements of an obviously non-dramatic nature, as well as with the still more elusive exigencies of whatever the current party line might be, it is small wonder that many playwrights sought refuge in remote times of the past. But the watchdogs of the party would have none of such shirking. Commenting on a meeting of stage managers held about that time, *Scanteia* of May 15, 1953, prescribed flatly that, "at the present time, the basic task is the creation of new shows, of original plays, with themes stemming from reality, from today's life of the people—plays that are of the highest interest to the working people."

As one American observer so wittily wrote of the accepted Soviet play, the proper theme is, "Boy meets tractor, girl meets quota." The play that won the R.P.R. Academy prize for 1949, and is still officially considered one of the best pieces to emerge under the present communist regime, is *The Miners* by Davidoglu. Its plot is simple: a production stalwart struggles against the twin adversities of bureaucratic routine and the political apathy of his fellow workers. In the end he unmasks the class enemy, and succeeds in firing the zeal of the other miners in behalf of socialist competition. Not very different is the subject of another very successful play, *The Lovers*, by Maria Banush. There we find a young woman who is "chief of cadres," that is, personnel manager with wide-ranging police powers, in an important enterprise, and who is in love with the engineer-manager of that enterprise. She is vigilant and has smelled out the class enemy. The manager is a decent man but lacks vigilance. Notwithstanding the want of proper support from her beloved, the heroine ends up by un-masking the class enemies, who are saboteurs and tools of the British-American imperialists.

Confined within such narrow patterns, it is not surprising that "pro-gressive" plays fail to attract the public. The outcome can be guessed by the most naive from the very opening lines. The "class enemy" is instantly recognized the moment he enters the scene. The ultimate victory of the "positive hero" is foreseeable, no matter how adverse the attendant cir-cumstances. Were it not that tickets are distributed free to selected groups of workers, soldiers, and school children, such plays—even Soviet importa-tions—would be presented to empty houses, no matter what efforts the official press might make to boost them. "All too often," complained the literary magazine *Flacara* of September 16, 1950, "important spectacles are played before houses that are not full, whereas at others the public is so numerous that many must renounce buying tickets." We need hardly point out that "important spectacles" are either Soviet plays or local "pro-gressive" ones, and that the "others" are the world-renowned classical plays.

Of course, it can not be officially admitted that it is precisely the im-position of rigid nonartistic tenets that is accountable for the unpopularity of "progressive" pieces. The fault, according to the party mouthpieces, lies with the authors. "The most numerous and serious deficiencies of our new stagecraft," proclaimed *Contemporanul* of June 20, 1952, ". . . stem from the lack of attentive study of reality in the perspective of the working class conception of life. The great deficiency of many dramatic authors is that they do not persevere in constantly raising their ideological and political level. . . . Political and ideological training is for the playwright an instru-ment for the knowledge and understanding of reality." Here as elsewhere, the prescribed cure is not less ideology, but more. It is because the Ru-manian dramatic author is weak in dialectic materialism, that, as *Scanteia* of March 21, 1953, complained, "the luminous figure of the advanced man of our times appears to stand out so poorly in our plays and on our stage."

Caught between the exigency of staging ideologically correct plays by Rumanian playwrights, and that of box-office success, theatre managers are understandably reluctant to do what is officially expected of them. *Scanteia* of May 21, 1953, observed wryly that during the 1952–1953 season even the National Theatre of Bucarest "failed to present a single new original play inspired by the construction of socialism in our country." Earlier, *Contemporanul* of June 20, 1952, had in vain denounced "a grave and blameable bugbear of our theatres that consists of a cosmopolitan attitude of ill will and contempt toward original dramatic creation."

In a determined effort to remedy these things, a conference of stage authorities was called in Bucarest in June 1954. The final findings stressed anew the need for new plays "topically inspired," apt "to teach the working people to fight with greater determination . . . for a new life, to be more vigilant against the perfidious machinations of the class enemy." This, the findings stressed, must be done by presenting more Soviet plays and plays that "reflect the life of today of the Soviet people, the constructors of communism."

Not only Soviet playwrights, but also Soviet stage managers and players are the constant models for their R.P.R. counterparts. Indeed, as far back as 1951, the presence in Rumania of special and permanent Soviet counselors for the theatre was known to be one of the features of the R.P.R. stage. And, in addition, the official drama critics likewise intervene directly in dramatic creation: "The critics of the party press," stated *Contemporanul* of June 20, 1952, "have helped Davidoglu to improve his play considerably, and to make of the second version of his *City of Fire* one of the foremost plays of our literature."

Actors, too, are forced to acquire a solid grounding of Marxist-Leninist doctrine, in addition to seeking inspiration from Soviet performers. They are required to attend special courses. As *Scanteia* of May 21, 1953, prescribed, "In order to identify themselves in their acting with the best sons and daughters of the people, in order to unmask all that is rotten and backward, in order to realize creations of great art, apt to exalt the spectators, actors must struggle to become themselves advanced people, of a high ideological, cultural, and professional level, people in whom the highest feelings of the people shall vibrate, people animated with the most burning interest in the construction of the new life—following the example of the great Soviet actors."

The end result of this constant and all-embracing interference of the party in the theatre is that the public is increasingly reluctant to attend the theatres to be subjected to propaganda in the guise of entertainment. In an attempt to win back the public, it became the general rule that the first few showings of a play would be acted by the players with every due respect for the official requirements, with the ideological contents stressed with proper decorum. But, after a play had been seen by the authorities and the official critics, the actors would change the whole spectacle, introducing "business" apt to amuse the public, ad-libbing, and altering the rhythm, pace, and impact of the piece. This was successful for a while, and, to the amusement of alert theatregoers, troupe after troupe literally "got away with murder."

But an alert woman journalist, Margareta Barbuta finally got wind of this. In a scathing article, published in *Contemporanul* of March 17, 1950, she thundered against the "degradation" of one particular play that was meant to be a "powerful social drama," into "a police comedy." She lashed out at the actors who at later showings of a play "sacrifice the idea" for the sake of making thereof a "commedia dell'arte," by introducing their own lines, and thus "misleading the public." The vigilant newspaperwoman conceded that "our public no doubt likes to be made to laugh," but, she pointed out, "laughter must be a sharp weapon directed against the exploiting class, against the remnants of the past, not a narcotic that puts class vigilance to sleep."

The article stirred up a tremendous uproar in stage circles. Many were the actors—some of the most prominent among them—who hastened to perform self-criticism in open letters to *Contemporanul*. The dean of the Rumanian stage, Maximilian, admitted in writing that the whole thing was due to the fact that Rumanian actors "do not have constantly in mind the example of Soviet actors." Stage Manager Sica Alexandrescu, another veteran of the theatre, blamed the "degradation" on the fact that "certain sections of the public still preserve the remnants of an old education."

Yet the phenomenon persisted, once the initial furore died down. As recently as the summer of 1954, *Contemporanul* was moved to take up arms once again against the system. A general press campaign against the "degradation" of the stage was unleashed. Some newspapers went so far as to advocate introducing a "record of impressions," in which the public might set down impressions, criticisms, and suggestions following performances at all theatres. The literary magazine itself, in its issue for July 2, 1954, was of the opinion that the "cultural activists" of the local people's councils should make a point of "checking the content and orientation of works performed in the theatres."

The variety theatres and revues, too, must fall in line, and, in behalf of socialist construction, put on shows of topical interest from the point of view of the regime. They are, indeed, considered to have an even more direct impact than the drama itself, their position in relation to the legitimate theatre being approximately that of political cartoons in relation to serious painting and sculpture. Not even puppet shows are exempt from this all-pervasive ideological contamination. As one instance, we find *Scanteia* of July 1, 1954, solemnly "panning" one puppet play for "making poor use of political satire on international themes." "The public," the official paper of the Central Committee, then pointed out, "would greet with the same interest satirical anti-imperialist tableaux, which are entirely absent in this play."

Going all the way down the intellectual line, we might add that even the circus is expected to do its part. Reporting the opening show of the R.P.R. State Circus, *Romania Libera* of November 8, 1954, voiced displeasure at the performance of the clowns: "The comic numbers must take their place among the satirical weapons, and contribute by way of wholesome laughter to the education of the masses."

Under the circumstances, it is but to be expected that productions for the screen, whose importance as political propaganda material hardly needs emphasizing, are the object of still greater official solicitude than the other forms of mass entertainment. The four existing film studios of the R.P.R. plan their production as a veritable military campaign might be planned, and nothing is left to chance. Scenarios and releases come under the direct authority of a General Directorate for Cinematography, and there is a special Directorate for Film Scenarios in the R.P.R. Ministry of Culture. Incidentally, the Film Center at Buftea, near Bucarest, is scheduled to become "the largest and most modern in South-Eastern Europe," according to official statements.

"On August 9, 1952, Niculae Belu, chairman of the Cinematography Committee," wrote *Romania Libera* of August 12, 1952, "expounded the cinematography plan for 1953–1955 at the Writers' House. The writers will complete 42 scenarios representing the fight for socialist construction, 14 with subjects illustrating the revolutionary struggle of the Rumanian people, and 6 for animated cartoons." Just like that—not one more, not one less. And, of course, as *Gazeta Literara* of July 8, 1954, made it clear, "in our scenarios and films, the hero of our epocn or socialist construction must appear in all his plenitude."

Just how bad these maqe-to-order scenarios are we can well imagine. Indeed, we may cite the high autnority of the critic Cronmalniceanu, whom we have aiready mentioned earlier in this cnapter. Writing in *Contemporanul* No. 28/1954, he states unamoiguousiy: "Many of our scenarios, especiaily tnose devoted to certain episoaes in tne struggle of the working class, are along the lines of a hybrid genre—neither artistic film nor yet documentary, but rather an odd combination of both." Bad as the scripts are, the resulting films are worse still. Crohmalniceanu goes on: "It must be said that the text of the first published scenarios is in the majority of cases superior to the subsequent transposition into films."

Even the communist promoters of the Karlovy-Vary film festival of 1954, desirous though they were to make awards to screen productions from each and every one of the people's democracies, could not do better for the R.P.R. film industry than a "special mention" voted for *The Nephews of the Bugler*, with a book by Cezar Petrescu. That same year, R.P.R. State Awards could be given to only a few "shorts." There seems to be a limit to the bad art that even a communist jury can swallow, even though it corresponds to ideological standards.

Rumania's musicians, painters, and sculptors thought at first that the communists would not bother them to the extent the writing fraternity was being circumscribed in its artistic activity. How wrong they were! One of the first blows came from a certain Rudascu, a communist and an art critic. Writing in *Contemporanul* of November 11, 1949, he chided the naive artists and rudely brought them to their senses: "They tell themselves that if the creative artists in other domains of art, notably the writers, might at a pinch need certain theoretical ideological knowledge, those who work with colors and with forms . . . can very well do without. Their art being less explicit and more susceptible of subjective interpretation, the ideological level of the artist will not be perceptible, they thought." A grave error, stormed Rudascu, for Marxist-Leninist critique has proven that, faced with a work of art, be it a picture or a symphony, it can very well reflect the artist's ideological level. Hence it behooves all plastic artists to study Marxism-Leninism seriously, because only thus can they attain truly superior art—art, that is, "imbued with the party spirit."

As for musical creation, Sabin Dragoi, who later was appointed Director of the R.P.R. Folklore Institute, had this to say in *Romania Libera* of October 15, 1951: "Owing to the right policy of the working class party, music is increasingly becoming an asset of the people—an active factor in tne construction of socialism in our country. . . . Directed and constantly assisted by the party, making use of the admirable example of Soviet artists, our artist of today comes ever closer to the people. . . . The love for tne country of liberty and peace, the Soviet Union, love for that banner-bearer of peace, Joseph Visarionovitch Stalin, our people's ardent love for the fatherland, and their grim determination to fight against the warmongers, are all mirrored in numerous works of Rumanian composers."

They are indeed, if the titles of the compositions are any clue. "Under the Sun of Peace" is the name of a composition by Hilda Jerea, "A Summer Day at a Collective Farm" that of a piece by Zeno Vancea, "Song for Stalin," that of a contribution by Anatol Vieru, awarded the R.P.R. State Prize for 1949. There is also a "Song of the Partisan of Peace" by Ion Chirescu, and "The Party Flag" by Matei Socor.

All further comments became superfluous in the face of the resolutions adopted by the Committee of the R.P.R. Composers' Union, in February 1952. This called upon all Rumanian composers to "struggle intransigently against every manifestation of formalism, impressionism, atonality, and cosmopolitanism, against bowing and scraping before decadent bourgeois art," after admitting that "composers have need, in their creative activity, of a critique of principles based on Marxist-Leninist aesthetics," and ended by demanding that all musical creation be "put in the service of the fight for peace and for socialism."

Music literature must likewise conform to party requirements, no matter how authoritative the imprint under which it appears. Thus, for instance, the magazine *Muzica*, the organ of the R.P.R. Composers' Union, came under violent attack in 1952 from *Contemporanul* for "lack of combativity and of militant spirit." The editors of *Muzica* were upbraided for "failing to analyze the problems of our musical creation in the light of the theses on literature and art that are included in the report presented by Comrade G. M. Malenkov at the 19th congress of the Communist party of the Soviet Union." They were no less bitterly reproached for not devoting a single article to "combating the influences of bourgeois ideology in our music, manifest in the form of cosmopolitanism, nationalism, impressionism, and so forth." On another occasion, *Contemporanul* took offense at the deficiencies of light music, likewise "infected with cosmopolitanism," and in its issue for September 19, 1952 demanded that the appropriate organs of local people's councils "be on watch, at popular balls, social occasions, restaurants, etc., to make sure the music is not infected by the microbe of adverse ideology, and that every musical manifestation be, on the contrary, a means of educating the masses."

No particular improvement seems to have resulted from this cry of alarm for, almost one year later, *Viata Capitalei* of July 4, 1953, also com-

plained of the "pernicious influence of American jazz and other decadent
Western music" on Rumanian popular tunes, and called upon the Directorate for Music of the Arts Committee to "enhance its vigilance and
check more often all concerts of popular music."

The musical authorities of the R.P.R. are strongly in favor of what is
known as the "mass song," usually a sort of topical propaganda cantata
for soloists and choir, a dreary and grimly serious version of the delightful
West Indian calypso genre. Composers are constantly urged to concentrate on such pieces, and even the most mediocre have a good chance of
a State Prize. A recent isue of *Contemporanul* (October 15, 1954) scolded
Rumanian composers for turning out gay dance tunes instead of, for instance, celebrating the "last elections for the people's councils." Earlier,
the same magazine prescribed that composers, in order to become "true
artist-citizens, veritable tribunes of the people," should study on the spot
the new life they must celebrate, preferably by working themselves at a
collective farm or industrial plant. The composer should "ceaselessly strive
to perfect his ideology and his art"—in that order.

The plastic arts, too, have sunk to the prescribed level of socialist realism, under constant pressure from the communist party and under the
equally inescapable example of Soviet art. As *Scanteia Tineretului* of December 18, 1954, told its young readers, "the party schools and the articles
in *Scanteia* and *Lupta de Clasa* have helped our plastic artists to understand the principles of Marxist aesthetics." And, of course, "the example
of Soviet art is of great assistance to the development of our plastic arts
along realist lines. . . . The visit of Soviet artists and critics . . . and the
friendly directives they have given our own creative artists have solved
many of the problems posed to our plastic arts."

The end result of all this extraneous—and inescapable—meddling can
occasionally be seen by the Western public, for the R.P.R. art authorities
are more than eager to stage exhibitions abroad, to display the current
level of socialist realism achieved by Rumanian artists. Paintings have
such titles as "The new members arriving at the collective farm" (by
Iosif Bene), "Ilie Pintilie in the Doftana prison" (by G. Saru), and "The
Grivitza strike of 1933" (by Gavril Mickloszy). Of course, portraits of
Lenin and Stalin and lesser communist luminaries abound. Of course, too,
such portrayals are apt to entail occasional risks. Such, for instance, was
the case of the painting of "Ana Pauker visiting a collective farm," which
was exhibited by the artist, G. Lazar, barely a week before the purge of

Ana Pauker, and which was described at the time by sculptor Boris Caragea as being "sunny, full of optimism, the joy reflected on the faces of the children and peasants showing clearly the close bonds existing between the communist leaders and the people." (*Contemporanul*, May 23, 1952.)

Other themes are "sure-fire" successes. Thus the monumental bas relief by Sculptor Baraschi, immortalizing the "liberation" of Rumania by the Soviet army and featuring a Soviet tank surrounded by smirking and gesticulating crowds, was awarded the State Prize for 1953, and now stands in Bucarest's University Square.

Paintings of still life, nudes, and landscapes, having no political content, are frowned upon. For, as *Scanteia Tineretului* pointed out, they belong to the past, whereas "our art was salvaged by the party of the working class, which took into its hands, at the same time as it took up the destinies of the Rumanian people, the problems of art, raising them to the level of state problems." Such old-fashioned paintings, when they still occasionally crop up in exhibitions, are described as "schematic works, lifeless and alien to reality, put together according to old patterns and formulas." But even paintings that conform to the current official requirements must show that the artist's heart is in them. Otherwise they are dismissed curtly: "True life is supplanted by pose, by the declamatory rhetoric of certain characters portrayed, which because of this appear unconvincing."

Posters and political cartoons, having a more obvious propaganda value, hold a place of honor among the plastic arts, in Rumania as elsewhere in the communist-dominated sphere. *Contemporanul* of October 8, 1954, carried an understandably indignant article, decrying the fact that the officially published album *Plastic Art in the R.P.R.: 1944–1954* did not include cartoons.

The arts in the so-called Rumanian People's Republic are, by overt official admission, called upon to perform certain very precise functions, wholly subordinate to political ideology. Freedom and sincerity of expression, so essential to artistic creation, are replaced with conformity. Inspiration stems solely from rigid and arbitrary tenets of so-called socialist realism. The painter, the composer, the writer, and the actor must hold on as best they can to the prescribed party directives, if they want to make a living by their particular skills and gifts. Artistic creation becomes a purely alimentary pursuit. Deliberate abstention is almost as dangerous as deviation. "One of the most frequently observed tendencies is manifest in the lack of creative activity displayed by certain artists," growled *Contemporanul* of July 30, 1954, warningly.

Such, as we shall presently see, is also the role officially assigned to the sciences under the current dispensation.

It may be said that the sciences enjoyed a measure of tolerance up to the year 1948, the party being concerned up to that time mainly with attracting collaborators from among those prominent in the various fields of scientific endeavor. But, at the same time, the country's scientific institutions were being infiltrated with more dependable specialists. Once the Republic was proclaimed, early in 1948, the whole picture changed almost overnight.

The first step was to do away with the Rumanian Academy and replace it with a newstyle institution called the R.P.R. Academy, modeled after that of the Soviet Union. The avowed purpose of this institution is to bring the "party spirit" into every field of scientific endeavor. As Academician Professor Constantinescu-Iash put it, in his report on the activities for 1953 of the Academy's History, Philosophy, and Juridical and Economic Sciences section, "Our entire labor is and will be subordinated to the main task, which is to serve the cause of the party with devotion."

The second purpose of the R.P.R. Academy is twofold: on the one hand, it is to promote the exclusive influence of Soviet culture; on the other, to eliminate all Western cultural influences from every domain of science. In the words of *Romania Libera* for December 7, 1954, "The broadening and constant improvement of our relations with the Soviet Union constitutes the guarantee that our cultural life will develop in all its aspects."

A special Rumanian-Soviet Institute of Studies has been set up. Its task is to make available translations of Soviet works, not only into Rumanian, but also into every one of the country's minority languages, and to provide textbooks, periodicals, and other publications, either in translation or in compilation, for various schools and courses. Aside from the vast output of this Institute, the R.P.R. Academy publishes some forty periodicals, all in the spirit of Marxism-Leninism and covering every conceivable subject matter. In 1951, the R.P.R. Academy set up what is described as an "Evening University for Marxism-Leninism."

The process of training new generations of scientists imbued with the spirit of dialectic materialism goes hand-in-hand with the weeding out of older elements. It has become increasingly evident that the overwhelming majority of men and women who attained a measure of prominence in the scientific field prior to the advent of the communist regime, almost all educated and trained in Western universities are, so to speak, constitutionally unadaptable from the point of view of the regime, no matter how earnestly they may try to cooperate. This is hardly surprising. It is true that examples abound, not only in the countries that have fallen under communist rule, but throughout the free world, of scientists of the first water who display a political "blind spot" that makes them willing dupes of the communist illusion. But in most cases, the acquisition of a true scientific outlook, which implies not only objectivity but also integrity, precludes adherence to the rigid, arbitrary, partisan, pseudo-scientific standards prescribed by Marxism-Leninism. Under communist rule, the humility of spirit implicit in the scientific approach becomes a different kind of discipline. Utter political compliance reaches into the inmost recesses of the spirit. Blinkers are substituted for the academic cap and gown. Any inner conflicts that arise must be solved in favor of the political requirements, no matter how strong the evidence to the contrary. The resulting abdications of the spirit have a cumulative effect. It is not a happy one. Nor can it in the long run turn to the advantage of the totalitarian regime and its works. And these things have to be personally experienced to be fully grasped. If only the Western scientists who, willingly or unwillingly, have fallen into the toils of the communists could return to the free world, what a story they would have to tell! As it is, it takes an unusually high degree of discernment to appreciate these things from the outside. It is easy enough to subscribe mentally to the principles of Marxism-Leninism when one enjoys the benefits of academic freedom the while. This accounts, no doubt, for the many theorists of communism still to be found among the honored scientists of the free world.

Of these things, the communist leaders are only too well aware. The Western-trained scientist of the old school is outwardly honored by them —but only insofar as he is willing and able to discard and publicly repudiate all he truly stands for, proclaiming instead the officially prescribed verities. But at bottom he is not trusted, no matter how he may humiliate himself to prove his adherence. The percentage of the reliable kind of pseudo-scientists a communist regime can truly count upon is small among those educated in an atmosphere of academic freedom. Hence the urgent need to replace the "old-timers" with young people untainted by "bourgeois ideology." The crux of the problem is how to train these rising generations, how to teach them the requisite skills and techniques—the fundamental knowledge available only through the medium of old-school teachers. The communist answer to this problem is direct. The savant, the professor must be brought to his knees. If he does not bow—and bow publicly—he must be broken. There is no compromise.

In an article published in *Romania Libera* of July 3, 1949, Professor Dr. Stefan Nicolau, a prominent Rumanian scientist, announced the new creed: "Any honest man in our country knows that Soviet science, the vanguard of the world's progressive science, must provide the model for every true servant of culture." Thereafter, all newspapers featured letters from scientists renowned in every field, openly and emphatically endorsing this now sacred tenet, each vying with the rest in terms of adulation and abasement. One of the most abject, Academician Professor of Mathematics Grigore Moisil, glibly stated: "In the science founded upon dialectic materialism we shall find the directive of our scientific activity."

But even Moisil was later publicly abused for not having mentioned Russian scientists in one of his books except in the bibliography, and for having instead referred constantly only to Western savants in the course of the work itself. *Contemporanul* of March 27 and April 3, 1953, raked the hapless Academician over the coals so violently that he had to perform penance loudly and prolongedly in order to reinstate himself.

Also in 1949, the linguists were brought in line. The French-language *Bulletin Linguistique,* which appeared in Bucharest, was accused by *Lupta de Clasa* of cosmopolitanism, and all its collaborators were subjected to the bitterest criticism. The magazine had to cease publication, and all its contributors were forced to beat their breasts in open letters to various other periodicals.

In 1950 came the turn of the technicians and engineers. *Contemporanul* of April 7, 1950, assailed the presence of cosmopolites in the Bucharest Institute of Construction and called upon the individual professors involved to recant or resign. Some of the culprits showed spirit and refused to admit they had erred. Their colleagues rose in wrath against them and denounced the "reactionary conception that led them to reject just criticism." The official view prevailed.

Scanteia of June 28, 1953, next found fault with the Institute of Biochemistry, where "party life" was found to be deficient. The Institute was grimly told it should "apply itself consequently to the principles of dialectic materialism in its work." It hastened to do so in no uncertain manner.

Some time before that, the official organ of the central committee of the Rumanian Workers' Party had asailed the country's historians as a group. In the issue for May 15, 1953, *Scanteia* called for "a thorough acquisition of party spirit," needed in order to be "freed from the burden of non-Marxist conceptions." Historians were also urged to "increase their vigilance against the remnants or influences of foreign ideologies, doing away with any kind of liberalism toward them, and thus stepping on to the road lighted by the example of Soviet historiography and by the genial ideas of Leninism-Stalinism." Historians must at all times "use Marxist doctrine in interpreting facts." Coining a contemptuous term for a troublesome reality, *Scanteia* dismissed "factology" as being "an immediate remnant of bourgeois historiography, a profoundly anti-scientific and reactionary method, camouflaging an unwillingness to participate in the shaping of a truly scientific history for our people." The meaning of these objurgations is crystal clear. It is an open invitation—indeed, an order— to falsify historical data, to set at nought the record, to invent if need be, with the purpose of "shaping a truly scientific history."

The R.P.R. regime, like all so-called people's democracies, spends an impressive amount of energy, ingenuity, and substance on the dissemination of "culture." For the official designation of this instrument of communist propaganda, it has coined the appropriate barbarism "the culturalization of the masses," and there is a special Directorate in the Ministry of Culture handling the various media. Fully one-sixth of the total expenditures in the State budget for 1953 was allocated to "social-cultural needs" (the figure given by *Contemporanul* of August 20, 1954, was 15.9%).

Though the principal agency, ARLUS, or the Rumanian Association for Friendly Ties with the Soviet Union, has been active since the end of 1944, it may be said that the drive for "culturalization" went into high gear in the year 1948. ARLUS, whose activities are devoted to disseminating throughout Rumania the "most advanced science and culture of the world," numbered 125,000 members by 1945. According to official data, the membership rose to 1,700,000 by 1948, and by the end of 1955 stood at 6,000,000, that is, the equivalent of 40 per cent of the entire population. In 1948, all Western institutes of culture were closed down, and in Bucarest, for instance, many persons who used to be regular patrons of the British, American, Italian, and French libraries were arrested by the police.

ARLUS now has agencies in all cities and in most villages, all actively spreading Soviet Russian culture. Its publishing concern, *Cartea Rusa* (the Russian Book) had, by the end of 1954, distributed no less than 1,900 separate titles, totaling 25 million copies. And *Cartea Rusa* handles but part of the immense output of translations from Russian, for there are a number of other publishing houses engaged in covering the fields of literature, science, politics, and so forth. ARLUS, in addition to this, and aside from also publishing a number of periodicals in Rumanian and in all other languages spoken in the country, is active in the exchange of visits, exhibitions, lectures, shows, and so forth, between Rumania and the Soviet Union. Each year it organizes the varied programs that mark the Rumanian-Soviet Friendship Month.

In 1948 all the existing cultural institutions in Rumania's cities and villages were transformed into centers of "progressive" culture. Since then, their number has grown so that at this time there is not a collective farm, plant, enterprise, or administration that does not have at least its own "red corner," where lectures, film shows, radio programs, readings, and the like are enjoyed in common. The accent is on "visual agitation." In urban and rural areas, special installations, consisting of public address systems broadcasting official propaganda, fill the air with their constant clamor. In the late afternoon, after the day's work is over, they go into action, and it becomes impossible to get away from the ubiquitous voice of the regime. This is especially true in the winter months on the land, when agricultural work is at a standstill. Willy-nilly, the peasants must gather, too, at the village cultural center, to see some propaganda film, listen to some lecture, or a reading from *Scanteia*.

In the cities, workers of various institutions, enterprises, and plants, once their regular stint is over, must attend meetings and sessions where, stupefied with fatigue and their bellies rumbling from hunger, they must sit through endless dreary lectures, movie shows, or readings. There is no escape. Not only the party's voice, but its eyes and ears are everywhere. The regime's watchdogs are constantly on the alert, and both the public and the agencies involved are immediately rebuked for the slightest sign of remissness. Not only must the privacy of the individual citizen be systematically invaded, but the invaders must do a thorough and satisfactory job.

Occasionally, however, the public finds it advantageous to comply voluntarily with the purveyors of indoctrination. Such "successes" are duly noted with approval. We find an ironically revealing instance cited by *Viata Capitalei* of December 9, 1953. Describing how in the bitterly cold winter of that year some forty housewives of the Tudor Vladimirescu raion of Bucarest were found gathered at the local "No. 1 agitation point," the newspaper said: "One after another they took place on chairs around the table or on the armchairs in the room. It is warm here, because Comrade Maria Varlan, who is the 'responsible' of the point, takes good care of this." Leaving aside the straight-faced acceptance of the presence of two score housewives in search of a little warmth as evidence of their interest in political agitation, the report pointed up the fact that it was up to the "responsible" of the "agitation point" to see to it that the place was comfortable. In other words, the newspaper apparently found it perfectly natural that a public building happened to be adequately heated simply because the caretaker was "vigilant," and saw fit to approve an obvious exception to the general rule, disregarding the sorry implications.

Prominent in the field of "culturalization" is the Society for the Dissemination of Science and Culture, set up in 1949. Organized and functioning along the lines of the Soviet "Universal Society for the Dissemination of Political and Scientific Knowledge," its main purpose is to combat "obscurantism and ignorance", or religion, and to propagate Marxist-Leninist political doctrine. It operates principally by organizing lectures and issuing pamphlets. According to *Contemporanul* of June 25, 1954, the Society in its first five years of activity, had sponsored 570,000 lectures throughout Rumania's cities and villages, with a total attendance of 53 million listeners, and published 170 tracts, each with an edition of 20 to 30 thousand copies.

The publishing of books was aptly described by *Romania Libera* of November 24, 1952: "The new regime of popular democracy has transformed the problem of disseminating books into a considerable State problem." Indeed, between 1949 and 1953 the regime's publishing concerns issued more than 13,500 separate titles with a total of almost 250 million copies. This impressive output of communist propaganda is handled by some 12,000 "popular" libraries, not including the libraries of the various individual trade unions, which in 1952 numbered not less than 6,000.

There are special courses for librarians. The "responsibles" in charge of libraries are expected to act as door-to-door salesmen, cramming propaganda books into the empty pockets of the citizenry. Certain books, like certain official publications and periodicals, are required reading in all institutions. There is no escape, for special meetings are called every so often, where each is quizzed exhaustively by the "activists" on the contents of the prescribed work. This applies to collective farms, theatre troupes, miners' collectives, university faculties, and state store personnel equally.

Under these circumstances, it is hardly a matter for wonder that even the poorest novel, providing it "has what it takes" from the point of view of communist propaganda, can reach impressive editions. In 1944–1945, the average edition of a novel translated from Russian was perhaps 6,000 copies. Nowadays it is 50,000 copies. This development provides the clue to the "popular success" enjoyed by so many mediocre Western writers in the Iron Curtain countries at this time. All that is needed is to be considered a "progressive" by the literary authorities of the communist regimes. Literary merit is unimportant. Small wonder that there are publishing concerns flourishing now throughout the free world solely on the strength of sales within the Soviet empire, whose "stable" of authors are practically unknown in the West. There are rich rewards for the "progressive" scribe in the people's democracies, and the temptation to the unscrupulous hack writer of the West is great indeed.

The conclusions are obvious enough. The meaning of culture in the people's democracies is different from that generally understood in the free world. "Culture" means just one thing in the R.P.R.: communist indoctrination of the masses.

5

religious life

Long before the Soviets came to power in Russia, Lenin had made clear both his own conception of the Divinity and the attitude of the Communist party toward religion. In a letter addressed to Maxim Gorki in December, 1913, he stated:

> The idea of God has always lulled and dulled the "social feelings" by substituting the dead for the quick, and it has always been the idea of slavery—the worst kind of slavery, that without issue. The idea of God has never "tied the individual to society" but has always shackled the oppressed classes through faith in the divinity of the oppressors.

Though for tactical political reasons Lenin had merely advocated the separation of Church and state, he made it clear that, "As for the socialist party of the proletariat, it considers that religion is not a private matter." Indeed, as may be found stressed in "Socialism and Religion" in *Novaya Zhizn* (New Life), No. 28 of December 3–16, 1905, the party "cannot and must not remain indifferent to irresponsibility, to ignorance, or to dark fanaticism in the form of religious beliefs."

The communists have remained faithful to this ideological position. They remain determined ultimately "to extirpate the last vestige of religious beliefs," as Nikita Khrushchev himself declared in the Decision of November 10, 1954, of the Central Committee of the Soviet Union's Communist party. Nonetheless, both in the Soviet Union and the people's democracies, a policy of gradual change has been adopted. The immediate goal, the initial phase, entails the thorough subjection of the Churches to the state, and their use for the propaganda purposes of the regime. To reach this end, an entire series of means, legal as well as direct, have been found suitable, and the communist regimes have not stopped short even of outright mass persecution.

If at first sight the Rumanian administration's policy toward the Churches may appear to differ from one denomination to another, the ultimate aim remains the same in all instances, and the differences are basically only in the methods used. Where dogma stands in the way of compromises between the faithful and clergy of a denomination on the one hand, and the administration's orders on the other; where compliance entails setting at nought the essence of the faith; the conflict becomes acute. It then takes the form of persecution. Such has been the case for the Catholic Church.

The Orthodox Church, the Protestant denominations, the Jewish faith, and even the Mohammedans could apparently be subjected to regulations that, though entailing painful diminutions, fall short of annulling their dogmatic fundamentals. Hence a difference of regimens has resulted, which certainly does not correspond to any intention of the administration to persecute certain denominations to the advantage of others.

We propose to portray the R.P.R. government's policies toward the country's religious life, by examining the concrete facts pertaining to the various Churches. In so doing, we trust that the broad lines of an over-all action will become clear, and that the reader will be able to grasp the full extent of what is assuredly one of the most serious aspects of the present plight of the Rumanian people.

The great majority of Rumania's population belongs to the Orthodox Church. The figures shown by tne census of December 29, 1930, within the borders of that time, are as follows:

Orthodox Church	72.6%
Greek-Catholic Church	7.9%
Roman Catholic Church	6.8%
Calvinist Church	3.9%
Lutheran Church	2.2%
Unitarian Church	0.4%
Baptist Church	0.3%
Lipovan Church	0.3%
Jewish Faith	4.2%
Mohammedan Faith	1.0%

(Cf.: *Populatia Romaniei*, Manuila & Georgescu, Bucarest, 1938)

The regime of the Rumanian Orthodox Church, as well as the division of its sees, within the country's integrated borders at the end of World War I, was defined in the Statute of Organization of May 4, 1925, which, with small subsequent modifications, remained in force up to the time of the changes introduced by the Groza government.

That government, notwithstanding its reiterated benevolent declarations and in spite of all reassuring appearance, never in reality ceased its policy of subjugating the Rumanian Orthodox Church to its own ends. In this field as in others, it proceeded systematically, in accordance with a well-laid plan.

The initial phase was marked by mass purges of the Orthodox hierarchy and clergy—similar to the purges carried out in other bodies (army, magistrature, education, etc.). In this manner, the administration secured control of leadership, by the installation of sure and devoted elements in all key positions. It was only the second phase that was marked by the introduction of a new legal regime, which gave the Rumanian Orthodox Church the modified standing that tallied with Communist interests. This new standing and organization could, obviously, not stop short of reducing the religious and educational role of the Orthodox Church to an absolute minimum. This, in turn, could lead only to a gradual transformation of that Church into an instrument of propaganda, and finally into a mere tool of the administration's basic policy: the ultimate communization of Rumania. It is obvious, too, that the third phase must necessarily follow: the rulers of the Rumanian People's Republic, following the example available in the Soviet Union itself, must seek to assign to the Orthodox Church a place similar to that which it has in the U.S.S.R.

The first concern of the Groza government was to secure the compliance of the entire Orthodox clergy, from the highest prelates to the last village priest. It was hoped that the prestige of the Church might be used on behalf of the government's aims without resorting to spectacular legislative measures that could not fail to dismay public opinion.

A first step in this direction was an appeal addressed to the clergy, inviting them to adhere politically to the new government. The so-called "Union of Democratic Priests," however, failed to gain much of a following, in spite of all high-sounding promises, and in spite of the presence of one of the principal promoters of that "Union," the Reverend Burducea, as Minister of Cults in the Groza government.

Faced with the fruitlessness of this action, and seeing that the clergy as a whole showed a marked aloofness to political blandishments, the government decided to take direct steps, attacking resistance by wholesale purges. Means had to be found to get rid of the highest prelates themselves.

Investigations were initiated against some, obliging the victims to resign their pastorates in sheer desperation. Such was the case of the Metropolitan Bishop Irineu Mihalcescu, Archbishop of Iash and Suceava (July 22, 1947).

In March 1947, the then Minister of Cults, Radu Rosculetz, a member of the Liberal dissident group under Tatarescu, made known his decision to submit to Parliament two draft laws. The first concerned the pensioning of priests; the other provided for a redistribution of sees and set up new rules for episcopal assemblies.

The first became law (No. 166/1947) in short order. It provided an age limit of seventy years for all clergy. Exceptions might be made, upon advice from the Minister of Cults, in favor of such prelates as "have had an exceptional activity." Clearly, this provision gave the government a free hand to rid itself, with a show of legality, of any resistance in high quarters. And indeed the Metropolitan of Oltenia, Nifon Criveanu, and Bishops Lucian Triteanu of Roman, Cosma Petrovici of the Lower Danube, and Gheronte of Constantza, were ousted almost immediately.

Then, in view of the Episcopal and Metropolitan elections scheduled for November 1947, the second draft law announced by the Minister of Cults was carried through and put into effect. Up till then, episcopal assemblies had been elected by the faithful, who delegated their members for a three years' period. Now, in the terms of the new law, these assemblies were to be made up with a de jure majority, for they had to comprise members of parliament, ministers of state, and state under-secretaries belonging to the diocese. Thus, both in these assemblies and in the National Church Congress, which likewise had to include members of parliament and of the government, the regime in effect obtained a free hand.

The significance of the episcopal elections was underlined in no uncertain fashion by the Communist press. For instance, *Universul* of August 28, 1948, stated:

> . . . The conduct of the country's destinies falling to the hands of
> the party of the working class and of the democratic parties and organ-
> izations, special attention was given to the renewal of the upper cadres

of the Church in the elections that took place in November 1947, when three hierarchs of the people entered the synod.

These "popular" prelates were Firmilian, Metropolitan of Oltenia, Sebastian Rusan, Bishop of Maramuresh, and Justinian Marina, Metropolitan of Moldavia. We must dwell a moment upon the personality of the last-named. A simple priest in the Ramnic eparchy, Justinian Marina had been closely connected with the dissident "peasant" formation headed by Anton Alexandrescu, who had dropped out of the National Peasant party. He succeeded in becoming at one stroke Metropolitan Bishop of Moldavia, without having shown the least prominence or especial merit as a churchman. On May 24, 1948, he was elected Patriarch of the R.P.R. Orthodox Church, succeeding the late Patriarch Nicodemus. As Patriarch, Justinian Marina, who had by then asserted himself publicly as a devoted partisan of the regime, was certainly the right man in the right place, in the eyes of the Groza government. Already he had revealed himself by the pastoral of March 14, 1948, in which he glorified the draft constitution of the R.P.R. From his latest and most exalted throne, he has rendered yeoman services to the regime, both by his words and by his deeds. No more devoted tool could a Communist regime find anywhere.

Thus, on the occasion of his enthronement, on June 6, 1948, Patriarch Justinian not only appealed to the Uniate (Greek Catholic) faithful, urging them to pass to the Orthodox Church; but he thundered against the Concordat, denouncing loudly the alleged inequality set up among denominations by that accord with the Holy See. The new Patriarch, it should be noted, has also shown himself to be a fanatic partisan of the closest possible ties with the Orthodox Church of the Soviet Union.

The publication of the new regulation of cults in the Official Gazette of August 4, 1948, marked the opening of the "legislative" phase proper. That decree formally established a privileged de jure position for the Orthodox Church, by comparison with the other—minority—denominations. In practice, however, the Orthodox Church was to be subjected to the same drastic limitations and controls as the other cults, in its organization and functions.

Article 22, which provided that "for the creation and functioning of eparchies (dioceses, superintendencies, etc.), an average of 750,000 faithful shall be reckoned for each such eparchy", provided thereby also a legal

basis for a new incorporation of Orthodox eparchies. And, indeed, this
new measure was carried out by the decree No. 244, published in the
Official Monitor No. 217, of September 18, 1948. This decree abolished
the Metropolitan See of Suceava and the Episcopal See of Maramuresh,
and set up a single eparchy instead: the Archbishopric of Suceava and
Maramuresh. A second decree, published in the Official Monitor of February 5, 1949, set forth the new bases for the "economic-administrative
organization of the Orthodox Cult", and at the same time once again
redistributed the Orthodox eparchies. As a result of these two decrees,
through a reshuffling of eparchies, the Bishoprics of Husi (established as
early as 1598), of Caransebes, and of Maramuresh, were abolished.

Finally, the Law on Cults, whose Article 58 abrogated "the provisions
of the law No. 68, of March 19, 1937, for the organization of the corps
of army chaplains", abolished at the same time (Articles 59 and 60) the
Orthodox Military Episcopate whose seat was at Alba Iulia. Aside from
these dispositions of a general "organizational" character, this law set up
in great detail a thoroughgoing control over the entire activity of the
hierarchy and clergy. Its provisions were to be put into effect either directly
by the Ministry of Cults or by the local authorities.

The law likewise abolished theological seminaries of secondary grade
(Art. 53) as well as certain schools of university rank, known as theological
academies. It left in existence but two theological university institutes.
Subsequently three such institutes were permitted to operate, in Bucarest,
Sibiu, and Cluj, in addition to one monastic seminary at the Neamtz
monastery, and one each at the Plumbuita and Agapia convents for nuns.
To these institutions we might add a number of schools for cantors, that
is, church singers. (*Universul* of September 28, 1951.)

In order to grasp the full significance of these measures, it should be
recalled that up to that time there had been an Orthodox seminary in
operation at almost every metropolitan and episcopal seat in the country.

The statute for the organization and functioning of the Rumanian
Orthodox Church, provided in the new law on cults, was approved by
a decree of the Grand National Assembly, dated February 23, 1949, and
published in the Official Gazette of February 25, 1949. The new regulations
entailed a marked diminution of the purely religious activities of the Orthodox Church. The number of sees was reduced from 19 to 14. The title
of the Episcopate of the Lower Danube, incidentally, was changed to the
Episcopate of Galatzi, as a gesture of courtesy toward the Soviet Union.

This was a significant move, for following the annexation of the three South Bessarabian districts by Russia in 1878, though the seat of the see was moved from Ismail to Galatzi, its ancient and eloquent title had remained unchanged. On the other hand, conditions for setting up new parishes were made more difficult, Article 49 requiring, for the creation of a new post of parish priest, a village population of 400 families, instead of 200 called for thitherto.

Lastly, all priests were placed in a situation wholly provisional and uncertain. Article 123 provided that priests and deacons hold provisional tenure for a five-year initial period, after which they are required to follow certain "special courses", and pass examinations entitling them to permanency. Following a further period of five years, another series of "special courses" are provided, prior to examinations in view of promotion. The ultimate sanction against those who fail to take the courses and the examinations is "the definitive expulsion from the ranks of the clergy." For a priest to be transferred to Bucarest from the provinces, he must, in addition to these courses and tests, go through yet another cycle of training and pass "a special examination". Furthermore, in order to qualify, the priest is required to have carried out what is described as an "exceptional" church activity for fifteen years (Article 125).

The nature of the "special courses" mentioned above was made clear from the very beginning, as indeed was that of theological education in general under the new regime. Thus, at the opening of the courses at the Bucarest University's Theological Institute, on January 30, 1949, the official address emphasized that one of the Institute's principal tasks was to give special attention to a new kind of training and orientation, both pastoral and social, for the clergy, to guide the latter "in the service of the people and of peace." In discussing the special missionary courses set up at that time, *Universul* of February 26, 1949, stressed that "the need for these courses had been increasingly felt of late, because a new and proper orientation of the clergy had become imperative, in all directions in which the people's democracy seeks to raise the masses of the people."

Within the framework of the regulations described above, the authorities proceeded with a thoroughgoing purge of the Orthodox clergy, with the concomitant promotion of compliant elements. As early as February 22, 1948, *Scanteia* had defined the administration's official position with regard to religion and to the clergy in general. An article titled "Concerning Religious Liberties" had proclaimed: "Our clergy has before it the example of the Orthodox clergy of the Soviet Union." It also remarked that the party of the working class could not remain "indifferent to the various prejudices and mystic beliefs fostered in the ranks of the workers by the bourgeois-landowning regime."

Thus, on the example of the Soviet clergy, the mission of the Rumanian Orthodox clergy is now a twofold one: On the one hand it will have to foster increasingly close relations with the Orthodox Churches of the neighboring countries, and especially with that of the Soviet Union, as well as with those of the Near East. On the other hand it will have to act wholeheartedly in support of the actions undertaken by the "Partisans of Peace". The latter task my be presumed to be of the utmost consequence politically.

The increasingly frequent reciprocal visits and talks that have been arranged in recent years between the higher prelates of the various Orthodox Churches illustrate eloquently enough the active pursuit of the first part of the mission. But it is in their capacity as "fighters for peace" that the hierarchy of the Orthodox Church and, indeed, the clergy of all other denominations in the R.P.R., are expected to show their mettle. As may be seen from the lengthy reports in the R.P.R. press, the theme of all sermons and pastorals, the tenor of all interdenominational meetings, and even the works of the Holy Synod itself (whose meeting of June 6 and 7, 1954, was related in *Romania Libera* of June 11, 1954) center upon the "Peace Movement." It is hardly a random result, any more than it is a simple coincidence, that it is precisely those clerics most zealously active in this field of endeavor who are promoted in the hierarchy. Among such faithful auxiliaries of the regime in the R.P.R. Orthodox Church, the most notable are: Sebastian Rusan, elected bishop and soon thereafter Metropolitan Bishop of Moldavia and Suceava; the Archimandrite Valerian Zaharia, enthroned as Bishop of Orades on November 25, 1951; and Alexandre Ionescu, appointed Vicar of the Bucharest Patriarchate. Their names are to be found, together with that of Patriarch Justinian Marina himself, on the very short list of Orthodox prelates decorated on June 7, 1953, for "meritorious patriotic activities and for contributions to the cause of peace." (Cf. *Scanteia*, June 20, 1953)

The communist administration does not hesitate to ask other kinds of propaganda assistance from its supporters among the clergy, as witness the pastorals issued for Easter and Christmas in 1952 by Patriarch Marina, in which he castigates "those American leaders who advocate and urge, in the name of a false science, that one-third of the people now living should be killed off," and denounces "the Herods of our time, who, headed by the rich of America, control the riches of this earth." It is in line with such endeavors, too, that Alexandre Ionescu, the Vicar of the Patriarchate, gave favorable testimony, in March, 1952, before the French courts, in a case involving the communists.

But these flagrant instances do not in any way mean that the Rumanian Orthodox Church is wholly in the service of the communist administration. Indeed, there is much evidence that stubborn resistance is being encountered among both the faithful and the clergy, and that this continued resistance marks, in fact, an upsurge of religious feeling. Already a number of high prelates have been thrown out of office. Already many priests have been jailed or placed in camps. This is not entirely unknown even outside Rumania. A Vatican broadcast of January 6, 1953, stated that there were at that time some three hundred Orthodox priests held in concentration camps in the country.

Under the circumstances described above, it becomes clear that the apparently privileged position of the Orthodox Church in Rumania, by comparison with that of the Catholic and Uniate Churches for instance, conceals a very dismal reality. The communist action is aimed against religion as such. Its actual development is merely a matter of opportune tactics.

The Bucarest government, in its desire to eliminate all possibilities of organized resistance to its policy of communizing the country, decided to begin a relentless campaign against the Catholic faith. This is a phenomenon common to all the captive countries.

Catholicism, by its international character and by the Western conception it represents, constitutes not only a close and constant bond with the free world of the West, in spite of the "Iron Curtain", but also a significant rallying point for an important proportion of Rumania's population, desirous to maintain intact the moral values threatened by communism.

The Catholic faith is represented in Rumania by the Roman Catholic Church which, according to the census of 1930, numbered 1,250,000 souls, and by the national Greek Catholic Church which, according to the same census figures, numbered 1,430,000 faithful. It represents therefore a very real force, well and truly organized, which would not allow itself to be subjugated without resistance.

This was officially recognized by no less an authoritative spokesman than the present First Secretary of the P.M.R. and former Prime Minister, Gheorghe Gheorghiu-Dej, who at the time was an important member of the government. In a public statement, on February 22, 1948, he openly admitted that the Catholic Church constituted one of the few forces in Rumania able to stand up against communism.

Hence the goal of the Bucarest government is precise, to weaken the Catholic Church in Rumania in order to render it inoffensive. To attain this end, the communists are proceeding in accordance with a well-established plan, involving several steps. First comes an action of a general character, striking at its organization and subjecting to the most rigorous control the exercise of its powers. A second step is nothing less than the suppression of the Uniate (Greek-Catholic) Church.

In the pursuit of this destructive work, the authorities are making full use of the classic means available to totalitarian regimes. The opening shots were a propaganda campaign, cleverly amplified, carried on parallel with an action of intimidation based on abusive steps directed against the hierarchy and patrimony of the Catholic Church. The moment the proper "atmosphere" was judged to have been created, legislative measures followed, setting up the "legal" framework of the initial project.

The slander campaign against Catholicism began discreetly, with certain sly insinuations like those made by Petre Groza on the occasion of the visit to Rumania of Patriarch Alexei of Moscow in May and June of 1947. It continued afterwards, gaining momentum and widening in scope and intensity, by various statements issued by several members of the government; it culminated in a concerted press attack.

Among the government's oratorical tactics we must cite the declarations of Gh. Gheorghiu-Dej before the National Assembly, on the occasion of the passing of the Constitution (April 1948), and those of Stanciu Stoian, Minister of Cults, on the occasion of the election of the new Patriarch, on May 24, 1948. In the course of a broad tour of the international horizon, Gheorghiu-Dej said, among other things: "The Pope will undoubtedly find occasion to assail our constitution because it does not tally with the Vatican's tendencies, which are to interfere in the internal concerns of various countries under the pretext of evangelizing the Catholic faithful." "Who knows", added the orator, "whether the Vatican will not consider anathematizing us on the pretext that our constitution does not provide for the submission of our fellow countrymen of Catholic persuasion to the political directives of the Vatican, or because we do not allow ourselves to be tempted by America's golden calf, to the feet of which the Vatican would bring its faithful."

Stanciu Stoian, for his part, contended that "world reaction is trying to make especial use of two religious instruments: the Roman Catholic Church and the Oecumenical Movement. The Vatican's action can not leave us indifferent when it attempts to interfere with and to pass judgment upon our democratic regime. Nor can we remain indifferent when the so-called Oecumenical Movement desires to annex (Greek) Orthodoxy to the other weapons of Anglo-Saxon imperialism."

By that time (end of May 1948) the campaign against Catholicism had widened in scope. Part of the hierarchy of the Rumanian Orthodox Church had seen fit to enter the arena and take a hand in a struggle whose political character was undeniable. The new Patriarch, Justinian, was launching appeals, inviting Greek-Catholics to "rejoin" Orthodoxy. On the occasion of his enthronement, Patriarch Justinian alluded—on June 6, 1948—to the Concordat "imposed upon our people by the Pope of Rome with the connivance of the former regimes, whereby the popish see was awarded greater rights than our own Church."

In order to understand the intervention of certain Orthodox prelates in this question, we should recall that the upper hierarchy of the Rumanian Orthodox Church had previously undergone an extensive "purge." The following from the communist paper Universul of August 28, 1948, is enlightening: "The guidance of the country's destinies having been taken up by the hands of the working class and of democratic organizations, special attention is being given to the renewal of the high cadres of the Church. This was evidenced by the elections which took place in November 1947, when three hierarchs of the people entered the Synod. This concern of the working class for the destinies of the Church culminated on May 24, 1948, when the new Patriarch of the Rumanian People's Republic was elected in the person of His Holiness Justinian."

Alongside this, to enforce its effect and create an atmosphere of terror, a whole series of administrative actions were taken, aimed both at the personnel and the patrimony of the Catholic Church. Thus in a single diocese in the course of a few months—May 1947 to January 1948—no less than twenty-two priests were arrested. By March 1948 their number grew to 92.

Particular mention must be made of the unlawful arrest of the French Ascensionist monks, headed by Father Laurent, who were conducting an institute for Byzantine studies in Bucarest (Fall, 1947).

Instances of the manner in which the administration interfered in exclusively religious concerns of the Catholic Church must include the cases of the prefects of Turda and Hunedoara, who, at the time of the trials rigged against Iuliu Maniu and other leaders of the National Peasant Party, summoned the representatives of the clergy and requested that they demand the death penalty for Maniu in their sermons (November 1947).

Yet another form of abuse was the requisitioning of Church-owned buildings. Thus, in Timishoara the building that housed the Catholic Seminary was taken over by the authorities on October 30, 1947, and assigned to the Medical School. It was only after long and tedious protests that a part of the building was put at the disposal of the seminary; the greater part, however, passed under the administration of the medical school.

In line with the persecutions directed against the Catholic clergy must be considered, too, the decree issued by the Ministry of Cults, dismissing from service and depriving of their living a large number of priests, whose names appeared on a list published in the Official Monitor for March 31, 1948.

Special attention was given by the government to the Catholic press, which was progressively suppressed until, by May 1948, but one magazine, the *Children's Paradise*, remained. This magazine too, edited by the Jesuits of Bucarest, saw its pages reduced from the usual 24 to the heavily censored material barely sufficient for 8, before it too was suppressed at last. The Bucarest administration then considered the first stage of the plan completed. It was decided to transform the legal basis of the Church. The liberal legislation on the books would be replaced.

Before proceeding the Bucarest regime had to repudiate such obligations of an international character as existed in this field. Under the Concordat between the Vatican and the Rumanian State, of May 10, 1927, ratified in 1929, the statutes of the Catholic Church in Rumania and its relationship with the State authorities were defined in great detail. On July 17, 1948, a communique of the Council of Ministers made known that, "in order to accomplish the constitutional provisions relating to the untrammeled liberty of religion, the Council approves the abrogation of the law of June 12, 1929, concerning the approval of the Concordat with the Vatican; the denunciation of that Concordat; and the cessation of the application of the provisions contained in that Concordat, as of the date of its denunciation." The decision of the Bucarest regime was a flagrant violation of the provisions of Article 23 of the Concordat itself, which recognized the right of the contracting parties to denounce the accord, but called for six months' notice in such an event.

The abrupt termination of the Concordat is to be explained when the contents of that accord are examined. In addition to clauses concerning the organization and the functioning of the Catholic Church (Articles 1 through 10), it contains certain provisions concerning confessional teachings (Art. 19) and referring to diocesal seminaries (Art. 16), as well as some relating to the administration and general conduct of welfare organizations, foundations, hospitals, convents, etc., functioning under the direction of the Catholic Church of Rome (Art. 14). In each of these fields the organs of the church enjoyed full freedom of action, initiative, and leadership, within the general framework of existing legislation, and in harmony with the powers of control and the directives of the various government departments.

The unilateral denunciation of the Concordat was the signal for the opening of a violent press campaign against the Vatican. Caricatures of an exceptional vulgarity appeared. For instance, the official communist paper, *Scanteia,* showed the Sovereign Pontiff, with an American flag in his tiara, bowing down and kissing the hand of Secretary of State Marshall. Articles began to pour out praise of the "liberating action" of the government and to denounce alleged interferences of the Holy See in the internal affairs of various countries. The Patriarch Justinian himself, upon returning from the Moscow congress, in August 1948, declared that "the political interests pursued by the Vatican are alien to the very spirit of our Christian faith. Hence the patriarchs and representatives of all Orthodox Churches hailed with joy the Rumanian government's decision to eliminate completely the possibility of the Vatican's interference in the internal concerns of the Rumanian Popular Republic."

In this artificially created atmosphere, which lacked all real acceptance in Rumanian public opinion, the government proceeded in the shortest possible time to promulgate two laws destined to lay the bases of the new regime of cults and schools. Of course, these two decrees signified at the same time a heavy blow struck at the independence of Catholicism in the Rumanian Popular Republic. Without entering into a detailed analysis of these decrees, we must examine here the provisions that have bearing upon the problem which makes the object of this study, and the application that was given to these provisions.

The decree, which appeared in the Official Monitor for August 3, 1948, transfers to the exclusive conduct and control of the state the entire system of schools, many of which belonged to the various Catholic communities (art. 35). The application and enforcement of this law, as the Minister of Public Instruction himself testified, was designed and elaborated "upon instructions from the Central Committee of the Workers' Party." It took immediate effect throughout the country. Commissions appointed to this end by the Ministry of Public Education first proceeded to close and seal the buildings of all private schools, and then made inventories of their entire contents, which was to be transferred to state ownership. This procedure gave rise to innumerable and serious abuses. For instance, buildings that housed both schools and other religious establishments were considered by the authorities to belong in their entirety to the school, with the sole exception of rooms reserved exclusively to actual religious practices. At one such institute, Notre Dame de Sion, the nuns were allowed to retain the use only of the chapel and of their personal cells. And while the inventory was being drawn up, no one was allowed to leave the buildings of the institute. The nuns were even prevented from accompanying the funeral procession of one of their own number. When the inventory was finally drawn up, the nuns were allowed to leave the premises only after submitting each time to a close personal search.

Such taking of inventories provided a pretext for instituting against Catholic personnel divers court proceedings, and numerous arrests followed. We may cite the case of Mother Clemence de Sion, the principal of the Bucarest institute, who was subjected to a severe investigation, together with several other nuns of the institute, on the pretext that they had destroyed the archives of the school (August 11, 1948). Father Arion Trifas, former principal of the Catholic Seminary of Iasi, was likewise arrested for having allegedly attempted to conceal a part of the seminary's possessions (August 26, 1948).

The wave of arrests of Catholic priests continued throughout the months of August and September. At the same time, the Ministry of Cults dismissed from their posts a large number of priests, especially former teachers of Catholic seminaries. We cite the case of Fathers Maximilian Simonic and Ion Farcas, parish priests in the Timisoara district, who were accused of "anti-democratic attitude," and indicted on September 8, 1948.

The reform of the schools, as we shall presently show, not only had the effect of abolishing all activities of the Churches in the field of teaching, but also provided occasion for numberless abuses and acts of terrorism.

Together with the reorganization of schools, new rules were provided for the general regime of cults, in the decree issued by the Presidium of the National Assembly, published in the Official Monitor of August 4, 1948.

The new law, although it asserts from the very outstart that it "guarantees freedom of conscience and religion" (article 1), in fact goes on to curtail most drastically all means of manifestation of the divers faiths, striking at their organization, and subjecting them to a rigorous administrative and police control. Starting from the premise that all denominations, with the exception of the Orthodox Church, "in order to organize themselves and to function, must have previous recognition by decree of the Presidium of the Grand Popular Assembly" (article 13), the law goes on to state that "in certain well motivated cases" such recognition may be withdrawn in the same way.

This basic principle established, the conditions under which the various Churches may organize themselves administratively are set forth. The criterion is provided in article 22, which says that "for the creation and functioning of any denomination, an average of 750,000 faithful shall be considered as constituting a see." Thereby, the Roman Catholic Church which in the terms of the Concordat was guaranteed six sees (the archbishopric of Bucarest, the bishoprics of Iash, Alba-Iulia, Timishoara, and Oradea, and the Gherla bishopric of Armenian rite), had to submit to a considerable reduction in the number of its dioceses.

The law also provides for the abolition of seminaries (article 53) and reduces to one the number of Theological Institutes of university rank of the Catholic Church and of other denominations in Rumania. At the same time, religious instruction in the army is eliminated, the function of army chaplain being abolished altogether.

Once the principles of organization are disposed of, the law proceeds to regulate the conditions in which the various denominations may function in the country. Their entire activity is subjected to the most thoroughgoing administrative control, reaching from inscriptions, symbols, seals, and stamps, through ritual books and pastorals, all the way to congresses and meetings of prelates. At the same time, the law forbids all relations that are not strictly "of a religious nature" between the country's denominations and foreign countries. Such ties are thenceforth placed under the "control and approval of the Ministry for Foreign Affairs" (article 40). (Under the Concordat all communications of the Catholic sees, clergy, and faithful with the Vatican were completely free.) Aside from the control of religious ties abroad, article 42 provides that "assistance and gifts received from abroad by various religious denominations in the country, or those sent by the latter abroad, shall be controlled by the state."

The law gives prominence to provisions governing the passing from one faith to another. Thus, article 27 provides that when 10% of the faithful of one community pass to another cult, a proportional part of the property of that denomination becomes the property of the other. Should a simple majority of the faithful of one denomination pass to another, then the local buildings and other possessions of the community, together with the church itself, become the property of the other. Finally, in cases where 75% of any community become converted to another faith, the entire local property of the abandoned denomination becomes the property of the second. All instances mentioned above "shall be controlled and solved by the local popular courts."

We shall mention, finally, the provisions of article 36, which call for the transfer to the state of all the property of "such denominations as may disappear or whose recognition shall be withdrawn." The whole of the law's final portion will be found to constitute a powerful and far-reaching weapon for the governmental abolition of the Greek Catholic Church.

In connection with the application of the law on denominations, a decree which appeared in the Official Monitor of September 18, 1948, established the number of Roman Catholic sees at two, and Greek Catholic sees likewise at two. As the result of this decree, and on the basis of the law No. 166 of 1947, the Roman Catholic Archbishop Alexander Cisar of Bucarest, and Bishop Augustin Pacha of Timishoara, as well as the Greek Catholic Bishops Traian Frentiu, Alexander Rusu, and Ion Balan, were summarily ousted from their high offices and "retired" by governmental action. As a matter of fact, the communist press had long been carrying on a heated campaign against Bishop Pacha, as illustrated by the newspaper *Luptatorul Banatean*, of August 15, 1948, which accused this high prelate of having consistently maintained a "clearly anti-democratic attitude". Another Catholic prelate, Mgr. Ion Scheffler, the Apostolic Administrator of Oradea and Satu-Mare, had been suspended from his post some days before (Official Monitor of September 16, 1948).

Whereas the law on education completely ended all possibilities for the Catholic Church to continue in the field of education, the law on cults regulated the organization of the Church itself, reducing it considerably and subjecting it to a rigorous control by the state in all its specifically religious activities. In addition, a new decree concerning the nationalization of all medical institutions was designed to eliminate the servants of the Church from yet another field: that of health.

The Official Monitor of November 3, 1948, published the decree for the nationalization of all private health institutions, which "pass into the property of the state as common possessions of the entire people, free of all encumbrances and charges, under the administration of the Ministry of Public Health."

This decree nationalized, among others, the following Catholic hospitals and Sanatoria: St. Vincent de Paul and St. Joseph, in Bucarest, St. Joseph in Oradea, the hospitals of the monks of the Order of Charity of St. John the Divine in Oradea, Satu-Mare, and Timishoara, St. Anne's hospital in Timishoara, St. Vincent's hospital of Miercurea Ciucului, the Maternity hospitals of Targul Mures and of Cluj, etc. etc.

As a consequence of the above, a decision of the Council of Ministers was issued on July 29, 1949, which prohibited the further functioning of fifteen Catholic orders and congregations, listed by name in article 1, as well as of such other Catholic monastic communities "as exercise an activity in the field of education, of health care, and of social assistance." The members of these orders and communities, notwithstanding any rules of their congregation to the contrary, were directed to regroup themselves within 15 days in one or another of five communities—two male and three female—if they desired to continue a monastic life (article 2). Those monks and nuns who did not wish to continue pursuing "the religious life" could apply for integration in "the field of labor". Those unable to work would be sent to asylums for the old and infirm.

On order from the Ministries of Cults and of Domestic Affairs, who were charged with carrying out the provisions of the decree, the authorities proceeded to act. The order was put into effect with unprecedented brutality, especially as the majority of the monks and nuns involved refused to establish residence in the communities indicated by the authorities. The extensive real estate and buildings owned by the various Catholic orders were confiscated.

As a result of these measures, the Roman Catholic Church of Rumania was deprived of the services of most of its higher prelates and of an important proportion of the members of its religious orders. Only two bishops remained: Martin Aron and Anton Durcovici. They came under constant attack by the communist press. For instance, Bishop Aron was denounced as a "reactionary leader", in *Scanteia* of December 9, 1948, by one Csiko Nandor, a member of the political secretariat of the so-called Magyar Popular Union.

In carrying through to the end this imposition of administrative control upon the Catholic Church, the Bucarest government soon reached the point of open conflict in matters involving basic tenets of dogma and canonical rules. This was occasioned by the submission by the Catholic Episcopate, for the requisite ratification by the Ministry of Cults, of the draft statute for the organization, conduct, and functioning of the Catholic Church in the Rumanian People's Republic. In accordance with the disposition of article 14 of the Law on Cults, the draft statute was forwarded on October 27, 1948, for "examination and approval". The proposed statute contained 46 articles, which referred, not only to the Roman denomination, but also to those of Greek and Armenian rites. It included, of course, the act of faith of the Catholic Church as well as the traditional norms of organization. The modalities of internal functioning and the specific attributions of the several ecclesiastical authorities were set forth in detail, in accordance with the established canons of the Church. In other words, the authors of this draft statute showed clearly that they fully meant to respect and comply with the legal principles of the R.P.R., in so far as these did not infringe rules and tenets established by canon law.

In the reply of the Ministry of Cults, issued after much delay in January, 1949, the administration recommended nothing less than the radical modification of 42 articles, and went to the length of even requiring the suppression of certain of them.

According to the Ministry of Cults, all dispositions bearing on the following issues had to be abrogated:

1) The general dogmatic position of the Catholic Church;
2) The Papal dogma and the canonical attributes of the Holy Father;
3) The norms applicable to the Greek Catholic Church;
4) "The right to give religious instruction . . . in all schools".

In general, the Ministry displayed especial susceptibility even in matters of terminology, reacting unfavorably to every term used in the draft statute that might seem disrespectful toward the laws of the R.P.R., or even of a nature to run counter to the official atheistic views. Thus, the expression "the community of the faithful" was found unsuitable and it was recommended to be changed to "the faithful," in the text of article 30.

In his reply, dated February 24, 1949, Bishop Aron Marton of Alba Iulia, after expressing his "deepest sorrow to find that the Greek Catholic bishops are prevented from expressing their opinion" concerning the draft statute, firmly refused to reach any compromise whatsoever on points connected with the primacy of Papal jurisdiction, with the exclusive right of the Holy Father to appoint bishops and to establish the number of dioceses, and with the liberty of relations with Rome, all of which constitute fundamental elements of Catholic dogma.

It was this exchange of correspondence that marked the sharpening of the conflict between the state authorities and the Catholic episcopate.

One of the first spectacular results of this difference was the decision of the Ministry of Cults, published in the press on May 29, 1949, whereby Bishops Aron Marton and Anton Durcovici, three canons, and 132 priests and administrative officials of the Roman Catholic Church of Rumania were struck out of the budget retroactively, that is, as of February 1, 1949, for "anti-democratic attitudes." *Scanteia* of May 29, 1949, justified this measure in a lengthy article, showing "that the regime of popular democracy cannot and does not tolerate the enemies from within and without the country to take advantage of any of our democratic liberties to mask their actions directed against public authority, against peace, independence, and liberty, against the united struggle for socialism carried on by the working people".

Finally, the two Roman Catholic Bishops were arrested, on June 20 and 26, 1949. Their real offense was—as Cardinal Tisserant testified before the Eucharistic Congress of Nancy—that "they refused to accept arbitrary state control over the Catholic Church and its organizations."

In recounting this last phase of the conflict between the Roman Catholic Church and the Bucarest government, we have simply followed its main line: that which concerned the protagonists. In fact, however, the persecution of Catholicism went much deeper. We have mentioned the measures decreed against various churchmen, and the abuses practiced against many members of the monastic orders. Alongside these administrative abuses and chicaneries, the government continued arresting members of the clergy. According to a Vatican estimate, by the beginning of July 1949, there had been arrested in Rumania no less than six hundred priests and members of religious Orders, since the advent to power of the Communists. (*Le Figaro*, July 23, 1949). A few days previously, *Osservatore Romano* (June 29, 1949) had stated: "By now, we are in an extremity. It is obvious at this time that the Rumanian persecutions have taken proportions that set them above all others . . . against the Catholic Church." The reference is, of course, to the persecutions suffered in the other "satellite" states.

The propaganda campaign that marked the initial stages of the persecution directed against the Catholic Church continued throughout the later phases. In fact it continues unabated to this day. From the very beginning, the entire press, literature, and even the plastic arts have been mobilized against the Church of Rome.

To cite but a few early instances at random, the annual state exhibition of plastic and decorative arts, held in June 1949, occasioned great official commendation of certain cartoons exhibited. One, a series of drawings which showed the Pope eating macaroni that assumed the shape of the dollar sign, was asserted by *Flacara* (June 25, 1949) to be "a model of caricature realization". The same issue of *Flacara* also carried what is described as "The song of the Catholic missionary", from the pen of the poet Radu Teculescu:

> I say unto you, "Peace to you," and I enter the city
> With a machine-gun hidden in my bag
> And with a cross in my right hand . . .
> I say unto you, "Peace to you! Strike out a sin
> "Alongside our American brethren engaged in the great crusade.
> "What matter if they command?
> "What matter if some of you must fall?
> "It is a law God-given to this world:
> "Some with the deed and sacrifice,

Others with dollars and the Word."
There!
I have unmasked for you the Catholic missionary.
Behold his words, Comrades.
Comrades, wherever you may meet him,
Spit him in the eyes
As you would a slobbering, honeyed beast.
And let your hands grip deep his throat,
And, wordless, smite him to the ground!

This, at the lower end of the scale.

At the highest, let us quote the words of the R.P.R. Patriarch Justinian Marina himself:

> . . . The Vatican is the center of the oldest imperialist tradition, which has not hesitated in the least to use every means of the capitalist system to commercialize holy things, with the help of the 'Bank of the Holy See' and of other enterprises that have common interests with Anglo-American financial circles. To that end, Pope Pius XII does not hesitate to use any means whatsoever, even though it be contrary to the letter and spirit of Holy Writ.
>
> (*Informations Roumaines*, Bulletin of the R.P.R. Legation in Paris, August 26, 1949)

Following the arrest of the two bishops, the government felt the Catholic Church, thus decapitated, would be more easily subjugated. The test was to come in connection with the campaign for signatures on behalf of the "Stockholm Appeal," launched by the so-called Permanent Committee of the World Congress of Peace Partisans. The Catholic hierarchy, represented by Monsignor Boga, Vicar of the See of Alba-Iulia, and Monsignor Glaser, Administrator of the former See of Iash, made known the position of the Church with regard to the idea of peace. In a circular they issued, they denounced the tendentious nature of tne Stockholm Appeal in measured and dignified terms. But the Militia succeeded in preventing the reading of this circular in the churches on April 23, 1950. Faced with the determined attitude of the Catholic leaders, tne administration had to resort to the familiar tactic of persecution and tne concomitant encouragement of such elements as seemed disposed to collaborate. A richly documented study of these events may be found in R. Janin's "L'Eglise Catholique en Roumanie," in *La Documentation Catholique* No. 1092, of April 8, 1951, which we have used throughout and to which we direct the attention of the reader.

One notable development was a meeting staged at Targu-Muresh on April 27, 1950, where a group of Catholic laymen and priests, under administrative pressure, declared themselves in favor of the "cause of peace" and even of "integrating the Catholic Church to the legal system of the Rumanian People's Republic." This assembly went to the length of setting up a "Catholic Action Committee," the chairmanship of which was given to the Archpriest Andrei Agotha, the principal animator of the congress. Agotha was promptly excommunicated by the Pope, yet the newly organized committee, strongly supported by the government authorities, proceeded to launch a spirited campaign for the realization of the Targu-Muresh resolutions.

As should have been expected, the attempt to gain approval from the Catholic hierarchy failed. For his determined stand, Monsignor Boga was thrown in jail on May 11, 1950. Monsignor Glaser, who had courageously denounced the Targu-Muresh congress from the pulpit, was felled by a stroke two weeks later. Archbishop Cisar was interned at Orastie. Bishop Schoefler was placed under custody at Baia de Cris soon thereafter. On June 28 an "espionage and treason" trial was rigged before the Bucarest military court, in which the members of the Nunciature were implicated.

Direct action and "legal" procedures continued side by side. On July 4, 1950, the Bucarest and Alba-Iulia episcopates were faced with the amended draft statutes drawn up by the R.P.R. Ministry of Cults to regulate the functioning of the Catholic Church. By and large, the new regulations appeared to respect the dogmas and traditions of the Church of Rome. However two short provisions annulled in effect all semblance of independence. The very last article—No. 29—provided that "the approval of the Ministry of Cults is required" for putting into effect the 14 articles referring precisely to the creation and modification of ecclesiastical divisions, to the appointment of the clergy, from parish priests to bishops, to the regimen of the congregations, to the administration of Church property, to the meetings of the clergy, and so forth. On the other hand, article 23 provided that "The bishops may communicate with the Holy See in conformity with the rules provided by article 40 of the Law on the general regulation of cults," which, as we have seen above, prescribed the intervention—hence the control—of the Ministry of Foreign Affairs.

On the same day—July 4, 1950—the Ministry of Foreign Affairs of the

R.P.R., alleging that "the members of the Apostolic Nunciature of Bucarest had taken advantage of their diplomatic status to interfere in the domestic affairs of the R.P.R., initiating, leading, and taking active part in the machinations of the group of spies sentenced in the aforesaid trial," requested formally that the Nuncio, Monsignor Gerald Patrick O'Hara and Monsignors Del Maestri de Schonberg and John C. Kirk, the auditor and the secretary of the Nunciature, leave Rumanian soil within three days. The full text of the note was published in *Universul* of July 6, 1950. Thus, through a domestic measure and an international act, the R.P.R. government broke off in one day all direct connections between the Vatican and the Catholic Church of Rumania.

As the Catholic hierarchy failed to act on the draft statutes, the "Catholic Action Committee" again stepped into the limelight. On July 28, 1950, it launched a manifesto, charging "certain leaders of the Church" with "carrying on a policy hostile to peace and equally hostile to the Church, which they would like to transform into a tool of British and American warmongers." The manifesto further expressed "great satisfaction with the proofs of understanding and good will displayed by the R.P.R. government," and ended with the resolution "to continue the struggle until the resolutions of Targu-Muresh shall be put into effect, both for the good of our Church and of our fatherland, as well as for the benefit of all peace-loving brethren."

Thereupon the communist administration abandoned all pretence. On the one hand, it made sure that all priests supporting the Catholic Action Committee continued to enjoy their livings, and even went to the length of restoring certain Church property. On the other, it descended with every means of totalitarian terror upon those who remained opposed. On August 20, 1950, eleven Franciscan friars and one priest were sentenced to terms ranging from three to sixteen years' imprisonment. The parish priest of Bacau, for having read Monsignor Glaser's statement from the pulpit, was sent to the Danube-Black Sea canal. At the canal, there were already by that time a number of priests and even nuns among the growing contingents of slave laborers, while many Jesuits and Franciscans were scattered through the country's jails and forced labor camps. This twofold attitude, of persecution toward the true Church and of encouragement toward those who were ready to set up an illegitimate faction in defiance of the Holy See, was to become the determined policy of the communist regime with regard to the country's Catholics.

At a meeting of the Catholic Action Committee at Gheorgheni on September 6, 1950, it was decided to call a general congress for the purpose of approving the statutes concocted by the government. But the lively resistance of the clergy and faithful prevented the holding of that congress in December as scheduled. It was finally held on March 15, 1951.

As was but to be expected, the firm stand of Rumania's Catholics was countered with an aggravation of persecution. This reached a climax at about the date set ultimately for the general congress. On March 8 the Italian Franciscan friar Gatti—who was replacing at the Italian church of Bucarest the Reverend Father Mantica, who had been expelled in January 1951 together with the Reverend of the Lazarite Schorung Order, and the Reverend Baral, an Assumptionist—was arrested. In Timishoara, Monsignor Iosif Waltner, Monsignor Albert Borosh, and the Reverend Father Ion Heber were arrested on March 10, while Monsignor Iosif Plesz, the vicar, was placed under custody. At the same time, Fathers Emeric Sander and Albert Gajdaly, of the Episcopal Curia, were arrested in Alba-Iulia; in Iash Father Clofanda was seized by the police.

Such was the atmosphere in which the "Extraordinary General Assembly of the Catholic Statute" met in Cluj on March 15, 1951. Attended by 224 priests allegedly delegated by the regional conferences of Bucarest, Timishoara, Oradea, Targu-Muresh, and Brashov, the meeting passed a resolution setting up a so-called Directing Council of the Catholic Statute. To the chairmanship of this body, made up of 14 priests and 13 laymen, Archpriest Grigore Fodor was elected. The Directing Council was entrusted with the task of taking the necessary steps in view of "proceeding without delay to integrate the Church to the legal order of the state, in response to the fervent wishes of all peace-loving Catholics in the country."

In his address, Father Fodor hinted broadly that the action of the R.P.R. government was but part of a general campaign against the Church of Rome common to all the people's democracies. "We, Catholic laymen and priests of the R.P.R. cannot remain behind our brethren of Hungary, Czechoslovakia, and Poland, who have found the right way of harmonious collaboration between the Church and the state, a collaboration whose purpose is to serve the sacred cause of peace." (Cf.: *Informations roumaines*—the news bulletin of the R.P.R. legation in Paris—No. 746 of March 19, 1951.)

The ambiguously named Assembly of the Roman Catholic Statute—that group of priests and laymen favoring collaboration with the communist administration, and enjoying the support of the regime—attempted to make a number of appointments to various ecclesiastical posts, notably the appointment as vicar of Canon Traian Jovanelli, and as chancellor of Father Andrei Horn-Despina. However the Holy See, condemning the entire action, declared such appointments invalid and excommunicated the appointees. Nonetheless the "Catholic Action Committee" went on to endorse the decisions of the heads of Rumania's other denominations, who, at a meeting staged on December 19, 1950, had declared their readiness to support the action of the World Peace Committee. It adhered immediately to that "Christian initiative of the other cults of the R.P.R. and approved with joy the Law for the Defense of Peace, recently voted by the Grand National Assembly." (Cf.: *Universul*, December 27, 1950). The "Statute" continued along this line, publicly advocating the conclusion of the Kremlin-initiated Peace Pact (*Informations roumaines* of April 21, 1951), and taking active part in all demonstrations connected with the successive World Peace Congresses.

It should be noted that the Law for the Defense of Peace, which was passed by the R.P.R. Grand National Assembly on December 15, 1950, provided the authorities with a series of "legal" oppressive means. Vaguely worded provisions punish "the dissemination of tendentious or invented reports apt to serve the warmongers' interests, and all other kinds of manifestations in behalf of unleashing a new war" with prison terms ranging between 5 and 25 years, in addition to the confiscation of all or part of the offenders' property. Although the "Catholic Action Committee" saw fit to "approve with joy" this remarkable law, the R.P.R. government has not yet found it opportune to "legalize" the situation of the Catholic Church of Rumania. This is an eloquent tribute to the brave resistance of the clergy and the faithful.

The persecution of the clergy and the faithful continues unabated, rising occasionally to truly spectacular forms. Thus the mass "espionage trial" opened before the Bucarest military court on September 10, 1951, resulted in severe sentences handed down to Bishop Augustin Pacha of Timishoara, Monsignors Iosif Schubert, Albert Borosh, and Iosif Waltner, and of the Reverends Pietro Ernesto Gatti and Ion Heber, as well as to a number of laymen implicated and found guilty as charged. Monsignor Pacha, then 81 years of age, was sentenced to 18 years' imprisonment. Gravely ill, he was set free on July 31, 1954, only to die soon thereafter.

By the beginning of 1952 it became known to the Western world that all the Roman and Greek Catholic bishops of Rumania had been arrested or sent to camps—some even to the Soviet Union. The Vatican Radio confirmed the facts in a broadcast of February 25, 1952. On March 27th the Pope, in an apostolic letter, "Veritatem facientes," addressed to the Catholic clergy and faithful of Rumania, stressed "the great dangers to which are exposed the sacred rights of the Catholic faith, and in particular the liberty that is its due," in that country.

According to data published by the Reverend don Brunello in *La Chiesa del Silenzio* the losses suffered by the Catholic Church in Rumania by January 31, 1953, were as follows: The Papal Nuncio expelled; all archbishops and bishops either arrested, sentenced, or deported (three reportedly dead in prison) 55 priests slain, 250 dead dispersed, 200 at forced labor, and 200 in prison; the Greek Catholic (Uniate) churches and parishes taken away and given to the Orthodox Church; 300 Latin rite churches requisitioned by the state; Catholic education, charitable institutions, and press wholly suppressed. (Cf. *Documentation catholique* No. 1156, September 20, 1953).

The newspaper *Deutsche Tagespost* of December 18–19, 1953, stated that a brigade made up solely of Catholic clergy under various sentences had been working at the Danube-Black Sea canal. Initially composed of 450 priests, the brigade lost 215 dead at the work site.

In August, 1954, the octogenarian Monsignor Vladimir Ghika, well known for his important humanitarian work both in Rumania and abroad (notably in France) died in prison. Earlier that same year, on January 7, the last surviving Rumanian Catholic Archbishop, Monsignor Alexander Cisar, had also succumbed.

It is needless to go on with a detailed examination of the available evidence. It should be amply evident by now that, officially designated as one of the principal foes of the very concept of "popular democracy," the Roman Catholic Church of Rumania is left headless and effectively cut off from the Holy See. It may be written off as a vanquished foe, felled by the ruthless advance of "socialist construction." And yet the Catholic Church continues to live on in the Rumanian People's Republic, with courage and confidence in its divine mission.

The Greek Catholic, or Uniate Church, which, ever since the end of the 17th century (1698), has played an essential role in the cultural, political, and religious development of Rumanians in Transylvania, had established, by the end of the 18th century, direct relations between Rumanians and the cultural centers of the West, especially Rome. It supported a strong and significant Western current in Rumanian literature, known as the Transylvanian School. This in turn was instrumental in the development of national sentiment, not only in Transylvania, but also in the Rumanian Principalities, throughout the 19th century. Following the union of Transylvania with Rumania, in 1918, the Uniate Church continued as an enlightened center of patriotism and high moral values.

According to the figures for 1938, there were 1,725 Greek Catholic churches, served by 1,594 priests, 34 canons, and 75 prelates. The faithful numbered at the time of the 1930 census, 1,430,000.

The organization of the Uniate Church, as it was guaranteed by the Concordat, was as follows: a Metropolitan see at Blaj, titled, in order to maintain the historic tradition, the Metropolitan See of Alba-Iulia and Fagaras; four suffragan bishoprics—of Oradea Mare, Lugoj, and Gherla, with the residence at Cluj, and of Maramuresh with the residence at Baia-Mare.

To suppress this important and venerated organization the government undertook a vast program. We shall have to distinguish two distinct phases in the development of events: the first, beginning with the appeals made to the faithful of Uniate denomination to pass to Orthodoxism, starting in May 1948, and leading to the Congress of Cluj, on October 1, 1948; the second, the events which followed that Congress and which led to the de facto and de jure suppression of the Greek Catholic Church of Rumania.

The Centennial of the meeting of the Field of Liberty, held on May 15, 1948 (when Rumanians under the leadership of the Orthodox Bishop Saguna and of the Uniate Bishop Lemeny demanded the recognition of their rights as a nation), saw the launching of a formal appeal inviting all Greek Catholics to join the Orthodox Church. "Today," said the appeal, "when the Rumanian Popular Republic guarantees equal rights, political, cultural, and religious, to all, no matter what their creed or race might be, to persist in the spiritual disunity which stemmed from the grave jeopardy in which the Rumanians of Transylvania found themselves in 1700, means to desert the united front of the new destinies that our working people are creating for themselves in the dawn of the future."

It is not necessary to stress the feeling of profound sorrow and concern aroused among Transylvanian Rumanians by this appeal, couched in the terms of a fatherly call. All realized that it was the opening shot of the coming struggle, all the more so as it came precisely on the occasion of the centennial of an event that marked the real unity then existing among Transylvanian Rumanians, notwithstanding their differences of creed. And indeed this true character of the appeal was shortly to be made quite manifest, when the administration and police began a huge campaign to ascertain the views of all Greek Catholic priests in the matter of passing to Orthodoxy.

The appeal was renewed on the occasion of the enthronement of Patriarch Justinian Marina, on June 6, 1948, when the new Patriarch stated, among other things: "What separates us at this time? Nothing but the faithful submission you still give to Rome. Give back this loyalty to the Church of our nation, the Church of our Forefathers and of yours.

"The energies we have all spent up till now in defending the national and religious identity of our nation let us henceforth spend—under the paternal protection of the Rumanian state, of the Popular Republic of Rumania—only in consolidating the sovereignty and the national independence of our democratic state.

"The widest prospects open before us and before our future activity, once we no longer work in isolation, abandonment, and persecution as we have in the past . . ."

These appeals were given the widest publicity, the press devoting numerous and lengthy articles to the event. When, in reply, the Uniate Episcopate attempted to argue against these official theses, and to answer the appeals with its own views, it was simply prevented from doing so. Administration and police authorities prohibited all circulars and pastorals on the question. Thereupon, the Uniate leaders proposed to address a collective pastoral to their faithful, setting forth the official position of the Greek Catholic Church. "The government censor's office refused approval for the printing of the pastoral, although it had not the least polemic and still less political character." (Memorandum of the Uniate bishops, addressed to the President of the Grand National Assembly's presidium on October 7, 1948.)

In step with this press campaign, which went to the length of uttering threats against the Uniate churchmen, the political organization began to attempt to interfere in the purely religious affairs of the Greek Catholic Church. Thus an illegal attempt was made to replace the Church's personnel with "members belonging to parties of the government bloc, and eliminating our priests from the administration of the Church's parish properties" (Memorandum cited above).

When the leaders of the Uniate Church saw that they were to be denied the right to circulate their reply to the appeals and to the press campaign that had been launched against their Church and themselves, they had to resort to sermons and canonical visits, in order to enlighten their faithful. Particularly active in this direction was Monsignor Ion Suciu, the vicar of the Blaj Metropolitan See. The results were not long in appearing. On September 3, 1948, a decree of the government put an abrupt end to the Reverend Father's mission, suspending him from his high office.

At that moment, the action against the Catholic clergy and congregations had already become considerably more precise and systematic. The authorities of state distributed throughout Transylvania so-called "delegations" which the members of the Greek Catholic clergy were required to sign in blank. These were to designate the names of two churchmen for each administrative district, who, though they might be unknown to the signatories themselves, were to represent the latter at a meeting called in Cluj on October 1, 1948, a meeting whose purpose was, as the document stated, "the return of the Greek Catholic Church to the Orthodox Church."

In order to obtain the signatures, the authorities resorted to acts which went all the way from promises of material advantages to the most direct threats. These were followed up with mass arrests. In order the better to give a picture of the behavior of the police authorities in this action, we shall quote from the note of protest handed by the Apostolic Nuncio on October 2, 1948, to the Ministry of Foreign Affairs of the Rumanian Popular Republic:

> "The priests were in many instances brought by force to the local prefectures. In the offices of the Sigurantza (state security police) they were intimidated, threatened with imprisonment, with separation from their families, with deportation, and even with death. Those who resisted the initial acts of violence were thrown in underground cells, ill-treated, subjected to exhausting questioning, and finally set free only when, broken down by the inhuman treatment of their jailors, they accepted to sign." The note adds that "these offenses, knowledge of which soon spread throughout the country, were confirmed by officials of the Bucarest Patriarchate and by members of the so-called 'Congress for Union with

the Orthodox Church' of Cluj. Some of the latter themselves displayed
visible marks of the duress they had suffered."

It should be noted that these things started and developed at a moment
when the Uniate prelates were busy trying to comply with the formalities
required by the law concerning cults, of August 4, 1948, of which we
have written above.

As we have indicated and as the memorandum of the Uniate bishops
quoted above asserts, "the immediate agents of this campaign . . . did not
scruple to confess that this is an action by the government for the abolishment of the Rumanian Uniate Church—something that might not be be-
lievable, had they themselves, deputies, inspectors of security, etc., not
amply proven it by the coercive measures resorted to, and the impunity
this wave of illegalities clearly enjoys, in pursuit of an obvious goal. The
fully conclusive evidence in our possession leaves no margin for doubt."

The campaign reached paroxysmal heights toward the end of September. Between September 26 and October 1, the emissaries of the Ministry
of Cults, local authorities, and the agents of the Directorate of the People's Security (the new form of the state security police, established by
decree on August 28, 1948) stepped up their activities in the attempt to
bring the Uniate clergy to sign the delegations. Acts of terrorism multiplied. The case of Bishop Suciu may be cited in this connection. This
reverend gentleman, on the morning of September 27, "following the consecration of the church of Copacel (District of Fagaras), was roused before daylight and taken by the organs of the security police to an unknown
place, where he was held for two days in a cellar, in order to prevent him
from getting in touch with the clerics and the faithful." And to show the
treatment meted out to other priests, we may consider the case of the
Reverend Canon Tamaian, of Oradea, and of his colleagues, Barbul and
Ghilea, who were tortured by the police authorities, endlessly questioned
under strong spotlights, held in underground cells, subjected to torture by
electric apparatus, and so forth in an attempt to make them sign their
adherence to the fateful decisions scheduled to be taken at Cluj. Bishop
Iuliu Hossu of Cluj was confined to his house, from September 30 to
October 4, and thus prevented from getting in touch with the clergy and
faithful under his pastorate. In addition, some thirty priests and laymen
of Cluj were jailed because, unaware of the measures taken against their
bishop, they attempted to see him at his residence.

Similar abusive and utterly illegal measures were taken against the delegates themselves, as is indicated in the Apostolic note cited above. Thus the Reverend Father Ion Florea, one of these delegates, was reported to have told a friend of his in Bucarest how certain delegates were taken from their homes by the police, without being allowed to take even a change of clothes, taken to Cluj, and from there to Bucarest, where they were held incommunicado at the Athenée Palace hotel.

Such was the atmosphere in which the Congress of Cluj met on October 1, 1948, to decide the passing of the Uniate clergy and faithful to the Orthodox Church.

On October 1, 1948, 38 prelates, canons, and priests, allegedly "delegates of the more than 400 churchmen of Transylvania, the Banat, Crisana, and Maramuresh," met in the gymnasium of the Gheorghe Baritziu school in Cluj. The meeting was to decide and put into effect the matter of passing to the Orthodox Church. Interestingly enough, the number of delegates—thirty-eight—was exactly the same as that of the Archpriests who assembled at Alba-Iulia on October 7, 1698, in a synod headed by Bishop Athanasius Anghel, and who drew up the manifesto declaring the union with the Church of Rome. This obviously intentional similarity was subsequently shown to have been contrived, for the minutes of the Cluj meeting enumerated but 37 priests, while the delegation that went to Bucarest seems to have numbered only 36. The dubious note is further enhanced by the fact that the actual number of priests who supposedly signed the "delegations" differs in the several articles signed by the participants themselves and in the lists annexed to the official texts of the congress. This in turn indicates the methods used in gathering the signatures in behalf of the delegates. The spurious nature of the entire affair was later confirmed by the numerous protests that were immediately forthcoming from churchmen who had been fraudulently represented as signatories or who had been coerced by threats into signing.

According to Universul of October 15, 1948, the congress, "after several hours taken up with the problems posed," resolved "unanimously and with great enthusiasm . . . the reentry into the bosom of the Rumanian Orthodox Church, and the definitive severance of the ties with Papal Rome."

The debates were presided over by Protopope Traian Balascu, who launched an appeal addressed to all Greek Catholics in the country, saying: ". . . Aware of the working of destiny that herald a shining future for our people, we have approached, trembling with divine awe, the problem of the imperious need to reclaim the spiritual unity of the Rumanian nation. . . . We, the undersigned, churchmen answerable before God and the conscience of our people, met together in divine spiritual concourse, upon this first day of October . . . resolve and effect our return into the bosom of our mother, the Orthodox Church.

"With unlimited love for you, clerics and laymen of the Rumanian Greek-Catholic Church, we beseech you to follow our example, and we most earnestly urge you to do likewise in all confidence, thus showing yourselves to be true and worthy servants of the people and real sons of God." There follow 423 signatures of Uniate priests who passed to Orthodoxy.

The following day, the delegation arrived in Bucarest and was met at the station by the capital's clergy, headed by the Protopopes and Counsellors of the Patriarchate.

On Sunday, October 3, the synodal session took place, at which the delegation presented the proclamation voted at Cluj. Divine service was celebrated subsequently in the church of St. Spiridon-the-New.

On this occasion the synodal act was read accepting the proclamation of "return" to Orthodoxism, setting forth the re-establishment of unity of faith and the reception into the bosom of the Rumanian Orthodox Church of all who should desire to break with the Church of Rome.

The list of delegates who signed the proclamation is as follows: Protopopes Traian Belascu, Aurel Drumboiu, and Nicolae Jangalau; and the priests: P. Vascu, V. Moldovan, Z. Hentia, P. Madincea, Laurentiu Pop, I. Onisor, I. Cristean, P. Pop, Z. Borzea, Al. Stupariu, E. Colceriu, S. Santoma, E. Muresan, Cornel Cernescu, T. Ploscariu, I. Vatu, C. Puscasu, V. Tr. Pop, Mircea Filip, Cornel Pop, Roman Nemes, V. Ienciu, Octavian Gherasim, Sabin Trutia, Vincent Torutiu, A. Coman, G. Zagrai, I. Florea, I. Andrasiu, V. Negrea, V. Plesug, Al. Farcasiu, I. Pop, and D. Glodean.

As early as October 2, 1948, Mgr. Gerard Patrick O'Hara, the Apostolic Nuncio in Bucarest, protested by verbal note, under No. 2130/1948, to the Ministry of Foreign Affairs against this "carefully prepared action, cleverly coordinated . . . against the Catholic Church of Greek rite." The Note after invoking the argument of the international obligations undertaken by Rumania in article 3, Section 1 of the Peace Treaty, and the guarantees set forth by the government of the Rumanian People's Republic in article 27 of the Constitution, and articles 1 and 2 of the

Law on Cults, refers to "the action undertaken, not merely by certain irresponsible elements, but by the civil authorities themselves." It goes on to state that, "faced with this unqualifiable attitude" of government organs, the Papal Nunciature, "on behalf of the Holy See and in the name of the entire Christian world, protests with all the energy demanded by the circumstances against such procedures, unworthy of a civilized state."

To this note, which, though severe in substance, maintains correct diplomatic form throughout, the Bucarest government answered with unusual violence and in a style entirely alien to the customary language of chancelleries.

After describing the protest of the Nuncio as "an interference in the domestic affairs of the Rumanian Popular Republic and an attempt to attack freedom of religion," the Bucarest government "rejects the manifest calumnies contained in this note" and states that "these defamatory assertions are a new proof of the antagonistic attitude systematically adopted by the Apostolic Nunciature toward the Popular Republic of Rumania and toward its reforms and realizations in democracy."

The reply further notes that "the Apostolic Nunciature, being but the diplomatic representative of Vatican City, cannot take upon itself to speak 'on behalf of the entire Christian world,' as it does in its Note." Finally, after "denouncing . . . the attempted blackmail embodied in the threat that the alleged violations of religious freedom in the Rumanian People's Republic 'will presently alienate the world's public opinion,'" the reply states that "this is in line with the campaign carried on by the imperialist circles and their agents against the democratic achievements of the Rumanian People's Republic," and concludes: "The government rejects in the most determined manner this Note . . . both as to its form and as to its contents, considering it to constitute an act of provocation against the Rumanian State and people."

The reaction of the Greek Catholic Bishopric was a bold and determined one. On the one hand, the high prelates proceeded to excommunicate the churchmen who had abandoned the Uniate Church. On the other hand, they addressed on October 7, 1948, a memorandum to the President of the Grand National Assembly's presidium, Professor Parhon. A second memorandum, signed also by the prelates of the Roman Catholic Church, was addressed to Prime Minister Petre Groza.

The memorandum addressed to Professor Parhon contained an indignant protest against the persecution to which the Greek Catholic clergy was being subjected, and a categorical declaration in which the Uniate bishops asserted they "are firmly determined to remain the pastors and sons of the Church of Jesus Christ, undivided from Catholic unity . . . firmly persuaded that in this Catholic Church, to whose service we are dedicated in life and in death, we serve the people and the country, as we have unwaveringly done hitherto."

Patriarch Justinian appointed Thursday, October 21, to be the day for the celebration in Alba-Iulia of "the reintegration of the Rumanian Church of Transylvania." On that occasion a motion was voted wherein those present declared: ". . . We break for ever our ties of all nature with the Vatican and with Papal Rome . . .

"We incorporate ourselves with our whole being to the Rumanian Orthodox Church . . .

"From this day on, all Rumanians are united . . . in loyal obedience to the demands for a new life of our beloved Rumanian People's Republic . . . To the members of the High Presidium of the Rumanian People's Republic and to the country's government, we bring our devoted thanks for the liberties assured to all the sons of the people, liberties which have rendered possible the achievement of unity within the Rumanian Church."

Dr. Coriolan Tatar spoke in the name of the laymen who passed from the Uniate to the Orthodox Church. The solemnities ended with the consecration of the Orthodox Cathedral of Alba-Iulia as "the Cathedral of Reintegration of the Rumanian Church of Transylvania."

The Congress of Cluj set off violent attacks against the clerics who remained loyal to the Greek Catholic Church. The strongest administrative pressure was also brought to bear upon the Uniate faithful to make them adopt the Orthodox faith. The primary goal was to bring about the legal conditions specified by the Law on Cults for the transfer of Uniate properties and churches to the Orthodox Church.

Faced with the stubborn resistance of the Greek Catholic clergy, the authorities resorted to mass arrests. During the night of October 27, Bishop Suciu was once again seized. The following night, Bishop Valeriu Traian Frentziu of Oradea, though 74 and seriously ill at the time, was taken into custody together with his secretary, P. Foishor. Other arrests followed shortly thereafter. They included Bishop Ion Balan of Lugoj, Iuliu Ratziu, the Vicar of Timishoara, Curator Ladislau Taglasiu, Protopope Ion Deliman of Arad, Canon Nicolae Branzeu of Lugoj, and the

Reverend Iosif Vezog. Bishop Hossu and Bishop Vasile Aftenie, the Vicar of the Blaj Metropolitan See for the O'd Kingdom, who were in Bucarest for the formalities connected with the presentation of the statutes for the Uniate Church, were also arrested by the local police. Finally, the last Uniate bishop still free, the Reverend Alexandru Rusu, was taken into custody. Available data show that during the month of November, 1948, some 600 Greek Catholic churchmen were under arrest.

Scenes of a rare savagery marked this campaign of violence. For instance, the Reverend Father Hyeronimus Susman, a distinguished graduate of the theological academy of Blaj, who had finished his studies in 1948 and had been ordained that same year, preached an impassioned sermon in the village of Asnip, not far from the city of Aiud, exhorting the faithful not to abandon their Church and to refuse to sign any form of apostasy. He was thereupon surrounded by the police and, when he attempted to escape, was shot down.

In Blaj, the *Institutul Recunostintei*, belonging to the congregation of nuns of the Order of the Immaculate Virgin, saw scenes of unprecedented barbarity when the local authorities arrived to evacuate the buildings and take them over.

The dissolution of the religious community at the Monastery of Bixad, in the district of Satu-Mare, center of the Basilian Order, was likewise marked by acts of appalling cruelty.

To buttress the campaign of abuse and persecution, the government took official measures designed on the one hand to encourage passage from the Uniate to the Orthodox Church, while on the other hand punishing attempts at resistance. The Ministry of Cults announced that Greek Catholic clergymen would receive their salaries upon embracing the Orthodox Church, the moment their names were communicated to the Department by the Church authorities. This constituted a new and very strong means of exerting pressure upon Uniate churchmen. Yet many not only abstained from answering all appeals to embrace Orthodoxy, but also, when they were signed by fraud and forgery on the lists of adherents, voiced their protest with the utmost courage and in spite of all personal risks involved. It was not long, in the face of such determined opposition, before the government press had to renounce publishing lists of Uniate priests who had allegedly passed to Orthodoxy.

Resistance was equally strong in the ranks of the laity. Such Greek Catholic churches as remained open were filled to overflowing. Parishioners protected their incumbents as best they could, defending and hiding them from the authorities with every available means. Faced with this resistance, the Ministry of Cults took the decision on October 18 to alter the manner of computing the number of those passing from the Greek Catholic to the Orthodox faith. Thenceforth, only the heads of families were counted, in order to determine the proportion of converts to those adhering to the Uniate Church. In this way the task of the authorities was considerably lightened, as it was much easier either to forge the signature of only the head of a family or else to obtain it under threats, than to secure the signatures of the entire family in each case. Thus, by fraud or violence, the procedure required by the law concerning cults for the transfer of property from one denomination to another was carried out with an outward show of legality. The cathedrals and churches in the principal centers of the Uniate Church were first closed, then handed over to the Orthodox clergy for their own use.

The official Monitor for November 8, 1948 published the decision of the Council of Ministers whereby an end was put to the mission of Bishop Iuliu Hossu. Thus the last of the Greek Catholic bishops was ousted from his post. The other three, Bishops Rusu, Frentiu, and Balan, had been pensioned on September 18 of that year.

In order to end the *de jure* existence of the Rumanian Uniate Church, a decree (No. 358, December 1, 1948, issued by the Presidium of the Grand Assembly) declared null and void all dioceses, chapters, and religious communities, as well as all other institutions of the Greek Catholic Church (article 1); and also provided (article 2) that all properties pass immediately to the state, with the exception of parish buildings and other similar edifices, which were given to the Orthodox Church. This measure was legally based upon the provisions of article 13 of the Law of Cults, and not upon the argument of the "return" of Uniate parishes to the Orthodox Church. Here is article 13, mentioned above:

"Religious cults, in order to organize themselves and to function as such, shall previously be recognized by a decree of the Presidium of the Grand Assembly, issued upon recommendation by the government, on the advice of the Minister of Cults.

"In well motivated instances, this recognition shall be withdrawn with the observance of the same forms."

Finally, all the high prelates of the Uniate Church were thrown into jail or sent to camps. Bishop Vasile Aftenie died in the Vacaresht prison on May 10, 1950, and the Vatican Radio announced the death of Bishop Frentziu on June 10, 1951. Later it was learned that Bishops Balan and Suciu had also succumbed in the Aiud and Vacaresht prisons respectively. This announcement was made by the Catholic international news agency KIPA, on February 13, 1952. Like their spiritual leaders, the great majority of the Uniate priests remained faithful to their Church. They too were thrown into prisons and labor camps, and many have perished.

Thus another phase—the most fearsome assuredly—in the fight of the R.P.R. dispensation against the Catholic Church came to a close. But, as we have pointed out earlier in this chapter, this too must be understood to be but a step toward the regime's objective, the eradication of religion itself.

While the communist regime was doing its utmost either to control or suppress the churches that represent the overwhelming majority of the Rumanian people, it was also carrying out systematically a parallel action against the other denominations represented in the R.P.R.

Thus, the law for the reform of education (August 3, 1948) abolished without discrimination all denominational schools. The law on cults (August 4, 1948) put the same controls and thoroughgoing regulations upon every manifestation of religious life, whatever the denomination. Lastly, the decree of November 3, 1948, by nationalizing all health and sanitary institutions, invaded and took over a broad and very important field of activity occupied by the various denominations.

In order to convey an idea of the degree of supervision to which all religious denominations are subjected, we shall quote the text of the decree No. 37, for the organization of the Ministry of Cults, published in the Official Monitor of February 5, 1949. Here is the part relating to the department's powers:

> The Ministry of Cults is the public service through which the State exercises its right of surveillance and control guaranteeing the use and exercise of freedom of conscience and of religion.
> To this effect—
> It supervises and controls all religious cults and their institutions—communities, associations, orders, congregations, and foundations of a religious nature, whatever their kind may be;
> It supervises and controls the special religious education of the personnel of all religious denominations;

It approves the founding of new religious communities, parishes, and administrative units, the creation of new personnel posts, and the appointments, whether they are paid by the state or not, in the services of the various denominations;

It supervises and controls all funds and possessions, whatever their origin and nature may be, of the religious cults;

It assumes the task of watching over the relations and correspondence between the cults of the country and those abroad;

It has various other tasks in connection with religious cults.

It was in this spirit that the various Protestant denominations, the Armenian-Gregorian Church, the so-called Old Style Cult (Lipovan), the Jewish and Mohammedan Rites were organized. Each had its statutes approved on the same day—June 1, 1949—with the exception of the Augsburg Evangelical Church, which was duly authorized on June 6 of that year. These statutes all provide for complete independence from any religious authorities outside the country, with the notable exception of that given the Armenian Church, whose central residence happens to be in the Soviet Republic of Armenia. Each and every one of the texts fully confirms the control of the state.

A statute approved on November 14, 1950, federalized the Baptist, Seventh Day Adventist, Bible Christian, and Pentecostal denominations. The Federation set up by the statute constitutes the representative organ that defines the relations between the several denominations and the state authorities.

In the light of the realities, the joint statement issued on June 23, 1949, together with the Orthodox leaders, by the heads of the denominations that had had their statutes approved, provides a striking instance of sinister irony. "The regime of popular democracy of the R.P.R.," that statement asserted, "translates into fact the provisions of the R.P.R. Constitution, and guarantees effectively freedom of conscience and freedom of religion throughout our country, by assuring the various denominations the right to organize themselves in accordance with their own rules, in conformity with their own teachings, canons, and traditions." (*Documentation Catholique*, July 17, 1949.)

It is hardly surprising to find all these denominations presently enrolled in the government's "peace campaign," each with its mission well defined. They have had to give repeated proofs of devotion to this propaganda issue. On June 23, 1953, for instance, some 500 representatives of the various Churches met in Bucarest in order, as *Scanteia* of June 25, 1953, put it, to "debate their various tasks in the fight for peace of our people and of all peoples of the world." The participants, according to the official report, "brought out in their discussions the diverse forms in which the servants of the Church, no matter what Cult they may serve, support the actions related to the struggle of all peoples for the maintenance and consolidation of peace in the world. They demonstrated at the same time their entire adherence to the actions designed to mobilize our whole people around the grandiose aims of the struggle for peace."

It cannot be denied that in Rumania, as in all the other European countries that have fallen behind the Iron Curtain, religion was an effective, organized obstacle to communism. It is unfortunately equally undeniable that the communist government of Bucarest has, like the rest of the Kremlin's puppets, to a large extent succeeded in eliminating that obstacle. This deliberate and ruthless action of a government imposed from without, had and continues to have the manifest character of a systematic suppression of religious freedom. Like all other fundamental liberties and human rights, freedom of religion is a thing of the past in the Rumanian People's Republic.

education

In pre-communist Rumania, education, directly inspired by Western pedagogical theory and practice, was primarily aimed at developing the individual child's personality as harmoniously and as freely as possible. The entire school system was designed to provide not only the inculcation of knowledge, but also the means of acquiring the basic formative elements necessary to round off the student's mentality. Such was the fundamental preoccupation that helped to shape both the structure of Rumania's educational system and the spirit that animated it. It explains, at the same time, the orientation of that system—particularly in the high school or secondary phase—toward the humanistic disciplines.

Legislation seeking to establish the closest relations between schooling and everyday life, and assure the maximum possible freedom and variety in the educational field, encouraged and even actively supported private schooling, whilst at the same time constantly improving the educational system provided by the state. Many of the existing private schools were denominational; not a few were operated by Western religious orders long established in Rumania. The Western European tradition is clearly discernible in the country's schools—from elementary spelling classes to the highest university courses—ever since the first Academy was set up in Cotnari, in the Principality of Moldavia, in 1562.

Following World War I and the Union of all Rumania's historic provinces, it became necessary to systematize and unify educational work, and a number of reforms were introduced, the aim of which was to make all levels of schooling universally available to all social categories without distinction, stressing the merit system as the final determinant. Rumania's schooling was divided into elementary (primary), secondary (high school), and higher (university) education.

The first included kindergartens, elementary schools, special schools for adults, schools for handicapped and backward children, and for the abnormal. Elementary schooling was free and compulsory. It was provided both in state and private schools as well as at home. Elementary schools comprised two cycles: the first covered four grades; the second three complementary grades, provided for such pupils as did not go on to secondary schooling.

Secondary schooling included high schools proper, known as *lycées* and *gymnasia* (the latter having but four grades, while the former had eight), junior colleges for future school teachers, theological seminaries, military schools, and special trade, industrial, agriculture, and professional schools. This phase comprised normally either seven or eight grades, with the exception noted above. It was designed to provide elements of general culture, rounded off with the requisite practical learning.

Higher education was available in the form of universities, special schools as, for instance, polytechnic institutes, and academies and institutes for advanced and specialized learning.

It can truly be said that Rumania's educational system following World War I could be compared with that of most European countries. Education was highly regarded, the teaching profession was rightly honored, the standards were creditable. Social or pecuniary circumstances did not stand in the way of merit. The son or daughter of the poorest peasant or mechanic could and often did go to the highest academic honors. State grants and scholarships, as well as private endowments, opened the way to those who aspired to learning and showed aptitude.

Such was the liberal educational system in existence in Rumania when the communist-dominated government was forcibly installed in power in the spring of 1945. It was destined to be utterly destroyed, wholly recast on the pattern required by the communist regime. At first it was deemed expedient to proceed softly, outwardly leaving the system intact. But, though the form was allowed to subsist, the content was adulterated beyond recognition almost at once. We can discern an intermediary phase that began on March 6, 1945, and closed with the introduction of the Law for Educational Reform on August 3, 1948.

A survey of the educational policy of the communist government during this period shows two parallel trends. On the one hand, a general action of a negative character may be discerned, aimed at a purge both of the educational personnel and of the existing curricula. On the other, there was a limited, even timid, drive to introduce certain novel institutions corresponding to the new ideology. In this phase, the intervention of the regime in educational matters did not amount to an actual structural reform, but rather took the form of *de facto* measures. Obviously enough, this was in accordance with the regime's program as a whole, which initially avoided any too spectacular measures, in order not to alarm public opinion before gaining a strangle-hold on power.

The general action took the form of a severe purge of all categories of teachers and an attempt to "re-educate" those left. At the same time the student body was subjected to a thoroughgoing sifting, the remaining university students and high school pupils being then organized into associations, brigades and groups, controlled by communist elements. Then came a gradual change—limited at first—in the existing curricula, and the similarly gradual introduction of new textbooks slanted in accordance with the official tenets.

At the same time, the government, through the Ministry of Education, decided to set up various novel educational institutions, as, for instance, the unified gymnasium, the schools for illiterates, and, finally, the schools for party cadres. Concomitantly a series of cultural institutes were established, which in reality were nothing but centers of communist propaganda.

The aim of the communist government was a far-reaching one. It was to destroy the entire edifice of Rumanian schooling, which was considered a "bourgeois" formation, and then, in a second phase, to replace it with a new educational system. Hence it was logical that the initial accent be placed on a negative action, while the "creative innovations" remained limited in scope.

The first victim was the teaching profession. A series of purges resulted in the ousting of the great majority of teachers, from those of university rank all the way down the line to village grade-school instructors, and their replacement with trusties of the regime. However, in spite of inducements of all sorts, ranging from special conditions for party members and supporters in the matter of acquiring the necessary degrees, to actual appointment regardless of possession of suitable titles, replacements fell far short of requirements. It was necessary to abolish courses and chairs, thus doing away with the need to furnish personnel in special fields held to be non-essential by the authorities. A typical instance of mass purges was provided by the School of Letters and Philosophy of the Bucarest University, where no less than 80 percent of the old staff of professors and instructors were eliminated.

In order to leave no possible loophole for certain categories of teachers that might be exempt from governmental control, a decree of June 24, 1948, authorized the Ministry of Public Education to suspend the operation of any foreign-owned school in the country. The state became legally the lessee of the closed foreign schools insofar as the actual buildings were concerned, while the foreign principal concerned remained merely the legal owner. This measure occasioned a series of unparalleled abuses, which were to reach a climax following the introduction of the Law for Educational Reform on August 3, 1948. All foreign schools were closed down and their staffs asked to leave the country. Acts of brutality accompanied the measure, especially directed against the various monastic orders.

The measures taken against foreign schools were manifestly aimed, not only at eliminating all but state controlled education from Rumania, but also at perfecting the break of cultural ties with the West, an action initiated by the closing of the Rumanian schools of Paris and Rome and by the cessation of existing Rumanian lectures at all Western universities. This gave reality to the formula proposed by Teohari Georgescu, then Minister of the Interior of the Rumanian People's Republic, before the student congress of Iash: "In our epoch, the light no longer comes from the West but from the East."

The methods applied were similar in respect to the student body. First came the purges, then those "cleared" were "organized." The magazine *Studentul Roman* of July 2, 1948, blandly stated: ". . . We know, for instance, that of the 37,000 students registered at the various departments of the Bucarest University there remain 24,000, following the expulsion of some 13,000." At the Bucarest University, as in every school throughout the country, the students were organized in associations comparable to the communist-type trade unions, and in April 1948 the U.A.S.R. (Union of Student Associations of Rumania) was set up. It was given a periodical of its own, *Revista Elevilor*, and began to organize special exhibitions, sports events, meetings, lectures, and so-called scientific and literary competitions. Presently the students were "permitted" to join the "Democratic Front."

While the measures described above were being applied to the teaching profession and the student body, the progressive purge of curricula and of school manuals was also undertaken. The various stages of this reform may be discerned with little difficulty. In the first place, the Education Ministry withdrew each year the authorization to use certain didactic manuals issued for previous years. At the same time appeared the first attempts to introduce sole authorized textbooks, that were later to become a feature of education in the "People's Republic of Rumania."

Also in line with the systematic drive of communist propaganda, the Russian language was introduced as a required subject in Rumanian schools. Here the educational authorities were faced with grave difficulties. There simply were not enough teachers to go round, Russian having at no time in the past been widely spoken in the country. To remedy this lack, the Rumanian-Russian institute organized in haste special streamlined one-month courses for prospective teachers of Russian. The incompetence of such "quick-order" language teachers need hardly be emphasized. As a matter of fact, the year when Russian was introduced, candidates for the high school baccalaureate examination were informed, on the very eve of the tests, that they might select either French or Russian. The Ministry's last-minute communiqué specified that answers to the Russian examination could be given in Rumanian!

In this initial period, aside from the general policy affecting all branches of education, the only structural innovation was the creation of the unified gymnasium (junior high school). As early as 1945 secondary education had been explicitly separated into two cycles: the first or gymnasial cycle, and the Lycee (high school proper). For the first cycle there was set up now a unified gymnasium, which in its curriculum and attributes fused together the former "theoretical gymnasium" and the post-primary schooling provided by existing school laws, that is to say those three extra required years provided for children who did not intend to go on to high school, following completion of primary schooling.

Aside from this, the communist regime set up a number of special schools for political education, and a series of schools for illiterates. The latter were indeed organized by the Ministry of Education in collaboration with the Communist Party and with various organizations spawned by the latter, like "street committees," the "Association of Democratic Women," and so forth.

In addition to the above, and likewise outside the field of education as such, we must mention the different institutes of an allegedly higher cultural nature, that were introduced by the communist regime, which include the "Institute of Universal Culture," the "Rumanian-Soviet Institute for Higher Studies," and the "R.P.R. Institute of History." Last but certainly not least, there was the R.P.R. Academy, which was set up when the Rumanian Academy was abolished by law in 1948, and which was to become the docile many-purpose tool of the regime, operating throughout the cultural domain.

The official conception of education promoted by the Bucarest regime is that advocated by Soviet pedagogy. As Scanteia of July 11, 1948, put it, "To educate the young means to provide them with a class education in the spirit of proletarian morale; that is, of morality subordinated to the interests of the proletarian class war."

This statement of principles is elaborated in Indrumatorul Pentru Invatamantul Mediu (Directives for Middle Grade Teaching), published in Bucarest in 1948. Here we find the following: ". . . The education of the pupils (must be made) in the spirit of Marxist-Leninist science and in that of proletarian morale. Marxist-Leninist science being the most advanced science, hence the only one apt to provide a clear and proper view of all natural phenomena, of phenomena of social life and thinking, must constitute the principal element upon which the activities of the pupils shall be based. Proletarian morale, which the pupils must acquire, will develop a new youth, healthy and educated in the spirit of popular democracy, in the spirit of socialism."

The immediate aim of this kind of upbringing was indicated by Makarenko, the Soviet authority on pedagogy, whose works have become the teacher's bible in the R.P.R.: "We cannot stop at the pure and simple education of man. We have no right to develop our educational work without aiming at a well determined political goal." This "well determined political goal" was defined by another Soviet pedagogical writer, Kairov: "Communist education is the preparation . . . of future generations in view of their active participation in the construction of the communist society." Furthermore, Kairov asserted, education must become "a powerful combat weapon against the exploiters." These aims have been officially endorsed by the R.P.R. educational authorities. The special newspaper of the teachers, Gazeta Invatamantului, specified in its issue of September 23, 1949, that, ". . . children must be fully acquainted with the criminal intentions of the imperialist warmongers. They must know the whole rascally background of the plots hatched by the British and American bankers, and see clearly that these exploiters are the foes of progress and the enemies of mankind." In the pursuit of such ideals, the R.P.R. educational authorities could hardly stop short of the complete destruction of the existing "bourgeois capitalist" pedagogical system.

The text of the Law for the Reform of Education appeared in the Official Gazette for August 3, 1948. According to Gh. Vasilichi, who was Minister for Education at the time, this law ". . . must be classed among the great structural reforms of our economic, political, and social life. Initiated by the Rumanian Workers' Party and adopted by the government, it will play a prominent part in raising the cultural level of our people, and assist in directing the youth of our country on the way of socialist construction."

The tendency of the law to supervise the pupil closely and in accordance with a well-defined plan does not stop at the schoolhouse door. Public education also concerns itself with "guiding the use of the pupils' free time, by organizing extra-curricular activities, welding the school to the family and to the social life of the ambient." (Article 2.)

To attain the proposed aim, which is "the education of youth in the spirit of popular democracy", the new law provides four grades of schooling, thus maintaining—at least apparently—the grades of "bourgeois-landowning" education. Schooling is now "pre-schooling, elementary, medium, and superior."

"Pre-schooling is optional. It is organized for children between the ages of 3 and 7 in day nurseries and kindergartens." (Article 5.)

"Elementary schooling is of seven years' duration and free. Schooling in the first four elementary grades is general and obligatory." (Article 6).

"Medium schooling lasts four years and comprises four types of schools, to wit: (a) *lycees,* (b) pedagogical schools, (c) technical schools, and (d) professional (trade) schools." (Article 8.) This was reduced to 3 years in 1953.

"Superior schooling had two categories of institutions: (a) universities and polytechnics; (b) institutes for higher learning." (Article 16.)

"Studies at Universities and Polythechnics last four to six years." (Article 17.)

"Studies at institutes of higher learning last three to four years." (Article 18.)

With the framework of education as set down by the law thus officially sketched out, we may now pass on to an analysis of the practical application of the "reform." But, before that, we must understand, and hereafter constantly bear in mind, that we are indeed dealing with an over-all plan, comprehensive and established down to the minutest details. For it is a feature of communist educational conception that it lays down every particular, leaving nothing to chance or to individual initiative. Everything is "planned."

In the light of this insight, we shall see that the various grades of schooling do not represent separate units, designed to provide the most favorable means for the harmonious development of the pupils' personality at various ages, according to individual temperament. They stand, in fact, as parts of the same machine, intended for the mass production of a type, "the Communist man." The sole permissible difference among the thousands that emerge from the schools of the Rumanian People's Republic is to be, according to the "program," merely in respect of the technical specialty of each unit turned out.

As a matter of fact, in our examination of the present educational system of Rumania, we shall encounter throughout, from kindergarten to University, a series of common elements, as a constant factor of all schooling. They are the Marxist-Leninist conception and, implicitly and explicitly, a boundless admiration for the Soviet Union.

Communist indoctrination must start in the kindergarten. As reported by *Scanteia* of September 15, 1948, Vasilichi, then Minister of Education, proclaimed that "the state must give particular care to the child's first steps in life . . . In bringing the children together in kindergartens and day nurseries, we teach them . . . to know the world that surrounds them, we discipline them, we train them for communal life." Just as it is in a factory or collective farm, the "working plan" is a basic feature of the infant school. Here, too, there are "required activities," and every moment of the toddlers' day is "organized." Instead of nursery rhymes, the tots learn to sing political flapdoodle in verse. Fairyland is the Soviet Union. Instead of the story of the Three Little Bears, they get the story of the Big Bear, and Stalin in his heyday was the fairy godfather.

At the same time, the children are taught early to hate and despise the "bourgeois" and the "capitalists", who are the communist substitute for the bogeyman and are invariably described as "the wild beasts". The first seeds of anti-religious notions are also sown at the earliest stage into the child's naturally receptive mind. Great efforts are made to increase the number of infant schools to carry on this "struggle against mysticism, superstititon, and obscurantism". According to *Gazeta Invatamantului* of December 31, 1953, there were 5,781 in operation by the end of 1953.

With respect to grade schools, the Education Law of 1948 brought in an innovation: the number of classes in secondary or high schools was reduced, and the lower grades were transferred to the elementary schools. Because of the great shortage of school buildings, this has resulted in a sharing of existing accommodations, to the detriment of all concerned.

The law proclaims that elementary schooling is free, and the first four grades obligatory. In reality, pupils of the upper grades, the fifth, sixth, and seventh, are constantly and insistently "advised" to contribute to the school's expenses. Soon after the publication of the law, indeed, the then Minister of Education showed, in an article titled "All children of school age to school!" which appeared in *Scanteia* of September 23, 1948, that, "through a well-organized propaganda, the parents and all villagers must be persuaded to assist their school, for it is that school which will enlighten and educate their children. Let those who have more give more . . ." The idea was put into practice without waiting for the parents to be persuaded by propaganda arguments. The procedure was much more effective and ingenious. *Gazeta Invatamantului* of September 16, 1948, stated editorially that: ". . . Under the leadership of the Party Organizations and at the insistence of the Educational Sections, with the collaboration of the mass organizations and of the UTM (the "Union of Working Youth") and UFDR (the "Union of Democratic Women of Rumania") hundreds of thousands of voluntary labor days were forthcoming for transporting materials needed in the buildings, for furniture repairs, and for cleaning the premises." And, to leave no doubt as to the "voluntary" nature of this work, the editorial went on: . . . "Almost everywhere where there was need, parents and the young were mobilized to work for their school. In many places, the salaried personnel formed veritable labor units on the spot."

School curricula have been changed to conform to the "highest pedagogical science." We should mention in the first place the elimination of all religious teachings, obviously considered "harmful or useless." This is confirmed in the article cited above. In the words of Vasilichi: ". . . As is known, the church's conception of the world and of nature is a metaphysical and idealist one, whereas the scientific conception of the world and of nature is that of dialectic and historic materialism. These two conceptions are diametrically opposed, and to go on propagating both in the tender minds of children means to bewilder these minds with grave confusion, which is apt to prevent them from acquiring a knowledge of all that science has produced to our day, and from further developing it."

Hence a clear cleavage is in order. "Religious propaganda, which is to be carried out in churches and prayer houses, is . . . one thing. Learning and culture, which must be taught in schools, under state direction and control, are another."

However, with religion eliminated, and with the humanities fallen in neglect, new horizons are opened to the tender minds of the children by the teaching of the Russian language. For the law provides that, beginning in the fourth year of elementary school, the Russian language is a required course (article 6). In other words, in the future, every Rumanian will have had to take at least one year of Russian.

"The introduction of the Russian language, beginning with the fourth elementary grade," announced Mihail Roller, "will help our pupils to acquaint themselves with and benefit from the great scientific conquests of the Soviet Union. It will assist tomorrow's citizens to prevail themselves in their activities, in every walk of life, of the great experience of the country of socialism, that is evolving toward communism." (*Scanteia*, August 4, 1948.)

Yet another article, published in *Scanteia*, of August 21, 1948, enthusiastically hails the introduction of Russian in elementary schools. Its author quotes in support the following statement of Majakovsky: "Even if I were a Negro of advanced years, I would still study with pleasure and zeal the Russian language, for it is in that language that Lenin spoke." This is truly an unanswerable argument!

But, while the Russian language is in principle only one of the required courses in the program, in fact all other disciplines are so presented and taught as to face the pupil at every step with the shining example of the Soviet Union.

And the propaganda on behalf of the Soviet Union is not limited to textbooks. It is present in every imaginable guise and at all times, so that the pupil becomes literally enveloped in this atmosphere both in and out of class. To convey some idea of the methods employed, one may turn to an authorized description of the inside of a typical classroom. Upon entering the class, the pupil's eyes are drawn to the red flags, the communist slogans, and the pictures of the Soviet leaders, of Marx and Engels, and of the current leaders of the Rumanian People's Republic. Elaborating, *Gazeta Invatamantului* of September 30, 1949, said: "Everywhere, clean premises, fresh painted, show concern for a good start of the school year. The schoolhouse walls are this day bedecked with greenery, with slogans, and with the traditional 'Welcome' signs. . . . The opening of the school year is marked with a display of red and tricolor flags, nicely draped around the schoolhouse . . . High-pitched children's voices intone the R.P.R. and Soviet hymns."

In this kind of setting, the teacher must do his best to provide his class with the prescribed indoctrination. He has no initiative to take, but must conform strictly to whatever he is instructed to do. The constant fear of "deviationism" besets not only the members of the teaching profession, but also the highest authorities of the R.P.R. educational system. Even a compilation translated from the works of Soviet authorities and made into a textbook presents dangers. The safest thing obviously remains to stick to the simple translation of single approved works. This, indeed, meets with the approval of the R.P.R. Ministry of Education.

The better to understand the kind of knowledge currently inculcated in elementary schools in Rumania, we shall now turn to some of the prescribed manuals at present in general use.

Here, for instance, is the very first textbook to which children are exposed, the ABC manual (*Abecedar*) issued by the State Publishing House in 1950. Instead of presenting some of Rumania's heroes of the past, the primer speaks of the "great learned men and fighters," Marx and Engels on page 74; of Lenin, whom "all who work love and remember," and "whose teaching guides all working people," on page 77; and of Stalin, "the best friend of the children," who is "Comrade Stalin, whom all workers love with an untold love," on page 78.

In a similar way, the primer tells of the glories of the Soviet Union, of the deeds of valor of the Soviet army (pages 40, 41, and 42), before coming out with a poem to the soldiers of the R.P.R. (page 43). In all seriousness it proclaims that May 9 marks the Independence Day of Rumania, when the country was so generously helped by the Soviet Union (page 70), thus implying there existed a Soviet Union at the time of the war of Independence of 1877–1878. Thereafter, on pages 53 and 81, the primer shows the portraits of Ana Pauker and Vasile Luca. The subsequent purge of the two formerly prominent communists resulted, of course, in a purge of later editions. The pattern however is the same, though the stress is placed more on "collective leadership" than on individual leaders nowadays.

The pattern holds good for more advanced textbooks. The *Rumanian Language Textbook* prescribed for the Seventh Grade of elementary schools (State Publishing House: 1949) mentions ten classical writers as against thirty-one "progressive" prose and poetry writers (of which 18 are Rumanian and 13 foreign authors). In addition to praising the Soviet Union at every step, the manual stresses the alleged historic friendship between Rumanians and Russians, while damning everything of an "imperialistic" nature, especially coming from the Western world. The predilection for "progressive" authors as against the classics is no accident. According to *Gazeta Invatamantului* of July 10, 1954, at the Rumanian language entrance examination for higher education, high school graduates are required to pass written tests on the works of six classic authors and fourteen communist writers.

History manuals are of the same tendentious character. For instance the *History of the Middle Ages* for Grade Six (1952 edition) treats the outstanding events up to the XVIIth century in strict accordance with Marxist-Leninist doctrine. "The monasteries were nests of superstition" (page 10). The Crusades sought to liberate Jerusalem ostensibly because, "according to a legend, Jesus Christ, the mythical founder of the Christian religion, was supposed to have been buried there." In reality, however, they were after the "gold-filled cellars" of the Middle Eastern cities and of Byzance (page 101). As for the Jesuit Order, "lowly flattery, corruption, fraud, calumny, and even threats and, in case of need, poison and the dagger, were their normal fighting weapons" (page 245).

Not only the Church and the monarchs of the middle ages, but also medieval cultural movements and their promoters are treated with the utmost contempt. Lorenzo de Medici was "a crafty and clever politician who would stop at nothing to gain his ends . . . He surrounded himself with painters, learned men, and poets, so that they might magnify and flatter him" (page 198). The Tsars of Russia, on the other hand, are treated respectfully, in accordance with accepted Soviet views, and everything Russian is held up for admiration. The student is given the impression that even in the middle ages the "light came from the East."

But if the slightest slip is made by the authors of any school book, in the sense of moderating the hostile attitude toward everything Western, the regime's watchdogs are instantly up in arms. An editorial in *Gazeta*

Invatamantului of January 25, 1953, for instance, took offense at the statement made in the *Textbook of Modern and Contemporary History* for the Seventh Grade to the effect that "the capitalist states proceeded to gain new colonies in order to provide for part of the jobless workers of the metropolis." This, the teachers' newspaper remarked, is to veil over the realities. Colonial policies were exclusively motivated by "maximum profits and the tendency of imperialists to dominate and exploit other peoples."

The 1949 edition of the *History of the R.P.R.* for seventh grade students provides a further instance of communist pedagogy. It is the collective work of several authors headed by Academician M. Roller. One striking feature is the disproportionate amount of space devoted to the contemporary epoch, in contrast to that devoted to Rumanian history prior to the end of the 19th century. For this, there is an explanation: the manual deals with events up to the year 1949, hence the authorities consider it proper to treat the "realizations" of the Groza regime, the various strikes in the period between the two world wars, or the formation of the "Tudor Vladimirescu" Division, on Russian soil, from Rumanian prisoners of war, indoctrinated with the communist faith, at greater length than, say, the reigns of Mircea the Old (1386–1814), of Stephen the Great (1457–1504), or of Michel the Brave (1593–1601), which merely enhance the place of Rumanian history in the history of the world. Anyone, indeed, expecting to find in this textbook the victories won by the princes mentioned above, would be disappointed. But, in exchange, the reader may find, on page 253, that "the fights of the striking railroad workers, in 1933, inscribed one of the great pages of glory of the people of Rumania." For the benefit of those who might not be aware of this event, it should be said that it refers to a strike at the Bucarest railroad yards and workshops, on February 15 and 16, 1933, which occasioned some clashes between the strikers and the police. The official exaggerations hinge on the fact that among the leaders of the strikers brought to trial on that occasion there were some of today's notables, such as Gheorghiu-Dej, Chivu Stoica, etc. The clue is provided on page 251 of the textbook.

On the other hand, the authors do not hesitate to falsify recorded history in order to present in glowing colors Rumanian relations with Russia. For instance, the whole of Moldavia's past is misrepresented, so as to avoid any mention of that principality's eastern part, which later came to be known as Bessarabia. Where it is impossible to omit the event, the rape of Bessarabia by the Russian Empire in 1812 is mentioned as follows: "Fighting between Russian and Turkish armies continued to the end of 1811, and peace was concluded in Bucarest (1812), liberating new territories from the Turkish yoke." (Page 118.)

The union of Bessarabia to Rumania (1918) is presented thus: "The reactionary Rumanian government, taking advantage of the difficult military situation of the young Soviet Republics, attacked them and occupied Bessarabia, smothering with armed force the revolutionary Soviet resistance, which had been born and developed during the revolution." (Page 229.)

The brutal Soviet ultimatum to Rumania, of June 1940, is recounted for the benefit of the student as follows: "On June 27, 1940, following the agreement between the Rumanian and Soviet governments, an end was put to the territorial conflict between the two countries—a conflict that originated in Rumania's armed intervention against the Soviets, in 1918." (Page 261.)

These are but a few samples dealing with one issue. It would take volumes to go into the details of all the falsifications and misrepresentations to be found in the book. In fact, the entire part devoted to the Groza government is fabricated out of whole cloth. For instance, the coup d'état of August 23, 1944, carried out by King Mihai, with the support of the leaders of the democratic political parties, Messrs. Iuliu Maniu, D. Bratianu, and Titel Petrescu, is recounted in the following words: "As a result of the crushing of the German and Antonescu forces, the Antonescu government was ousted and a new government was formed on August 23, 1944." (Page 266.) And again: "The military action, in view of the coup d'état, had been prepared by a commission in which, together with certain high-ranking army officers, the Communist party was also represented." (Page 274.) And, finally: "In reality, the leaders of the National Peasant and Liberal parties were hostile to the act of August 23, 1944." (Page 275.)

It is a noteworthy peculiarity that the phrases used to describe the Maniu trial in this book, have been borrowed from the high-school history textbook of 1947. Although the latter had been issued prior to the sentence in the trial, the 1949 manual found the authors with no need to make any changes whatsoever—a clear enough indication that the sentences had been prearranged, just as the trial itself was rigged. Here is what the textbook has to say: "The people of Rumania, in their effort to make a definitive break with the anti-democratic regimes of the past, could not rest content with simply dissolving this Party [the National Peasant Party]. Maniu, Mihalache, and the other members of the party's leadership could not escape responsibility for all their crimes, before the righteous justice of the people." (Page 301.)

In view of the great importance accorded to the study of Russian, a review of the contents of a Russian-language manual is in order. Let us turn to the one designed for the elementary fourth year, edited by the Rumanian-Soviet Institute of Studies, published by the "Russian Book" in 1948. The book is quite ably contrived so that the student becomes gradually familiarized with Russian names and customs, the latter being skillfully alternated with the Rumanian counterparts. As in a Rumanian primer, immediately following the alphabet and the rudiments of the language, propaganda is introduced. Thus, on page 32 there is a short composition about the city of Moscow, and on page 71 there is a description of the rest center of Artek, in the Crimea, where young pioneers who have worked well in their kolkhoz and have learned well, spend their well-earned vacations. Then, on page 80, there is the indispensable article on Lenin, followed a few pages further on by one devoted to Stalin's childhood (page 88). But the "Anglo-American Imperialists" are not forgotten either. The very last lesson comprises a poem to be memorized by the pupils, who thus can start the vacation marking the end of the school year with this final memory. The poem is entitled "The little Negro boy"; it is on page 91, and its translation is as follows:

"I live, oh, I live in America,
I, John, the little black child;
And to the distant schoolhouse
I always must go on foot.
Bells are heard in the streets;
Streetcars go everywhere;
But, alas, the conductor
Will not allow Negroes to ride.
Not allowed! Not allowed! Not allowed!
And here, oh here, in America,
In all the huge cities and towns,
There are numberless white children
All playing in gardens and parks.
They play ball and make merry
But we blacks may not join them.

Not allowed! Not allowed! Not allowed!
But we all know from hearsay
There is one land in this world
Where men are of different colors
Yet all lead the same good life."

The little Negro's Eldorado, as the reader will have guessed, is the Soviet Union.

The final pages of this manual announce a competition among school children, organized by ARLUS, in celebration of Rumanian-Soviet friendship. The text says: "We owe to the Soviet Union the liberation of Rumania from the Hitlerian yoke, the winning of national independence, political and economic. The great Soviet experience in the construction of socialism stands as an example before the People's Republic of Rumania, in the struggle for the establishment of a higher order: the socialist order." (Page 94.)

One of the means most favored for spreading and sinking Communist propaganda into the minds of the young is this system of competitions. The prizewinners are rewarded with Russian books or translations from Russian authors.

Such in broad outline, is the program of communist propaganda in elementary schools. One would be inclined to consider it fairly comprehensive and exhaustive. Yet, the restless and eager mind of the "cultural responsibles" must seek control over the children even outside the school. Hence the creation of the "Pioneer" organizations.

The Central Committee of the Rumanian Workers' Party, in the plenary session of December 22–24, 1948, "entrusted the sole Marxist-Leninist organization of the Working Youth with the task of creating and guiding the Pioneer organization (children between the ages of 9 and 14), which will be inspired by the wonderful experience of the Pioneer organizations of the Soviet Union." (*Scanteia*, May 4, 1949.)

The first detachment of Pioneers began to be organized toward the end of April 1949. One year later, according to data quoted from *Gazeta Invatamantului* in *Adevarul* of May 2, 1950, the number of Pioneers had risen to 130,000. By 1953, there were more than 700,000 Pioneers in Rumania. Units are led by instructors who all are members of the Young Workers' Union. Each Pioneer gives a written pledge to carry out tasks assigned to him. Aware of the importance of emulation among the young, the educational authorities were certainly shrewd in designating but a small proportion of Pioneers at the beginning. The other pupils may well be expected to overbid their enthusiasm for communism, in order to attain the coveted distinction of being a Pioneer. What, then, do the communists count to gain from this institution? The answer is not far to seek. "The Pioneers", wrote Alexandru Draghici, a member in the Central Committee of the Rumanian Workers' Party, "must acquire all those wonderful traits that characterize communist morale. . . . Pioneers must grow and develop in such a way that, at a certain age, they can enter the ranks of the Working Youth Union, then those of the Party, to work and struggle for the exalted cause of communism." In conclusion, according to the article printed in *Universul* of May 3, 1949, what is desired for the Pioneers is "education in the spirit of a glowing love for the most advanced country of socialism, the Soviet Union, the country which defends the peace and independence of peoples, which liberated us, and which is continually helping us to achieve a new life."

The motto of the Pioneers, indeed, is "In the fight for the cause of Lenin and Stalin, forward!"

But, if the Pioneer's "love" is directed toward the Soviet Union and toward the Rumanian Workers' Party, the authorities do not omit to foster a feeling of hate in the children's hearts. Thus, Gheorghe Florescu, member of the Central Committee of the Rumanian Workers' Party, stated that, "The Pioneer's patriotic education must inspire him with deadly hatred for the enemies of our country and of the working people, the Anglo-American imperialists and their despicable servants inside and outside the country." (*Scanteia*, May 4, 1949.)

But every effort of the people responsible for education to bring up the children of the Rumanian People's Republic in these views still seems inadequate to the authorities. There is every evidence of a constant and haunting obsession, a fear that a moment's slackening of attention may leave the children free to get contaminated with "bourgeois-landowning" ideas. Hence the ceaseless appeals to teachers and especially to parents, and the reiterated admonitions, urging them, "conscious of their great responsibility . . . to give wholehearted support to the Pioneer organizations to bring up the children in a spirit of love for Pioneering; to instill in the children's consciousness the burning zeal to be awarded the red necktie of the Pioneer, that fragment of the workers' red flag." (*Scanteia*, May 4, 1949.)

As is only to be expected, the Pioneers enjoy a favored place in school. This is overtly admitted by the authorities. An article in *Gazeta Invatamantului* of June 10, 1949, states: "Thus, some teachers and instructors make it a point in class to stress the differences between Pioneers and the rest of their pupils. Pioneers are protected in various ways, manifest to all. The rest are humiliated and discouraged with the constant refrain, 'Well, of course, what can I ask of you who are not a Pioneer?' "

"The result of such an attitude," the article goes on with a show of concern, "is disastrous. A gulf is created between Pioneers and non-Pioneers, leading to consequences entirely contrary to those counted upon." The animosity between Pioneers and non-Pioneers seems in effect to be far deeper than an outside observer might be prepared to believe. For, as the article goes on to show, "Another serious mistake is to pursue the Pioneers too assiduously in every class activity; then, at the slightest slip, inherent to any child, to scold them, saying, 'Shame on you! You, a Pioneer, to do such things?' In such cases the other pupils will follow the teacher's example and will lie in wait for the Pioneers on every occasion, to pounce on them with glee at the slightest mistake."

It is the Pioneers who edit the wall newspaper, who decorate the school, and especially the Pioneers' Room, with red flags, slogans, portraits, and so forth. They also are "a valued assistance of the didactic cadres in their work in behalf of communist education," according to *Gazeta Invatamantului* of February 18, 1955.

The reality behind this high-sounding formula is in fact the encouragement of spying and tale-bearing, not only against the Pioneer's schoolmates, but against the teachers and even the parents. It is no less than a highly complex system of espionage.

Concrete examples are not lacking. Here is one taken from a letter to the editors of *Licurici*, the children's magazine, of November 7, 1949. Maria Grigorescu, a schoolgirl from Iash, writes: "Some of my schoolmates come to class with unprepared lessons. For instance, Elena B. was unable to answer a question in geography class. She had done no homework, thinking she would not be called out. That is what she always did—she never prepared her lessons when she already had a mark in the catalog."

The French newspaper *France-Soir*, in its issue of March 15, 1949, published the statements of a French technician, who had lived in Rumania some time. This is his story: ". . . A good part of these courses is devoted to a strange subject of learning: denunciation. Teachers are taught to 'tell on' their pupils and their families; the pupils are taught to spy on their teachers, their families and friends, and even on their own families. On several occasions I had at my home such unfortunate teachers who were forced to comply with this regime, and who would come to weep at their ease before a neutral. 'If I were to cry at home,' said these victims . . . 'my servant, my son or my daughter might be tempted, willy-nilly, to speak of it and, so, to denounce me unwittingly.' In such an atmosphere it has become impossible for parents to discuss anything with their children, to try to reason with them, or to give them the benefit of their experience. They would be too much afraid to let slip a word or a phrase which, retold in school, either textually or in an 'ideological' guise, might mean imprisonment and sentencing to some heavy penalty. Many such cases have already occurred."

Perhaps the most significant indication of the importance officially accorded the Pioneers is that the government has given the use of the royal palace of Cotroceni, in Bucarest, to that organization.

We cannot close this chapter concerning the education of children of tender age, without making it clear once again that all books, magazines, and films officially designated for them are either of actual Soviet origin or else abound in fulsome praise for the U.S.S.R.

The first magazines issued especially for the Pioneers, *Licurici* and *Pogonici*, have the mission "to bring the children close to the revolutionary transformations that are taking place in our country, in order to make them participate therein with all their force, and to prepare them to defend these achievements if need be." This injunction may be found in *Scanteia Tineretului* of September 26, 1950. The organ of the U.T.M. further advised the editors of these children's periodical that "communist education is their basic task," and scolded them for not having sufficiently insisted upon "planting in the children's souls the implacable hatred against the bandit plots of the imperialists."

Such children's publications have a truly impressive circulation. The newspaper *Scanteia Pionierului* and the magazine *Cravata Rosie* and *Luminitza*, for instance, had circulations of 300,000 copies each in 1953. The *Editura Tineretului* publishing concern of the Union of Working Youth Central Committee, in seven years of activity, brought out some 200 titles and over four million copies, according to *Gazeta Invatamantului* of April 30, 1953.

This means of communist education is supplemented in various other ways, including special radio broadcasts, meetings, lectures, and so forth. Unfortunately, while learning all sorts of things beyond their years, such as the communist interpretation of international developments, of life on a Chinese collective farm, and the living standards of Venezuelan oil workers, the children are very poorly schooled in such elementary subjects as the Rumanian language, mathematics, and the like. Small wonder that such "deficiencies" must be denounced again and again in the R.P.R. press, and that every session of graduation examinations marks an outbreak of alarming reports in the newspapers, stressing the ignorance of the candidates.

The behavior of school children between the ages of 8 and 14 is a subject of perennial and apparently fully justified complaint. "There are still pupils and students who think it is a brave thing to affront a teacher," complained *Gazeta Invatamantului* of September 4, 1954, "and to show disrespect to the didactic cadres. Some students are unseemly and show improper attitudes toward their female colleagues." And *Scanteia* remarked glumly that even in 1954 there were still many students who stay away from class, show up wholly unprepared at examinations, and fail to pass the tests in two or even three subjects. "They become truants, shirkers, and cheats, and have an impudent attitude toward their teachers."

This ever recurring theme of disrespect toward the teachers is noteworthy. It is, of course, the expectable result of the officially encouraged role of informer. When from the very inception of the communist regime the school children have been incited to act as spies, sneaks, and party stool pigeons, what standing can the teaching profession have in their eyes?

As we have already indicated, it is the high school system that has suffered the most radical changes under the communist regime. The accent now is on technical high schools of various sorts; agricultural, cooperative, vocational, and trade schools have largely superseded the former classical medium or secondary schools. According to *Scanteia* of September 16, 1948, "In view of the urgent need for intermediary cadres in production, this type of schooling will have a preponderant role in secondary education." Indeed, as *Gazeta Invatamantului* of February 11, 1955, reported, there were in Rumania, at the opening of the 1954–1955 school year, 265 trade schools with a total attendance of 77,000, and 286 medium technical schools with a total attendance of 80,700 students. From the time of their first introduction, such schools, though under the authority of the Ministry of Public Education, were organized, operated, and financed by various technical departments. But six years' experience showed that the results left much to be desired. Hence, in February 1955 a joint decision of the Central Committee of the Rumanian Workers' Party and of the R.P.R. government was issued, reorganizing the technical medium schools.

According to the text published in *Gazeta Invatamantului* of February 11, 1955, "The schooling aimed at training skilled workers and medium technical cadres needed in the national economy, in health protection, and in the development of the people's culture will comprise three types of schools: Professional schools for apprentices, technical schools for skilled workers and technical personnel, and technical schools for master-workers." Such schools are designed to operate in conjunction with the larger enterprises, plants, mechanical centers, tractor stations, and so forth. The respective enterprise has the responsibility for the proper operation of the schools, but their coordination from the point of view of their educational curricula is the responsibility of the Ministry concerned in each case, while the Ministry of Public Education is left with but a control role which includes approval of textbooks and the like. Graduates of such schools, with the exception of those for apprentices, may qualify for higher education of university rank.

It should be noted that in the field of medium schooling, as in all other fields of endeavor, there is open discrimination in favor of students of "acceptable" social origin. In the first place, the children of "workers" and "poor peasants" enjoy preference, while those of "bourgeois" family background are systematically discouraged. This has been openly affirmed by the highest authority. Florica Mezincescu, then Assistant Minister of Education, wrote in *Gazeta Invartamantului* of September 23, 1949: ". . . It is not a matter of indifference to us who enters high schools. We must watch the social composition of the student body, which must represent the great mass of the working people, which has the guiding role, then the working peasantry, their ally, the state's public servants of all categories, and the small artisans who march in step with the constructors of socialism." And *Scanteia* of August 26, 1948, was still more explicit: "At high schools, in the middle Eighth Grade, assignment of places, following entrance examinations, shall be made with the proviso that 50 per cent of available places are reserved for the children of workers under collective working contracts, of poor peasants, and of public and private office workers that belong to unions and lack the necessary means. Once this 50 per cent of available places . . . is completed, in the order of their classification, the rest shall be allocated to others, likewise on the basis of their classification."

In high schools, as throughout the educational field, students are required to fill in forms showing their "social origin" at every step. There are, indeed, special "class committees" operating in high schools, formed of students who have shown themselves particularly proficient in Marxist-Leninist doctrine. These bodies of future "activists" are the repositories of "proletarian vigilance," and act as veritable screening units, ferreting out signs of "bourgeois and reactionary sabotage" among their fellow-students, the teachers, and the parents. They operate under the direct supervision of the communist "responsible" of the school.

We have examined at length some of the typical textbooks prescribed for elementary schools. As we might expect, the same features are to be found, amplified, elaborated, and confirmed in the manuals of the medium schools. Indiscriminate admiration for everything Soviet and specifically Russian, the concomitant denigration of all things Western, and the systematic belittling of religion and everything connected with the Churches are, indeed, to be found in all textbooks, whether scientific, literary, or technical. Here are a few instances.

Describing the new Geography Books, *Gazeta Invatamantului* of September 30, 1949, proudly pointed out that "in the new geography manuals may be found problems that were never mentioned in the old textbooks. . . . The people's struggle for national and social liberation . . . occupies an important place. . . . The people's victories in this continued fight are indicated." The Soviet Union provides study material for one whole year's course; the rest of the world is squeezed into a course of exactly the same duration. Characteristic is "the radical transformation" caused by the "application of Marxist-Leninist science to the study of geography."

Rumanian language and literature textbooks stress the approved "progressive" writings of the regime's accredited writers to the detriment of the classic authors. The thinkers and writers of the past are either belittled as "reactionaries," or else "interpreted" in terms of the current political dogma. Even the foreign languages, such as are still taught, are presented in manuals abounding in political irrelevancies. These manuals refer at every step to the Soviet Union, to Pioneer activities, and to social problems, discussed in the communist style. Among the "French authors" presented in extracts for the students' edification are Marx, Engels, Lenin, and . . . Maurice Thorez. As for Rabelais, according to the prescribed *French Literature Book* for the last grade of high schools, "he shows us two social types constantly antagonistic in an oligarchic society: the rapacious rich man and his poor victim." The textbook opens with a quotation from Jdanov and closes with a fragment by Leonov concerning criticism and self-criticism.

Even arithmetic is not exempt from this all-pervading political angling. Every approved textbook features problems that involve data culled from the activities of state enterprises, collective farms, and the like, with production norms and delivery quotas cropping up again and again to bedevil the budding mathematicians of the R.P.R. Current events must be brought in at every step by the teachers, and "examples taken from the every-day life of the workers, from international developments, and from the various forms of production" have to be dragged into even anatomy or astronomy courses.

With such claptrap interlarding the textbooks, it is obvious that everything pertaining to Western pedagogy is officially considered obnoxious. The authoritative *Gazeta Invatamantului*, in its issue for January 1, 1953, described the noted Belgian pedagogue Decroly as "one of the most disgusting representatives of imperialist pedagogy," and dismissed John Dewey as "one of the most typical exponents of pragmatism, a servile lackey of the trusts."

What of those who must dispense the "new education" prescribed by the regime, the members of the teaching profession? Their lot is not an enviable one. As far back as 1947, the Ministry of Public Education brought out a "Rule Book for Cultural-Educational Work in Secondary Schools," by which they have to conduct all their activities. The booklet states unambiguously on page 5 that "the pages that follow contain remarks having the sense, not of mere recommendations, but of . . . a compulsory character." Foremost of the innovations introduced by this Rule Book is the "educational counselor," who is appointed for each school from among the teachers of "verified democratic convictions," that is, having the confidence of the Communist party. This functionary is the true head of the school, the principal being but a figurehead. It is he who exercises the "guidance and control" service, to which the Education Law of 1948 devotes an entire chapter.

All activities, inside and outside school are closely supervised and "planned," not only the school principal, but the communist organization assuring the system of checks and counter-checks at every step. The accent is placed upon the "ideological contents" of all schooling, and the school's unions, U.T.M. (Union of Working Youth), and Pioneer organizations participate in every decision. The party line, whatever it happens to be at any given time, must be strictly adhered to. All slips, "deviations," or other failures are immediately punished. With everyone spying and reporting on everyone else, it is not difficult to imagine the atmosphere in schools.

The school authorities interfere even in the home life of students, harassing their parents, "educating" them in the "new spirit," and reporting anything suspicious they observe. This business of dogging the students' families in and out of season raises a problem that to this day has not been satisfactorily solved from the point of view of the authorities, and still persists as a thorn in the side of educational "responsibles." It is naturally the "bourgeois" and "kulak" influences at home that must be put down at all costs. But there is also "agitation work" to be performed by the members of the teaching profession; they must be prepared to "sell" and "boost" the regime's topical propaganda themes, by house-to-house methods. These additional chores make the overworked teacher's life burdensome indeed.

The varied activities required from the teacher make necessary an infinity of special courses and training programs that have little or nothing to do with actual instruction in class-room subjects. Even prior to the introduction of the Reform Law, as far back as July 1948, a center for teachers' instruction was set up in Bucarest. This started out with 114 teacher-students. By August that same year, there was one such center at every district capital, and a total of 25,000 teachers were put through the mill. Barely one year later, the Minister of Public Education could announce that no less than 80 per cent of the country's teachers had been through the requisite cycle. Since then, this type of extra schooling and screening for members of the teaching profession has been constantly elaborated.

Yet, in spite of all efforts, the results still do not satisfy the party watchdogs. *Gazeta Invatamantului* of January 25, 1953 complained bitterly at the persistence of such sins as "objectivism" and "cosmopolitanism" among the country's teachers, and, in general, of lack of recognition and combativity when it came to "remnants of retrograde bourgeois ideology." It was in order to remedy these deficiencies and others that the R.P.R.

Council of Ministers issued a decision on July 30, 1954, aimed ostensibly at "assuring the stability of the teaching profession." It affects all teachers of elementary and secondary schools, and provides two forms of extra-curricular but compulsory activities for them. The first is a one-year's "qualification course," to be taken every five years, and the second is a "methodical activity" of a permanent nature. The one-year course consists of a stint of required reading and exercises, which is taken during the actual school year, and of a cycle of lectures, seminars, and practical work, which is scheduled during the summer vacation months. In other words, it means that the teacher does without a vacation every five years. It should not be thought, however, that it is only every fifth year that the members of the teaching profession forego their vacations. There are such summer chores as helping out in summer camps for children, and thus continuing the communist education of their charges, which are no less obligatory. The second phase consists of several more cycles of conferences, lectures, meetings, and so forth, carried out through "pedagogical circles" set up for each raion of the country. Four special institutes have also been set up—in Bucarest, Iash, Cluj, and Timishoara—to handle and systematize these activities.

It does not take a great deal of imagination to realize that a teacher's lot in the R.P.R. is no easy one. Harried by the educational authorities, constantly spied upon by colleagues and pupils, despised by all concerned in consequence, the man or woman who chooses the teaching profession is hardly apt to develop a very high morale as time goes on, no matter how dedicated he or she may be initially.

To round off the picture of the educational field and of the manner in which future generations are currently being shaped in Rumania, a glance at the physical training programs is in order.

The educational value of organized competitive sports has been widely recognized, and it is hardly necessary to point out that totalitarian regimes of every shade invariably make use of them for propaganda purposes. The pomp and pageantry attending all major sports events in Hitler's Third Reich and in the Soviet Union are all too familiar, and the concomitant political trappings have become almost commonplace even to the average movie-goer and reader of illustrated magazines in the Western hemisphere.

For a definition of sports and for an understanding of the part they are called upon to play under a communist regime, the most authoritative source is provided by the available official texts. Here, for instance, is "The decision of the Political Bureau of the Central Committee of Rumanian Workers' Party concerning the constant stimulation and development of physical culture and of sports," from *Scanteia* of June 26, 1949: ". . . The thorough-going organization of physical culture and of mass sports, in the present conditions of our country's development, is of great political importance, because physical culture and sports, guided by the Party, constitute a significant contribution to the formation of a new man, of a determined and active fighter for the construction of socialism." Then comes the basic act of faith: "The concern of the Party for the problem of sports and physical culture is inspired by the Stalinist conception . . . it is inspired by the genial teachings of the great leaders of the proletariat, Marx, Engels, Lenin, and Stalin, who have stressed the role of physical culture alongside ideological and political education and technical instruction, in the communist upbringing of the men of labor."

It is not surprising, therefore, that the Communist regime, as early as 1946, set up the so-called "Organization of Popular Sports," which, as was only to be expected, was placed "under the guidance of the Party and supported by workers' unions and by democratic youth organizations."

The results of this organization, however, were disappointing. Hence the Political Bureau of the Central Committee of the Rumanian Workers' Party presently announced that it ". . . considers that, on the basis of a proper guidance, the participation of athletes in the country's political and social life must be assured. Physical improvement and sports must become one of the important factors in the physical and moral toughening of the men of labor, and in the strengthening of our Fatherland, the Rumanian Popular Republic." Hence, ". . . with the aim of continually stimulating and developing mass physical culture and sports," it is resolved that existing sports organizations be recast, and that ". . . a Committee for Physical Culture and Sports be set up as an agency of the Council of Ministers, with the participation therein of representatives of the General Confederation of Labor, of the Working Youth Union, of the Army, of the Ministry of the Interior, of the Ministry of Education, and of the Ministry of Health." The resolution made it clear that the new committee would have as its primary task "to put into effect the policy of the party and of the government in the field of physical culture and of sports."

This decision of the Politbureau became law through the decree No. 329 of August 6, 1949. The Committee for Physical Education and Sports, according to that decree, ". . . leads and controls the activities of all physical culture and sports organizations." Its mission is to establish ". . . the norms and . . . necessary measures for the development of physical culture and of sports." It "studies, establishes, applies . . . taking example from the experience of Soviet sports and making use thereof, the new method of teaching and practicing physical culture and sports, in view of acquiring the most advanced sports techniques and of attaining the foremost physical culture." Furthermore, the Committee " . . . in collaboration with the Ministry of Public Education, establishes programs of physical culture and sports, and controls their carrying out, in all educational institutions of whatever category; it organizes, directs, and controls the technical teaching of sports, at all levels, taking measures . . . for raising the ideological level of these cadres and of the foremost athletes . . .

". . . It directs the sports press; it edits books, brochures, manuals, bulletins, almanacs, and other publications in connection with problems of physical culture and of sports; and it advises concerning publications of this nature, edited by other organizations and institutions."

The Committee is made up of a president, four vice-presidents, and twelve to eighteen members, appointed by the Council of Ministers. District committees for physical culture and sports are envisaged to function alongside the existing district "popular councils" (in Rumanian: "sfaturi populare," soviets in the Russian sense), while "local popular councils will have delegates for physical culture and sports."

Such is the framework in which organized sports of all kinds must be practiced in the People's Republic of Rumania. A resolution of the Committee for Physical Culture and Sports, published in the Official Bulletin of February 2, 1950, asserts control over the organization of physical culture and of sports. In accordance with this new directive, no sports whatsoever may be practiced except within sport associations, sport collectives, and sport circles. The first of these institutions may only exist "within the framework of the General Confederation of Labor, alongside workers' Unions, according to production fields, and within the framework of the Ministry of National Defense and the Ministry of Internal Affairs." "Sport collectives" in rural areas are to function "alongside State Agricultural Farms, machine and tractor stations, collective farms, and cultural centers." In the field of education, ". . . within the framework of elementary, medium, and upper schools, there will be set up sports collectives and circles." Article 7 of the Resolution provides that "medium grade schools will organize sports collectives, and elementary schools, sports circles." These are to come under the control of the school management," . . . and in cities and districts under the control of the educational sections of the local Popular Councils and Committees for Physical Education and Sports." The purposes and tasks of the latter organizations are to be found in Article 2 of the Resolution, which provides that all activities will be carried out ". . . with a view to forming constructors of the socialist society, multilaterally developed, healthy, strong, and full of life, devoted to the utmost to our Fatherland and to the Rumanian Workers' Party . . . and in the spirit of unswerving faith in the victory of the international proletariat, in the struggle against exploitation, for the defense of peace, liberty, and progress, of devotion and love for the great Stalin, leader of genius of the peace front, democracy, and socialism throughout the whole world, and for the Great Country of victorious socialism, the Soviet Union."

Well might the Western reader wonder what all these high sounding aims have to do with the world of sports. But, be that as it may, this much is clear: the communist regime, in this field as in all others, strives to achieve a twofold end—on the one hand, the servile copying of available Soviet models, and, on the other, a new means of shaping tomorrow's communist fighter. To meet these requirements, the Council of Ministers, in its session of April 14, 1950, approved "the Regulations of the State Sports Complex, 'Ready for Work and for the Defense of the Rumanian People's Republic.'"

The Resolution of the Council of Ministers, published in the R.P.R. Official Bulletin of April 27, 1950, provides that ". . . The Ministry of Public Education will take steps for the adoption, prior to May 1, 1950, of state programs for physical education, in schools of all kinds, to the provisions of the Complex 'Ready for Work and for the Defense of the Rumanian People's Republic.'" Article 5 of the Resolution specifies that ". . . all typical school program rules for the methodical teaching of gymnastics and sports, established for physical culture and sports collectives, shall be adopted, and provisions for their printed issuance in large editions shall be made."

The "Complex" referred to is the Rumanian translation of the "Complex of Sports Rules" that constitutes the basic program for physical education in the Soviet Union, and which is commonly known as the "G.T.O." As *Scanteia Tineretului* for June 7, 1949, explains, these regulations "comprise the simplest sports contests, accessible to the great mass of the citizens." They are divided into three categories, the first of which was established in 1931, in the U.S.S.R. The regulations for the "State Sports Complex," set forth the aims of this "Complex." In addition to "the education of the workers in the spirit of true patriotism and of proletarian morale," and in "boundless" love for the Soviet Union and "The Great Leader" Stalin, its task is "to combat cosmopolitanism in sports, which takes the form of servility toward the decadent sports of the West."

Whereupon the regulations proceed to set forth organizational details:

"The Complex 'Ready for Work and for Defense' is constructed on the principle of the continuous multilateral physical education of the population, beginning at the age of 15, and is divided into the following grades:

a) 'Be prepared for Work and Defense,' whose aim is the correct physical development of young boys and girls;
b) 'Ready for Work and Defense,' First Grade, whose aim is the multilateral physical development of the workers . . .;
c) 'Ready for Work and Defense,' Second Grade, whose aim is to assure a high degree of multilateral physical development of the workers and to contribute to the acquisition of proficiency in sports."

Then the regulations go on to provide a series of tests and rules for obtaining the insignia, and the rights and duties of those attaining these distinctions. The emblem may be withdrawn from those guilty of certain deviations "incompatible with the dignity of a citizen of the R.P.R." or with "sports morale."

Under such regulations, how are sports practiced in the R.P.R. nowadays?

Certainly the most popular sport is association football (there are some 5,000 clubs in operation). In *The Economist* for July 11, 1953 we find a comprehensive report thereon. The article opens with a quotation from *Scanteia* to the effect that even in the first division "games have in general been played on a low technical level." The explanation, according to the R.P.R. sheet, can mean but that "the remnants of bourgeois sports practices have given rise to unhealthy manifestations which have nothing in common with the new sport, or the healthy spirit of hundreds of thousands of young sportsmen educated by the democratic people's regime." The article adds: "These *unhealthy manifestations* are not, as one might innocently suppose, just foul play, engaging the referee in fisticuffs or throwing things at him, but *the low political level . . . in the activities of the players in the social field.*"

"The behaviour of the clubs themselves" causes *Scanteia* much grief: "for it seems that they are set on winning their matches. At all costs they are determined to exceed the norm; and they therefore seek, by means of all sorts of extravagant promises, to entice the best players away from the opposing teams. Such practices are apparently not in themselves so bad," but, as *Scanteia* points out, the "fluctuations and transfers" take place "on an unprincipled basis' which has given the star players the impression that, for them everything is permissible on the football field." And club managements "in their impetuosity for victory" "at all costs" rush to the defense of the culprits. Moreover, "Party and State activists with responsible posts" who happen to be on a club board of directors, or who are football fans, "have lost their objectivity and political clarity, and have taken up a partisan and inadmissible attitude in covering up and even encouraging these unsporting practices."

"Have they forgotten," asks *Scanteia*, that their duty is "to combat the spirit of competition between teams?" Have they forgotten that they must be "guided by Stalinist teaching concerning Socialist competition?" Furthermore "the lack of ideological vigilance" of many of the activists on the directing boards of football clubs is so great that they allow themselves to be "influenced by so-called 'sports technicians' and 'stars' soaked in bourgeois ideology, to such a degree that they resort to unprincipled interventions" in their favour, and "tolerate the reintroduction of the competitive spirit of the teams, which is completely contrary to the spirit of collaboration and reciprocal aid that is a specific part of the Party line and spirit in sports matters."

Scanteia made responsible both the Central Commission of the Sports Federation (CCFS) and the individual sports club managements for this sorry state of affairs. The communist sheet recommended, too, that a first-class player develop "the well-developed conscience of a patriotic citizen with a high political and ideological standard." And the British magazine cites the revealing argument with which *Scanteia* closed its tirade: "The absence of close coordination between sports education and political education represents a danger to the work of the communist education of the great mass of young people."

The regime realized from the very beginning the need for finding a more or less adequately qualified personnel to replace throughout the administration the officials destined to be purged. To satisfy this need, the Law on Education provides the creation of "special schools and courses." Article 26 of the law states: "There will be set up in certain centers, for the workers, special two-year schools. These schools are designed to give students a preparation equivalent to secondary schooling. Those who successfully pass the entrance examinations may become pupils. Pupils of these schools will be taken out of the production process. They will be supported throughout the period of their student status by the respective Ministries (departments) and enterprises. Graduates of these schools may enter admission examinations for higher education (universities)."

Article 31 provides a still more radical innovation: "To answer the urgent needs of the country's economic and social life, schools may be set up with a duration of studies shorter than that provided in the present law, under conditions that shall be established by special laws."

As a consequence, all kinds of so-called special schools have already been created, so that, by now, an important number of posts in the administration, especially responsible ones, are held by graduates of these novel institutions.

As early as 1947 special high school evening courses were introduced for the benefit of public servants. The reason was obvious enough. Extensive purges had already seriously depleted the civil service. Existing laws and regulations which, at that stage, could not have well been ignored or changed without gravely diminishing the regime's ostensible position, required candidates for certain administrative posts to be at least high school graduates. The need was urgent: trusted minions of the regime had to be provided with the requisite diplomas without delay. All too many of them were barely literate, hardly able to spell. The answer was found in these three to four weeks' cramming courses.

According to classical Marxist doctrine, class consciousness constitutes the basis of political consciousness. To this Lenin adds that, in order to develop political consciousness, class consciousness must be aroused through education, for otherwise we have but economic insight on a purely corporative level. Hence the interest displayed by the communists in party schooling. Such schooling of a "partisan" character is provided for every echelon, from the base organization of individual enterprises, through raion and region party committees, and on up to the Central Committee, constituting the so-called "links" in party education. At the lowest level are the discussion circles that include all party members, and constitute a general initiation phase. Immediately above are the study circles, where various political problems of a precise nature are delved into exhaustively. There such works as *The History of the Communist (Bolshevik) Party of the USSR*, Stalin's biography, Stalin's *Economic Problems of the USSR*, and the *Decisions of the Nineteenth Congress of the Soviet Union's Communist Party* are dealt with at length. During the 1954–55 school year, the *History of the Rumanian Workers' Party* study circles were for the first time organized. Party evening schools also come under this general heading. At the highest level are the one-year party schools and the party universities.

The regional party schools (one-year courses) are designed to train cadres for the regional party apparatus, for raion committees, and for party organizations of various sorts of a local nature. Such high-ranking institutions as the "Stefan Gheorghiu" party school and the "A. A. Jdanov" school of social sciences (both have courses covering three years) rank as higher educational establishments. The "Stefan Gheorghiu" school has a journalism section, a "finishing course" for secretaries of raional and city party committees (one year), as well as a four-year course requiring no attendance. In addition to the above, there are "night universities" for the study of Marxism-Leninism (set in 1949–1950), of which one operates in conjunction with the R.P.R. Academy.

The student body is formed of party members, party candidates, and even non-party individuals. According to *Lupta de Clasă* of October 1954, there were a total of 328,301 students attending these party schools, of whom 233,361 were party members, 4,855 candidates, and 90,105 non-party individuals. The faculties are composed of specially trained and qualified personnel, selected from the "active of propagandists," whose main concern, in addition to a thorough familiarity with the prescribed classics, must be effectiveness as propagandists and constant agreement with the current party line.

While in general the study material and methods remain the same, it is interesting to note that during 1954–1955 the accent was on Lenin's works and on individual study (though the latter had hitherto been deplored officially as "bourgeois").

"The reform of education," observed one high party official in *Scanteia* of September 16, 1948, "introduces structural changes also in the institutions of higher learning."

It most certainly does. Though the law formally states that institutions of higher education "are designed to prepare cadres for the teaching personnel of medium and especially higher education, higher cadres of specialists and researchers in the various branches of science" (article 17), in reality they are intended simply to turn out "cadres" thoroughly imbued with Marxism-Leninism for the state apparatus, and production technicians. As one of the top-flight exponents of the regime, wrote in the magazine *For Enduring Peace and for Popular Democracy*, September 30, 1949, "The envisaged purpose of the new education is the formation of trained cadres corresponding to the tasks that fall to the constructors of socialist society."

In order to assure the unchallenged primacy of the communist doctrine in education, eliminating any "ideological competition" of "bourgeois" origin, the law provides in article 20 that "all higher education will comprise minimum analytical programs (i.e. curricula), obligatory and unified, prescribed for all chairs of the same specialty." And article 21 elaborates: "For each discipline (subject), students will be provided with required minimum manuals and treatises." It is hardly necessary to point out that such a system eliminates all possibility for instructors to present in their courses any personal ideas, resulting from the studies undertaken. Furthermore, even personal interpretations or individual presentations, at variance formally in any way, in any field whatsoever, are explicitly prohibited. In other words, the most stringent and restrictive norms are formally imposed, from which the slightest deviation is beforehand expressly branded as heretical.

With Marxist-Leninist doctrine supreme in every department, and with anything remotely resembling Western influences carefully eliminated, what is the current aspect of higher education in the R.P.R.?

According to the decision of the Education Ministry, dated October 15, 1948, ". . . Higher education comprises the following institutions: 1) universities, and 2) higher institutions of learning." (Article 1.) "Universities comprise several faculties (schools), and the latter may have a number

of sections each. Universities are under the authority of the Ministry of
Public Education." (Article 2.) "Institutions of higher learning shall have
one or more faculties (or departments); the faculties may have several
sections each. Institutes of higher learning are under the authority either
of the Ministry of Public Education or other Ministries (government departments)." (Article 3.) "Universities and institutes of higher learning
will be headed by rectors, and their component faculties by deans." (Article 4.)

Aside from Bucarest, there are universities in the cities of Iash, Timishoara, and Cluj, the latter having also a University where courses are
taught in the Hungarian language. As for the Institutes of university rank,
they may be found, in addition to the university cities, in various industrial, mining, and agricultural centers and in other localities, where the
students can be given the necessary practical training.

The stress on technical learning has led to a continual increase in the
number of specialized technical institutes, which have come to supplant
what were formerly integral parts of the universities, that is, the component schools or faculties. During the 1954–1955 school year, according
to official figures issued, 36.6 per cent of the total body of students of
university rank were registered with the polytechnic and technical industrial institutes, 24.6 per cent with the higher pedagogical institutes, 12.7
with the agronomical and forestry institutes, 15.3 with the medical, physical education, and pharmaceutical institutes, and 2.6 with the art institutes. This excessive specialization was from the very beginning the characteristic trait of higher education under the regime of popular democracy.
It was then hailed by the communist press as "a great clarification of
higher schooling." In reality, of course, it works to the obvious detriment
of what is commonly accepted to be a general culture, to say nothing
of that which in the West is described as a liberal education.

But let there be no mistake in regard to the results. True, the new educational reform deliberately aims at the prevention of a general culture in the
Western sense. In exchange, all graduates of university rank in the R.P.R.
are provided with a deep insight and understanding of Marxism-Leninism,
intended to replace advantageously such a "bourgeois and imperialist"
background.

To regulate the awarding of university degrees and titles, a whole series
of ministerial directives and decisions have been successively provided. The
final result of this progressive manipulation has been that today higher

education in the Rumanian People's Republic has an aspect identical with that in the Soviet Union.

What of the titles themselves? A directive issed by the Council of Ministers, published in the R.P.R. Official Bulletin of January 17, 1950, provides that: ". . . In order to receive the diploma (awarding the title) of engineer, physician, professor, architect, chemist, biologist, jurist, etc., graduates of higher institutions of learning must pass a state examination." (Article 1.)

"The state examination may be taken by graduates of institutions of higher learning who have passed all final yearly examinations and have filed within the required term their diploma work or project." (Article 3.)

Candidates may present themselves for this examination at most twice, within a term of two years. Those who fail to pass "remain in the field of labor with only the title of graduates." (Article 12.)

It is obvious that the required state examination is in effect the equivalent of the former master's degree (license) with, however, a greater emphasis on the precise professional field.

Article 6 indicates the nature of the state examination: "The state examination consists of the following tests:

a) a test concerning the bases of Marxism-Leninism;
b) an oral test in the basic specialty of the graduate. The candidate will be questioned about his diploma thesis or project;
c) an oral test in some specialty selected by the candidate and connected with his basic subject;
d) a pedagogy test for candidates who intend to enter the didactic cadres."

The enumeration indicates unambiguously that Marxism-Leninism is the principal required subject at all categories of examinations, whatever the candidate's chosen field may be. Those who wish to specialize further are provided by the law with doctorate courses, which may be taken by "any graduate of higher learning who successfully passes the entrance examination. The number of available doctorate seats will be established by the Council of Ministers, according to necessities. The duration of doctorate courses will be three years." (Article 23.)

The decrees Nos. 13, 14, and 15 of the Presidium of the Grand National Assembly, published in the Official Bulletin of January 17, 1950, reorganize this sector of higher education, destined "to prepare cadres of high scientific qualifications."

Decree No. 13 provides that, "with the aim of preparing the cadres of specialists and researchers necessary for the institutions of higher learning and scientific institutions of the R.P.R., the educational (academic) degree of 'aspirant' is hereby created." (Article 1.)

This "aspirancy" is organized alongside universities, educational institutes, or scientific research institutes of the R.P.R. Academy, on the basis of a decision of the Council of Ministers. That directive will also decide ". . . the specialties wherein aspirants will be prepared, as well as the number of places for each special field." (Article 2.)

Originally the duration of the courses for "aspirancy" was set at three years. The Decree No. 241/1953 issued by the Presidium of the Grand National Assembly created three forms of "aspirancy"—a) requiring attendance, with a duration of three years; b) requiring no attendance, with a duration of four years; and c) reduced to one year, specially designed for members of the teaching profession. Graduates of schools of higher educational level may qualify as "candidates of science" without formal inclusion into the "aspirancy" system.

Aspirants who finish their courses and successfully defend their thesis will be awarded the title of "Candidate in Science." Admission to aspirancy is based on a competitive examination, to which only persons of not more than forty years of age and who possesses a diploma of higher learning may present themselves. "The admission competition will consist of the following tests:

a) the bases of Marxism-Leninism;
b) the selected specialized subject;
c) the Russian language."

Throughout the duration of the courses candidates receive state scholarships and are required to carry out a didactic activity. Those who succeed in obtaining the title of science candidate will be required to work for five years in one of the institutions of higher learning or of research.

Seeing that many of the university professors and lecturers lack the doctorate, they are thus provided with the opportunity to "qualify." That such is indeed the purpose of the legislators is made clear by Decree No. 14, which sets up special conditions for university professors and lecturers.

Decree No. 15 organized the Doctorate "as a degree of learning." The required course of studies is three years, devoted to the preparation of the thesis. Candidates for the doctorate are to take part in an entrance examination; they must be either "science candidates" or holders of "an equivalent title from abroad, recognized by the Ministry of Education." The entrance examination comprises tests similar to that for "aspirancy."

The above review of legislative provisions governing "aspirancy" makes it once again obvious that the deliberate intention is to regulate everything pertaining to higher education, both by general provisions and by others of an exceptional nature. In other words, while tomorrow's generations are provided with one regime, today's favorites are exempted therefrom. Such indeed is the case of the organization of the doctor's degree. For, once the objective conditions for this degree are established, a special article intervenes to set up an exception. This is article 10 which states: "The Ministry of Education may likewise confer the title of doctor on persons who, though they may not fulfill the conditions set forth in the present decree, nevertheless have to their credit some original work of great scientific, literary, or artistic value." Knowing that the value of any production is judged according to partisan standards, we see that any favorites of the present regime can be made to fit the required conditions to be awarded doctors' degrees.

These "normal" steps in higher education could not cope with the urgent need for trusted administrative personnel. In order to fill responsible posts with devoted partisans, whose qualifications are flagrantly inadequate, a series of temporary laws have set up special "short-order" courses and exceptional conditions of promotion.

After all, no matter how the academic field is reorganized, and no matter what special facilities are afforded to those favored by the party for responsible positions, a certain intellectual ability and a certain minimum basic schooling are indispensable even in the acquisition of the new type of academic titles. But corners must be cut wherever this is at all possible.

Thus, on the authority of Decree No. 388, published in the *Official Gazette* of October 11, 1949, the title of engineer may be conferred upon certain technicians of a standing comparable to that of a foreman, who have eight years' experience in their particular specialty and who can pass a test. The title may also be conferred on persons "presenting evidence of at least five years' practice or activity in technical services or bureaus." It goes without saying that the requisite qualifications also include evidence of the candidate's status in the party. And, as is also but to be expected, the examination comprises the fundamentals of Marxism-Leninism and of the candidate's special subjects—in that order. The organization of this transitory schooling and its very nature make it particularly difficult to classify in any scheme of education. The fact that, on one hand, this category of schooling does not require any certificate of prior studies while, on the other hand, the titles it confers are equivalent to academic degrees, emphasizes its ambiguous character. These diploma mills may therefore be considered a distinct section of the field of education.

It is not necessary to enter into details or to examine the many kinds of schools that have been set up or projected to cover the section. Something, however, must be said of the "two years' faculties for workers." *Contemporanul* of December 30, 1949, stated that "these special courses for workers are intended to form, within a short period, exploitation engineers of the worthiest elements among workers in the various enterprises." They function "alongside the institutes of higher learning of similar types, in the university centers."

There are also special "accelerated" law schools in operation, set up to provide the necessary personnel for the various courts, that is, the so-called people's assessors, who, though lacking legal training of a formal nature, form the majority of all quorums of judges. Such short-order law schools have been set up in Bucarest, Iash, and Cluj, the one in Cluj having a section operating in the Hungarian language for the benefit of the Magyar Autonomous Region."

An entire network of special evening courses, paralleling the respective university departments, has been established for the benefit of would-be students employed in the "field of labor" who, in addition to being high school graduates, are "recommended by the enterprise or institution where they are employed, upon advice from the union committee." Graduates of these evening schools, whose courses generally cover a four years' period, have "the same rights as graduates of day courses." In other words, university-type diplomas are made available to trusted party members "on the job," in order to fill the regime's very real need for reliable and devoted "production cadres."

For the formation of "cadres" of another type—party activitists and party agitators—there is the "Stefan Gheorghiu Higher Party School" which functions under the direct control of the Central Committee of the

Rumanian Communist party. This "party university," to which admissions are made on recommendation by the Central Committee on the basis of "requisite training and record in party work and of activity in the social field," has become, so to speak, a reservoir of party functionaries for central and regional agencies, as well as for the party press and other propaganda media. The courses provided are the history of the Soviet Union's Communist party, universal history, the history of the R.P.R., political economy, dialectic and historical materialism, international relations, political and economic geography, the workings of the regime of popular democracy and of the party, Rumanian language and literature and, of course, Russian. The diploma issued to graduates is the equivalent of a university diploma.

The "A. A. Jdanov" School likewise operates in direct conjunction with the Central Committee. It is designed to provide "theoretical cadres for the party's central institutions, for the conduct of party schooling, for scientific work at the center and region organs, heads and teachers for party schools, lectors and lecturers for State higher educational establishments, editors for ideological magazines, and leadership for the propaganda sections of central publications," according to the authoritative *Lupta de Clasa* (issue for September 1953). The courses are almost the same as those of the "Stefan Gheorghiu" Institute, except for those given in the third—and last—year, which are more highly specialized.

It is not surprising to find that all this para-educational apparatus is set up for the exclusive benefit of trusted party members and presumptive recruits. The discrimination, however, does not end there. We have already pointed out that deliberate discrimination exists throughout the field of medium and high school education. This is even more evident in higher education where prospective students are screened with the utmost care. Indeed it is next to impossible for anyone whose social and family background is not "acceptable" from the point of view of the communist regime to register as a student with any university department, let alone to graduate. An extensive biography must be furnished by all candidates, including the answers to a most exhaustive questionnaire of more than one hundred separate questions. Scholastic merit plays no role. The stress is laid on recommendations from the unions (the UTM has the weightiest say in the matter), on commendable activities (for instance in the Pioneer organization), and on social origin. The purpose, officially avowed, is to exclude so far as possible students of a "bourgeois-landowning" back-ground. *Scanteia* of November 18, 1948, made this absolutely clear in an article devoted to the subject of entrance examinations at the universi-ties: ". . . But, aside from these (the sons of workers and of working peasants), certain well-to-do misses and young masters, who imagine that . . . education is what it was in the past, registered for the entrance ex-aminations. Undoubtedly the new examination commission will know how to select true talents and those candidates who are truly devoted to the cause of the people."

It is the official educational policy to "homogenize" not only the student body, but also the courses provided in the universities and institutes of university rank. That is to say, as in the case of medium or high schools, the tendency is to introduce "sole authorized manuals" for every branch of science, for each separate subject, all based squarely on Marxist-Leninist foundations. As the authoritative *Lupta de Clasa* (Series V, XXX: 3) put it, "The Law for the Reform of Public Education . . . introduced the principle of compulsory curricula and sole manuals for university courses, corresponding to the scientific level demanded by the socialist or-ganization that is being built in our country."

The most practical solution was found in simply translating into Ru-manian the corresponding works used in the Soviet Union and imposing them as the sole authorized textbooks. Professor Salageanu, in his capacity as the Rector of the "C. I. Parhon" University of Bucarest, stated in *Gazeta Invatamantului* of November 13, 1954, that "the specialized ma-terial translated from the Russian language are of great help to the pro-fessors and students." He marred the effect of this remarkable bit of understatement by adding that a total of 57 courses and textbooks had been translated and made available for the R.P.R. higher educational system during the year 1952, that the number for 1953 was 63, and that a further 76 were "planified" for the year 1954.

An important role in this regard is played by the collection of manuals for university courses, published by the Institute of Rumanian-Soviet Studies of the R.P.R. Academy. The most recent index of titles issued in translation from Russian during the 1947–1954 period comprises about 6,000 works, covering the field of science and technology. The works have been issued either in the collection mentioned above or as parts of various separate series.

In their lectures, courses, and seminars, members of university faculties must, of course, hew close to the Marxist-Leninist line. There is no room for any opinion that, from the point of view of the prescribed doctrine, is even remotely or potentially controversial. At every turn, whether in relation to medicine, history, philosophy, architecture, or mathematics, the absolute superiority of the accepted Soviet authorities must be stressed *ex cathedra*, while any divergent doctrine or theory evolved in the Western world must be vigorously denounced as backward, tendentious, or wrong.

More than anyone else, university professors, instructors, and lecturers must step warily. They are watched closely and constantly for the slightest sign of deviation. Seeing that even at this late date the great majority is constituted by men and women educated and trained in Western universities, or at the very least imbued with the Western ways, theories, and practices that used to prevail in the academic field of pre-communist Rumania, they are particularly vulnerable. They are cursed with the original sin of heresy by definition. An inadvertent slip brings swift and merciless retribution. No matter how great a devotion they might show to the party, no matter how exalted their academic standing, they are publicly brought to book by the party's ideological watchdogs. Whereupon they must perform public penance, disavowing themselves in an orgy of "self-criticism" in writing, never sure whether this will be acceptable and bring about absolution, or whether it might spell dismissal and final disgrace.

The roster of intellectuals who have at one time or another during the last ten years been stretched on the Procrustean bed of communist ideology for public opprobrium is an impressive one. It reads, indeed, like a veritable academic *Who's Who*. It covers every domain of intellectual and professional endeavor. It includes members of the R.P.R. Academy, former R.P.R. envoys abroad, former members of the R.P.R. government, and Rumanian savants of universal stature.

The initial denunciation of "deviationism" is apt to come literally out of the blue. It may take the form of a bitterly critical article in some specialty review, written either by a member of the editorial staff or by a faculty colleague of the "accused" (who is apt to be raked over the coals for heresy himself soon thereafter); it may come as a resolution of some student union or the UTM; or it may be initiated during the discussions at some congress or convention. No matter in what form it comes, the man or woman under indictment is not considered to be a "defendant" in the usual sense of the word. There is no defense available in the sense of an explanation. There is, above all, no defense conceivable in the sense of attempting to prove one's expressed views are the right ones. The accused must plead guilty, must beat his or her breast with a loud show of repentance, must admit the "error," proclaim unambiguously that the accusers were right. Controversial discussions are inacceptable. Of course, Soviet authority is the ultimate one, and opposing Western views are wrong. Humble pie must be consumed on the rostrum, abject promises of future conformity must be made in the forum.

Here are a few instances of the official attitude toward various fields of academic learning, as well as some examples of what can befall those educators found guilty of heresy.

As quoted in *Universul* of September 18, 1948, Academician Professor P. Constantinescu-Iash, in his capacity as President of the Bucarest Institute for Universal History, laid down the law for teaching history at universities in the following terms: "Marxist-Leninist teachings, as formulated by Marx, Engels, Lenin, and Stalin, are the best directives for all men of science, and, therefore, for our historians." And, according to a survey issued by the R.P.R. Academy's Institute of History and Philosophy in 1950, the principal task of Rumanian historians is "to acquire Marxist-Leninist culture and the conquests of Soviet science, in order to assure the development of historical science in the R.P.R." On the authority of Gheorghiu-Dej, it behooves Rumanian teachers of history to show that the Roman conquest and occupation of Dacia (which gave the Latin character to Rumania) amounted to a mere episode of imperialist invasion, looting, and exploitation, and that, furthermore, "for over a thousand years the territory of our country was subjected to incursions and depredations by the Roman conquerors, by the Turkish invaders, and then by the 'civilized' imperialists, French, British, and German." As the overthrow of the Roman Empire marked the earliest "liberation" of the provinces that were to become Rumania, so, of course, the crushing of the Axis by the sole might of the Soviet armies heralded the "liberation" of Rumania in our own days. The prescribed line of endeavor for both historians and archaeologists is to play down the Latinity of Rumanian origins, stressing instead their alleged Slavonic character. As another R.P.R. academician and university professor, L. Rautu, put it, ". . . the theory of the Rumanian people's latinity has been used to isolate Rumania from her neighbor and natural ally, and to create scientific support for the expansionist plans of the Western powers, particularly those of France." The "natural ally" being, of course, Russia, all this must be changed from now on. Woe to those who might run counter to these approved views. The matter was summed up by yet another academician, Professor Mihai Roller, writing in *Contemporanul* of October 28, 1949: "Some still display remnants of the old theory which claims that the scholar may withdraw to the study of archaeological finds of four thousand years ago, estranging himself from everyday struggles. Such an attitude means to break with the people, to break with the present struggle of the people for culture." Putting the matter in a nutshell, Professor Roller concluded, "We must be fighters in science, not mere narrators of 'objective' reports," because, in his own words, "to study history thus means to consider this science as a weapon of the ideological front, placed in the service of the working class, in the service of socialist construction."

This trend is a general one, and it is constantly accentuated. Writing in *Contemporanul* of December 31, 1954, Professor Traian Savulescu, President of the R.P.R. Academy, announced: "In the field of historical and economic-philosophical research, the R.P.R. Academy will carry out, during the year 1955, a more sustained activity in behalf of the study and application of the all-conquering Marxist-Leninist teachings."

As for the teaching of philosophy, an authoritative article in the magazine *For a Lasting Peace, for a People's Democracy*, of September 30, 1949, stated unambiguously that "Reactionary philosophy has been ousted from our universities, together with its exponents." One practitioner who fell afoul of the party line in this field was Academician Professor Mihai Ralea, former R.P.R. minister to Washington. Notwithstanding his most assiduous efforts to conform, he was denounced in print by a colleague, L. Rautu, as follows: ". . . the psychology course of Academician Mihai Ralea contains numerous mistakes in the presentation of the Marxist-Leninist point of view . . . the course still bears strong traces of cosmopolitanism and bourgeois objectivism." Since then Professor Ralea has gone to great lengths to rehabilitate himself in the eyes of the educational authorities of the R.P.R. The first of a series of articles on American psychology he published in the R.P.R. Academy's periodical *Studii* (III/1952) bears the revealing title "Aspects of the American Cannibalistic Psychology," and the second (II/1953) is titled still more elegantly "The Amoral Aspect of Psychology in the Phase of Capitalist Putrefaction."

The social sciences, as might be expected, have become increasingly important, this being the domain in which Marxist-Leninist teachings are of particular significance. In one year alone—1953–1954—thirteen new chairs were established in this field of study in the universities and institutes of university rank. The manner in which the social sciences must be taught, as well as the distribution of component subject matters came under review by no less an authority than the Central Committee of the Rumanian Communist Party, which in August 1953 issued a special decision reorganizing the social science chairs throughout the higher educational establishments. An authoritative article in *Studii* (July–September 1954), reviewing the results of the first year of this reorganized academic sector, specified that "a permanent task of the chairs of social sciences is to participate actively in the struggle caried on in the institutions of higher learning in behalf of a materialist science and for the extirpation of cosmopolite elements from education."

With regard to another discipline, philology, of which almost all prominent practitioners have been officially condemned at one time or another for the sin of "cosmopolitanism" or another unforgivable heresy, we shall quote without comments a statement by Academician Professor C. Balmus, holder of the chair of Classic Philology at the Bucarest University, as published in *Romania Libera* of October 29, 1949: "From my very first contact with Soviet Science, I understood that everything I had learned in the bourgeois schools of my own country and abroad was but a collection of falsehoods and errors. I understood too that in order to advance in the way of true scientific research I must first, as Lenin said, throw into the trash-can of history the errors, false conceptions, and faulty interpretations contracted in the backward world of bourgeois 'science.' I learned, and I still learn with each passing day, to renounce the old habits of thought and investigation. I learned, and I am still learning each day, that the sole method of scientific research is the method of dialectic and historic materialism, which opens in all domains the most brilliant perspectives, and which stimulates the spirit in the most fruitful manner. On comparing in my own field, the history of Greco-Roman civilization, the results of bourgeois science with those of Soviet science, I gained the unshakable conviction that Soviet science is the most advanced in the world. The bourgeois so-called science has placed itself in the service of the trusts, in the service of the Anglo-American cliques that push toward war, that dream only of ways to prolong the inhuman exploitation of the working masses. Thanks to the aid received from Soviet science, my eyes were opened to the immense danger of cosmopolitanism and of servile grovelling before 'western science,' that ideological tool of Anglo-American imperialism. Lastly, by reading the works of Soviet scholars, I deepened and strengthened my conviction that there is no such thing as an apolitical science situated above classes and peoples. True science is realized starting from the positions of the working class."

Turning now to the positive or exact sciences, where the uninformed might imagine there is really no room for political ideology, we shall quote again from the authoritative *Contemporanul*, in whose issues for February 17 and 24 and March 3, 1950, a series of articles analyzed the "problem of courses in higher technical education." Andrei Mihailescu, the author begins by justifying his critical study: "To discuss what is being taught at our technical institutes and the manner of those teachings is not, as some short-sighted people might think, a purely specialized matter."

"We are therefore directly interested," he goes on, "in the kind of knowledge the students are to acquire, in the spirit in which this knowledge is imparted to them, and, finally, in the manner in which that knowledge is connected with the problems of our economy and whether there truly exists a guarantee that it will serve for the construction of socialism and not against it. There are still some people who imagine that the technical field is a domain where the party spirit and the class content of the manner in which problems are posed and solved, do not apply. If you speak to them of such things, they shrug their shoulders and reply with naïveté (real or feigned) that, after all, a given material will always bend or give under certain stresses and loads, whether the phenomenon occurs under a capitalist or a socialist regime. Likewise that a motor works according to certain principles that apply in either hypothesis, that a certain industrial chemical preparation is put together according to an established formula in both cases, and so forth. Such an argument in this case, if it is not manifestly ill-intentioned, is certainly childish."

Having thus stated the prescribed position, and following the equally prescribed anathema pronounced against cosmopolitanism which, ". . . in countries that in the views of the imperialists should have remained in a semi-colonial state, tends to transform science and technique into loud advertising, into a low commercialization," the writer proceeds to analyze a number of university textbooks for technical subjects.

The course of Elements of Public Utilities by Engineer Professor Emil Blitz comes under his displeasure. ". . . We shall first discover here that servile grovelling before the West. The author deals with various public works installations in Boston (U.S.A.), Frankfurt-am-Main . . . But, if the abundance of examples, names, and procedures inspired by the advertising prospects of the imperialist trusts cram the manual of Professor Emil Blitz, we must take a candle to seek out data that show use of the immense experience of the Soviet Union. It is manifest that, willy-nilly, nationalist-bourgeois tendencies go hand-in-hand with cosmopolitanism." In the end the reviewer relents to the extent of admitting that the incriminated manual of Professor Blitz shows evidence of improvement, ". . . especially as the final lessons become increasingly guided by Soviet experience."

Yet if certain courses show "improvement," those of other professors indicate a too deeply rooted bourgeois education. Such is the case of Professor H. Teodoru's course: ". . . Here the traits criticized above, and which can be traced throughout the lectures covering several years, derive from an old professorial activity and engineering practice. More than that, the lecturer rejects the criticisms made by his own students or else takes a trifling attitude toward them, thus showing that the cosmopolite and nationalist-bourgeois attitude is deeply ingrown in the teacher's mentality."

Criticisms of other courses are in the same vein. Thus, ". . . Engineer Borneanu, in the preface to his course on Reinforced Concrete, does not even mention the Soviet experience, but waxes lyrical in his praises of Western capitalist technique." And in the course on Hydraulics of Engineer Dorin Pavel: "Throughout the course . . . American specialists, English and French specialists keep cropping up as though they were at home. Nowhere is any Soviet research even mentioned."

So Andrei Mihailescu reaches the sorrowful conclusion: "We shall never succeed in constructing a socialist industry if we seek to apply the technical rules of engineers of American and British trusts."

Even mathematics are not exempt from criticisms of a similar character. Two of the most noted mathematicians of the R.P.R., both members of the Academy and, oddly enough, both former R.P.R. chiefs of mission abroad, Professors Grigore Moisil and S. Stoilov, have come under fire for alleged deviations. Other notable holders of university chairs who have also come under criticism for their courses include such names and specialties as Professor R. Codreanu (biology), Professor Dorin Pavel (hydraulics, construction materials), and Professor Florica Bagdasar, former Minister of Public Health under the present communist regime (psychiatric medicine). The list can be continued indefinitely: it is still growing as these lines are being written. We shall conclude the list ourselves, however, with what is probably the most unbelievable instance of all: the case of Dr. N. Blatt, Professor of Ophthalmology at the Medical Institute of Timishoara, and director of the *Ophthalmological Review*. The occasion to censure Professor Blatt's activity was seized upon by the R.P.R. Academy, to set an example and to lay down the norms that must regulate all scientific activity in the country thenceforth. Here are the pertinent quotations from the Report of the Medical Science section of the R.P.R. Academy, published in *Romania Libera* of June 30, 1949:

". . . It (the *Ophthalmological Review*) publishes articles especially in French and English, maintaining the old bourgeois-landowning tradition of discounting the national language . . . It is clear that such a cosmopolite position, being antipatriotic, cannot be accepted by the men of science who are close to the people.

". . . The sole aim of the *Ophthalmological Review* is manifestly that of propagating cosmopolitanism, the deadly enemy of science; to propagate dependence upon and subservience toward the decadent bourgeois culture of the West. And this, in order to make the readers believe that the most important achievements in the realm of ophthalmology are due exclusively to the science of capitalist countries.

". . . It is small wonder that the cosmopolite attitude of national nihilism of the *Ophthalmological Review* and of its director wins approval and encouragement in Western imperialist circles. The evidence may be found in a review which came out in the 'American Journal of Ophthalmology' for April 1949. This American magazine, which pretends to be purely 'scientific', is not at all ashamed to publish a purely political review concerning the *Ophthalmological Review*. In it, satisfaction is expressed because the majority of articles are in French and English.

". . . A critical analysis of the *Ophthalmological Review* reveals at the same time how servility toward the imperialist West finds its most appropriate medium in men who lack patriotism and constructive spirit—men who move within the narrow circle of certain mercantile and career interests. The director of the *Review*, Dr. N. Blatt, represents the typical scientist of this kind."

The end result of this "conclusive evidence" of harmful activity on the part of the medical journal, its director was branded as one who had ". . . proved through his activity that he is unworthy to educate young people," and a distinguished career came to an abrupt end.

The intellectual and spiritual degradation of the people involved in this system needs no elaboration. It is the exact opposite of academic freedom, of candor, of true intellectual integrity.

What are the results of the academic system described above? With the accent in every course, in every discipline, placed heavily on Marxist-Leninist "teachings," the rest, that is the student's chosen field of specialization is provided only in its barest essentials. Examinations and tests bearing on the subjects as such have become a mere formality, and an absolute minimum of knowledge is considered satisfactory, provided the student is proficient in the elements of Marxist-Leninist dogma. It is more important to have a good standing in the Union of Working Youth than to be thoroughly familiar with, say, the principles of electronics or obstetrics.

Much ado is made of the "festive atmosphere" reigning at examinations. As described by *Scanteia Tineretului*, organ of the Central Committee of the UTM, in the issue of September 13, 1949, "the hall is adorned with pictures and slogans. The candidates take a place before a table draped with red cloth, on which a vase with flowers stands. Present in the hall are representatives of the Rumanian Workers' Party educational section, of the Union of Working Youth committee, of the faculty, and of the teachers' union."

In this inspiring atmosphere, the university faculty must strive, like any other "workers' collective", to meet the quota, to surpass the planned norm. As the gang of laborers is expected to move so many cubic meters of earth, as a team of tractor drivers must plough a prescribed area in a given time, so must the professors turn out a satisfactory percentage of graduates. The examiners are, on the one hand, careful not to give bad marks to any candidate who is well thought of by the party organizations or whose parents are highly rated by the regime; on the other hand, seeing the competition that must exist between the various departments, they must do their utmost to secure success for the largest possible number of their own students.

The press is most insistent on educational results, and anxious to register the proportion of promoted candidates, proclaiming it as yet another "success" of the regime of popular democracy.

Now and again, however, the system backfires with such devastating effects that even the party press must sit up and take adverse notice.

This, indeed, happens oftener than one might expect, for there is hardly an article to be found in any communist publication, on any aspect of life in the R.P.R. that does not show an odd contrast between the optimism of proclaimed "successes" and dour criticism of observed "failures" and "deficiencies." In matters relating to the academic field, as in every other domain, the criticism is never leveled at the system itself, but always at the manner of its practical application. It is only the highest authorities in the Kremlin that may reverse themselves—and the rest of the communist-dominated sphere—on any issue of doctrine. For the R.P.R., as for the other "people's democracies," the current party line is absolutely right by definition; only the interpretation or execution thereof may be criticized.

And so, every so often, we come across an article like that in *Gazeta Invatamantului* of December 11, 1954, which sourly denounces the notion held by "certain university students" who, though their record of studies is bad, "consider that their healthy origins (as sons of workers) gives them the right to be advanced without learning." The article even goes to the length of chiding certain UTM organizations for failing to take a stand on this matter. We hasten to add, however, that the writer of that article was herself a secretary of the Union of Working Youth Central Committee, by name Cornelia Mateescu.

And here is a still more revealing instance: writing likewise in *Gazeta Invatamantului* (issue of September 30, 1949), an R.P.R. university professor had this to say: "It is a sad but undeniable reality that the majority of our students present themselves in an altogether unsatisfactory manner, both from the point of view of their learning and from that of the maturity of thought we are entitled to expect from people who pursue specialized studies over a number of years."

Some part at least of the blame for this "sad but undeniable reality" must certainly be attributed to the system. And it is not only in the "homogenized" character of the overwhelming majority of today's student body, resulting, as we have seen, from the deliberately applied policy of checks and screenings, that the reason for the prevailing poor scholastic showing and lack of maturity must be sought. The truth is that, at the level of higher education, as throughout the entire schooling system, the communist regime lays altogether too much stress on extra-curricular activities.

Pursuant to the policy of occupying the students' free time with political activities and training, the communists started "organizing" the student body from the very moment they were installed in power.

The initial organization, the "Communist Youth Union", was dissolved as early as 1945, on account of what was officially described as "the narrowness of its scope." It was superseded by "a new and broader youth organization without a class character," which was titled "Tineretul Progrexist" ("Progressive Youth"). This, in turn, was found inadequate. In the words of the Resolution of the plenary session of the Communist party Central Committee of December 22–24, 1949: ". . . This form of organization was harmful to the working class and to the young democratic movement, whose combativeness and vigilance it weakened by allowing its ranks to be infiltrated by elements alien and even inimical to the (working) class. Even certain party members sank into this heterogeneous mass, losing their combativeness and class consciousness."

A thorough house cleaning was indicated. The Resolution continued: ". . . Faced with this situation, the party leadership set itself the task of creating the Union of Working Youth (UTM), sole organization of the young workers . . . to unite and educate young workers in factories and plants in the spirit of class struggle, in the spirit of Marxist-Leninist teachings, and of love and devotion to the party."

Alongside the Union of Working Youth, there were set up various kindred formations, grouping together young farmers ("Tineretul satesc"— "Village Youth"), school children ("U.A.E.R."), young Hungarians ("Tineretul I.P.M."), as well as a university student organization.

Within this general framework of youth organizations, the organization of the university student body proper likewise went through several phases. Following the directives of what was known at the time as the Bloc of Democratic Parties, the Democratic University Front was set up. Its press organ was *Studentul Roman*. This body took in hand the entire apparatus of student assistance, that is, the cooperatives (that of Bucarest, *Solidaritatea Studenteasca*, being the most notable), the aid institutions, the cultural teams, the theatrical groups, and so forth. Strongly supported by the government, the Front succeeded in imposing its views in all decisions taken by university authorities, its representatives entering even such bodies as the University Senates, the Council of Professors, and the Council on Higher Education.

Following the resolution of the congress of Cluj, in May 1947, the Front was transformed into the National Union of Rumanian Students (U.N.S.R.).

Both the Democratic Front and its successor, the U.N.S.R., aimed at the most direct and constant supervision of the student body, even during vacations, and even outside the academic centers. As early as 1946 it began to create district student circles which, in districts where universities existed, were placed under the control of the latter.

During vacations, moreover, students organized in labor brigades were being sent out to work on national projects that were given such names as Gheorghiu-Dej, Vasile Luca, and Ana Pauker. These projects were designed to become patterns for "finishing schools" of communist education for the participants. Hence the great care displayed by the communist leaders in the composition of brigade commands and in the selection of elements forming the so-called guidance collectives. As *Studentul Roman* of July 2, 1948, put it, the mission of these stalwarts was "the task of dynamizing (sic), enlightening, and educating the masses."

Such was the situation up to December 1948, when the plenary session of the Central Committee of the Communist party voted a Resolution, "concerning the Party's activities in the ranks of youth," which decided the unification of all existing youth organizations. The Resolution acknowledges that ". . . the U.N.S.R. and the U.A.E.R. have achieved certain positive actions in the field of creating a democratic spirit in schools and universities." However, ". . . lacking the foundation of a clear political line, being unconnected with the working youth through a single organization, and leaving the door too widely open to all students and pupils, without distinction of political views, these organizations were unable to carry out decisively a consequent political and cultural-educational activity while, owing to deficient vigilance, their ranks could be infiltrated by elements inimical to the Party, and the spirit of sacrifice for the cause of the working class . . . vigilance and implacable class hatred against the exploiters, against war-mongering imperialism, and against the agents of the class enemy, inside and outside the country."

The intention was to allow only the most thoroughly screened elements to enter the new organization, excluding all who do not actually belong to the "workers." The Resolution lays this down in so many words: ". . . the members of the single organization of working youth will be recruited from the ranks of young workers and poor peasants, of the better elements among the middling peasants, of young employees, of pupils and students closest from the ideological point of view to the proletariat."

The Resolution further defines the activity the new organization is expected to carry out in the educational field. The party's concern in this respect is obvious: ". . . Special attention must be given to the proper communist education in elementary schools, in high schools, and in institutions of higher learning. The single working youth organization must give its support to the application of the educational reform initiated by our Party, maintaining close contact with the appropriate organs of the Ministry of Public Education, by means of periodic consultations to be organized under the direction of the Central Committee of the Rumanian Workers' Party."

On March 19, 1949, in the presence of the government, the Congress of the Single Revolutionary Organization of the Working Youth of the R.P.R. opened in Bucarest, and the new organization was formally constituted. There can be no doubt that, in thus unifying the country's entire youth in a single organization, the regime gained immense means of control. Yet the haunting fear of "bourgeois infiltration" was not abated. By the beginning of July 1949, less than four months later, an overhaul of the membership appeared called for. A decision of the plenary session of the Central Committee of the Communist party directed that a new registration of members was to take place "in order to strengthen the class character of the UTM (the Union of Working Youth), to raise that organization's authority among the broad masses of young workers, to eliminate from its ranks inappropriate elements . . . to strengthen its mobilizing power, with the aim of an increasing contribution to the struggle carried on by the Party for the construction of socialism in our country." (*Scanteia*, July 7, 1949.)

Finally at the beginning of 1950, the Central Committee of the Communist party decided to group the student body into unions. The decision, asserted the R.P.R. press, raised "lively enthusiasm" among the students. "The integration of the students into unions," states one of the Resolutions voted on this occasion, "will model their socialist attitude toward labor." "Organized in unions," states another motion, "we shall fight wholeheartedly for the common cause—for peace—and against Anglo-American imperialist warmongers."

Such, then, are the principal concerns prescribed for R.P.R. university students. Statutorily, they are expected to become "constructors of socialism" rather than good construction engineers, and to "fight wholeheartedly against Anglo-American imperialist warmongers" instead of fighting disease, soil erosion, or plain ignorance. It is in such academic endeavors that the R.P.R. educational system reaches its heights nowadays.

press and radio

Expanding the provisions of the 1866 Constitution, the Constitution of 1923 devoted three articles (Arts. 5, 25 and 26) to freedom of the press. Neither censorship nor restrictions of any other nature whatsoever were countenanced, and freedom of the press was guaranteed to all citizens without distinction, both substantially and explicitly. Under this regime, and up to the time of King Carol's dictatorship, the press flourished and attained a standing comparable with that in most countries of the West. In every field, whether purely informative, political, economic, educational, or scientific, Rumania's newspapers, periodicals, and other publications enjoyed the services of writers of adequate professional qualifications. In pre-war Rumania more than 1,300 periodicals appeared, 140 of them dailies, and there were more than 2,250 magazines and other specialty reviews.

This serves to explain why, notwithstanding the dictatorial regimes that intervened from 1938 to 1944, the coup d'état and armistice of 1944 sparked a lively resurgence of the press. Within a few days, such new democratic dailies as *Democratul, Curierul,* and *Jurnalul de Dimineata* reached the 100,000 mark. A similar popular demand greeted the organs of the democratic parties, like *Dreptatea, Liberalul,* and *Libertatea.* One of these newly established newspapers, *Curierul,* reached the hitherto unparalleled circulation figure of 350,000 copies by September, 1944.

This rebirth of the free press was, of course, fostered by the reintroduction of the provisions of the 1923 Constitution, no less than by the guarantees extended by the Allies at the conclusion of the armistice agreement, with regard to the exercise of human and civil rights and of national sovereignty. This promising situation was unfortunately not destined to endure.

Let us note a significant feature of the brief period that saw the restoration of a free press in Rumania. One of the first measures taken by the coalition government brought to power following the coup d'état was the abolition of the Propaganda Ministry. All matters relating to the various news media were taken over by the Ministry of Foreign Affairs, mainly in order to facilitate the work of foreign correspondents and to assure that government interference with the press be kept at the absolute minimum level dictated by the existing state of war with Nazi Germany. In other words, aside from the customary war censorship exercised by military personnel, there was no administrative censorship whatsoever in effect during that time. This conformed to Law No. 462, published in the Official Bulletin (*Monitorul Oficial*) No. 218/1944.

It was not long, however, before the Allied (Soviet) Control Commission stepped in to change matters. Acting under the guise of the joint commission, the Soviet occupation authorities, working hand in glove with the local communists, proceeded to curtail the freedom of the press in a number of ways, both directly and by devious means. Article 16 of the armistice agreement allowed great latitude to the authorities, specifying that "the printing, importation, and distribution in Rumania of periodical and other publications . . . radio broadcasts, and postal, telegraph, and telephone communications shall be carried out in agreement with the High Allied (Soviet) Command." In addition, Annex F of the agreement stated: "The Rumanian government and its organs shall act in accordance with all instructions of the Allied Control Commission that result from the Armistice Convention."

Despite all protests and efforts of the Rumanian government, the Soviet officials of the Control Commission contrived to exercise an increasingly stringent censorship upon all means of communication, notably the press. The Soviet occupation forces having begun issuing a daily newspaper of their own, *Graiul Nou*, soon after the armistice, this Rumanian-language sheet took a hand in the matter. While every kind of pressure was being exercised against the official Rumanian news agency *Rador*, *Graiul Nou* started intervening in the country's domestic concerns by issuing general directives and injunctions.

One after another, the democratic dailies that incurred the displeasure of the occupation authorities were suspended or banned outright. Thus

Democratul was suppressed for allegedly offending the Soviet army, and its managing editor was jailed, while at the same time the property both of the paper and its editor was confiscated.

Curierul, after suffering constant harassment, had part of its premises taken over by the Red army paper and the communist party organ. *Viitorul* was suppressed at the direct instance of the Soviet legation. *Universul* was suspended and ultimately forcibly "purchased" by a communist organization. In the provinces, the same thing happened to many local newspapers, the most flagrant instance being that of *Gazeta Transilvaniei*, the oldest Rumanian-language newspaper, which came out in Brashov.

One most effective device in constant use was the refusal by the Soviet authorities to permit the issuance of avowed organs of the democratic political parties. This ban was soon extended to cover all independent dailies for which permits were requested by prospective publishers. The communist and pro-communist press enjoyed the utmost favor.

But Soviet censorship was not restricted to Rumanian periodicals and publications and the *Rador* news agency. It affected the dispatches of foreign non-communist correspondents too. Not only were whole passages favoring the National Peasant, Liberal, and Social Democratic parties systematically deleted from such dispatches, but the Soviet censors went to the length of altering and even substituting texts destined to be sent abroad.

The while, entry permits for foreign newspapermen were obtained from the Soviet occupation authorities with ever greater difficulty. Foreign reporters who insisted on being objective and outspoken found themselves faced with outright threats, and quite a few were forced to leave the country. The Soviet censorship also took steps to curtail the free entry of foreign publications and periodicals. This soon reached the point where foreign printed matter from non-Soviet and non-communist sources was almost wholly suppressed. Innumerable protests from the governments, the news agencies or the newspapers involved were registered, all without the slightest result.

Sabotage of the free press was likewise carried on as a deliberate policy by the local communist party. Here, too, the devices and means used were many and varied. In the main this sabotage took the following forms: The communist-dominated printers' unions systematically refused to set or print any articles or news items that dealt with the abuses committed by the Soviet occupation authorities, or denounced the illegal actions of the Communist party. Workers who refused to obey such bans were subject to severe manhandling at the hands of the thugs. The communist sheets would themselves initiate some bitter and virulent polemic against one or more of the democratic or independent papers; when the periodical under attack retaliated, even in the most urbane manner, a complaint to the Allied (Soviet) Control Commission would follow, and the result would be that the paper opposing the communists was suspended or banned for a longer or shorter time, according to the seriousness of the issue involved, the charge being that of "disturbing the peace."

The allocation of newsprint provided perhaps the most direct means of pressuring or favoring the press. The occupation authorities made the freest use of this device to reduce the circulation of anti-communist papers while boosting the communist and pro-communist sheets. An additional advantage was derived by the favored communist papers: the excess of newsprint they got could be and almost invariably was resold at a handsome profit.

The end result of this deliberate and systematic drive was that soon after the Groza communist-dominated administration was installed in power, almost the entire metropolitan press of the democratic parties was suppressed. There was one exception: *Libertatea*, the organ of the Social Democrats, but it went over to the communists about that time. The provincial press suffered a similar fate. More than fifty periodicals, representing every shade of the anti-communist opposition, as well as independent groups, disappeared.

The installation of the Groza regime saw the re-establishment of the Ministry of Propaganda. Within this department, a Press Directorate, set up by a decree published in the Official Gazette No. 67 of March 27, 1945, was assigned "the function of conducting and coordinating all work connected with the domestic and foreign press." The legislative and administrative measures taken by the Groza regime, added to the mounting terror to which the press and all its auxiliaries were subjected, had the expected outcome: communist policy and doctrine could no longer be openly opposed. Even a neutral or objective stand became an impossibility.

The compulsory prior authorization for the issuance of any publication thenceforth became the legal prerogative of a special commission that functioned in the Propaganda Ministry. All periodicals being required to renew existing permits, it was a simple thing to do away with them by simply refusing such renewals.

In addition to the control exercised by the communist-dominated printers' unions, another device was used. The government began requisitioning or confiscating outright the more important printing establishments, which were then handed over to the communists. Thus in Bucarest the printing shop of *Curierul* was taken over by *Scanteia;* the *Adevarul* (Dacia-Traiana) presses were taken over by *Romania Libera* and *Viata Sindicala;* and the same thing befell the larger provincial concerns throughout the country. The pretext in each was that the former owners were "fascists" or "reactionaries"—meaning simply that they were anti-communists.

The distribution of newsprint continued to be a most effective means of muzzling all opposition. It was handled during the period by a government commission staffed exclusively with communists. The most flagrant discrimination was overtly practiced. Communist sheets were allocated quotas three or four times larger than their actual needs, while the opposition would be doled out quotas barely covering 20 per cent of their circulation. Newsprint was then sold at a very high premium on the black market, the communists pocketing the profit.

Censorship of a military nature was taken over by a special agency titled the Military Press Censorship. Set up by Administrative Order No. 3395, published in the *Official Gazette* No. 67 of March 22, 1945, this institution was officially designed to answer "the need to assure strict application of the armistice agreement with the governments of the United Nations, and . . . the need for preserving the secrecy of military operations, domestic order, and state security, as well as that of maintaining good relations with the Allied and neutral nations." The powers of the commission were extensive. They included "supervision of the conditions and manner in which publications of every description, both Rumanian and foreign, are published and distributed throughout the country." They likewise covered such things as "the withholding from publication and circulation of any texts, drawings, cartoons, engravings, and so forth, apt to cause offense to Allied nations or to nations with which Rumania maintains diplomatic relations, or to the representatives thereof." In a general way, the commission's business was "to authorize the publication of any sort of printed matter." It had full latitude to prohibit the issuance of any publication, newspaper or other, as well as the publication of certain (un-specified) news items or articles. The sanctions it wielded included: repri-mand, temporary suspension, revocation of license. Branch offices of this commission functioned throughout the provinces under the authority of the local prefectures.

The outcome of this far-reaching censorship was that clearance became necessary for absolutely every item printed in a newspaper, including ad-vertising copy, private announcements, and the like. Of course, the red tape involved had the result that dailies could no longer appear on time, and when they did come out at all, after two or three separate siftings of their content, all newsworthy items had been deleted or altered beyond recognition.

If at any time the censors' office felt that the editors were recalcitrant or not prompt enough in obeying and carrying out injunctions, the solu-tion was handy: the paper was simply suspended for a longer or shorter period. Under such circumstances, it is not difficult to understand how editors could be compelled to print all sorts of prescribed and ready-made propaganda material, favorable to all things pertaining to the Soviet Union and to Soviet interests in general. It was either include what you were told or scrap the entire issue; dance to the Kremlin's tune or goodbye newspaper.

The sole Rumanian news agency, *Rador*, was placed under the control of a government commissioner whose job it was to sift all incoming and outgoing news, except of course that of the Soviet news agency, *Tass*.

On top of every other kind of chicanery, a most effective means of curb-ing the opposition press was the prevention of its distribution by strong-arm methods. Postal authorities played their part by dumping out the bundles of papers sent to the provinces, and there were always on hand gangs of toughs to beat up newspaper dealers who might insist on putting up for sale any particular paper that had incurred the displeasure of the communists. The readers themselves were exposed to serious trouble if they kept copies of incriminated newspapers about. In case of a search by the police, such material was instantly seized upon as evidence. In other words, possession of a copy of an opposition paper constituted of itself *prima facie* evidence against anyone who might be under suspicion for one reason or another.

The newspapermen themselves, of course, were among the first to feel the full weight of the totalitarian regime that was entrenching itself in power. Law No. 102 and Order No. 3595, both published in the *Official Gazette* No. 34 of February 12, 1945, defined the manner in which the press was to be purged of "fascist" elements. Promptly upon coming to power the Groza administration set up its own "purge commission" and by the end of 1945 the roster of working newspapermen had been pretty thoroughly sifted. Independent journalists went in fear of their lives. Many were picked up by the police at their offices, at home, or off the street, and disappeared off the face of the earth. Thenceforth newspapermen could exercise their profession only if they belonged to the communist-controlled unions. Their freedom to associate, which had been maintained even under the preceding dictatorial regimes of Carol II and Antonescu, went by the board.

The prevailing situation was summed up by Reuben H. Markham in *Rumania under the Soviet Yoke* (Meador: Boston 1949) as follows: "A worthy account of the efforts of Rumanian newspapermen to preserve a free press during the three years following August 1944 would be one of the noblest and most heroic chapters in the history of world journalism. The pro-democratic journalists and printers faced every obstacle, including violence of the most vicious sort. Every independent newspaperman had to leap at least six hurdles: the Russian censors, the Communist censors, the syndicate of journalists, the printers' Union, Communist shock troopers, and prison. These obstacles faced him every day!"

Much the same could be said of the typographical workers who stood out against the orders of the communist-dominated unions. There are numerous cases on record of arrests on trumped up charges, of beatings, and of other kinds of violent coercive means used against anti-communist printers, linotypists, and print shop workers.

The readers interested in learning further details of the manner in which the communists proceeded to do away with the freedom of the press in Rumania might leaf through the pages of the U.S. State Department Blue Book, *Violations of Peace Treaty Guarantees of Human Rights*, No. 4,376 of November, 1951.

In an attempt to restore some semblance of freedom of the press, the Moscow Agreement of December 26, 1945, mentioned that "the reorganized government (of Rumania) should give assurances concerning the grant of freedom of press." In a statement issued on January 8, 1946, the Groza government duly gave such assurances. The situation, however, did not visibly improve.

True enough, the National Peasant Party was permitted to renew issuance of one newspaper, *Dreptatea*, in Bucharest and another, *Patria*, in Cluj, while the Liberals also had *Liberalul* in Bucarest and *Natiunea Romana* in Cluj restored. The independent Social Democrats, however, were not authorized to publish a party organ. There were at that moment 26 dailies in the entire country. Of these the communist-dominated administration had no less than ten in Bucarest alone, as well as 9 weeklies and semi-monthly magazines. Six of the existing periodicals could be described as more or less independent. In Cluj, where the communists issued twelve periodicals in Rumanian and Hungarian, *Patria* had to close shop during the summer of 1946, under the repeated assaults on its premises and equipment by communist strong-arm squads. A few months later *Natiunea Romana* succumbed in its turn to the same tactics.

Meanwhile, the restrictions on newsprint continued as before, and opposition papers could not cope with the demand. *Dreptatea*, for instance, was being sold on the black market at ten times the set price a copy. Meanwhile too, opposition newspapermen were being excluded from the professional unions in ever greater numbers.

The censorship, not content with suppressing all political opposition stemming from domestic sources, spread the ban to cover official statements by Western governments. A communique issued by the U.S. Department of State on June 20, 1946, states the following: "We understand that it was forbidden to publish the texts of the American and British notes, and that it was even forbidden to send the texts to the censor. The order added that any newspapers would be immediately and permanently suppressed if they attempted to publish the British and American notes."

It was during the period covered by the elections of November, 1946, and the signing of the peace treaty in Paris, on February 10, 1947, when the Groza regime was supposed to have respected such things as the basic human rights and civil liberties, that the final chapter of the liquidation of the free press in Rumania was played out. The two opposition dailies, *Dreptatea* and *Liberalul*, disappeared in the summer of 1947. At that moment their joint circulation had fallen to 60,000 copies. The independent press was suppressed out of hand at the beginning of 1948. It then numbered *Jurnalul de Dimineata, Momentul, Fapta, Finante si Industrie,* and *Bursa,* whose joint circulation was barely 120,000 copies. The remainder of the independent newspapers had to play the part of an intermediary in the covert suppression of what little still remained of the liberty of the press. The regime during that period had to take into account three factors then still weighty: it had to keep up appearances before the West, it had to give some semblance of satisfaction to public demand and taste, and it had to conceal the true extent of the process of communization which was already in full swing.

Some of the independent newspapers, notably *Semnalul, Cotidianul,* and *Era Noua,* with a total circulation of 110,000 copies, joined the communist bandwagon. Others, such as *Universul, Timpul, Adevarul, Ultima Ora,* and *Argus,* were simply taken over by the communists under their existing mastheads. Their circulation was approximately 200,000. Yet another category had previously belonged to the crypto-communist splinter parties or to front organizations. They included *Frontul Plugarilor, Natiunea, Dreptatea Noua, Unirea, Drapelul, Poporul, Aurora,* and *Libertatea.* Their estimated joint circulation was some 60,000 copies at the time. These newspapers did not last long. Once the People's Republic was proclaimed in 1948, fellow-travelers no longer had a place; the crypto-communist publications disappeared completely by 1952.

While the non-communist press was being destroyed, the dyed-in-the-wool communist publications underwent a process of vertiginous development. The three chief newspapers, *Scanteia, Romania Libera,* and *Viata Sindicala,* were in full swing by the end of 1944, alongside the Soviet-Rumanian sheet *Veac Nou.* By 1949 the roster was completed with *Glasul Armatei, Contemporanul, Romaniai Magyar Szo, Scanteia Tineretului, Libertatea, Scanteia Pionierului, Neuer Weg, Gazeta Invatamantului, Urzica, Scanteia, Satelor,* and so forth. By then the total circulation of these papers reached about 1,500,000 copies, and the communist weeklies had another 1,200,000.

One of the innumerable notes addressed to the Bucarest regime by the United States Government, dated April 2, 1949, stated unambiguously that "The disregard shown by the Rumanian government for the rights and liberties of persons under its jurisdiction . . . has indeed become so notorious as to evoke the condemnation of free peoples everywhere." In reply the Bucarest government said that such assertions "merely repeat the inventions and the slanderous press of the imperialist monopolists," and pointed out that the R.P.R. constitution provided full guarantees for the rights and liberties of all citizens, the workers having fullest access to the press. In conclusion, the R.P.R. communists said that only "fascist-type" organizations opposed to the democratic liberties of the people were being rigorously suppressed.

The Rumanian People's Republic has different definitions for the freedom of the press, human rights, and other fundamental liberties from those generally accepted in the West. Wholly subservient to the Kremlin, it has adopted wholesale the notions prevalent in the Soviet Union.

As in the Soviet Union, in today's Rumania the press is subservient to the Communist party. Aside from the over-all control by the police organs, and the direct check afforded through the Press, Information, Agitation, and Propaganda sections of the Central Committee and Political Bureau of the party, it is customary for the chief editors of the metropolitan newspapers to be high-ranking party officials. The regional and local press gets its instructions through the administrative organs of the party.

The Decisions issued in March, 1951, by the Central Committee of the "Rumanian Workers' Party" (Communist party) have this to say concerning the press: "Following the example of the Bolshevik press, editorial offices must see to it that all material appearing in print, from the editorial articles down to the last information item, be penetrated with the high principles and spirit of the party." This official view was subsequently voiced by the then chief editor of the authoritative *Scanteia* in a "Press Day" address (May 5, 1952): "The press must defend the party line as it would the very apple of its eye, and must educate the workers in the spirit of uncompromising struggle against any deviation or influence alien to the party line." Under such circumstances, the notion of censorship, as it is commonly understood in the West, does not apply in a people's democracy, where the press is simply an integral part of the body politic itself.

The first step in this direction was marked, following the establishment of the R.P.R. as such, by Decree No. 62, published in the *Official Gazette* No. 131 of June 8, 1948, which set up the Ministry of Arts and Information. This was followed by Decree No. 64, published in the *Official Gazette* No. 42 of February 19, 1949, which placed both the *Rador* agency and the State Enterprise for Press and Publicity, *Slova*, together with the Graphic Arts Industrial Center, directly under that Ministry. In February, 1949, too, the name of the Press Directorate was changed to "Directorate of Press and Printing."

There followed a reorganization of the Ministry, which transferred the

Directorate to the bureau of the Council of Ministers. In this guise, as an organ of the highest government authority, the Directorate of Press and Printing was given its final form by Decree No. 218, published in the *Official Gazette* No. 32 of May 23, 1949. Among the current legal powers of this General Directorate, are the following: ". . . To edit the *Official Bulletin* (i.e. the *Official Gazette*) of the R.P.R; to approve the publication of all printed matter (newspapers, periodicals, . . .), and to take measures in view of the observance of legal printing conditions; . . . to approve the sale and distribution of books, newspapers, and all other printed matter, and the import and export of newspapers; . . . to regulate working conditions for . . . the wholesale newspaper trade; . . . to edit and distribute to the press the official communications of the Council of Ministers." (Article 1.)

It is interesting to note that article 3 states that "the functions of the director and deputy director, and the organization and operation of the services of the General Directorate of Press and Publication shall be established by decision of the Council of Ministers."

In other words, it is currently the Council of Ministers that establishes, without further legal limitations and at its own discretion, the workings of the General Directorate, hence of everything connected with the press. Since there are no longer any press organs that do not depend directly upon the Communist party, political control is exercised either directly by the central organs of the party or through the official voice thereof, *Scanteia*.

The Graphic Arts Industrial Center, mentioned above, was set up as the final authority in the matter of printing, as the sole authorized agency to decide questions about the use of typographical material and equipment of all sorts, by Order No. 37,388, published in the *Official Gazette* No. 69 of November 5, 1949. It had originally been set up as a state production unit by Decree No. 128, published on July 12, 1948, and was then integrated as part of the Ministry of Arts.

In February, 1950, a "Directorate for Publishing, Distribution, and Typography" was created as a bureau of the Ministry of Arts. In March that same year, this became a bureau of the Council of Ministers, and was titled the General Administration of Publishing, Industrial Reproduction, and Book, Magazine, and Newspaper Distribution. This new and cumbersomely titled agency took over the powers of the Graphic Arts Industrial Center, which was dissolved.

Decree No. 62, published in the *Official Gazette* No. 26 of March 17, 1950, established the powers and activities of this General Administration as follows: ". . . to direct, plan, and coordinate the work of all publishing houses; . . . of all printing establishments, manufacturers of ink and other types of supplies; . . . to furnish plants within its field of activity with machinery and supplies; . . . to direct and organize the distribution of books and newspapers; . . . to make proposals concerning the importation of books, periodicals, newspapers, and other printed matter for the approval of the Council of Ministers; . . . to establish, together with the proper labor unions, wage schedules, as well as regulations and directives concerning working conditions in publishing houses, in the printing industry, in the book trade, and in newspaper sales." A Decree of the R.P.R. Presidium, No. 19, published in the *Official Gazette* No. 22 of February 16, 1951, added the supervision of copyrights to the above. This additional jurisdiction includes publishing contracts of authors, the number and size of editions, and the amount of royalties.

In view of the fact that a decision of the Council of Ministers, No. 768, published in the *Official Gazette* No. 22 of July 14, 1950, placed all paper production under the regime of state planning, it is obvious that at the present time every phase of the press is thoroughly in the hands of the party. Indeed a so-called Center for Press Distribution and Mailing was set up as one of the services of the General Administration.

In August, 1952, following a joint decision of the Council of Ministers and the party's central committee, the "Center" was placed under the authority of the Ministry of Posts and Telecommunications, and its title changed to General Directorate for Press Distribution and Mailing. This agency, which operates throughout the country in close collaboration with the local people's councils, as well as with the party organs, now handles all subscriptions to the various newspapers and other publications.

Thus "planned" from top to bottom, the number of newspapers has been sharply reduced. There are at this time 42 dailies, of which 9 are metropolitan newspapers, as against 141 (of which 21 were metropolitan) before World War II. Existing magazines represent but approximately 10 per cent of the pre-war number. Moreover, aside from insignificant details, all newspapers nowadays are but specialized editions of *Scanteia*. Likewise such publications as those of individual unions, farms, and plants, and the various "wall newspapers" that have become a feature throughout the industrial and agricultural field.

On the other hand, the decrease in the actual number of papers has been accompanied everywhere by a prodigious rise in the circulation figures. In 1955 there were 376 periodicals issued in Rumania, including the 42 dailies mentioned above. Minority language groups have the following share: Magyars—approximately 30 (8 dailies); Germans—4 (2 dailies); Yugoslavs—2 (1 daily); Jews—5 (two in Yiddish, two in Rumanian, and one in Hungarian); Ukrainians—2; Armenians—2; Greeks—1. To these we must add the periodicals of the R.P.R. Academy and of the Soviet-Rumanian society ARLUS, which likewise appear in Magyar and German editions. The total circulation of periodicals, including dailies, was officially given as 4,500,000 in 1950. The partial figure for the first four months of 1955 was given by *Scanteia* of May 5, 1955 as approximately 5,500,000.

In 1950, on the party's initiative and with the allegedly voluntary contributions raised from the "workers," the construction of a gigantic polygraphic combine was begun. This combine, named the "Casa Scanteii I. V. Stalin," was partially inaugurated the following year, and is still to be completed. It is planned to be the largest such combine in all South-Eastern Europe.

The *Scanteia* publishing concern was established on April 1, 1954, by the Central Committee of the Rumanian Workers' Party. This concern, which is part of the party's central financial system, represents an important source of income.

A word remains to be said about the wall newspapers mentioned above. These are in the form of bulletin boards, and are edited by a "collective" and a "responsible," whose business it is to display the more important editorials from the metropolitan papers and articles contributed locally on the production problems and results of the unit. The main purpose of these wall newspapers is to boost "socialist competition" and whatever drives are promoted by the party. The contributors to this special type of press have been described by *Agerpress* as "a new army of journalists of the modern type, reared and educated by the party." There are at this time several tens of thousands of them. Another propaganda device in use for some years now is the leaflet distributed by special trucks to farm workers in the field during the "agricultural campaigns."

Under the conditions described, here is how a newspaper operates: Aside from the "collective" made up of the entire personnel, editorial, administrative, and technical, there is a so-called editorial collegium, headed by the chief editor. There are daily editorial conferences, and it is customary to plan the material to be printed. Such plans, weekly, monthly, or half-yearly, must be approved in advance by the party. The planning of each issue is the responsibility of the editorial secretary. As we have shown in another chapter of this work, each newspaper has an unlimited number of "volunteer correspondents."

The main result of this is a tone of uniformity that is striking. Every editorial of every paper might have been written by the same person, for all the differences to be observed. Even the makeup of newspapers is similar. Most papers have the same four pages, and exception is made only on special occasions, as when some important speech must be printed in full, some outstanding party document must be made public, or some party festivity must be publicized.

It is obvious that newspapermen under this regime are but party functionaries, who have no latitude whatsoever in their work. The slightest slip may be fatal. Legally, such slips may be construed as coming under such provisions of the R.P.R. Criminal Code of 1948: Articles 204–209 (crimes against the state security); Article 183 (defense of common property); or Article 225 (offenses against the security of foreign states, the peace, and good international relations). Mistakes made by newspapermen may further be prosecuted under the provisions of the Decree Concerning Crimes against the State Security, published in the *Official Gazette* No. 68 of September 12, 1950, and under those of the still more drastic Law for the Defense of Peace (published in the *Official Gazette* No. 117 of December 16, 1950).

Concerning the actual access to information of newspapermen, we should remark that a number of decrees and decisions issued by the R.P.R. administration are secret, in virtue of the provisions of Decree No. 112, published in the *Official Gazette* No. 304 of December 31, 1948. The *Official Gazette* itself, where all such legislation or statutes or regulations are printed, has not been available to the public since January, 1952. Indeed, newspapermen may not even consult the "morgue" of their own paper without a special authorization. As in other people's democracies, the collection or use of statistics other than those issued by the Central Directorate of Statistics is expressly prohibited in the terms of Decision No. 1298/1953.

Add to the above restrictions the fact that the unauthorized "purchase, possession, or handing over in any manner" of typewriters and other polygraphic devices constitutes a criminal offense (Decision No. 583, *Official Gazette* No. 51 of June 9, 1950). As for translators, they too may work only if they possess a special certificate (Decision No. 2238/1952).

A special decision was issued by the central committee of the Rumanian Workers' Party in 1951, concerning the "formation of new cadres of newspapermen." Under its terms, the newspapers themselves must concern themselves with this matter. Special facilities were made available in June, 1953, when the press section of the Bucarest University was promoted to the status of a special school with studies covering a five-year required course. Editorial writers in responsible positions are required to follow the courses of the A. A. *Jdanov* Institute, which turns out the party's highest cadres. The "Syndicate of Professional Newspapermen" was dissolved in March, 1949, following a decision of the General Confederation of Labor. Consequently, a "Union of Syndicates (labor unions, that is) of polygraphy, of the press, and of cultural institutes" was set up. To this all newspapermen must belong in order to exercise their profession.

The public taste, as we have already indicated, is not consulted in matters pertaining to newspapers. Subscriptions are obtained on the principle of "buy it or else . . ." and it is hardly necessary to add that the party has an infinity of means of applying pressure to recalcitrants, and of making the whole process appear a "voluntary" one. In this way, the much trumpeted "ties with the masses" are effected.

Something remains to be said now about *Agerpress*, which replaced the news agency *Rador* in 1949. At that time, under the terms of Decree No. 217, published in the *Official Gazette* No. 32 of May 23, 1949, *Agerpress* (we write the name with the normal double s at the end, though its official title is "Agerpres") was set up as the "Rumanian Press Agency of the Council of Ministers of the R.P.R." Article 2 of the decree gives it the following powers: ". . . the reception, transmission, and distribution of all news items and press pictures, foreign and domestic, political, economic, cultural, and so forth." This right belongs "exclusively" to Agerpress: "news transmitted or distributed . . . may not be used in any form except on the basis of a contract signed with Agerpress." Article 6 specifies further that "the mode of operation of the agency, as well as the functions of its directors and deputy directors will be established by decision of the Council of Ministers." This decree was cited as an instance of "a directed regime of information" in the special UNESCO study *Les Agences Télégraphiques d'Information* (October, 1953).

In October, 1950, a "coordination agreement" was signed by the information agencies of the "people's democracies," including Agerpress and Tass. The agreement calls, among other things, for the introduction of special Soviet "coordinating editors" in each of the Iron Curtain countries, who play the part of advisers within each of the local press agencies.

The most legitimate activities of non-communist foreign correspondents in a "people's democracy" are considered to come under the heading of espionage, and any unauthorized information concerning the country's life is a breach of state secrets. This has become evident in Rumania following the setting up of the popular democratic republic. Not only has it become a matter of the utmost difficulty for a foreign correspondent to work in Rumania even for a limited time, but all foreign news agencies not communist ceased to function there in 1950. Unfortunate individuals who, as Rumanian citizens, represented non-communist news associations have either fled the country or been tried and sentenced to long terms of imprisonment.

The British and American information offices in Rumania were closed down on March 3, 1950.

A list of the principal periodicals, dailies and others, that currently appear in Rumania, all controlled communist publications, follows:

Scanteia, daily, issued since 1944 as the official organ of the Central Committee of the Rumanian Workers' party, circulation approximately 1,000,000 copies.

Romania Libera, daily, issued since 1942 (started out as a clandestine paper); now the organ of the people's councils (Soviets), circulation about 180,000.

Unirea, daily, organ of the "Jewish Democratic Committee," issued since 1945.

Munca, daily, organ of the Central Council of Trade Unions (formerly titled *Viata Sindicala*, first a daily then a weekly paper), circulation 200,000 (in 1949).

Scanteia Tineretului, daily organ of the Central Committee of the UTM (Union of Working Youth, the R.P.R. equivalent of the Soviet Komsomol), formerly appeared under the title *Tinarul Muncitor*; circulation 300,000 (in 1954).

Informatia Bucurestiului, daily organ of the Bucarest party committee and people's council, brought out 1953 to replace *Universul*, which was suppressed at that time.

Apararea Patriei, daily organ of the Ministry of the Armed Forces, formerly *Glasul Armatei*; circulation (1949) about 80,000.

Elore, Hungarian-language daily (party and people's councils) formerly titled *Romaniai Magyar Szo*, circulation 46,000 (mainly in the Magyar Autonomous Region).

Neuer Weg, German-language weekly (party and people's councils), started out as a crypto-communist paper and organ of the German Anti-Fascist Committee; circulation about 30,000.

Veac Nou, bi-weekly organ of ARLUS General Council; circulation: 93,000 in Rumanian, 20,000 in Hungarian, and 7,000 in Ukrainian. It has a special illustrated monthly edition for farmers (200,000 copies). It started in 1944.

Contemporanul, weekly organ of the Ministry of Culture, started publication in 1946, current circulation about 40,000.

Gazeta Literara, weekly organ of the Writers' Union since March, 1954.

Gazeta Invatamantului, weekly organ of the Ministry of Public Education and of the Teachers' Unions since March, 1949.

Scanteia Satelor, weekly supplement of *Scanteia* specially addressed to the farmers; circulation (1949) 150,000.

Scanteia Pionierilor, bi-weekly annex of *Scanteia* for children in the Pioneer organization, issued since 1948; 200,000 circulation.

Urzica, semi-monthly satirical and humorous R.P.R. version of Soviet Krokodil, printed since 1949.

A *Scanteia* editorial of May 7, 1954, provides the best description of the current R.P.R. conception of radio broadcasting. This description has the merit of being official. "A cultural instrument of immense penetrative force," it states, "the radio constitutes a powerful means of influencing the masses ideologically, of disseminating the Marxist-Leninist teachings, and of educating the workers in the spirit of socialist patriotism, proletarian internationalism, and love and attachment for the great Soviet Union."

To attain this level the communists had to proceed step by step. First the existing broadcasting facilities and radio enterprises had to be seized and transformed into state monopolies; then special committees to handle the various phases of radio broadcasting had to be put in exclusive control; and finally new installations and sets had to be provided, while the existing transmitting and receiving equipment had to be physically altered so as to exclude Western broadcasts and thus confine the captive audience to the wave lengths on which approved programs are broadcast.

Following the coup d'état of August 23, 1944, the Rumanian Broadcasting Company (Societatea Romana de Radiodifusiune), which had been set up in 1927, regained in principle the autonomy and freedom of action it had enjoyed prior to the outbreak of the Second World War. This status lasted barely two months. During this brief interlude it was subject only to an administrative control by the Press and Information Service of the Ministry of Foreign Affairs, which was itself set up by Decree No. 2462 of 1944. By October, 1944, the Soviet Military Mission, alleging "military requirements" and "reasons of security," was already seriously hampering operations. Military control was introduced and an agency of the Office of the Council of Ministers took over the supervision of radio broadcasting.

Shortly after the advent of the Groza regime, the Soviet occupation authorities handed radio censorship over to the Ministry of Propaganda, which had been re-established, as related earlier in this chapter. From then on, Rumania's radio broadcasting was administered precisely as though it had already become state property, and all appointments were thenceforth made by the government.

The assurances given by the Groza government pursuant to the Moscow agreement of December, 1945 included the use of broadcasting facilities "by all political parties represented in the government, impartially, for the dissemination of their political views." Access to broadcasting facilities however continued to be unavailable to any non-communist group or person throughout the pre-election period that followed.

It is interesting to note that during the years 1944–1947 the broadcasting station known as *Radio Romania Libera*, which had functioned clandestinely since 1941, continued to function in disregard of existing laws and regulations as an independent communist outlet.

The constitution introduced in 1948 provided in Article 6 that all radio broadcasting installations and facilities became state property. This provision was subsequently embodied in Article 7 of the 1952 constitution, and is still in effect at this time. Pursuant to this provision, broadcasting was placed under the direct control of the reorganized Ministry of Arts and Information. This was effected through a special law passed on June 11, 1948, and through Decree No. 62, published in the *Official Gazette* No. 131 of June 8, 1948, which reorganized the ministry itself.

A change was introduced later by Decree No. 64, published in the *Official Gazette* No. 42 of February 19, 1949, which set up a special department for the network of radio stations and amplifiers. In May, 1949, another change was introduced by Decree No. 216, published in the *Official Gazette* No. 32 of May 23, 1949. The Ministry became known thenceforth as the Ministry of Arts, and a special Radio Committee was set up, as a service of the Office of the Council of Ministers. This made radio broadcasting a state monopoly wholly subservient to the government itself. Though up to this time there is no television broadcasting in Rumania, televising was included specifically in this statute.

Article 4 of Decree No. 216 specifies the duties of the Radio Committee as follows: "To assist in carrying out the policies of the government by producing and broadcasting programs, in Rumanian and in the minority languages of the country, of a nature apt to educate, organize, and mobilize the working people in behalf of the construction of socialism in the R.P.R.;

". . . To make known beyond the borders the achievements of the R.P.R. in its struggle for peace, democracy, and socialism;

". . . It shall support and organize scientific activity in the field of radio and television, collaborating with the R.P.R. Academy, the Ministry of Public Education, the Ministry of Arts, the Ministry of Industries, and all other state organs and institutions."

The Radio Committee furthermore was given the exclusive right to approve broadcasts produced, and to set up radio transmitters.

Yet another change was introduced by Decree No. 116, published in the *Official Gazette* No. 41 of May 13, 1950, which placed the technical questions of setting up local relay stations and loud-speaker systems under the Ministry of Communications. In April the following year, Decree No. 30, published in the *Official Gazette* of April 6, 1951, transformed this to the Ministry of Posts and Telecommunications. However, aside from this purely technical side of radio installations, the Radio Committee remained in full charge of policy in the matter of broadcasts. The production of equipment was handed to the Ministry of Electric Energy, while the formation of specialized "cadres" for the various technical branches was under the Ministry of Public Education.

Decree No. 462, published in the *Official Gazette* No. 44 of October 31, 1953 reorganized the Ministry of Culture, and the Radio Committee itself was transferred to this newly set up department as a General Directorate.

So much for the formal aspect of the evolution of radio broadcasting under the communists. What of the results?

It must be pointed out in the first place that, in addition to the problems involved in making radio programs strictly conforming to the requirements of the party line palatable to the audience, the regime was faced with a shortage of technical equipment. Such equipment had in the past been imported from the Western countries with which the R.P.R. no longer had trade relations. In order to make full use of the radio as a propaganda medium, a great deal of new equipment was necessary. The answer was found in what is referred to as *radioficare*, a barbarous term coined by the regime's propagandists by analogy with *electrificare*, denoting the network of local transmitters and loudspeaker systems designed to carry the authoritative voice of the party to the remotest corners of the country at a minimum cost.

Organized on the Soviet model, the R.P.R. radio functions on three planes:

1) the central broadcasting system, comprising the group of transmitters of the Bucarest-Brashov (Stalin) region;
2) the regional system, the broadcasting stations of Timishoara, Craiova, Cluj, and Iash;
3) local broadcasting, that is the *radioficare* centers, which relay programs to their subscribers by wire.

The years 1948–1950 were marked by two unsuccessful one-year plans. This period saw little progress in the field of radio, aside from the tightening of the central organization in the form of a Committee which functioned as a service of the Office of the Council of Ministers, and the installation of three new transmitters, imported from the Soviet Union, totaling 205 kilowatts.

The first five-year plan (1951–1955), which comprised the electrification program, brought an upsurge of effort to the field of radio. As we have shown above, the various phases of the process were distributed among a number of governmental departments. 1950 indeed marked the first "Radio Day" to be introduced in Rumania. The work started off rather unimpressively at first. The five-year plan, which favored heavy industry to the detriment of consumer goods, showed scant results in the field of radio. By the summer of 1952 all that had been achieved was the installation of one single regional transmitter of a mere 20 kilowatts.

That summer there was an outburst of official criticism directed against the central radio authorities. There was a dearth of equipment and little or nothing was being produced. By 1953, however, results began to be forthcoming. *Casa Radiofoniei,* the central Broadcasting House, was finally completed in Bucarest. The *radioficare* program went into high gear. Transmitters totaling 170 kilowatts were set up. Foreign broadcasts began in real earnest. The government, in order to stimulate the effort, began awarding honors and medals to people engaged in the various phases of broadcasting.

The year 1954 saw the installation of the Cluj and Craiova studios, and the beginning of work on the Iash station. Local radio facilities progressed and reached out into the rural regions. A large number of so-called amateurs' clubs sprang into being, all, of course, under strict party control and supervision.

Here, according to official figures, is the progress of *radioficare:*

Year	No. of centers	Loud-speakers
1949	34	?
1950	44	16,000
1951	78	40,000
1952	160	65,000
1953	300 (approximately)	240,000
1954	700	390,000 (approximately)
1955 (1st quarter)	?	430,000 (approximately)

And here, likewise according to official data, is the over-all picture of the listening audience served. The figures include both individual subscribers owning radio sets and installed loud-speaker systems. The density refers to the number of sets of both types per 1,000 inhabitants.

Year	No. of subscribers	Density
1952	426,700	25.8
1953	660,000	39.6
1954	930,000	55.5
1955 (1st quarter)	1,000,000	58.6

In addition to the above, which may be described as the captive audience, there are of course the clandestinely owned receiving sets. The number of such undeclared radios was estimated during the war years at between one-third and one-half the number of legally functioning radios. It must be understood in this general connection that in Rumania, as in a number of other countries, the system of registering privately owned radios prevailed, the registrants being required to pay a small fee as subscribers of the national broadcasting system. There was a considerable proportion of people who deliberately evaded such registration and payment. Although it has become practically impossible to replace deteriorated parts, the presumption is strong that there are still many such clandestine sets in operation at the present time. Even the severe controls obtaining under the communist regime, which make the legal purchase of radio parts, when they happen to be available, a major transaction, it may be taken for granted that the number of people who still risk their necks to listen to foreign broadcasts is far from insignificant. There was, for instance, a communiqué issued as late as December 11, 1954, by the R.P.R. Ministry of Posts and Telecommunications, granting such clandestine owners of radios a term to legalize their situation. The term of grace expired on December 15, 1954, but the authorities did not reveal how many people had responded.

Another remark is in order. At the beginning of 1953, when the pre-war level was reached at last, the density of radio receivers in Rumania was still very low. It was in fact the lowest in Europe. It remains to this day unimpressive by world standards. This situation is further aggravated by another factor: whereas the majority of sets in operation in Rumania prior to World War II included short-wave reception and were of relatively high quality, the radios manufactured at the present time are mostly of very poor quality.

Under the communist regime, only a small number of sets come in from abroad. These were, during the years 1947–1949, of Soviet manufacture or assembled in Rumania from parts sent in by Soviet Russia. Only at the beginning of 1953 did radios begin to be brought in from Czechoslovakia, and fairly acceptable sets made in Rumania. The published results of the economic plan for 1954 mention that the manufacture of radio receivers had grown by 211.8 per cent above that of the previous year.

In the spring of 1949, "workers" might purchase Soviet sets, upon presentation of a certificate from their union, for 6,528 lei, which at that time represented almost two months' wages for an unskilled worker. By 1954, the price of radios then available in state stores varied between

750 and 2,500 lei, that is, two to six months' wages of an unskilled worker.

Under such circumstances, it is not difficult to appreciate the advantages derived from the "radiofication" network mentioned above. With a minimum of equipment, a large audience can be reached for propaganda purposes, a captive audience in the fullest sense of the term. For, needless to say, what this audience is fed through the medium of radio is, no matter what the nature of the program, exclusively slanted along current party lines.

Yet the results obtained are invariably considered to be meagre by the communist authorities themselves. For instance, a joint decision was issued on September 15, 1951, by the central committee of the Rumanian Workers' Party and the R.P.R. Council of Ministers (Decision No. 965/1951), severely criticizing the results achieved in the field of "radiofication" during the years 1949–1951. Much the same criticism was voiced by *Scanteia* in an editorial devoted to Radio Day on May 7, 1953, which took to task the various government departments involved as well as the Radio Committee itself. These criticisms were leveled both at the paucity and poor quality of equipment, and at the broadcast programs.

As is shown in the preceding tables, a measure of improvement has been registered since that time. However, the goal set for the end of 1955 in the field of "radiofication"—2,000 centers and 1,000,000 loud-speaker systems—still seems wildly improbable.

In the matter of radio programs, too, there is ample evidence to show that the communist authorities are far from pleased with the results obtained. Thus an article published in *Contemporanul* of September 2, 1955, over the signature of one of the top functionaries of the General Broadcasting Directorate, stresses the grave inadequacies generally found in local broadcasting stations.

The current yearly rates paid by listeners for the privilege of having a radio, set by Decision No. 91 of the Council of Ministers, published in the *Official Gazette* No. 21, February 12, 1955, are: (a) for a crystal set —440 lei (about one month's pay for an unskilled worker); farm workers pay only 104 lei; (b) for a set with tubes—2,204 lei (farmers belonging to collective farms pay only 220 lei); (c) a *radioficare* loud-speaker system —1,104 lei (installation is without charge). Theatres, public halls, plants, and shops are charged twice to eight times these rates, but hospitals and elementary schools are exempt from all payments.

The programs given in exchange show less concern with tastes of the listeners than with "educating" the audience to "socialist consciousness." While seeking to "raise the cultural level of the masses" according to the gospel of Marx and Lenin, even diversion is expected to have a "constructive" character. Obviously this raises an almost insoluble problem. When the party line, slogans, and attendant ritual must be introduced even in sports broadcasts, musical programs, and literary hours, the boredom level is quickly reached, no matter how open-minded the audience may be. In a country like Rumania, where the captive audience can hardly be described as favorably inclined, the difficulties faced by the radio authorities are not hard to imagine. Though a totalitarian regime has no scruples about riding rough-shod over the public's likes and dislikes, it cannot really expect that sheer verbal repetition of the blessings of life under a people's democracy, and of the miseries inherent in bourgeois capitalism, will ultimately result in persuasion. Attempts must be made to find the "subtle approach."

At first this was tried out, but during the years 1948–1953 the tone was deliberately changed. With Stalinolatry then at its height, a truculent, snarling note was adopted. In all fields, the stress was exclusively on Soviet achievements, with the concomitant denunciation of all things Western. On Sundays and other holidays, even Rumanian music was banned from the air, and Rumanian listeners were deliberately bullied with Soviet and Russian names hurled at them at every turn and in every imaginable connection. Communist theory and the party line, dry and uncompromising, were the central theme in all programs. But in the end this proved unavailing. Official displeasure was voiced by *Scanteia* of May 7, 1953: all radio programs were found wanting; they were empty of interest, unrelated to the every-day life of the workers; they even introduced errors and falsifications of the party line in their frantic efforts to drum it into the public's heads. A new approach was in order. Greater variety must be introduced. Education must be made palatable to the various categories addressed: party workers, farmers, housewives, members of the armed forces, children, and so forth.

One result was that in 1954 the number of broadcasting hours increased considerably, and variety was introduced. Cultural broadcasts (music, theatre, literature, and lectures) came to total almost three quarters of the actual broadcasting time. Of course "socialist construction" still had to be boosted in every possible way. The accent however shifted somewhat. Audience participation was introduced. Quiz programs appeared. Even a carefully groomed socialist version of the soap opera came into being. The general effort was directed toward making radio broadcasts as "lively" as possible, while keeping them in step with the current party requirements.

With the regional broadcasting joining the increased output of the central broadcasting system, a considerable amount of ingenuity had to be mobilized. The local stations, each under the constant supervision of the regional radio committee, which in turn is directed by the local party organs, work in close cooperation with the General Directorate of Broadcasting. They make extensive use of local talent, and do their best to cope with the demands of their audiences.

Broadcasts beamed to listeners abroad are put together by a special editorial board. Their aim is threefold: to tell the world of the accomplishments of the R.P.R.; to give propaganda support to the foreign policy objectives of the Soviet bloc; and to maintain contact with communists and fellow-travelers throughout the world. The last two purposes explain both the languages selected for broadcasting, and the varying length and contents of the broadcasts.

Foreign broadcasts began in 1948 in Russian, German, French, and English. In 1949 Greek and Serbian were added, and there were broadcasts in Italian and Yiddish. Since 1954 ten languages have been in use, Spanish and Arabic being added to those already mentioned. The number of broadcast-hours has steadily increased, though it remains unimpressive to this day—somewhat in excess of 100 per week.

During the years 1947–1948 an illustrated weekly, *Secolul Radiofoniei*, official organ of the former Rumanian Broadcasting Company, and an independent periodical, *Radio Azi*, made a brief appearance. Since their suppression there is only a weekly radio program (*Programul de Radio*) published in Rumania. This is brought out by the General Directorate of Broadcasting.

As one might expect, the communists are making efforts to coordinate broadcasting activities within the Soviet bloc. An agreement was signed between the radio authorities of Soviet Russia and those of the R.P.R. on April 4, 1949, as a consequence of which Rumanian stations broadcast and relay a considerable amount of material prepared in the Soviet Union, while certain Rumanian programs are broadcast from Moscow and other

Soviet stations. Notably during the years 1949–1952, Station Bucuresti II relayed propaganda broadcasts to Greece and Yugoslavia.

An arrangement for radio cooperation was signed by the broadcasting authorities of Rumania and Bulgaria as early as 1948, and following the break with Tito, Radio Tirana was afforded much assistance from Rumania. The year 1951 saw the beginning of reciprocally relayed broadcasts between Rumania, Czechoslovakia, Poland, Bulgaria, and Hungary, mainly beamed at the Western world.

Rumania has been a member in the International Radio Organization since 1946. This organization, known as OIR, is controlled by Moscow and designed to coordinate the broadcasting activities of the communist bloc as a whole (Eastern Germany has belonged to it since 1952, and communist China since 1951). In 1948, the European Broadcasting Convention was concluded in Copenhagen, and the R.P.R. is a member thereof. In 1954 the R.P.R. Radio began collaborating with certain capitalist countries, like France, Sweden, Denmark, and Egypt.

In addition to the severe punitive measures taken against clandestine listeners to broadcasts from the free world, the R.P.R. has done its share of jamming. As far back as 1945, the communists considered listening to broadcasts from the free world as evidence of anti-communist feeling. Then came the Law for the Defense of Peace (published in the *Official Gazette* No. 117 of December 16, 1950), which made listeners to foreign broadcasts liable to arrest and to sentences up to 25 years at hard labor. Denouncing one's neighbor became an officially prescribed act of civic virtue. The summer of 1952 saw the installation of a number of jamming transmitters, notably in the larger urban centers. Nonetheless, while some such centers have become almost wholly isolated from foreign broadcasts, there are to this day parts of Rumania where the effects of this interference are completely absent.

There is one fact that may be taken as evidence that the R.P.R. authorities are still considerably irked by the evils of clandestine listening to free world broadcasts. Every now and again there are sudden outbursts of polemics from the R.P.R. radio, in reply to some particularly telling foreign broadcast or program. At all times, as the Director General of the R.P.R. Broadcasting stated as late as 1955, "it is an honor duty for . . . radio workers to put on the air more and more combative broadcasts, to unmask concretely the aggressive policy of the imperialistic circles and their machinations against peace."

Communist stations currently broadcasting in Rumania are:

Radio Romania (Bod, Brashov)—wave length 1935 metres; 155 kilocycles; 150 kilowatts.

Radio Bucuresti I—wave length 285 m.; 1025 kilocycles; 5 kilowatts (?). A new station with the same wave length was set up in 1953.

Radio Bucuresti II—wave length 351; 854 kilocycles; 150 kilowatts. Situated at Tancabeshti, near Bucarest.

Radio Romania Libera—48.3 metres, 6210 kilocycles, 5 kilowatts—foreign broadcasts in six languages.

Short-Wave Station, titled Station A at one time, 32.4 metres, 9250 kilocycles, 4 kilowatts, foreign broadcasts in six languages.

Short-Wave Station, titled Station B at one time, 25 metres, 11,955 kilocycles, 0.1 kilowatts, no foreign broadcasts since 1953.

Short-Wave Station, name unknown, 31.35 metres, 9570 kilocycles, 100 kilowatts, began broadcasting for foreign listeners toward the end of 1953; currently broadcasts in six foreign languages.

Short-Wave Station, name undisclosed, 50.17 metres, 5979 kilocycles, 50 kilowatts, started broadcasting for foreign listeners toward the end of 1953; currently broadcasts in six foreign languages.

Timishoara, regional, relays, and international. Wave lengths 285 and 397 metres; kilocycles: 1052 and 755; kilowatts: 1 and 50; foreign broadcasts in six languages.

Cluj, regional and relays, 261 metres, 1151 kilocycles, 20 kilowatts (?); broadcasts in Rumanian and Hungarian since March, 1954.

Craiova, regional and relays, 206 metres, 1457 kilocycles, 20 kilowatts (?), in operation since November 7, 1951, the "Cluj Regional Studio" has functioned since June 7, 1954.

Unidentified Station—202 metres, 1484 kilocycles, power unknown, apparently a frequency band used in common by several stations, for relays of domestic broadcasts.

Radio Free Greece (Timishoara) details unknown, broadcasts of Stalinist propaganda for Greece, in the Greek language, were heard for a time, starting end of 1951.

Anti-Tito Station (Timishoara) 540 metres, 557 kilocycles, power unknown, broadcasted in Serbian (15 minutes daily) during the Kremlin-Tito break.

Iash, regional and relays, details unknown, in the process of completion at the end of 1955.

Note: Program I for home listeners is currently broadcast on the 202, 206, 397, and 1935 metres bands;

Program II for home listeners is currently broadcast on the 261, 285, and 351 metres bands.

Foreign broadcasts: 28.3, 32.4, 31.35, 50.17, and 397 metres bands.

the R.P.R. constitution

The full significance of the radical innovations enacted by the communist-dictated constitution of 1952 can hardly be appreciated without at least a cursory survey of Rumania's constitutional history. Initiated by the introduction of the short-lived constitution of 1948, the break with the past was completed in the current statute. Before proceeding with an analysis of the R.P.R. constitution of 1952, we must therefore give a brief sketch of Rumania's constitutional background.

Rumania's first constitution, introduced on June 30, 1866, was inspired by the constitution of Belgium, then considered one of the most modern, and best suited to the aspirations of the newly organized state. As amended in 1879, 1884, and 1917, it was based upon the principles of national sovereignty and independence, of representative government, separation of powers, and political and individual liberties. The monarchy was declared hereditary, the king inviolable, and responsibility vested in the government. The constitution, whose supremacy over other laws of the land was recognized, could be amended only by a specially elected constitutional assembly. The vote for the election of the Chamber of Deputies became universal, equal, and obligatory.

The second constitution, enacted on March 29, 1923, was in effect a revised version of the first, adapted to conditions obtaining after World War I, notably the inclusion of the provinces of Transylvania, Bessarabia, and Bucovina in the country's national territory. The main principles—

democratic representation, separation of powers, and guaranteed political and personal rights—were extended and defined more clearly. The executive, legislative and judiciary, were defined as follows:

a) The hereditary monarchy, assisted by the government, whose members were appointed by the king and which was responsible to parliament, whose confidence it required;

b) The Chamber of Deputies (elected by the people by direct, universal, equal, and secret vote) and the Senate (partly elected and partly appointed *ex officio* on the basis of past services to the country of the appointees);

c) The judiciary, headed by the Supreme Court, whose members throughout the entire hierarchy enjoyed personal immunity and inamovability. The courts could invalidate all rightfully challenged government acts, and the Supreme Court could declare any law unconstitutional and thus void it.

This regime of democratic and constitutional monarchy, based on direct popular participation and control, guaranteed as a matter of course all personal liberties. Freedom of conscience, of religion, of expression, and of association were specifically prescribed by the constitution, as were property rights, the inviolability of the home, freedom of movement, of residence, and of work. Violations of these personal and civic rights were made punishable by law, and redress through the courts was readily available to the individual.

The 1923 constitution remained in force until 1938, when it was replaced with that enacted on February 27, 1938, which, together with a concomitant series of authoritarian laws, marked the advent of King Carol's personal dictatorship. It was designed to introduce the single party system.

On September 5, 1940, the 1938 constitution was suspended by the dictatorial regime of Marshal Antonescu, which was to last through the war years, until its overthrow by the August 23, 1944, coup d'état.

With the arrest of Marshal Antonescu and the signing of the armistice that brought Rumania into the Allied camp, a decree issued by the king on August 31, 1944, and published two days later, restored the personal and civil liberties embodied in the constitutions of 1866 and 1923. By then, overwhelming Soviet occupation forces had overrun the country, and events that ensued ran against the reestablishment of anything remotely resembling a democratic regime.

The communist-dominated Groza government, forcibly imposed by the Kremlin, proceeded to liquidate all political opposition, to suppress all liberties, to exile the king, and, following what have been described as one of the most fraudulent elections known to history, set up a Grand National Assembly. Acting as a rubber stamp, this assembly obediently voted, and the government promptly promulgated, the constitution of April 13, 1948. This statute, though differing in many respects from the Soviet constitution, was clearly inspired by it. Its main purpose was to set up, with a semblance of democratic forms, a totalitarian dictatorship of the Communist party.

As in the Soviet Union itself, the Communist party of Rumania, calling itself the Rumanian Workers' Party, was legally set up as the sole source of power and authority. Designating and controlling the election of the Assembly's members, which in turn "elected" the Presidium (endowed with the functions and prerogatives of the head of state), in whose hands lay the appointment of a Council of Ministers, the latter in effect carrying out both the executive and the judicial functions of government. Thus the Soviet juridical system, which admits no separation of powers in the state, and which provides for effective control by the single party in power, was formally introduced in Rumania. The country itself was formally renamed the Rumanian People's Republic.

The 1948 constitution prescribed a number of personal rights and liberties which, however, were automatically negated by the manner of their enforcement. More significantly, it listed a series of concomitant duties, notably the duty to work, which could be, and subsequently was, construed as authorizing forced labor. As most of the salient innovations of the 1948 constitutions were featured also in the constitution of 1952, they will be discussed in connection with the latter statute.

On July 19, 1952, the Rumanian Workers' Party made public the draft of a new constitution, which comprised an introductory chapter and ten main headings, with a total of 105 articles. With the greatest attendant publicity, the draft constitution was ostensibly submitted to public debate. The regime's propaganda machine spared no device in inviting comments, suggestions, and discussions of the project, prior to the actual vote by the Grand National Assembly. The whole procedure was conducted unilaterally by the communists, under precise instructions from the party's central organ, and one would seek in vain the actual contributions by the people of Rumania themselves to the proposed charter. Indeed, even in the course of the debates staged by the Grand National Assembly, the draft—which was discussed and voted within the space of a few brief hours—was modified only in a few minor particulars, most of which merely accentuated the authoritarian and Soviet-inspired character of the charter. The constitution was voted unanimously by the Assembly and came into effect on September 24, 1952.

The 1952 constitution consists of an Introductory Chapter and ten Chapters, titled as follows:

1) Social Organization;
2) Organization of the State;
3) The Supreme Organ of State Power in the Rumanian People's Republic;
4) The Organs of State Administration of the Rumanian People's Republic;
5) Local Organs of State Power;
6) The Judiciary and the Office of the Public Prosecutor;
7) Fundamental Rights and Duties of Citizens;
8) The Electoral System;
9) The Emblems, Flag, and Capital of the Rumanian People's Republic;
10) The Procedure for Amending the Constitution of the Rumanian People's Republic.

Like the above, the constitution of 1948 was also divided into ten parts called "Titles," and the chapter headings of the 1952 statute closely follow the names of the previous one (though the contents differ in detail); the 1952 text is closer to that of the Soviet Union's constitution, and the Introductory Chapter comes as a highly significant innovation. The U.S.S.R. constitution has 13 chapters, the three titles missing from the R.P.R. constitution of 1952 being those that deal with the federal organization of the Union Republics and Autonomous Republics which, of course, do not apply to Rumania.

The Introductory Chapter, which does not exist in the Soviet constitution, is common to the basic charters adopted in all the Soviet Union's "satellites". Its main purpose is to express in servile terms the alleged "friendship" toward, and "alliance" with "the great Soviet Union", whose "historical victory over German fascism", together with "the liberation of Rumania by the glorious Soviet army . . . allowed the working people, headed by the working class, led by the Communist party, to overthrow fascist dictatorship, to crush the power of the exploiting classes, and to set up the state of popular democracy, which corresponds wholly to the interests and aspirations of the popular masses of Rumania". It also stresses the friendship and alliance with "the countries of popular democracy, and a policy of peace and friendship with all peace-loving peoples." As for the state policy of the people's democracy, it is described by the preamble as aimed "at the liquidation of the exploitation of man by man, and at the construction of socialism".

The opening chapter furthermore attempts to justify the need for the new constitution, stating that, "The present constitution of the Rumanian People's Republic consecrates the results hitherto achieved by the workers, headed by the working class, in the work of building the socialist society in our country". In other words, it states officially that the socialist evolution had advanced so far in Rumania by 1952, that it could no longer be adequately covered and provided for by the constitution of 1948. It might be remarked that the socialization of the country could very well have been carried out under the constitution of 1948. The inference appears to be that while, as will be seen presently, the 1952 constitution comes much closer to that of the Soviet Union, and is hence a considerable forward legal step in the actual sovietization of Rumania, the statute itself was primarily introduced for its propaganda value, both at home and abroad. A comparative analysis of the 1952 constitution will indicate, too, that it is more radical and "advanced" than those of the other satellite countries, including the more recent one of Poland. It would appear, therefore, that Rumania has been given the dubious distinction by the Kremlin of acting as an experimental field and an example to the other enslaved countries of Europe.

The chapter, entitled Social Organization, which corresponds to Chapter 1 of the Soviet Union's constitution of 1936, is notable in that it sets forth the social reforms introduced, following the pattern established in the U.S.S.R. itself. Article 1 reproduces the first sentence of the Introductory Chapter, stating that the R.P.R. is a "state of the workers of cities and villages." Article 2 describes the "alliance of the working class and the working peasantry", in which the "leading role" belongs to the former, as the "foundation of popular power in the R.P.R." Article 2 states that the R.P.R. was born and consolidated as the result of the country's liberation by the armed forces of the Soviet Union, and owing to the subsequent overthrow of the "power of the great landowners" by the workers of cities and villages, led by the Rumanian Communist party. The power, adds article 4, is exercised "through the intermediary of the Grand National Assembly and the People's Councils," the latter constituting the "political basis of the R.P.R." This comes much closer to the Soviet constitution than the provisions of the 1948 constitution, which contained merely the general statement that "the power emanates from the people and belongs to the people". It still falls short of the Soviet constitution, however, in that it does not mention the "dictatorship of the proletariat."

Articles 5, 6, and 7 define the three "social-economic sectors" of the R.P.R., which are (a) the socialist sector, (b) the sector of "small merchant production," and (c) the "private capitalist sector." The socialist sector is, according to article 6, "founded upon the socialist ownership of the means of production," which may take the form of state property, cooperative property, or collective property. Here, the difference from the Soviet constitution is the recognition of the existence of a "private capitalist sector." Article 7, however, so extensively enumerates the fields of endeavor and the resources that are barred to private ownership and exploitation, that the "private capitalist sector" is effectively reduced to an academic existence, with the notable exception of small privately owned and operated farms, and workshops of minor importance. In this respect, the R.P.R. constitution goes considerably farther than the constitution of the other "satellite" countries of Europe.

Articles 8–12 deal with land ownership, article 8 stating flatly that "in the R.P.R. the land belongs to those who work for it." Article 9 regulates the standing and operation of collective farms (identical with the Soviet Union's own kolkhozes) and cooperative properties. Members of collective farms are permitted to retain private ownership of "the auxiliary economy situated" on the plot considered as belonging to their house, of the house itself, and of such "production stock, fowls, and small agricultural material" as may be permitted by the statute of the collective farm to which they themselves belong. They have only "the personal enjoyment" of the plot. This, and the fact that the extent of the outright ownership of the rest is specifically left by article 9 to the statute of the collective farm itself, makes the entire matter of what a collective farmer may or may not consider to be his private property entirely unclear and uncertain. From this point of view, the R.P.R. constitution is more drastic than those of the other "people's democracies."

Article 10 permits "merchant production" in the form of "small and middling peasant exploitations, in which land ownership is founded upon the personal labor of the producer, as well as of workshops of artisans that do not exploit the labor of others." Such private landownership rights, the article states, are protected by the state, "in accordance with existing laws."

Article 11 states unambiguously that it is a policy of the state to "limit and eliminate capitalist elements." Articles 12 and 13 deal respectively with other property rights and with the state plan. Article 14 states that foreign trade is a "state monopoly." Lastly, article 15 proclaims the Soviet principle that "he who does not work does not eat," and makes labor "a duty and a question of honor for every citizen able to work." It also states that the tendency is to apply increasingly the socialist principle "from each according to his means, to each according to his work."

The agreement of the above principles, as enunciated in Chapter 1 of the R.P.R. constitution, with the corresponding principles of the Soviet constitution is obvious enough. The toleration of a "capitalist sector" and, especially, of private tenure in land (small and middling farmers) must be attributed to the recognition by the communists of the inescapable fact that in 1952 Rumania was far from ripe for total socialization.

The chapter entitled Organization of the State, corresponding to Chapter II of the Soviet constitution, comprises articles 16 through 21, and opens with the reiteration that the "state regime of the R.P.R. is a regime of popular democracy, that represents the power of the workers." Article 17 goes on to describe this state as "unitarian, sovereign, and independent." Attention should be drawn here to the term "popular democracy" or "people's democracy" (the Soviet constitution speaks of the "socialist state"), which is to be found in other satellite constitutions, and which, in communist terminology, designates what can be described only as a preliminary stage in the "construction of socialism."

Article 17 enumerates the functions of a popular democracy, which in some respects may appear to go beyond the corresponding provisions of the Soviet constitution. We find, for instance, "enemies of the people" mentioned twice: (a) in connection with the "defense of the Rumanian people's independence and sovereignty" and (b) in connection with the "internal security" of citizens, when the charter proclaims that one of the state functions is to "neutralize and punish the enemies of the people." The introduction of these provisions in the constitution is tantamount to a recognition of the strong and widespread resistance to the communist regime. Since it is the most elementary business of any organized state to assure security against attacks from without and within, and since Article 17 itself states that ". . . the constitution and the laws of the country (are) the expression of the will and interests of the working people," why enunciate such notions at all?

Another interesting innovation is that the conduct of foreign affairs is specifically attributed, not to the state as such, but to the Presidium of the Grand National Assembly (art. 37). Here, too, there is divergence from the Soviet constitutional pattern.

Articles 18–21 deal with the territorial divisions of the country, 18 administrative divisions or "regions" being set up. Among these there is the "Magyar Autonomous Region," an innovation obviously inspired by the national-administrative division of the Soviet Union, but also by the need felt to give the Hungarian minority of Rumania a modicum of satisfaction. "Autonomous" is largely an academic notion in this connection, in view of the fact that, according to article 20 of the constitution, all laws, decisions, and ordinances passed by the R.P.R. central authorities are equally binding to all that live in the region. Furthermore, in the terms of the Law No. 77, of September 8, 1950, a "region" is defined as an "administrative and economic unit, circumscribed territorially, that carries out the policy of the party and government."

Article 22 states that the highest organ of state power in the R.P.R. is the Grand National Assembly which, according to article 23, is also the "sole legislative organ," and, according to article 24, elects the Presidium, forms the government, modifies the constitution, decides on matters of war and peace, establishes plans for the national economy, approves the budget, determines the number of ministries, their creation and fusion, decides on matters pertaining to the administrative division into regions, exercises amnesty rights, and generally controls the application of the constitution. It is "elected by the workers, who are citizens of the R.P.R., voting by electoral districts, in the ratio of one deputy to 40,000 inhabitants." Its term of office is four years (art. 25). It meets twice yearly (art. 28), but may be convened in extraordinary sessions by the Presidium (art. 29). Its decisions are taken by simple majority (art. 26). In practice, the Grand National Assembly's sessions have lasted two days, on an average, and its role has been obviously that of a legalizing rubber stamp, approving—with invariable unanimity—every measure set before it.

The Grand National Assembly validates the mandates of its members (art. 31); it may appoint investigation commissions (art. 32); its members are exempt from legal pursuit and arrest (art. 34); it elects the Presidium, which is composed of a president, two vice-presidents, a secretary, and thirteen members (art. 35). The Presidium, which is answerable for all its activities to the Grand National Assembly (art. 36) has, according to article 37, the following wide range of powers: it convenes the sessions of the Assembly; issues decrees; interprets the laws in force; decides on referendums; annuls decrees and orders of the Council of Ministers, when they are not in agreement with the law; appoints and relieves of their duties (on proposal from the Council of Ministers, and pending subsequent approval by the Assembly) the ministers that form the government; institutes and awards decorations and military ranks and distinctions, diplomatic ranks, and other special titles; decides on a state of war (between sessions of the Assembly, and on proposal from the government); appoints and demotes the supreme commander of the R.P.R. armed forces; orders partial or total mobilization; pardons and commutes sentences; ratifies and denounces international treaties; accredits and recalls plenipotentiaries of the R.P.R., and receives the letters of credence and recall of foreign representatives; and proclaims states of emergency on part or the whole of the national territory.

"The supreme executive and administrative organ of state power" is, according to Article 42, the Council of Ministers. It comprises, according to Article 43, the president and vice-presidents of the Council of Ministers (the number of the latter is unlimited), the president of the State Planning Commission, the president of the State Control Commission, the ministers, and the presidents of the State Provisioning Committee, of the State Grain Collection Committee, of the Committee for higher education, of the Cinematographic Committee, and of the Arts Committee. Responsible to the Grand National Assembly and to the Presidium (art. 44), it has the following powers: to coordinate and direct the activities of ministries and other subordinate institutions; to take measures in execution of the state plan, of the state budget, and the consolidation of the currency and credit system; to assure public order; to coordinate foreign relations; to establish the annual draft contingent and to direct the general organization of armed forces; and to set up committees and commissions as well as general directorates, for economic, cultural, judiciary, and military matters (art. 47). It is unnecessary to enumerate the individual ministries as they are set forth in article 50, because since the constitution came into effect, there have been a number of changes, ministries merged and new ones set up, a process that is still going on.

Chapter V deals with the local organs of state power, the local people's councils, the R.P.R. counterpart of the soviets in the USSR. Following the administrative divisions of the country, there are people's councils for regions, raions, cities, and villages (art. 51). Their members, called deputies, are elected for two-year terms (art. 52), in accordance with the electoral law. As for the elections to the Grand National Assembly, article 52 states that the electors must be "workers," considered as such by the party. The people's councils are simply the local organs of the communist party, whose role (art. 53) is to "guide the activities of subordinate administrative organs, local economic and cultural activities, and to assure the maintenance of public order," in addition to making the local budget and assuring the respect of laws and the protection of citizens' rights. They work through their executive committees (arts. 56, 57, and 59), and they are responsible both to the immediately superior people's councils and to the respective ministries (art. 62).

The role of the judiciary, according to article 65, is "to defend the regime of popular democracy and the conquests of the working people, to assure the respect of popular legality, of public property, and of the rights of citizens." It comprises "the Supreme Court of the R.P.R., the regional courts, the people's courts, and special courts set up by law," in the terms of article 64. All courts include (art. 66) people's assessors, "except in cases specially provided for by law." The Supreme Court is elected by the Grand National Assembly for a five-year term (art. 67), while the appointment of judges to the lower courts and to "special" courts, as well as the election of the "people's assessors," is left to be dealt with by special laws. This means, at this time, the amended Law No. 5, of June 19, 1952, which provides for the appointment of judges by the Minister of Justice, and for the election of the people's assessors (whose functions and standards of justice are political rather than legal) on proposal by either organs of the Rumanian Workers' Party or by organizations that are directly controlled by it. Since the election of members or the Grand National Assembly is similarly rigidly controlled by the single party or by organizations under its direct sway, the manner in which the entire system operates—directly or indirectly—is obviously designed to assure the basic principle of "no separation of powers."

Court proceedings are public, "except in cases provided for by law," in the terms of article 69, which also guarantees the accused the right of defense. "Court decisions are rendered in the name of the people" (art. 71).

The Prosecutor is appointed by the Grand National Assembly for a term of five years (art. 74), and as the Supreme Court has supreme control over all lower courts (art. 72), so does the Prosecutor General over all lower prosecutors (art. 74), whom he himself appoints for four year terms. The Prosecutor General is answerable to the Grand National Assembly and to the Presidium (art. 75).

First listed in the chapter on the Fundamental Rights and Duties of Citizens is the right to work, which, according to article 77, is "guaranteed by the existence and development of the socialist sector of the national economy, by the constant and systematic growth of production forces in the R.P.R. by the elimination of the possibility of economic crises, and by the suppression of unemployment." Next in order come the right to rest, based on an eight-hour working day (art. 78); the right to old-age insurance (art. 79); and the right to free elementary education (art. 80). "Absolute equality of rights" is assured to all "workers," regardless of their ethnical origin, who are citizens (art. 81); women have equal rights in all respects (art. 83). Article 84 guarantees freedom of conscience (making no distinction as between "workers" and others); it also states that education is separated from the Church, and that the Churches are to be regulated by law, as to their organization and manner of functioning. It is interesting to note that article 84, unlike article 123 of the Soviet constitution, fails to include the freedom of anti-religious propaganda.

Article 85 lists further freedoms: of speech, of the press, of assembly and meetings, and of "processions and street demonstrations." However, these rights are extended "in conformity with the interests of the workers," and they are "assured" by "placing at the disposal of the working masses and of their organizations printing presses, paper stocks, public buildings, streets, means of communication, and other material conditions necessary to the exercise of these rights."

Article 86, while permitting the formation of various associations (with the textual exclusion of those "of a fascist or anti-democratic character," membership in which is "punishable by law"), formally prescribes that "the most active and conscious citizens of the working class and of other strata of workers join in the Rumanian Workers' Party." This party is not formally described as communist, but as "the vanguard detachment of the workers in their struggle for the strengthening and development of the regime of popular democracy and for the construction of the socialist society." The final paragraph of article 86 is the truly significant one: "The Rumanian Workers' Party is the directing force of all workers' organization, *as well as of the state organs and institutions. Around it are grouped all workers' organizations of the R.P.R.*"

Continuing the enumeration of rights—and following in general the pattern set by articles 118–125 of the Soviet constitution—articles 87 and 88 guarantee respectively "personal inviolability," "inviolability of the home," and "secrecy of correspondence," to all citizens, and not only to "workers." The right of asylum is guaranteed to citizens of foreign states, "pursued for having defended the interests of the workers or for reasons connected with their scientific activities or for having taken part in the struggle for national liberation or for the defense of peace."

Finally come the duties of citizens. Article 90 prescribes respect of the constitution and of the laws of the R.P.R. as well as the duty to "safeguard, strengthen, and develop socialist public property; to respect labor discipline, and to contribute actively to the consolidation of the regime of popular democracy and to the economic and cultural development of the country." Article 91, after stating that military service is compulsory, elaborates this by proclaiming that "military service in the ranks of the armed forces of the R.P.R. is a duty of honor for every citizen of the R.P.R." This is enforced by article 92, which says, "The defense of the fatherland is the sacred duty of every citizen of the R.P.R." and adds that, "treason toward the fatherland, violation of the oath, passing to the enemy, prejudice brought to the state's military power, and espionage constitute the most serious crimes against the people and the state, and are punished with the fullest severity of the law."

The chapter on the electoral system opens with article 93 which states that elections for the Grand National Assembly and the people's councils are carried out by "universal, equal, direct, and secret suffrage." The voting age is fixed at 18, and the age of those elected at 23 (art. 94). Articles 95 and 98 stipulate that the electorate is formed of "all workers who are citizens." Article 96 grants equal rights to women, and article 97 extends these rights to members of the armed forces. Article 100 guarantees the right to put candidates up for election to "all workers' organizations: to the organizations of the Rumanian Workers' Party, to professional trade unions, to cooperatives, to youth organizations, and to other mass organizations, as well as to cultural organizations."

Articles 102, 103, and 104 deal respectively with the arms (in the heraldic sense), the flag, and the capital of the R.P.R. Article 105, the last, deals with the manner in which the constitution may be amended. A two-thirds majority vote of the Grand National Assembly is required for any constitutional amendment.

It will be readily seen from the above analysis that the salient feature of the R.P.R. constitution of 1952 is that there is no separation of powers under its system. Though it deals separately with the state's powers (art. 17), with the powers of the Grand National Assembly (art. 24), of the Presidium (art. 37), of the Council of Ministers (art. 47), of the people's councils (art. 51), and of the judiciary (arts. 64, 72, 73, and 76) all power finally converges in the hands of the single party, as it does in the Soviet Union, which served as the model. The single party in Rumania, as we have seen, does not call itself a communist party, but is content to refer to itself formally as the Rumanian Workers' Party.

As for the Soviet system, the point has been enunciated in no uncertain terms by no less an authority than the late Andrei Vishinsky: "The program of the All-Union Communist (bolshevik) Party rejects the bourgeois principle of the separation of powers." (Andrei Vishinsky, *The Law of the Soviet State,* Macmillan, 1948.)

From the texts quoted above, it is already evident that the Grand National Assembly wields, in the final analysis, not only the legislative powers, but also the executive and judiciary. In view of the fact that all elections, both for Grand National Assembly and for the local people's councils (soviets), are under the strict control of the Communist party or of organisms and organizations that are under its exclusive sway, it is impossible to speak of popular representation in the accepted sense of the term. The rights proclaimed in the constitution, both public and private, are negated effectively in actual practice. Even the right to work is a mere fiction. For, on the one hand, certain categories are effectively barred from regular employment, while, on the other hand, the conditions imposed upon the workers under the guise of "labor discipline" (a constitutional obligation) can be and in fact have been, so legislated and interpreted as to become tantamount to a regime of forced labor.

With regard to the constitutional duties, too, there is to be observed a notable denial of civil liberty, one that amounts to a formal annulment of freedom of conscience, namely the obligation imposed on all citizens to "contribute actively to the strengthening of the regime of popular democracy." This is, in fact, nothing short of a formal abolition of anything remotely resembling opposition, even passive non-cooperation. The same applies to the obligation to "safeguard and strengthen and develop socialist public property," to be found likewise in Article 90 of the constitution.

The exceptionally heavy penalties prescribed for what have come to be officially described as "anti-state activities," together with the peculiarity that all criminal provisions are deliberately worded as loosely as possible, result in a constant threat hanging over the heads of all citizens. The constitutional right of defense, laid down in article 69, has been shown in actual practice to be illusory. Official accounts of trials, published in the R.P.R. press, are on record to illustrate this fact. In no political trial yet held in Rumania, has the defense ever pleaded innocent. Rather it has invariably admitted guilt, as charged, and limited itself to a plea for leniency. The wide interpretation that the courts may legally give to the existing texts, coupled with the fact that the "people's assessors," who form the majority of every quorum, are primarily concerned with the political characteristics of the cases and of the defendants, allow the gravest injustices to pass for justice.

Such personal liberties as the "personal inviolability" and the "inviolability of the home," guaranteed respectively by articles 87 and 88 of the constitution, are set at nought by the every-day practices of the totalitarian police state. The "secrecy of correspondence" mentioned in article 88 is likewise known to mean the exact contrary, a strict censorship by the secret police. It is enough to enumerate such civil liberties as those mentioned in article 85, to have a list of activities universally known to be absolutely beyond the reach of the citizens of the R.P.R. Freedom of speech, of the press, of assembly and meetings, and of processions and street demonstrations must all be understood to mean, *strictu sensu*, that the citizens may speak, write, assemble, and demonstrate only as the party decrees. Indeed, not even then can such activities be rightly described as the exercise of a right, but as the fulfilment of a duty. For, when the party requires citizens (in their capacity as "workers") to make any statement, to write anything, to attend a meeting, or to go out into the streets and demonstrate, there is no holding back, and no job holder in his right mind will hesitate to comply, knowing full well that his living and even his personal safety may be at stake.

The constitutional distinction between "citizens" and "workers," which recurs throughout the 1952 charter, is yet another notable feature. It results, on the one hand, in the conference of certain civil rights to a circumscribed category of citizens. Article 94 specifically excludes from voting in elections for the Grand National Assembly "persons that have been deprived of electoral rights by the courts or that have been declared unworthy by law." Article 52 similarly limits voting rights to "citizens who are workers" in elections for the people's councils. This amounts to the legal elimination of all opposition to the regime. Again, it is the all-powerful party that determines who shall be a "worker" and who "unworthy" in the eyes of the law. There is, furthermore, no guaranteed permanence implied for the individual citizen under this system. The least deviation, the most involuntary infringement of the line set by the party, either by commission or by omission, may at all times cost the individual "worker" his relatively privileged status. Deprived of the right to regular employment, ineligible thereby for membership in one or another of the all-embracing unions or cooperatives, the delinquent loses all attendant privileges, such as preferential status in the matter of access to food, clothing and housing. Such a demotion has far-reaching consequences, not only from the point of view of the individual's civil rights, but also from that very immediate one of his and his family's economic circumstances.

But if the citizen's rights are highly contingent, the same can not be said of his constitutional obligations. Not only do his duties exist independently of any rights, not only do they far outweigh the rights, but they hang as a constant threat over the individual's head—open at all times to the widest interpretation in his disfavor. In other words, under the R.P.R. regime, as under every communist-inspired regime, the individual's rights are compressible and his duties expandible, at the discretion of the authorities.

Whether merely a citizen or also a "worker," the individual is at all times subject to the far-reaching consequences of a loosely specified "labor discipline," as we have seen. This situation has resulted in what can be described only as outright industrial and agricultural peonage. But that is not all. The R.P.R. Labor Code of 1950 provides—in Article 111—that "in exceptional cases" citizens may be called upon "to perform certain temporary obligations of labor," thus legalizing conscription of labor.

We must note, finally, that in foisting the 1952 constitution upon the people of Rumania, the communists have displayed ingenious foresight in at least one respect. By ostensibly submitting the draft to public debate, and by attributing it formally to the "results hitherto achieved by the workers," as the Introductory Chapter proclaims, they have contrived to give the constitution a formal aspect of public approval. The "debates" before the Grand National Assembly came merely as a climax. Gheorghiu-Dej himself told the Assembly that "more than 8,000 amendments and proposals" had been forthcoming from the people, and that these "had, in the great majority, been taken into account in drafting the final text." Hence, the Assembly was told it could accept the final text, "firmly convinced it was expressing the votes of millions of workers . . . who had already approved it." The Grand National Assembly passed the constitution, after less than two days of discussion—a *pro forma* discussion, according to the official accounts issued at the time—by unanimous vote. The text as voted was practically identical with the original draft. The 1952 constitution of the R.P.R. remains, however, an alien statute, contrary both to the spirit and to the traditions of the Rumanian people.

the judiciary

It is probably in the realm of justice that the Soviet-inspired innovations introduced by the R.P.R. communist regime have had the most striking consequences. Students of communist ideology and practice are of course aware that what the communists call "the most advanced" justice differs greatly, both in its conceptions of principle and in its manner of operation, from the legal systems elaborated in the Western democracies upon the foundations of classic Roman law and of traditional common law. A country like Rumania—where, up to the advent of the communist regime—the philosophic notions of justice, and their translation into legislation and judiciary practice had evolved in step with the Western world—provides a particularly striking instance of the thorough upset brought about by the enforced substitution of the "Marxist-Leninist historical imperative" for the moral ideals and the scale of values that formerly prevailed. The change is as absolute as the regime is totalitarian.

Here and there the familiar terminology persists, but the words no longer have their original meaning. There can be no justice, in the commonly accepted sense, in a state that discards the ethical ideas of right and wrong, that ignores the ideas of liberty and individual rights in the organization and exercises of its judiciary. No relationship can be found between the ethical notion of justice and the function of the judiciary under a regime of "popular democracy." Indeed it may be said that it is precisely this lack of relationship which is characteristic of the R.P.R. legal system. Certainly it is in this discrepancy that we find the diametrical opposition between the traditional and the "new" concepts of justice.

The last constitution in force in free Rumania, that of 1923, provided as a matter of course such guarantees as the principle of the separation of

state powers, the independence of the judiciary, the immovability of
judges, the control of the constitutionality of laws, and the legal responsibility of the executive. Like the old Constitution of 1866, it gave the
magistrature an independence that was no mere matter of form, but a
reality stemming from the very working of the fundamental charter.

As we have seen in the previous Chapter, the communist-imposed charter of 1952 does away with this entire system. Article 65 defines justice as
an instrument for the protection of the regime of popular democracy, of
the conquests of the working people, of popular legality, and of socialist
property. This definition is reiterated in the Law for the Organization of
the Judiciary, introduced on June 19, 1952, and modified on March 4,
1953. Article 2 of that law states that the primary mission of justice is
to defend the social and state structure and the socialist economic system.
Current R.P.R. doctrine, reproducing the legal theories officially accepted in the Soviet Union, strongly enforces this view. "The creation
of this proletarian state," proclaimed the authoritative magazine *Justitia
Noua* for 1954, "is not possible without the prior shattering of the state
machinery set up for itself by the bourgeoisie, of the bourgeois army, of
the bourgeois police and justice, of the bureaucratic administrative apparatus, of parliamentarianism." (Article by I. Ceterchi, 1954, page 585.)

In other words, the role of justice is primarily a negative one, but it
also has a positive role: to serve as an instrument of oppression in the
class war. Justice must be partial, it must be "partisan." Writing in *Justitia
Noua* for 1949 (page 65), a judge of the R.P.R. Supreme Court, I. Stoe-
nescu, made this clear: "In court decisions is expressed the attitude of the
governmental power toward certain social phenomena that come within
the sphere of activity of justice." And, elaborating Lenin's theory that
"Justice cannot be conceived independently of class," the same juridical periodical for December 1948 published the statement: "Justice becomes an organ for the execution of the will of the working class, its
method of action being that of Marxist-Leninist dialectic materialism,
the only method admitted by the ruling class, as the sole efficacious
method."

Under such a system it is obvious that the objective conscience of
judges applying legal texts impartially is replaced by the orders of the
communist party, posing as "popular legality." Indeed the very fact that
legality is thus qualified stresses the fact that we have here a legality that
is subordinated to a particular ideology—a far cry from the notion of

absolute justice as an ethical, rational concept. In the communist view, the law is simply a "superstructure," at all times correlated with the economic base. Hence legality merely confirms a given economic structure. Since policy itself is "the concentrated expression of economy," and the laws simply enforce policy, legality must have a substantially political role, for the laws themselves are "the means of enacting the policy of the dominant class." (Bratus, *Justitia Noua*, 1954, page 764.) That is to say, law is not an end in itself, and justice is no more than an instrument wielded by the government for its own purposes. The "popular legality" prescribed to the judiciary by Article 65 of the R.P.R. constitution does not mean the imposition of a rule of law, but of discipline. As one currently acknowledged author expressed it *Justitia Noua* for 1954 (page 769), "Socialist legality constitutes the indispensable condition for the realization of the policy of the communist party and of the government. . . . Juridical laws . . . express the scientific policy, that is, the policy of the communist party." One could hardly be more explicit.

It behooves all judges to enforce "popular legality" as the surest way to hasten the advent of communism, not because it expresses any ideal of justice among men. It is amply clear by now that this "popular legality" is the very negation of the idea of justice as conceived in the West and, formerly, in Rumania. This "popular legality" stands above the law, and places no burden of lawfulness upon the regime itself, since political expediency sways the very notion of justice. The results are unjust sentences for imaginary crimes, rigged trials, concentration and labor camps, and the rest of the repressive mechanism of the totalitarian communist regime. The only obligatory and permanent reference is to the consecrated writings of communist authority: Marx, Engels, Lenin, and Stalin, and then only in so far as these gospels can be made to fit the current party line in decisions of the party leadership. Any deviation is heresy, and heresy is a crime.

But, in addition to the obligation to conform to, and substantiate "popular legality," the judiciary must fulfil a task of education and propaganda in the exercise of their duty. Article 2 of the law organizing the courts is peremptory: "Through their activity, the courts educate the citizens of the R.P.R. in the spirit of devotion to the fatherland, of socialist construction, of the exact fulfilment of R.P.R. laws, of particular care for socialist property, of labor discipline, of an honest attitude toward civic and social duties, as well as of respect toward the rules of social coexistence in the state of popular democracy." It is clear from this text that the judge's appraisal is severely restricted. It is no less that Justice is a one-way proposition under the current system.

The criteria enumerated above are obviously more often than not in flagrant contradiction with the civil liberties and human rights as understood in the West, and as confirmed, for instance, in the United Nations Charter. In effect the educational task of the courts is to subject the people to the constrictive measures enacted by the administration, whose constant tendency is to suppress the individual as an autonomous personality. Severe sentences must be handed down to serve as an example and a warning. The arbitrary acts of the administration must at all costs be given legality. Defendants must be made to admit their guilt; parents must accuse their own children, and children must testify against their parents; husband and wife must take a stand alongside the administration against one another; men must denounce their neighbors. The righteousness of governmental measures of a coercive nature must be justified before public opinion from the bench.

This explains the publicizing of certain trials. Entire categories of citizens are forcibly brought into court to watch selected trials and to be intimidated by the severity with which those whom the regime considers to be its enemies are punished. In his role as a propaganda agent, the judge must promote conformity among the citizenry. He thus becomes the principal instrument of conscience violation, in pursuance of this forcible communist indoctrination. Under such conditions, it is hardly necessary to point out that a judge under a regime of popular democracy has little resemblance to his counterpart of the free world.

True enough, article 70 of the R.P.R. constitution proclaims, and it is echoed by article 6 of the Law for the Organization of the Judiciary, that "Judges are independent, and are subject only to the law." But we have seen above that this "independence" is a very special thing with a most peculiar meaning.

As a matter of fact, the suppression of the independence of judges is not solely a consequence of the legal system in force. It is at the same time a result of the kind of professional training now required of jurists. The high educational standards that formerly prevailed in Rumania's judiciary were found to constitute a dangerous weapon of the opposition, a means of resistance, and a veritable threat to the regime. Men trained for the Bench by Western standards have been systematically eliminated. Only people prepared in the new schools, proficient solely in such legal skills are required to expound and apply the "high advanced conquests of Soviet juridical science," the Marxist-Leninist teachings, and the decisions of the communist party's central committee plenary.

The study of law is organized to this end. Though the "higher juridical schools" that have taken the place of university law schools still function, the overwhelming majority of today's jurists are trained in the "short-order" one-year law schools set up by Decree No. 297/1948, or in the two-year schools that replaced them under Decree No. 370 of October 6, 1952. Such schools, functioning as services of the Ministry of Justice, are specially designed to turn out future judges and prosecutors. Their students are recruited from among industrial workers and collectivized or "poor peasants (article 3 of Decree No. 370/1952), so that graduates may presumably be favorable to the regime. Prospective judges and prosecutors are *expressis verbis* barred if they have any real previous schooling. The law required a minimum of four years of elementary schooling and a maximum of four years in secondary school as the entrance condition. It is not too difficult to imagine the kind of legal training that is built upon such educational foundations, and the nature of the mental "independence" resulting therefrom.

The R.P.R. constitution, as we have seen, requires the presence of "people's assessors" at all courts, except in cases otherwise provided for by law. The Law for the Organization of the Judiciary distinguishes between the judging of suits as to substance and the judging of appeals. The bench for the first category is composed of one judge and two "people's assessors"; for the second the quorum is three judges. Article 13 of the law states that people's assessors are elected on proposal by the Rumanian Workers' Party and by various organizations that are in effect but instruments of that party, such as trade unions, cooperatives, youth organizations, and so forth. Decision No. 365 of March 2, 1953, issued by the Council of Ministers provides that candidates for posts of people's assessors must be proposed in "popular meetings" held by the organizations mentioned. It also provides, however, that the minutes referring to such proposals must expressly mention the candidates' political affiliation and social origin. It is common knowledge that candidates are in effect put up for "election" by the Central Committee of the Communist party.

The "voting" is invariably unanimous; there are never any debates; no alternative candidates are nominated.

Elections of people's assessors for higher courts, such as the Tribunal of the R.P.R. capital, the regional courts, and special courts, are conducted—by open vote—within the competent people's councils. Here, too, the "elections" are always carried unanimously. People's assessors to the Supreme Court are chosen by the Grand National Assembly.

To qualify as a people's assessor, a person must be at least 23 years old (18 is the minimum voting age) and, as in the case of deputies elected to the Grand National Assembly, he or she must not have been defendant in a court sentence involving the loss of voting rights, and must not have been declared "unworthy" by law. People's assessors are accountable for any act that might be found to run counter to the party line, and are liable to criminal sanctions. They must in all cases carry out the party's orders. Though article 13 of the law states that people's assessors "are elected freely," the very next article proclaims that service in the capacity of people's assessor is compulsory. Even more so than career judges, people's assessors are therefore obedient tools of the party. Indeed, the entire procedure prescribed for their election and validation shows that they are mere party functionaries.

Under these circumstances, it is clear that the very title of "people's assessor" is a deliberate misnomer, notwithstanding the elaborate show of election. But then, as we have seen elsewhere, this applies equally to the so-called Grand National Assembly and to the people's councils themselves. As for the resulting "popular justice," it may well be said to be the precise opposite, the negation of everything implied by the words themselves.

Outnumbering the career judges two to one, the people's assessors, ignorant of legal matters and utterly submissive to party orders, represent in effect the active intervention of class war in all litigation, civil as well as criminal. As a result, R.P.R. courts play a role that differs widely from that of Western courts. Under a people's democracy the judge intervenes actively in all suits and trials, and the parties involved are no longer in a position, once the proceedings are set in motion, to bring to an end the litigation, say by out-of-court settlement. Even putting the opposing party under oath to testify no longer constitutes absolute evidence under this system. In all cases the primary interest is that of a third party—the Communist party. The court may at all times intervene and present its own evidence, continue a suit the parties might want to bring to an end, and thus substitute its own will (that is, the will of the Communist party) for that of the litigants.

The R.P.R. Constitution permits (art. 64) the creation of special courts. This means that special jurisdictions may be set up by law for trying a particular case, be it civil or criminal, or any particular person or group of persons, a thing expressly prohibited in the Rumanian Constitution of 1923. This fact alone indicates sufficiently the disregard for personal liberty, characteristic of the regime. At the same time it does away with the very notion of equality before the law.

The law of 1953 sets up the following jurisdictions for all manner of cases, both civil and criminal, that are not expressly referred by law to some special court:

a) The People's Courts for raions, cities, and city raions. These may judge all civil cases, no matter what their nature, except those arising between state institutions and nationalized and collective enterprises. The number of these courts, as well as the number of their sections is established by the Ministry of Justice (art. 19). They are composed "of a number of judges, and headed by a president" (art. 20).

b) The Tribunal of the R.P.R. capital (Bucarest) and the regional tribunals, each made up of one or more "collegia" of a civil and criminal nature, whose number is likewise fixed by the Ministry of Justice. These courts are in principle courts of revision, dealing with the cases handled by the people's courts of raion, city, and city raion. Exceptionally, they judge cases referred to them by law (art. 24). Their criminal collegium is of particular importance, its competence extending to decisions handed down by special courts like the people's tribunals for maritime, railroad, and river transport matters. Though they are from the hierarchic point of view immediately superior to the people's courts, tribunals of this category are not actually a second degree of jurisdiction; they are not courts of appeals proper. Copying the Soviet system, the R.P.R. judiciary does not recognize the right of appeal as such. This is a further means to ensure the complete subordination and conformity of courts.

c) The Supreme Court, which operates in Bucarest. This is composed of three collegia—criminal, civil, and military. Its president and judges are elected by the Grand National Assembly; its competence is multiple. It judges not only requests for revision of sentences and decisions passed by all other courts, and all cases referred to its jurisdiction by law, but it also instructs lower courts on the manner in which laws shall be applied.

The requests for review handled by the Supreme Court are essentially intended simply to assure "popular legality," that is to say, to ensure that in all cases the laws are interpreted and applied in conformity with the communist regime's ideology and aims. As *Justitia Noua* for 1954 (page 791) phrased it, the Supreme Court "promotes the policies of the party and government," and "assures the constriction of the private-capitalist sector to the point of liquidation." Leaving no doubt as to the true role of this highest and ultimate authority of the communist system of courts, *Justitia Noua* shows that its function is to break the people's resistance to communism. This is justified by the fact that the people, "through deeds and actions manifested in the most diverse forms, opposes a stubborn resistance to the construction of socialism."

The intervention of the Supreme Court as a reviewer of decisions by lower courts is not the result of action by the interested parties, but either by the R.P.R. Prosecutor General or by the President of the High Court himself. It is the latter who must introduce the request for review of a court decision that is considered to be "illegal and groundless." The criterion applied—and again we quote from *Justitia Noua* for 1954 (page 799)—is formulated as follows: "The rigorous application of procedural and substantive rules in solving a case must have a partisan character, and must be made from the positions of class war." In other words, consideration by the Supreme Court hinges, not on any legal issue, but solely on opportuneness from the political point of view of the regime. Furthermore, once taken under consideration, a case may be solved by the Supreme Court in a sense diametrically opposite to that of the original court decision. Evidence may be wholly reappraised, new elements introduced, and the very nature of the case may, on the sovereign appreciation of the Supreme Court, be changed. In criminal matters, the Supreme Court may increase or decrease the sentence; it may annul the sentence altogether; or send back the whole case to the prosecutor's office for further investigation and a new trial before another court (Decree 506/1953, modifying Article 406 of the Code of Criminal Procedure). Under such conditions, it is scarcely necessary to point out that the basic principles involving *res judicata* and double jeopardy are abolished.

What this entails in criminal cases is a veritable legal enormity: since resort to the Supreme Court does not come under any statute of limitations, anyone considered to be an enemy of the regime may be retried and sentenced anew at the very moment when he is about to finish serving his original term and to be released. Individual liberty is thus legally set at nought, for even a final court sentence becomes meaningless. This situation is admitted in so many words. "The dominant preoccupation of Justice," states *Justitia Noua* for 1954 (page 797), "is to apply juridical norms in the action of repressing inimical elements." And indeed, as can be seen from the above, there is no limit to what the Supreme Court can do to enforce "popular legality" in the "partisan spirit of class war."

As for the instructions the Supreme Court may give the lower courts, a procedure is prescribed by article 41 of the law. At least once every three months, the plenum of the Court must meet, in the presence of the Minister of Justice and the Prosecutor General, and the latter present their conclusions. Instructions thus handed down become rules of positive law, a veritable extra-legal source of legal prescriptions. In this way, there being no separation of powers in the state, the administration may enact and enforce any norms that may seem expedient politically, without having to put them through a show of legislative procedure. This does away with the principle of the pre-communist Rumanian Constitution concerning the authority to interpret the laws.

In certain cases expressly defined by law, the Supreme Court is called upon to judge, not only issues of law, but also the substance and facts involved. In such cases it functions much as do the lower courts.

From the above it must be concluded that the Supreme Court, at the same time an administrative, a legislative, and a political organ, is far removed from the High Court of Cassation of Rumania's former judicial system. Indeed one of the highest attributes of the former High Court of Cassation, the constitutional control of laws, is absent from the R.P.R. Supreme Court. Hence a powerful check upon abuses by the legislature is removed in the present totalitarian state, with the consequence that the last vestige of individual security is in effect abolished under the current regime.

d) The special courts mentioned earlier in this survey were instituted by law for certain fields of activity. They comprise military courts, railroad courts, and courts for maritime and riparian matters. Since, as we have seen, the R.P.R. constitution permits the creation of such special tribunals, it is impossible to define the rules governing their existence.

On the other hand, article 9 of the law for the organization of the judiciary permits hierarchically higher courts to remove from the competence of the lower any case pending before them, and either judge it themselves or send it for judgment to some other similar court. This legal provision amounts to yet another means, exercised through the intermediary of the judiciary, to deny justice to the citizenry by removing them unrestrictedly from their natural judges.

The most widely used of these special courts are the courts martial. In the terms of Article I of the law of June 12, 1952, "their purpose is to defend the social and state order of the R.P.R., to fight mercilessly against the enemies of the working people, as well as to strengthen the discipline and fighting capacity of the R.P.R. armed forces." Military courts, that is, have a prescribed role of political policing intended, not to mete out justice, but to repress and suppress the "enemies of the working people," a notion which, as we know, has a very broad meaning in communist parlance.

Consequently the number, location, and territorial competence of military courts is left indeterminate by the law, and such courts may be set up by the Minister of Justice, in agreement with the Minister of the Armed Forces, or of State Security (art. 3), as required. Judges of the military courts are appointed and transferred by the Ministers mentioned, and people's assessors for them are similarly appointed (art. 5). Hence both judges and assessors are wholly dependent upon the executive.

On the occasion of the introduction of the law of June 19, 1952, the doctrine concerning military courts was laid down before the Grand National Assembly. According to *Scanteia*, it was formulated as follows: "The sword of our military justice turns this day against the enemies of the people, that handful of worthless persons who envy our people their newly found happiness, and who hate our fatherland. It is in the first place the agents and footmen of American and British imperialists, the fascist and Titoist agents and spies, mortal foes of our people, who must be pitilessly struck by our military courts."

There are three categories of courts martial: a) the courts functioning in conjunction with large military units, and the courts whose jurisdiction is territorially defined; b) the courts set up for the existing military regions, for the navy, and for the units of the State Security Ministry; and c) the Military Collegium of the Supreme Court. The courts of the first category judge only the substance of cases, the others judge both substantive cases and cases submitted to them for review.

The partisan and inquisitorial nature of all these special courts results from the very competence given them by law. Thus, while the railroad courts and the maritime and riverine courts handle only certain arbitrarily defined categories of cases, the courts martial may judge, not only military personnel, but civilian offenders, men and women, in matters involving a most loosely defined state security. This very confusion of military order and domestic security indicates sufficiently the legal atmosphere that prevails in a people's democracy.

The entire function of the judiciary, hence the way of life imposed by law, are dominated in today's Rumania by that institution specific to communist regimes, the "Procuratura". This institution, which has no equivalent in Western legal systems, is the hierarchical apparatus topped by the Prosecutor General. In Rumania it was introduced by the law of June 19, 1952 (subsequently completed and re-enacted on March 4, 1953), on the model of the Soviet Union's system.

There is, as we have indicated, no real analogy between the "procuratura" and such institutions of the West as the French *parquet* and *procureur*, and the district attorney, the coroner, and the state prosecutor of Anglo-Saxon law. The procuratura, as set up by the R.P.R. constitution of 1952, and elaborated by the laws mentioned, is a special organ designed as a constant and ubiquitous means of checking all private and public life, and especially all court proceedings and decisions. It operates on the principle that "socialist legality" must be made to prevail on all occasions, exclusively and in an absolute manner. In the words of *Justitia Noua* (1951, page 955) this means "striking mercilessly at the enemies of the regime, at such elements as, through the remnants of their interests and mentality, still cling to the regimes of exploitation, and stand in the way of socialist construction."

The autocratic and totalitarian nature of the procuratura is defined in article 1 of the 1953 law, which provides that its powers extend over all state organs, all enterprises and cooperative organizations, and all functionaries and other citizens. The supreme head, the Prosecutor General, is essentially the agent of the party and government. He is, according to *Justitia Noua* (1951, page 958), "the political and class organ of the dictatorship of the proletariat."

Among other extensive functions, a prosecutor—for failure to attain the political purposes involved—may legally assail all normative measures enacted by local organs of the state, ministries, and state administration. To such ends, he may participate, with a consultative vote, in the meetings called by these organs for the elaboration of rules and regulations. Within five days following the signing of such normative decisions, the respective organs must forward all information to the prosecutor, who thereupon may enter a demand for review. In such cases, the act that fails to meet with his approval must be modified to conform with the prosecutor's observations. Should this not be done, the matter is referred to the immediately superior prosecutor, and may thus eventually come before the Grand National Assembly as the last resort. Aside from such direct control, the prosecutor may take cognizance of any complaints coming from the general public, and require the administration involved to make the necessary changes.

But the most significant power of the prosecutor is connected with criminal proceedings. He may intervene in all cases, at any stage of the legal procedure, and his directives become compulsory for all concerned (art. 7). He may initiate proceedings himself. Under these circumstances, the courts obviously lose all independence, since they must carry out the prosecutor's orders at all times. In practice, the prosecutor is virtually never absent in cases of arrests and inculpations carried out by the security police and the militia, ordering the steps to be taken as required by the party and government.

Furthermore, the prosecutor is the only person authorized to order that a person be kept in custody beyond the legal term, for criminal investigations (art. 8). It is difficult to conceive a more serious infringement of human rights and individual liberty.

But, in addition to the above, the prosecutor supervises all court proceedings, in order to make sure that, as *Justitia Noua* (1951, page 964) phrased it, "all those who by their deeds stand in the way of the regime" are duly punished. He may, that is, call for the review of any final sentence, and suspend any court decision, thus in effect annulling the legal security of the individual.

Lastly, the procuratura may substitute itself for the parties involved in any suit, by instituting or initiating further court procedures, as it may see fit (art. 9). Before all courts, the prosecutor (in Rumanian, *procuror*) is, in the words of A. I. Vyshinsky, "an agitator and a propagandist." How far-reaching the powers of the procuratura are, and how discretionary, is evidenced by the terms of article 11 of the law of 1953, which state that the orders of the Prosecutor General (in Rumanian, *procurorul general*) are compulsory, not only for all organs of the procuratura, but also for all investigating organs. Only the Presidium of the Grand National Assembly or the Council of Ministers may annul or suspend such orders (art. 12).

The exorbitant powers of the procuratura are matched by the methods it employs. Its doctrine is that laid down by that most notorious of the Soviet Union's prosecutors general, the late Andrei Vyshinsky, whose analysis was reverently quoted by *Justitia Noua* (1951, page 962). "The Procuratura is based upon its own organized active personnel, and upon groups of collaborators, in plants, factories, collective farms, transportation, institutions, and organizations . . . tens of thousands of volunteer activists, from among the country's most advanced citizens, stakhanovists and prominent workers of plants, collective farms, and state farms, who help the prosecutors vanquish the difficulties they encounter in this field . . . Thousands of *signallers* ensure that the procuratura can react swiftly."

Signallers, indeed. This means simply that the procuratura raises denunciation to the rank of a systematic state action, that the technique of the informer is encouraged and rewarded, and that the stool pigeon becomes an admired and praiseworthy civic leader.

What of the organization of the procuratura itself? Unlike the state prosecutors, district attorneys, and the *parquets* familiar in Western judiciary systems, who function in a purely legal capacity in conjunction with a court of law, the R.P.R. *procuror* is ubiquitous, and his name is legion. In addition to a powerful "central and directive apparatus," there is a vast and complex network of "local units."

The central office of the procuratura has 12 directorates, whose powers include: the direction of military prosecutions; state security and criminal prosecutions; those for the supervision of railroads, of sea and river navigation, and general policing activities; supervision of criminal court activities and of militia criminal investigations; the execution of penal sentences and of prison inspection; studies and statistics; and cadres and education. Each of these services is headed by a prosecutor, under the orders of the prosecutor general; together they constitute the operational staff of the center.

Within the framework and under the orders of these directorates are the "local units" of the procuratura, reaching down to the minutest territorial subdivision, through the raion, city, and so forth. The very numerous personnel includes prosecutors, assistant prosecutors, prosecutor's aides, chief investigators, and people's investigators, as well as military criminal investigators. Over this immense apparatus the Prosecutor General has absolute and final power: he confers grades, makes appointments, marks for advancement, controls all disciplinary action, and establishes uniforms and insignia. This special police corps of the judiciary in a people's democracy, this rigid hierarchy operating under a system of military rule, has no counterpart in the Western democracies; it is something without precedent in Rumania too. As we have seen in the chapter on the R.P.R. constitution, the head of this grim organization, the *Procuror General* or Prosecutor General, is appointed for a five-year term by the Grand National Assembly, and is answerable to that body and, in the intervals between its sessions, to the Council of Ministers, in whose working meetings he indeed participates with a consultative vote. This indicates sufficiently the essential role played by the procuratura in the R.P.R. state organization.

Pursuant to the provisions of the R.P.R. constitution, whose article 69 proclaims that "the accused is guaranteed the right of defense," the Decree concerning the lawyers' profession (No. 39/1950, published in the *Official Gazette* No. 11, of February 14, 1950) regulates the exercise of this "defense." This statute lays down rules that make it amply clear that the lawyers' profession under the current regime has but the name in common with the legal practice familiar to the West and to pre-communist Rumania.

In the R.P.R. the lawyer may not exercise his profession freely. He may not choose his clients, nor refuse a case. He is not bound by any notions of a professional secret. His office and home are at all times open to the visitations of the security police and militia, in search of data and evidence that need have no connection whatever with him personally. The government, through the Ministry of Justice, may use him at will for the promotions of the regime's purposes.

Under the terms of the decree mentioned above, the lawyers are organized in collegia, functioning in the district capitals and controlled by the Ministry of Justice (art. 3). The Ministry can at all times check on the activities of these collegia and of their members, and may take any measures it sees fit as the result of complaints against them. The Minister of Justice may even order the dissolution of a collegium. It is he, too, who decides the conditions of admission to the bar. Article 4 provides that "graduates of one-year law schools may register with the lawyers' collegia." As is the case with all other fields of endeavor, the manifest objective of the regime is to staff the lawyers' collegia exclusively with communist-trained, hence presumably "reliable" men and women, not with legally-minded and competent jurists of integrity.

Certain categories are expressly barred from the lawyers' profession: former landowners, manufacturers, merchants, and employers of labor, no matter what their social and political attitude may have been in the past. These people are *ipso jure* ineligible, let it be marked, not simply because they have been in the past members of a social class, but because they have been members of certain professional fields of endeavor, all of which were thoroughly lawful in pre-communist Rumania as they are now throughout the civilized world. Likewise barred are people sentenced for offenses against the political, social, or economic bases of the R.P.R.

Most revealing of all, however, is the provision of article 5 which prohibits the exercise of the legal profession to anyone guilty of any other kind of offense "that shall be appraised by the council of the collegium as rendering the sentenced person unsuitable for the lawyers' profession". This ruling by analogy (which is confirmed in the very first article of the R.P.R. Criminal Code) confers upon the council of the lawyers' collegium —itself but a tool of the Ministry of Justice—discretionary powers in the selection of those permitted to practise law. As a matter of fact, once admitted to the bar, all lawyers remain throughout their career subject to disciplinary measures, hinging not merely on reasons connected with their profession but on any deeds, attitudes, or manifestations indicating hostility to the regime (art. 48). The lawyer, in brief, must at all times obey the injunctions of the party authorities if he wishes to remain in practice.

Lawyers are enrolled in the collegium by decision of the council which must be confirmed by the Ministry of Justice (art. 9). The latter also establishes the requisite examinations and the examining commissions (art. 13). Thus from the beginning to the end, the independence of the lawyer is suppressed in the most thorough way that can be devised.

The exercise of the legal profession is likewise strictly regulated. In the first place, a lawyer may practise only within a collective lawyers' office. These are set up by the local collegium, and their organization and operation are regulated by decisions of the Ministry of Justice. They are headed by directors, working for a fixed rate of remuneration.

The right of the citizen to choose his lawyer is completely suppressed, as is the right of the lawyer to accept or refuse a client. Parties in a suit are represented in court on the basis of a written delegation, issued by the director and the secretary of the collective office (art. 23). There is no such thing as a general or a special power of attorney given by the prospective party—the delegation alone empowers the lawyer to represent a client. That is, the relationship of trust that exists between legal counsel and client is replaced with a task set by the state. In consequence lawyers' fees are not set in agreement between client and counsel, but unilaterally established by the director of the collective office, on the basis of a tariff approved by the Ministry of Justice. Fees are collected by the collective office only (art. 24), and the lawyer who actually handles the case receives but a portion thereof, set by the council of the collegium and likewise approved by the Ministry of Justice. The rest goes to meet various budget requirements of the collegium. In no case may any lawyer receive more than the monthly ceiling sum set by the collegium, no matter what fees he may actually earn. The only exceptions to this general rule operate in favor of individual lawyers who also hold high party rank.

Under a people's democracy lawyers no longer belong to what may be described as a liberal profession, but are indeed state functionaries of a special kind, carrying out set tasks and paid in accordance with government regulations. The law confirms this situation by formally prohibiting "the giving of consultations, the initiation of lawsuits, the drawing up of acts and requests, and, in general, the performance of essential legal services, otherwise than through collective offices" (art. 28).

As has been indicated above, the professional secret has gone by the board—or, to be accurate, a "partisan" conception of the professional secret has been introduced. The law now requires all lawyers to convey to the appropriate authorities any informations they may have concerning acts "endangering the domestic or external security of the state." Since this provision is purposely vague and undefined, no man can be sure that his lawyer will not betray him on the flimsiest pretext. Such a betrayal of trust is in fact to be expected, in view of the lawyer's constant need to ingratiate himself with the authorities in order to remain in practice. The result is that in seeking legal counsel, the citizen actually exposes himself to a potential trap.

The manner of presenting a plea before the courts must conform with the provisions of the law, and the law expects a lawyer to contribute to the "educational" and propagandist role of justice. Hence the lawyer's first concern is not the defense of his client's interests; his problem is not, in a criminal trial, to vindicate his client or to obtain a minimum sentence. On the contrary, he must plead for a harsh and exemplary punishment; he must, in all cases where this suits the purposes of the communist regime, plead guilty and admit the righteousness of the prosecutor's allegations. He must concentrate on pleading mitigating circumstances, notably on showing that whatever offense his client is supposed to have committed is the result of former corrupt education under the abhorred landowning-capitalist regime, or of British-American imperialist provocation. Such, too, is the standard plea of all accused in trials involving state security. The official published accounts of every political trial staged in the R.P.R.—and in the rest of the people's democracies—are invariable in this respect.

The defense lawyer, as often as not, is not even personally acquainted with his client, whom he must defend in virtue of the "delegation" by the collective lawyers' office. The line he is expected to take in the defense is to paraphrase the prosecutor's exposé, elaborating it and attempting to slip in a plea for mitigating circumstances, without attempting to disprove or discuss the accusations. A brochure was issued officially in Bucarest in 1950, concerning the espionage trial staged on June 28, 1950 before the Bucarest military court. Here are a few quotations *from the defense:* (My client is) ". . . corrupted by the rotten bourgeois morals, and lacks all patriotic feelings." (Another defendant) ". . . a highly trained spy, instigated and patronized by the Apostolic Nuncio." (The defendants are) "sold to the dollar; they serve the interests of American and British imperialists, to the detriment of the people's interests." (The defense) ". . . admits that the deeds of the accused are particularly serious . . . Behind him stand the true authors and instigators of these crimes, the British-American imperialists."

In the official brochure describing the trial of the group of "traitors" headed by Iuliu Maniu (Bucarest, 1947), we find one defending lawyer making the following statement: ". . . The accusation has succeeded in gathering so much evidence against the accused, and to bring out so well the exceptional gravity of the things imputed to them . . ." Another prominent communist lawyer, in a trial staged on August 7, 1950, based his plea on behalf of his client as follows: "The activities he is accused of and which he admits will no doubt result in severe punishment." This lawyer, incidentally, was none other than Paraschivescu-Balaceanu, the president of the lawyers' collegium. In that same trial, yet another defending lawyer, after duly admitting the "crimes" of his client, wound up his plea thus: "These are the elements evidenced by the accusation, and I request (the court) to bear them in mind in establishing the appropriate punishment for the accused."

It is needless to continue with such quotations; they are all too familiar to all who have ever studied the proceedings of any political trial behind the Iron Curtain. Not only the defense lawyers, but also all defendants involved in such trials invariably plead guilty before the court. So much for criminal trials of which the state is a part. What of civil cases between private parties?

In all civil suits, no matter what the evidence, the court's decision must favor the party closest to the standards set by the regime. The lawyer's plea hinges in all cases on "partisan" issues, and he may not make use of the evidence on file if that evidence runs counter to the aims of the communist regime. Official and officially approved publications confirm this, and furnish a vast variety of instances. Here is one. In a suit involving the annulment of a sale, the decisive argument runs as follows: "The powerful and infallible feeling of equity pleads in favor of the plaintiff, and demands that justice be on his side, regardless of, and above, all evidence in the file." Here is another way to determine a favorable decision in court: "The manner in which the plaintiff appeared in court, ill dressed and with a general aspect denoting poverty." (*Justitia Noua*, No. 3–4, 1949). In yet another case, bearing on the annulment of the sale of some real estate, the lawyer points out the social standing of the parties involved, and the court motivates its findings in consequence: "Through the information resulting and from the data of the suit, we find that the defendant—the purchaser of the plot—is a farmer who enjoys a good material standing in the village, while the plaintiff is a poor woman without any property of her own. In view of these facts, the court decides that the sale shall be annulled, and the plot be returned to the plaintiff" (*ibidem*).

With such non-legal and manifestly demagogical standards prevailing, the counsel's plea becomes simply a political address, and he may never insist on his client's legal rights when these are in any way at variance with the propaganda purposes of the regime, no matter what the actual provisions of the law may say.

Ministerial departments and people's councils are represented before the courts by their own juridical offices. The special law organizing these legal offices (Decree No. 86 of April 1, 1950) gives them very extensive powers. Not only do they represent their principals in all court proceedings, but they draw up draft laws, decrees, decisions, and instructions, and conclude agreements and transactions on behalf of the institutions they represent. Their personnel is drawn, not only from among graduates of university law schools, but also from among graduates of one-year schools of law. Selection is even more rigorously political than in the case of run-of-the-mill lawyers.

Decree No. 79 of March 31, 1950, introduced to Rumania a novel institution known as the State Notariate. Cumulating a series of powers that formerly were performed either by lawyers, notaries, court clerks, or notarial courts, the State Notariate now draws up and authenticates various legal documents for private parties, issues legalized copies of such documents, legalized signatures on acts protesting checks, promissory notes, and other such instruments. It also ascertains the dating of written acts, makes translations from foreign languages, and receives for deposit all kinds of documents. In this way a rigorous centralization of all legal activities of the citizenry is realized. Like all public institutions under a "people's democracy," the State Notariate is in reality but a subsidiary organ of the administration and operates under the orders of the Ministry of Justice. Its main purpose is to promote the interests of the regime, not that of private persons.

The entire organization of the Notariate is dictated by the Ministry of Justice. In addition to the principal local offices functioning in each district capital, article 4 of the Decision permits the Ministry to set up as many other offices as it may deem necessary. Subsidiary offices function wherever there are people's courts. Each State Notariate office is headed by a chief notary and staffed with notaries and secretaries. All are appointed directly by the Ministry of Justice and may at all times be dismissed by it. Among the conditions for eligibility to such offices, the law includes the requirement that appointees shall not have suffered a court sentence for "offenses rendering a person unfit" for this office. In other words, here again we have the arbitrary political criteria specified in the customary vague and indefinite terms of the law.

The functioning of the State Notariate is likewise subject to political criteria. The law provides that the notary must "verify" the contents of all acts prior to their effectuation. This verification must be made from the point of view of conformity with "the spirit of socialist legality" (arts. 1 and 11). In a subsequent set of instructions, embodied in Decision No. 1827, of July 12, 1950, the Ministry of Justice enjoined all notaries "to refuse the effectuation of the notarial act in all cases that might tend to create a situation contrary . . . to the rules of socialist coexistence or to harm the consolidation of socialist legality." This introduces the principle of the "directed" act, destroying thereby any semblance of liberty of contract.

The sphere of activity in which the regime's dictatorship is displayed in its most absolute form is that of economic production. This comes under the competence of a special organ called the State Arbitrage, which takes cognizance of all juridical relations between the various state institutions and enterprises, including cooperatives and all other organizations of a public nature, and the relations of the foregoing with private individuals. In general the State Arbitrage concerns itself with matters involving the application of the State Plan.

With a country's entire public and private life subordinated to the State Plan, the latter constitutes in effect the supreme law. Offenses against it are major crimes. It is the job of the State Arbitrage to check the operation of the State Plan. Not only does it judge litigation arising therefrom, but it also directs such matters as deliveries, execution of work projects, and services. All these are the result of contracts concluded between the individual organizations, plants, and enterprises.

A word of warning is in order here. Occidental jurists commonly make the mistake of confusing a contract concluded under a communist planned economy with the freely negotiated contracts familiar to the West. Nothing could be farther from the truth. In a people's democracy a contract is dictated by the conditions in which the State Plan is carried out. All elements in such contracts are imperatively determined by the planning authorities. The parties to the contract, the object of agreement, prices, and delivery dates are laid down from above. The contract itself is but a document of public administration that the parties involved must conclude and sign. It does not embody the freely expressed will of the parties but a specific application of the State Plan.

Hence the State Arbitrage is not, as its name might lead one to think, an organ designed to conciliate opposing interests, but one intended to promote the interest of the state. Consequently, the State Arbitrage does not appraise and judge. It orders. Its findings are discretionary acts. Should its findings show the existence of deficiencies in plan fulfilment, it simply informs the State Planning Commission of this, so that the deficiencies may be remedied. Or else it advises the Procuratura to set in motion the requisite punitive procedure. Or it may very well do both at the same time. In all cases, the State Arbitrage has a strictly "partisan" attitude toward problems submitted to its rulings. It is, in the words of *Justitia Noua* (1951, page 912), an instrument "of increased vigilance, for combating deviations from the party line in economic activities."

Article 1 of the law organizing the State Arbitrage defines its purpose as follows: "The State Arbitrage pursues the strengthening of popular legality, of plan discipline, of contract discipline, and of socialist administration, as well as the enhancement of the sense of personal responsibility." This indicates that the State Arbitrage, though apparently a juridical organ, must be located at the periphery of the judiciary. In reality it is but yet another political organ of the state, and it has neither independence nor impartiality. It carries out its "partisan" function without any concern for issues other than the fulfilment of the State Plan. In carrying out the purposes of the Communist party, it wields the methods of constraint of the totalitarian state.

The latest organization of the State Arbitrage is outlined in Law No. 5, published in the *Official Bulletin* No. 37, of August 5, 1954, of the Grand National Assembly. The provisions of this law are elaborated from time to time by decisions of the Council of Ministers. Prior to this, it functioned in virtue of Decree No. 122/1951 and of the rules and regulations published in the *Official Bulletin* No. 26, of March 18, 1950, authoritatively expounded in *Justitia Noua* for 1953. It is almost redundant to mention that all these texts are inspired by the laws of the Soviet Union, notably that of March 20, 1931.

The State Arbitrage operates through the following organs: a) the State Arbitrage functioning in conjunction with the Council of Ministers; b) that functioning in conjunction with the district Executive Committees; and c) that of a departmental character functioning within the individual Ministries and Cooperative Unions. It is headed by the Prime State Arbiter, who takes part in the meetings of the Council of Ministers (hence is manifestly an element of the executive), and elaborates the rules for all arbitrage organs.

The competence of the State Arbitrage is fixed by article 6 of the law of 1954. It extends, as we have said, to all litigation related to the fulfilment of the State Plan, including civil offenses like misappropriation and embezzlement. However, suits involving sums smaller than 2,500 lei, if they do not bear on the conclusion or refusal to conclude a contract; suits concerning state farms and collective farms; and suits resulting from the statutory operations of the State Bank do not come under its competence but go to the ordinary courts. Certain litigation is handled exclusively by the State Arbitrage of the Council of Ministers. These include suits connected with foreign trade, import and export; those in which one of the parties is the Ministry of the Armed Forces, the Ministry of Domestic Affairs, or the Directorate of Industrial, Agricultural, and Food Reserves.

In addition to the above, which are set down by law, the Prime State Arbiter holds discretionary powers in that he may remove any suit from the competence of State Arbitration offices functioning alongside the executive committees of the people's councils, and submit it for solution to the State Arbitrage connected with the Council of Ministers. In all cases, the procedure of the State Arbitrage is a summary one. The parties are summoned to appear, but their non-appearance does not prevent the handing down of the decision. The arbitration is not bound by the limits of the actual problem before it; it may proceed to solve any problems connected therewith. The decision may force the delinquent party to carry out the contract, by setting new standards if necessary; it may modify the existing contract in disregard of the will of the parties; it may annul the contract, and award damages. The decision of the State Arbitrage is final. The parties have no means of appeal whatsoever. Persons found guilty of failure to carry out the contract, that is, of failing to meet the requirements of the Plan, are handed over to the criminal courts. They are thereupon open to sentencing in accordance with the provisions of the law of April 30, 1949, concerning economic offenses.

What is more significant is the resulting fact that the most important field of activity—that which concentrates the entire economic life of a people's democracy—is statutorily subtracted from the judiciary as such. Litigation arising in this field is not solved by court judgment, but by dictatorial decisions handed down by an organ of the governmental power. Even litigation connected with foreign trade—that involving economic relations between state units and foreign parties—is subject to this authoritarian rule.

Official R.P.R. juridical doctrine readily acknowledges the State Arbitrage to be an instrument of the "dictatorship of the proletariat" (*Justitia*

Noua: 1951, page 311) and that it operates not only in accordance with the law, but also in compliance with "decisions of the government and party" (*Justitia Noua:* 1954, page 307).

We may well consider State Arbitrage to be the crowning glory of the legal system of the communist totalitarian state. It is certainly the most eloquent expression of the absolute power of the state over the entire activity, collective as well as individual, of the community. Neither private enterprise nor personal rights and initiatives can be conceived under such a system.

foreign relations

Soviet predominance in Rumania became evident long before the war in Europe came to a close. By its one-sided interpretation of the Armistice Convention signed on September 12, 1944, and by the Stalin-Churchill "zones of influence" agreement of the following month, the Soviet Union gained what was virtually a free hand in Rumanian affairs. Thus, up to the time when the peace treaty went into effect (September 15, 1947), the Kremlin exercised complete control in Rumania through the Control Commission and the local Communist party. It was the oddly named commission—in the armistice convention it was referred to as "the Allied (Soviet) Control Commission"—that kept the Groza administration in power in spite of its increasing unpopularity in the country and despite all objections raised by the Western Allies. From the very outset it became amply evident that the American and British representatives in the Commission were little more than observers, seldom if ever consulted by their Soviet colleague.

The Control Commission, although there existed a Rumanian commission for carrying out the armistice provisions and to act as a liaison office between the Rumanian and Allied (Soviet) authorities, had its own representatives in each of the country's major cities. These local representatives, while ostensibly supervising the implementation of the armistice provisions, actually acted as agents for the constant instruction and support of the local communists.

On August 20, 1945, the Groza government was officially "recognized" by Moscow. The Kremlin ostentatiously marked the occasion by raising the Rumanian representation in Moscow and the Soviet representation in

Bucarest to Embassy rank, notwithstanding the fact that, formally at least, a state of war still existed between the two countries, since the peace treaty had not been signed. The Soviet ambassador, who thus also became the dean of the diplomatic corps, was careful from the very beginning to give precedence to Moscow's principal agent in Rumania, the head of the Control Commission. This marked deference served to stress the true nature of what would otherwise have been a strangely hybrid situation.

Earlier still, the Kremlin established its primacy in Rumania by signing the economic collaboration treaty and the agreement on trade exchanges on May 8, 1945. The additional protocols set up the notorious Sovroms which, as we have seen in the chapter on the R.P.R. economy, secured a Soviet monopoly in all major fields of production. We have seen, too, how this ruthless exploitation of the country's resources, coming on top of the exorbitant "reparation" deliveries, was to bring Rumania to the status of a Soviet colony.

Under the circumstances, it is wholly permissible from a juridical point of view to question the validity of the economic agreements concluded in Moscow on May 8, 1945, since they were signed by the representative of an illegally constituted government. It is now public knowledge that the Groza government was imposed upon Rumania by the Kremlin's emissary, Vishinsky. For the details of this operation, the reader is directed to the Special Report No. 11, issued by the Select Committee on Communist Aggression, United States House of Representatives, 83d Cong., 2d Sess. In any case, as Rumania was at the time under the regime provided by the armistice convention, certain elements at least of her independence and sovereignty were lacking. An indication of the situation may be found in the fact that not a single one of the countries that had broken off diplomatic relations with Rumania on account of the war—with the notable exception of the Soviet Union—formally renewed them until after the peace treaty came into effect. The presence in Rumania of the British and American political representatives fell short of full diplomatic representation, in view of the concomitant presence of the "Allied (Soviet) Control Commission." In this same connection, it should be noted that the Soviet Union itself did not proceed with the conclusion of the Treaty of Friendship and Collaboration with Rumania until after the peace treaty became effective. Also it was only then that the Groza regime itself applied for membership in the United Nations.

The legitimacy of the Groza government was raised before it had been many months in power. It will be recalled that the King brought the matter to the attention of the three principal Allies on August 20, 1945. The Soviet refusal to consider the dismissal of the government the Kremlin itself had installed resulted in a deadlock: the King refused to work with that government for almost half a year.

Meanwhile, however, a delegation of that government was invited to Moscow, where it arrived on September 4. The discussions were originally to include such matters as Rumania's frontiers, German reparations due to Rumania, the repatriation of Rumanian prisoners of war, an exchange of populations between the Sub-Carpathian Ukraine (annexed by the Soviet Union) and the Rumanian province of Maramuresh, the import of 60,000 carloads of grain for the starving people of Moldavia, the regime of the Danube, the regime of the Straits—in addition to the "perfecting of Rumanian-Soviet relations and of the Sovrom agreements." The delegation returned to Bucarest on September 12, with little to show for the trip. The Soviet Union agreed to support the return of all of Transylvania to Rumania; it granted half the grain that was requested, in exchange for the immediate setting up of the Sovroms; it agreed to repatriate a tiny number of prisoners of war.

At the same time Stalin sent King Mihai a verbal message: the King was assured of Stalin's "confidence in his loyalty and friendship"; Stalin felt the King's demarche in view of Groza's dismissal was "the work of British and American pressure"; would the King reconsider the matter, under the circumstances? In other words, the Kremlin had decided to give the fullest support to the puppet communist-dominated government of Rumania come what may. It maintained this attitude even after the failure of the London conference of the Big Three foreign ministers. The outcome was the meeting in Moscow of December, 1945, where the Rumanian crisis was solved, as we have shown in a previous chapter, by the inclusion of one representative of each of the two major political parties in the Groza government. The outcome of that "solution" we have also already described.

In exchange, the Groza government gave its full support to the position adopted by the Soviet delegation at the Paris peace conference of August, 1946, which led to the conclusion of the peace treaty of February 10, 1947.

On February 20, 1947, a new economic agreement was signed between the Soviet Union and the Groza administration, increasing the volume

of trade between the two countries. Political changes of a far more spectacular nature were presently to overshadow this event.

By the end of that year the elimination of the democratic parties from
public life was an accomplished fact. Now, with the peace treaty in effect
and the Allied Control Commission safely out of the way, the communists proceeded with the maneuvers that were to culminate in the
forced abdication of King Mihai.

Soon after the People's Republic was proclaimed, a governmental delegation was invited to Moscow. There, on February 8, 1948, the treaty of
friendship, collaboration, and mutual assistance was signed between the
R.P.R. and the U.S.S.R. Ostensibly directed against any resurgence of a
military threat by Germany, and stated to be "in conformity with the
aims and principles of the United Nations Organization," this treaty,
which covered "any threat of repeated aggression," not only by Germany,
but also "by any other state that might join Germany, either directly or
in any other form whatsoever," was to have a validity of twenty years. It
was to be renewable by tacit consent for subsequent five-year periods after
its expiration. Article 5 speaks of the "reciprocal respect for the independence and sovereignty" of the contracting parties, and specifically of
"non-intervention in one another's domestic affairs." This treaty was to
provide the model for the others subsequently concluded between the
R.P.R. and the rest of the countries of the communist bloc. In effect it
bound the new People's Republic inextricably to the Soviet Union, a
situation that was to be reflected, as we have elsewhere pointed out, in the
very Constitution of the R.P.R.

The more recent treaty of "friendship and military assistance" concluded in May, 1955, among the communist bloc countries set up a single
joint military command. In fact, however, it cannot be said to go very far
beyond formally confirming a situation that had existed all along. Indeed,
it is clearly intended by the Kremlin as an additional formal means to seek
the dissolution of the NATO front.

As for the economic relations between the R.P.R. and the Soviet Union,
which, as we know, culminated in the Warsaw agreements of 1955, designed to counter the Marshall Plan, here is a list of agreements identified
so far:

An agreement on May 8, 1945, concerning trade for the years 1945–1947;
An agreement on January 18, 1948, concerning trade for 1948;

An agreement on January 24, 1949, concerning trade for 1949;

An agreement on February 17, 1950, concerning trade for 1950;

An agreement on March 15, 1951, concerning trade for 1951;

An agreement on August 24, 1951, concerning trade for 1952–1955;

In August, 1948, an agreement was signed between the R.P.R. and the Soviet Union whereby deliveries based on the armistice convention were reduced 50 per cent (for that year only).

In July, 1945, and in August, 1949 and 1952, the protocols for the Sovroms were signed (but their texts remain unpublished to this day).

On September 25, 1954, the Soviets agreed to "sell" to the R.P.R. their share in all but two of the Sovroms.

On September 27 and November 29, 1949, protocols concerning border delimitation were signed between the R.P.R. and the U.S.S.R. Their texts have so far not been published.

On February 2, 1947, a convention for navigation on the lower (maritime) Danube was signed (text published in *Monitorul Oficial* No. 85 of April 11, 1947).

The successive crises deliberately fostered in Rumania by the Soviet Union following the conclusion of the armistice of 1944, marked the start of a series of violations of East-West agreements. Though they were manifestly the results of outright acts of aggression by the Soviet government, these crises were treated at first by the Western Allies as mere local misunderstandings. Thus the bases for an endless succession of East-West "misunderstandings" were set quite literally by the situation that developed in Rumania.

The record of the significantly titled Allied (Soviet) Control Commission, as we have seen, is largely one of Western defaults and of mounting Soviet encroachments. When the crisis reached the point where the King of Rumania staged a "strike" against the illegal Groza government by refusing to work with its representatives and by appealing to the three principal Allied Powers for a solution, both the United States and Great Britain had already reacted with commendable spirit. Both had stated they did not consider the Groza government to be either representative or democratic.

On August 9, 1945, on his return from the Potsdam conference, President Truman had reported that, "it was reaffirmed in the Potsdam declaration on Rumania, Bulgaria, and Hungary (that) these nations are not to be the spheres of influence of any Power." And the newly appointed Secretary for Foreign Affairs, Ernest Bevin, told the British House of Commons on August 20, 1945 that, "the governments which have been set up in Bulgaria, Rumania, and Hungary do not, in the view of the British Government, represent a majority of the people." He added: "The impression I got from recent developments was that one kind of totalitarianism was being replaced by another."

The matter was threshed out at the London Big Three foreign ministers' conference in September of that year. Two months later it was taken up again at the Moscow conference. In the meantime, Secretary of State Byrnes sent Mark Ethridge, the editor of the Louisville *Courier-Journal*, to Rumania to investigate the situation. The findings of Mr. Ethridge were never published, obviously in order to avoid embarrassing the Moscow negotiations, as Mr. Ethridge had come to the conclusion that the Groza government was neither representative nor democratic, and that it did not meet the requirements of the Yalta "Declaration on Liberated Europe." The "compromise" reached in Moscow was little short of a triumph for the Soviet-imposed Groza regime. In exchange for vague promises, that government gained recognition by the United States and Great Britain. By mid-February, 1946, firmly entrenched in power, it began the liquidation of the opposition, introducing a regime of mounting terrorism.

Thereafter the United States and Great Britain protested unavailingly, in note after note, against the lawless acts of the communist-dominated Bucarest government. These protests were all rejected by the Groza government, secure in the knowledge that its repeated violations of solemn promises and undertakings were not merely condoned but inspired by the Kremlin. The election "campaign" and the spurious elections that brought the year 1946 to a close brought forth a renewed stream of British and American protests and official denunciations. The sequence of events was not affected thereby. It became clear at last to the Western Allies that the Control Commission provided wholly inadequate means for bringing the Bucarest regime to respect the basic human liberties and political rights of the Rumanian people.

What hope remained for improvement now turned on the peace treaty. Perhaps, since everything else had failed, the conclusion of the peace treaty might favor an East-West agreement and a relaxation of the mounting tension. It was believed in some quarters that the Soviet Union had perhaps a valid point in its insistence on "friendly" governments in the neighboring countries, notably those that had been Germany's satellites in the first stages of the war. This argument was indeed put forward in the United States Senate when the ratification of the "satellite" peace treaties came under discussion.

The Western Powers were in such haste that they accepted article 21 of the peace treaty, which gave the Soviet Union a privilege it had not formally obtained in the armistice convention of 1944, namely to maintain troops in Rumania, ostensibly for the purpose of controlling its lines of communication with the Soviet occupation forces in Austria.

Another noteworthy provision was article 40, which did not require the treaty to be ratified by the Bucarest government, but made its effectiveness contingent merely on ratification by the Soviet Union, the United States, and Great Britain. In exchange, the treaty included guarantees for the respect of political, religious, and publication liberties, and banned discrimination of all kinds (articles 3 and 5). An exception was made in the case of "fascist organizations" and it was precisely this loosely worded exception that was later to provide the pretext for gradually doing away with all opposition activities.

The Western Allies counted on the provisions of articles 37 and 38, which set up a commission made up of the chiefs of mission of the three principal Allies. The commission was to function for a year and a half following the coming into force of the peace treaty. It was to discuss and solve disagreements between the contracting parties in regard to the implementation of the treaty itself. The United States and Great Britain seem to have expected the commission somehow to force the Bucarest government to respect the provisions guaranteeing human rights and civil liberties in the country.

The treaty, signed on February 10, 1947, went into effect on September 15, 1947.

By then, the relations between Great Britain and the United States on the one hand, and the Groza government and, we might add, the Soviet Union on the other, had become more than a little strained. Notwithstanding the generous American shipments of food for the starving people of Rumania, there was no show of friendliness or cooperation from the communist-dominated regime. By the summer of 1947, the barrage of protest notes was in full swing again. The United States government denounced the manner in which the Groza government disregarded the peace treaty provisions, notably in the matters of illegal imprisonments and the treat-ment of political prisoners. The British government seconded these de-nunciations. Finally, the conduct of the Groza government led to the rejection of the R.P.R. request for United Nations membership. The Security Council turned down the request on October 1, 1947.

The forced abdication of King Mihai and the arrest of Rumania's op-position leaders now made it clear that the R.P.R. had in effect become a mere satellite of the Soviet Union. Protest notes and official denuncia-tions could no longer be expected to improve the situation in Rumania, Bulgaria, and Hungary. On March 29, 1949, the United States and Great Britain addressed a set of similar notes to the governments of Bucarest, Sofia, and Budapest, in which the long series of violations of international undertakings by the three satellite governments were recalled, and the latter were challenged to show what steps they were prepared to take to remedy the situation they had thus created in defiance to the peace treaty provisions. The British note to Bucarest minced no words: ". . . the dis-regard shown by the Rumanian government for the rights and liberties of persons under its jurisdiction . . . has indeed become so notorious as to evoke condemnation of the free people everywhere."

It had indeed. But this did not prevent the Groza regime from replying on April 18 that laws had been passed implementing the treaty provisions, that the fundamental liberties were assured by the R.P.R. constitution, and that the British and American accusations "do not correspond to reality, but repeat the inventions of the slanderous press of the imperialist monopolists." The following May 31, the London and Washington gov-ernments rejected the R.P.R. reply and stated that a dispute had in effect arisen with regard to the interpretation of the peace treaty provisions. Hence the R.P.R. government was requested to instruct its representative on the commission set up by article 38, to take part in discussions aimed at solving such divergences.

On July 11, however, the Soviet government stepped in to inform Lon-don and Washington that the U.S.S.R. would not take part in any dis-cussions of the Bucarest commission, since in its opinion the R.P.R. gov-ernment had faithfully carried out its treaty obligations. The Kremlin furthermore informed the Western Allies that it considered their action to be an attempt to interfere in the domestic concerns of a former enemy state. An official statement by the United States government was issued to the effect that the Soviet refusal to cooperate created the presumption of guilt both against the Soviet government and against the satellite governments themselves.

In the autumn of 1949 the United States and British governments addressed themselves to the General Assembly of the United Nations, asking that the entire matter be taken under advisement. When, in the course of that same autumn, R.P.R. membership in the United Nations once again came up for consideration, the United States opposed such consideration by the Security Council. By then, the Washington government had accumulated an impressive amount of evidence adverse to the R.P.R. administration. The Rumanian dispute was brought up before the United Nations General Assembly in the Fourth Ordinary Session, at the same time as the cases of Bulgaria and Hungary. An Australian proposal to appoint a special commission to investigate the matter of treaty violations was set aside, and a resolution (Document A/1025) was issued instead, referring the matter to the International Court of the Hague for a consultative opinion. The resolution also registered the refusal of the R.P.R. government to cooperate in the investigation of the accusations brought against it, and expressed growing concern over the situation.

Meanwhile, the United States and Great Britain having appointed their own members on the arbitration commission, pursuant to the procedure laid down in the peace treaty, the R.P.R. government, at the beginning of September, 1949, denounced this as open interference in the country's domestic concerns, and announced it refused to appoint a Rumanian delegate.

In January, 1950, the R.P.R. government, replying to a communication of the International Court of the Hague, rejected the request for information contained therein, alleging that the action taken by the U.N. General Assembly was contrary to the U.N. Charter, and the procedure before the International Court an interference in Rumania's domestic affairs. The R.P.R. refusal notwithstanding, the International Court reached a decision, which was made public on March 30, 1950. It confirmed the existence of a dispute within the meaning of the peace treaty; it agreed that the parties involved should therefore appoint members to the commission; but, in view of the R.P.R. refusal to do so, the Court decided the United Nations General Secretary could not appoint the third member to complete the commission.

The Hague decision or, to give its formal title, consultative advise, came before the United Nations General Assembly in the fall of 1950. The full text of the resolution adopted on November 3, 1950 reads:

> The General Assembly condemns the willful refusal of the Governments of Bulgaria, Hungary and Romania to fulfill their obligation under the provisions of the Treaties of Peace to appoint representatives to the Treaty Commissions, which obligation has been confirmed by the International Court of Justice.
>
> Is of the opinion that the conduct of the Governments of Bulgaria, Hungary and Romania in this matter is such as to indicate that they are aware of breaches being committed of those articles of the Treaties of Peace under which they are obligated to secure the enjoyment of human rights and fundamental freedoms in their countries; and that they are callously indifferent to the sentiments of the world community.
>
> Notes with grave concern that grave accusations have been brought against the Governments of Bulgaria, Hungary and Romania on these matters and that these Governments have not replied satisfactorily to the accusations.
>
> Invites the members of the United Nations, and in particular those which are parties to the Treaties of Peace with Bulgaria, Hungary and Romania, to submit to the Secretary-General all evidence which they now hold or which may become available in future in relation to this question.

The actual relations between the R.P.R. government and the United States and Great Britain were rapidly deteriorating. The war of notes went on apace. The Bucarest government took a series of measures to hamper the activities of Western diplomats in Rumania. In August the British chargé d'affaires was arrested before his recall was requested, on the allegation that he had been instrumental in the flight abroad of certain "enemies of the regime." In February that year the R.P.R. had announced its withdrawal from the World Health Organization, and in March the British and American press and information offices had been closed down. The repeated protests and denunciations that came from Washington and London all remained without results or effects. Then, on April 29, 1950, the U.S. Department of State retaliated: the R.P.R. trade office in New York was closed down. Barely a month later, the R.P.R. government countered this by asking that United States personnel in Rumania be limited thenceforth to ten persons. Promptly the Washington government replied by curtailing the comings and goings of R.P.R. diplomatic personnel in the United States. Next a number of British and American diplomats were expelled from Rumania on various charges, including espionage.

When the United States blockade of Korea was announced, the R.P.R. government made known it did not recognize that blockade, which it described as having been enacted on the basis of an "illegal" decision of the United Nations. American disapproval was marked at the beginning of 1951 by the maintenance of a chargé d'affaires in Bucarest, following the recall of the U.S. Minister. Time and again the question of withdrawing recognition from the satellite governments was raised in the United States during this period; but nothing so conclusive and drastic materialized, and things went on in the same unsatisfactory way as before.

The year 1951 saw the publication of an official United States compendium of material concerning the violations of the peace treaty provisions by the R.P.R. government, notably in regard to human rights, civil liberties, and the press. In the preface, the then Secretary of State, Dean Acheson, stated among other things: "The Rumanian government has, by terror and by various and devious devices, completely suppressed, abolished, and prohibited an independent press and the independent and free expression of ideas, whether in print or by any other media. The book-burning by the notorious Nazis in Germany, it now appears, is characteristic of the Communist regime of Rumania as well."

On September 24, 1951, an R.P.R. note abrogated the trade agreement with the United States, which had been concluded barely thirteen months before. Before the year was out, a new spate of notes were exchanged between Washington and Bucarest on the subject of the mutual security law, which the communists maintain was a form of aggression. The U.S. Blue Book mentioned above likewise came under fire from the R.P.R. regime, which expressed virtuous indignation at the very suggestion that it had in any way violated the provisions of the peace treaty. Yet another subject for recrimination was provided by the capture and trial in Rumania of a number of alleged American spies stated to have been parachuted into the country by United States espionage organizations.

Presently the Bucarest communists issued a White Book of their own, answering the charges brought against the R.P.R. regime before the United Nations. Again sinister influences in the United States and Great Britain were accused of seeking to overthrow the people's republic by force and of interfering in Rumania's domestic affairs. And, supported by the Kremlin on every occasion, the R.P.R. government sought again and again to gain admission to the United Nations.

With Stalin's death in 1954, an event that was to mark far-reaching changes throughout the communist bloc, came a series of renewed efforts by the R.P.R. dispensation to obtain membership in such international organizations as UNESCO and the ILO.

As might have been expected, the East-West talks of 1954 and 1955, held in Berlin and Geneva, provided occasions for the R.P.R. government to issue peremptory official statements fully supporting the position of the Soviet Union. It is indeed on this familiar note of slavish endorsement of every move of the Kremlin that we can most fittingly close this section of our discussion.

Praised by the communist press as "model international relations," the formal connections that have developed among the individual members of the Soviet bloc reflect increasingly the vassalage of these countries. This characteristic status of subjection became manifest as soon as communist-dominated regimes were firmly entrenched in power in each of the satellite countries. The creation of the Cominform in 1947 accented the situation. It also pointed up the fact that under communism, government and party are one and indivisible.

Incidentally, after the defection of Tito's Yugoslavia from the bloc, the Cominform headquarters was in Bucarest, and it was there that its publications, including the multilingual *For a Lasting Peace, for a People's Democracy*, were printed.

As established following the conclusion of the peace treaties with Rumania, Hungary, and Bulgaria, the formal relations between the satellite governments were set up on the same unvarying pattern as those we have shown to exist between the R.P.R. and the Soviet Union. The Bucarest regime concluded a treaty of friendship, collaboration, and mutual assistance with each of its fellow-vassals. Very similar conventions for technical, scientific, and cultural collaborations, and annual trade agreements round off the picture.

It was only in the spring of 1955 that this system of bilateral agreements was completed by means of the multilateral treaty of friendship, collaboration, and mutual assistance concluded in Warsaw by the Soviet Union, Poland, Czechosolvakia, Hungary, Rumania, Bulgaria, and Albania. This political instrument was shored up by the establishment of a joint military command which is wholly in Soviet hands.

In the economic field, the attempts at long-range coordination and integration led to the establishment of the Economic Council for Mutual Assistance. We might note in passing a significant remark recently vouchsafed by one of the top planners of the R.P.R., Miron Constantinescu. Writing in the *Cominform Journal* for September 9, 1955, he called attention to the "coincidence" that all the latest economic plans of the satellite countries come to an end this year, and opined that it would be the opportune moment to begin in real earnest the highly desired economic coordination among these countries, with each concentrating thenceforth on producing only such categories of goods as it is best fitted for, bearing in mind local raw material supplies and workers' know-how. This might be taken at least as an indication that much remains to be done in the domain of integrated over-all planning.

Returning now to the field of political relations, we shall observe that it has been the unvarying practice of the R.P.R. regime to extend immediate recognition to every successive communist regime that has come into being anywhere in the world, once the green light has been given by Moscow. Such recognition entails among other things, an exchange of full-fledged embassies. The R.P.R. government has recognized communist China, communist North Korea, and communist North Vietnam. In 1948, it hastened to recognize the "government" of General Markos, though the latter managed to maintain a foothold in Greece only so long as Tito's support was available. This did not prevent the Bucarest government from subsequently doing its utmost to establish diplomatic relations with the present government in Athens.

Inter-satellite relations are apt to be exorbitantly costly. The R.P.R. contributions to the reconstruction of North Korea have for years burdened the depleted resources of Rumania. The people of Rumania, themselves sadly in want of adequate food and clothing, have had the dubious satisfaction of making shipment after shipment of various commodities available to their fellow-victims of communism in the most unlikely corners of the world map. To North Korea alone, in the course of the year 1955, they contributed by official admission no less than sixty million rubles' worth of goods, in addition to a series of industrial plants set up there with Rumanian money and help.

Among the multilateral agreements concluded by the R.P.R. regime, we must mention the railroad transportation convention for Eastern Europe, concluded on October 13, 1947. The yearly conferences held in various satellite capitals since the date of its conclusion have become a permanent feature. Here, too, we must classify the Danube navigation convention signed in August, 1948, in Belgrade, of which we shall have more to say later in this chapter.

To complete the picture of the "new type" relations that have been set up within the Soviet bloc, here is a list of the bilateral agreements concluded by the R.P.R. with its fellow-satellites:

ALBANIA

Agreements on trade and payments April 4, 1949; March 26, 1952; April 22, 1954; and November 29, 1954.

BULGARIA

Protocol for trade and payments, March 2, 1945.
Economic Agreement, October 12, 1945.
Agreement for railroad and ferry traffic, August 6, 1946.
Agreement for air traffic, July 22, 1947.
Protocol for the export of electric power, October 10, 1947.
Protocols concerning the Craiova agreement, January 14, 1948.
Friendship, collaboration, and mutual assistance treaty, January 16, 1948.
Trade treaty, February 21, 1953.
Postal and Telecommunications Agreement, November 26, 1953.
Trade and Payments Agreement, May 23, 1954.
Long-Term Trade Agreement (1955–1957), July 20, 1955.
Protocol for the List of Exchanges, January 11, 1955.

COMMUNIST CHINA

Recognition extended, October, 1949.
Agreement on trade and payments, April 19, 1954.

CZECHOSLOVAKIA

Trade and Payments Agreement, November 9, 1945.
Extension of above, June 30, 1947.
Treaty of friendship, collaboration, and mutual assistance, July 21, 1948.

Trade and Payments Agreement, January 4, 1950; October 16, 1951; May 10, 1952; February 21, 1953.

Agreement for the regulation of trade exchanges, July 21, 1954.

NORTH KOREA

Economic agreement for North Korea's reconstruction, October 23, 1953.

EAST GERMANY

Protocol for the financing of trade payments, September 22, 1950.

Long-Term Trade Agreement (1952–1955), January 23, 1952.

Annual Protocol for the list of goods to be exchanged, September 20, 1952; March 28, 1953; June 1, 1954.

POLAND

Convention for civilian air traffic, August 29, 1947.

Trade and Payments Agreement, September 9, 1947.

Treaty of friendship, collaboration, and mutual assistance, January 26, 1948.

Convention for Economic Cooperation, September 10, 1948.

Agreement for Trade Exchanges and Payments, December 13, 1948; January 6, 1950.

Extension of Economic Agreement, August 15, 1951.

HUNGARY

Agreement of Trade and Payments, January 13, 1948.

Treaty of friendship, collaboration, and mutual assistance, January 24, 1948.

Agreement for Trade and Payments, July 7, 1948.

Treaty for the extradition of political prisoners, November 23, 1949.

Agreement for trade and payments, January 11, 1950.

Protocol for broadening the Agreement for 1951, September, 1951.

Agreement for trade exchanges and payments, May 10, 1952; May 20, 1954.

NORTH VIETNAM

Recognition extended, February 3, 1950.

The paramountcy of the "party line" is surely nowhere so clearly discernible as in Rumania's relations with Yugoslavia during the past decade. In hardly another instance have we seen the long-standing, traditionally close friendship between two neighboring peoples so thoroughly disregarded and set at nought in the sole interests of an alien ideology—indeed of a pseudo-ideology thinly cloaking a no less alien contest for power.

It will be recalled that the end of the war brought Tito to such prominence that it was thought he was slated to become the head of a Balkan confederation that seemed on the point of materializing, under the aegis of triumphant communism. It was in this atmosphere of speculation that a secret meeting was staged between certain of Rumania's communist leaders and Tito in the border village of Banloc, in the autumn of 1945. The object of this meeting was to discuss Yugoslav claims to the Rumanian Banat, Rumanian support of Tito's claims on Hungary, and Yugoslav assent to the basic proposals concerning the forthcoming Rumanian peace treaty.

All was still sweetness and light when Tito arrived in Bucarest on an official visit, to be received with the highest honors by his communist colleagues there, and to sign with them, on December 20, 1947, one of the familiar treaties of friendship, collaboration, and mutual assistance patterned by the Kremlin. But, by the time the Rumanian People's Republic was proclaimed, the rift in the communist lute had begun to be felt. The Danube conference in Belgrade, in the summer of 1948, was marked by unmistakable discord. On October 1, 1949, the treaty of friendship, collaboration, and mutual assistance was denounced by the R.P.R. In January of the following year, the long-standing agreements on railroad and postal communications were also denounced, and all traffic between the two countries was halted.

The communists of the R.P.R. and of Yugoslavia had been hurling insults and denunciations at each other across the border for some time already. Now "border incidents" of increasing violence and frequency began to claim victims from both sides. Refugees from each of the now openly hostile regimes began a strange two-way clandestine flight. From Rumania, anti-communist refugees crossed into Yugoslavia; from Yugoslavia, anti-Titoist communists fled into Rumania. A full-scale propaganda war, making fullest use of refugee groups, of press, radio, and even of loudspeaker systems and gigantic insulting political cartoons on the banks of the Danube, was waged for some years. The conflict grew in bitterness, though it can hardly be said that the people of either Rumania or Yugoslavia were in any way concerned with the issues at stake.

Official Yugoslav statistics published in 1953 show that a total of 1,560 Rumanians sought refuge in Yugoslavia during those troubled years. In 1948, 709 crossed the border; in 1949, 298; in 1950, 141; in 1951, 352; and in 1952 barely 60. This sudden drop was due to the extraordinarily stringent measures that had been taken by the R.P.R. authorities to secure the Rumanian-Yugoslav border: as many as 28 separate barbed wire barriers were counted at one spot; strips of constantly ploughed and bare terrain went the length of the land frontier, with searchlights, high watch towers, police dog patrols, mined areas, and so forth adding to the hazards of flight; the banks of the Danube were likewise under twenty-four hour guard, with speedboats armed with machine guns cruising all likely stretches; exacting security measures kept unauthorized people out of the entire border region.

Presently it became known that some refugees were being handed back to the authorities of the country from which they had fled, and that other refugees, instead of a safe haven, found forced labor awaiting them on the other side. A series of trials, both in Rumania and in Yugoslavia, brought short shrift to group after group of alleged spies and saboteurs from the other side. Yugoslav diplomatic representatives in Rumania and R.P.R. diplomats in Yugoslavia were subjected to various indignities by the local authorities. The temper and temperature of this cold war mounted steadily, both sides deliberately adding fuel to the fire, while claiming for themselves the highest purity of motives.

Then came the year 1954, and relations between the Kremlin and Tito underwent a sudden and dramatic change. By the summer of that year, there was once more a Yugoslav ambassador in Bucarest and an R.P.R. ambassador in Belgrade. Now normal traffic had to be established again, and the pending problems between the two countries once more came to the fore. Normal relations were resumed, and border incidents ceased, as though by miracle, almost overnight. The end of 1954 saw the conclusion of an economic agreement, fixing the volume of goods to be exchanged at a modest six million dollars. On December 31, 1954, Gheorghiu-Dej gave an interview to Tito's *Yugopress*, in which he showered words of high praise on the Yugoslav dictator, whom only a short while before he had been denouncing in the most virulent terms as a "Judas sold to Wall Street interests."

But now it was Tito's turn to be haughty: when the R.P.R. administration staged its festivities marking the "holy" day of August 23, in 1955, and the Soviet Union was represented by Nikita Khrushchev in person, Tito alleged that the press of current business was so great that no special Yugoslav representatives could be sent to Bucarest.

Yugoslavia, of course, had ample reason to bear rancor against the R.P.R. regime. The mass deportations of 1951 and 1952 struck heavily at the Yugoslav minority in the Banat, and the very numerous unfortunates, who were then forcibly removed from their farms and homes to be dumped in the arid regions of the Danubian steppes known as the Baragan, have yet to be compensated in any way. Here Tito undoubtedly has a well-founded claim against the communist regime of Bucarest.

A highly important issue is the problem of the Danube which transcends the mere riparian interests of either Rumania or Yugoslavia. We need not however enter here into the details of the century-long attempts to solve this problem on the international level, nor recall all the regimes that have at one time or another governed this important European waterway. It suffices to point out that navigation on this river, that flows through so many countries, has long been treated as an international problem of the widest interest, and no doubt rightly so.

With the penetration of the Soviet armies deep into Europe, commercial navigation on the Danube came to a virtual standstill, and the Danube problem became so to speak a touchstone of the Kremlin's approach to international organization as such. The New York conference of the Council of Foreign Ministers, held on December 12, 1946, decided that six months following the ratification of the peace treaties with Rumania, Bulgaria, and Hungary, a conference would be called to adopt a convention concerning navigation on the Danube. It was then decided that, in addition to the United States, Great Britain, the Soviet Union, and France, the riparian states, Bulgaria, Yugoslavia, Czechoslovakia, Rumania, and Hungary, would participate. Oddly enough, though both Germany and Austria were excluded, the Ukraine was admitted as a "riparian state."

The conference was held in Belgrade in the summer of 1948. Both the United States and the Soviet Union submitted draft conventions. It was the Soviet submission that was finally adopted. This entailed setting up a single commission for the entire navigable part of the Danube, and the abolition of the commissions that had functioned pursuant to pre-war conventions. We might note, incidentally, that the American draft likewise provided for the ending of the previously existing commissions. Separate administrations were established for certain parts of the river, composed of representatives of the riparian states. One such body was to administer the lower Danube, from Braila to Sulina; another the sector of the Iron Gates, from Moldova Veche to Turnu Severin. In the latter, representatives of the R.P.R. and of Yugoslavia were to participate.

Like the American draft, the Soviet project reasserted the principle of freedom of navigation; but the Soviet concept of freedom differs somewhat from that of the West, so it was not astonishing to find, for instance, that freedom of navigation and equality of treatment applied solely along the course of the river itself, not in the harbors. Once shipping entered a harbor, it could use port facilities, such as loading and unloading devices, storage, and so forth, only by virtue of agreements with the services handling the transports (art. 41). In other words, a ship once it has entered a harbor was at the mercy of the local "nationalized" services or companies, which were at liberty to set discriminatory tariffs favoring the shipping of certain states only.

Unlike the American project, the convention adopted in Belgrade restricted membership in the Danube Commission to riparian states, among which it numbers the Soviet Union and the Ukraine, with Austria to be included once its independence was confirmed by peace treaty. The Western suggestion that the commission be placed under the supervision of the United Nations was wholly ignored, and the adopted convention nowhere mentions the U.N. in its text.

The Soviet delegate, Andrei Vishinsky, summed up the situation bluntly, in reply to the protests of France, Britain, and the United States: "I would say in general that what is acceptable in the United States draft can be found in the Soviet draft, and what is not in the Soviet draft is not acceptable." He concluded with characteristic communist courtesy: "The door was open for you to come in; the same door is open for you to go out, if that is what you wish." The result was that the United States, Great Britain, and France did not recognize the convention as it finally emerged from the Belgrade conference; Italy, Belgium, and Greece added their protests to this refusal.

In the past, the Rumanian view had always been to eliminate foreign interference from the administration of the lower Danube, where the river flows entirely on Rumanian soil. In exchange, Rumania offered the requisite guarantees for the freedom of navigation and for equality of treatment of all shipping, and assumed responsibility for properly carrying out the hydro-technical work requisite for the maintenance of the water-way. This principle of national sovereignty is completely ignored by the present Danube Convention, notwithstanding the Soviet thesis expressed at Belgrade. This is obvious from the fact that the Lower Danube Commission administers the Sulina Channel which is wholly on Rumanian territory.

Signed in Belgrade on August 18, 1948, the Convention became effective on May 11, 1949. The first session of the new Danube Commission met in November, 1949, and the Western Powers took this occasion to register a protest on behalf of the free world. In their note, they maintained the view that the convention violates the rights of the following states: France, Great Britain, the United States, Germany, Austria, Italy, Belgium, and Greece, and in placing the Danube under exclusive Soviet control, it violates the provisions of the peace treaties with Rumania, Hungary, and Bulgaria. To this the Soviet government replied in March, 1949, indignantly rejecting the Western point of view and stating that this view had been duly rejected in Belgrade by the majority of the participating states.

It remains none the less evident that the Danube has in effect become a waterway wholly integrated to the economic and political purposes of the Kremlin, and can no longer be considered to be an international river.

Furthermore, as the Stalin-Tito conflict took shape, the Soviet government made the fullest use of the Danube Commission to put pressure on Yugoslavia. At the very first session, the secretariat of the commission —it was the Soviet delegate who was "elected" secretary—was transformed into an agency of administration and control. It is the secretary who establishes the agenda of the sessions; it is he who assigns tasks to the riparian states; and it is he who appoints personnel, without any prior consultation, in the intervals between sessions. The commission itself has little or nothing to do but ratify the steps taken by the secretary. With Yugoslavia in a minority of one, it is not difficult to see what this amounted to. Nor is it any wonder that a transportation tariff grossly favoring the Soviet Union to the detriment of all other riparian states was promptly adopted.

At the second session, held in the summer of 1950, with an agenda arbitrarily set up by the Soviet delegate, the Yugoslavs protested bitterly that the principle of equality was being set at nought. At the third session, staged in December of that year, the Soviet delegate-secretary merely gave reading to a report on the activities of the commission's bureau, which showed that the Yugoslavs were not represented at all. The brief session was devoted to ratifying the Soviet report.

The fourth session met on June 2, 1951 to adopt a series of navigation rules and regulations, which the Yugoslav delegation promptly denounced as discriminatory. The Yugoslavs also accused the Soviet Union of pursuing solely its own ends; they got nowhere, and withdrew in a huff. A series of Soviet proposals were adopted at the fifth session, in December, 1951, among them the unification of existing navigation rules, and the principle that damages to shipping be investigated solely by the owner-state, not by river authorities of the riparian states. Yugoslavia once again protested against certain health and customs regulations which it considered to be detrimental to itself. A surprise marked the session of June, 1952: a Yugoslav proposal to set up an executive committee, formed of representatives of all member countries, to supervise and control the activities of the commission in the intervals between sessions, was not immediately rejected. Not only was the proposal slated for subsequent study, but a number of Yugoslavs were appointed to posts on the commission. Later, however, though a special administration was set up in 1953 for the Iron Gates sector, the special study committee rejected the Yugoslav project entirely.

The conflict broke out anew at the seventh session, in mid-December, 1952. The temporary administration set up for the Iron Gates sector as early as 1945 had been broken up by the R.P.R. authorities, which had arrested or expelled a number of Yugoslav officers of that joint body. As the Yugoslavs rightly pointed out, the result was that traffic through the Iron Gates was threatened with complete stoppage. The rocky bottom of the Danube at the Iron Gates makes normal traffic practically impossible when the waters are low. Consequently a navigable canal was cleared near the Yugoslav shore, with a railroad line running alongside, assuring towing service by locomotives under all hydrographic conditions. The current there is so swift that low-powered tugs cannot come through under their own power, especially with strings of barges in tow. The installations of the Ship Canal are all on the Yugoslav shore, and the Yugoslavs repeatedly urged that Article 21 of the Danube convention be implemented by setting up the joint commission provided therein. The R.P.R. administration however had persisted in its refusal to negotiate this matter directly and bilaterally with Tito's regime. Thereupon the Yugoslavs demanded that their towing services be paid for, setting an estimated yearly sum of 72,000 Swiss francs for such payment, on the basis of an earlier agreement signed in 1934 between Rumania and Yugoslavia. By an odd coincidence, Yugoslavia was now accused of failure to pay its dues to the Danube Commission, and the sums allegedly owed by Yugoslavia were set at approximately the same figure as that claimed by Yugoslavia.

The deadlock was reached on October 1, 1952, when Yugoslavia simply refused to give towing service to non-Yugoslavia shipping unless immediate payment was made. The R.P.R. attempted to provide such towing service by means of an old tug, the "Vaskapu," but the Yugoslav authorities promptly refused to countenance such maneuvers, rightly pointing out the risks of accidents, which could do damage to the canal and its installations. Following the "Vaskapu" incident, the R.P.R. government agreed to begin negotiations, and finally the first agreement was concluded between Tito's Yugoslavia and one of the satellite states. A special Iron Gates administration was set up on the basis of the agreement signed on May 31, 1953. The new regime of the Iron Gates, in addition to establishing the principle of free navigation through the Iron Gates, gives a large measure of satisfaction to Yugoslavia's justified claims.

However, as we mentioned above, the Yugoslav draft project for procedure was none the less rejected, and almost immediately the Soviet delegation unexpectedly came forward with a proposal of its own to change the existing regulations, which up till then had appeared to be eternally sacrosanct. The Soviet draft met many of the main Yugoslav demands. A system of rotation was adopted for the designation of the secretary of the commission, and an executive committee was also set up. The new regime was adopted at the eighth session in July, 1953.

The very next session, in December, 1953, saw a Yugoslav elected to the post of secretary. The headquarters of the Danube Commission were also moved from Galatzi to Budapest. Thereafter, with most of the Yugoslav grievances solved satisfactorily, the 1954 and 1955 sessions of the Danube Commission became increasingly mild.

An agreement was signed between the R.P.R. and the Soviet Union on December 5, 1953, for the administration of the Lower Danube, including the Sulina channel. It was merely a ratification of the Belgrade decision of 1948, confirming a *de facto* situation.

The regime of navigation on the Danube is still far removed from anything resembling freedom and equality. The Danube Commission remains an instrument for the effective hampering of free and normal shipping on this important waterway.

Something now remains to be said about the relations of the R.P.R. government with various countries of the free world. Developments in this field come almost entirely under the heading of trade relations. The present section therefore must necessarily be a brief one, political, cultural, and social relations of the R.P.R. being confined to the Soviet-dominated bloc.

At the time of the armistice, Rumania had diplomatic relations only with such Western European regimes as were countenanced by Hitler's Third Reich. Neutral diplomats stationed in Bucarest and representatives of countries with which Rumania was not at war, seeing that in most cases their countries had no diplomatic relations with the Soviet Union, sought to leave Rumania as quickly as possible once the occupation regime got under way. While the armistice was in effect, connections with the free world were kept at a minimum, it being the deliberate policy of Soviet Russia to isolate Rumania in every possible way.

Starting out from such unpromising beginning, relations with the countries with which Rumania had been on traditionally friendly terms prior to World War II were far from amicable once they were renewed. Not only did it become the customary practice of the R.P.R government to arrest and harass Rumanian employees of the Bucarest diplomatic offices of such countries, but the authorities went out of their way to subject the diplomatic representatives themselves to many indignities and much vexation.

The case of France is characteristic. A representative of the de Gaulle government replaced the representative of the Pétain regime. But it was not long before the situation of the French legation became well-nigh intolerable. Rumanians employed there, as well as Rumanian employees of the French Institute in Bucarest, were placed under arrest on various trumped-up pretexts. A number of French citizens were also arrested and several were subsequently tried and sentenced on spurious charges. On November 19, 1948, the R.P.R. government denounced the cultural agreement with France. The French Institute was closed down, and the French teachers were expelled from the country.

Things came to a climax in 1950, when certain members of the French legation, the military attaché among them, were accused of espionage by the R.P.R. authorities. Following a rigged trial, a number of French citizens were sentenced to long terms of imprisonment. They were released only in 1955, when the French government suspended exports to Rumania—a measure, incidentally, taken in retaliation for the failure of the R.P.R. government to carry out the terms of the economic agreement that had been signed late in 1954. The end of 1955 found the Bucarest communists apparently once again anxious to step up the volume of trade exchanges with France.

Relations with Belgium and Holland were resumed by the R.P.R. government only after the peace treaty came into effect. They got off on the wrong foot, since on June 11, 1948, Rumania's industries were "nationalized" and this affected important Dutch and Belgian investments. Notwithstanding the repeated protests of Brussels and the Hague, citizens of both Belgium and the Netherlands have yet to receive a penny in compensation for their losses. This fact stands in the way of the conclusion of any trade agreements with these two countries. Indeed, both Belgium and Holland have yet another reason to feel they have a grievance against the R.P.R., the Danube convention adopted in Belgrade in 1948.

The normal diplomatic relations that existed with Spain prior to 1944 were continued until the spring of the following year, when they were brought to an end. In 1947, the Groza government extended recognition to the exiled Spanish regime set up in Toulouse. A representative of that body was indeed officially received in Bucarest, but he has not been much in evidence since his arrival there. The R.P.R. has no diplomatic relations so far with the Franco regime.

There are no diplomatic relations between Bucarest and Bonn (as of the end of 1955). Trade relations are currently governed by an agreement with a special quasi-governmental agency at Bonn. The Western German trade office in Bucarest, set up in 1955, was the first such agency to be opened behind the Iron Curtain. Having in the past faithfully followed the sinuous line set by the Kremlin itself, the R.P.R. government is currently making great efforts to increase trade exchanges with Western Germany, whose industrial products are badly needed in Rumania.

Since diplomatic relations with Switzerland had not been interrupted

by the war, they continued as before, once the R.P.R was formally proclaimed, though a marked note of strain and suspicion entered the picture.
It was the official feeling in Bucarest that the Swiss representatives were
"spies and agents of American imperialism." Two recent incidents brought
relations very close to the breaking point. In 1949, the Swiss authorities
got wind of the activities of a certain Solvan Vitianu, a secret agent of
the R.P.R., who, by devious and illegal means, gained information concerning bank deposits of Rumanian citizens in Switzerland, whereupon
the owners were subjected to every conceivable form of blackmail, threat,
and pressure to surrender their accounts to communist hands. Three days
after his arrest, the R.P.R. government, in an ill-considered last-minute
attempt to save this man, appointed him commercial counselor to the
R.P.R. legation in Berne. But neither this nor the subsequent arrest of
a number of Swiss citizens, and even the denunciation of the R.P.R.-Swiss
treaty of conciliation of 1949 availed. The spy was tried, sentenced and,
at the conclusion of his prison term, expelled from Switzerland.

The second incident occurred in 1955, when a group of anti-communist
Rumanian refugees attacked the R.P.R. legation in Berne, shooting the
chauffeur (who turned out to have been the local security chief), and
holding out on the premises for almost two days before finally surrender-
ing to the Swiss police. The Swiss refusal to extradite the four men involved brought forth a flood of furious invective from the Bucarest government, not only in the form of violent official notes but also in that of
calculated insults from the entire R.P.R. propaganda machine. One end
result of these two incidents has been that the effectiveness of the R.P.R.
legation in Berne as a center of political and economic espionage was
considerably impaired.

Diplomatic relations with Italy likewise continued throughout the war,
even during the interval between Italy's passage to the Allied side and
the Rumanian coup of August 23, 1944. With Italy under Allied occupation however, the Groza government viewed with suspicion any resumption
of normal contacts with that country. The moves against the Catholic
Church, discussed elsewhere in this book, resulted in the arrest of a number of Italian citizens. This brought protests from the Rome government,
and the ensuing tension culminated in the denunciation on March 4, 1950,
of the cultural agreement between the two countries. This meant the
closing of the Italian Institute in Bucarest.

The year 1950 also saw the defection of the first counselor of the R.P.R.

in Rome, a member of the central committee of the Rumanian Workers' Party, who sought refuge in Israel and refused to return to Rumania. Later, in 1952, the R.P.R. Minister to Rome also "chose freedom" and was granted political asylum by the Italian authorities, but subsequently he recanted and was escorted back to Bucarest by a couple of R.P.R. legation "couriers." Finally in 1955 Teodor Verche, one of the secretaries of the R.P.R. legation in Rome was discovered to have been an important member of a communist espionage organization.

Relations with the Holy See were extremely tense from the time the Groza regime was installed in power, with the communist authorities subjecting the members of the Apostolic Nunciature in Bucarest to every imaginable harassment and indignity. In 1947, a new Nuncio came to Rumania, Monsignor O'Hara, an American citizen. This did not prevent the R.P.R. regime from proceeding with the forcible abolishment of the Uniate Church that same year. As related in the chapter on religion, this brought protests from the Vatican, protests that remained without response or result. Not long thereafter a rigged espionage trial implicated the members of the Nunciature, and the Holy See was forced to withdraw its representatives from Rumania. To all intents and purposes, the relations between the Vatican and the Catholic Church of Rumania were thus willfully severed by the Bucarest communists.

Relations with Austria are currently "normal" but in effect limited to trade exchanges only. The same may be said of relations with the Scandinavian countries, which are even more scanty than those with Austria. Trade exchanges with Finland, with which country the R.P.R. has a tripartite agreement in which the Soviet Union is the third party, are of a more significant volume. We might mention incidentally that certain members of the R.P.R legation in Stockholm had to be recalled, since they were found by the Swedish police to be implicated in an espionage scandal.

With Israel, the R.P.R. relations have been somewhat less than cordial, in view of the problem of Jewish emigration from Rumania. An R.P.R.-Israel agreement had allowed some 120,000 Jews to leave Rumania for Israel by 1950. About 60,000 more are stated to wish to follow suit, and at the end of 1955 negotiations were being carried on on their behalf. The R.P.R. has been systematically persecuting, not only the Jewish faith as such, but Zionism as an organization. With the Zionist leaders in Rumania in and out of prison for the last few years, it can scarcely be said that the R.P.R. administration is making an effort to achieve really friendly relations with Israel.

Formal diplomatic relations exist also between the R.P.R. and the following countries: Egypt, Iran, India, Indonesia, Argentina, and Turkey. With Greece, though a trade agreement was recently signed, the R.P.R. had not yet succeeded in resuming diplomatic relations by the end of 1955.

It may be said in conclusion that, while it has successfully severed Rumania's traditional ties with the West, the communist government of Bucarest, though doing its best to duplicate the recent "smiling" attitude of the Soviet Union, has so far not gone beyond entering into a series of trade agreements with the countries of the free world.

the armed forces

It is not without significance that Rumania's first legislation providing for conscription and universal military training and service was enacted as late as 1864. Five years earlier, in 1859, the regular armies of the principalities of Moldavia and Wallachia had been merged into what was to become the standing army of Rumania. Both Moldavia and Wallachia had known the levying of troops in time of war since their beginnings as states toward the end of the thirteenth century. But, notwithstanding their stormy existence, neither Moldavia nor Wallachia had felt it necessary to keep up a standing army, aside from relatively insignificant bodies of guards maintained by the local princes. A large army was called for only in an emergency. In the event of imminent attack from abroad, the ancient law of the land required the services of all who could bear arms. Throughout the centuries, in the face of recurrent invasions by powerful neighbors bent on conquest, such haphazardly raised and trained Rumanian troops again and again proved their valor in battle in the defense of their homeland. It was regarded as a disgrace for any able-bodied man, whatever his station in life, not to undertake this traditional duty.

These circumstances fostered the traditional traits of the modern Rumanian army. It was a strictly territorial, non-political body, proud of its strong *esprit de corps*, whose officers and men were devoted to their own soil, to the fatherland, and to the throne. From the earliest times, as one noted Rumanian historian phrased it, "all were equal and brothers in arms, and the prince could raise the brave from the ranks to the nobility." Not only do many distinguished Rumanian families owe their origin to some simple yeoman ancestor promoted on the field of battle, but not a few of the princes of Moldavia and Wallachia have been of peasant ancestry. And this tradition has not been belied in modern times. One of the most brilliant commanders of the first world war, Marshal Alexandru Averescu, began his military career in the ranks, while two of the three Marshals of Rumania's army were sons of peasants. In the rest of the officer corps, the proportion was probably much higher.

The military law and regulations introduced in 1872, consolidating the principle of compulsory military service, and providing for the maintenance of a peacetime army which could be swiftly transformed into a war army, assuredly gave good results. The young Rumanian army gave good account of itself in the Russo-Turkish war of 1877, and later in World War I. The army as such never intervened in politics.

During the inter-war period, military matters were secondary among national preoccupations, and even when the clouds of World War II began to gather over Europe, little was done to reorganize and reequip the army. When, following the Ribbentrop-Molotov agreement of 1939, caught between the colossal pincers of the Red Star and the swastika, Rumania was forced to submit successively to the seizure of Northern Bucovina and Bessarabia, of Northern Transylvania, and Southern Dobrudja, her army had no choice but to withdraw and look helplessly on. This was a heavy blow to its morale.

However, with the outbreak of hostilities against the Soviet Union, in the summer of 1941, having been feverishly regrouped, re-equipped, and trained for modern warfare, the Rumanian troops fought valiantly for the liberation of the Rumanian provinces forcibly annexed by the Soviet Union. Even when it came to marching beyond the Dniester River, and notwithstanding the many natural misgivings, and in spite of the fact that there was no love lost between them and the Germans, the Rumanian troops fought well. They suffered immense hardships and their casualties were exceptionally heavy. (Although it is undeniable that the Rumanian armies were sent by Marshal Antonescu beyond the Dniester and far into Soviet territory, no formal military alliance existed between Rumania and the Third Reich.)

By the summer of 1944 it was obvious that the war was lost from the military point of view. The mounting reverses of the previous year, the long retreat, the turn of the tide in favor of the Allies both in the West and in the East, brought a sense of impending catastrophe. To the Rumanian troops, the coup d'état and the armistice of August 23, 1944, were to provide a further test. Though both officers and men abhorred the idea of being in the same camp as the Red army, the entire Rumanian army obeyed the royal command as one man. Hostilities against the Russians ceased instantly. While the troops on the Eastern front calmly awaited the outcome, those inside the country swiftly disarmed the German forces or drove them beyond the frontiers. Though the Soviet army has to this day failed to return many of the 130,000 officers and men whom they took prisoners, Rumania, instead of the 12 divisions pledged in the armistice provisions, put in the field between 16 and 20 divisions throughout the rest of the war against the European axis, thus becoming in point of numbers the fourth largest military force in the Allied camp. The Rumanian army fought its way into Hungary and Czechoslovakia ,and fought on to the end. Between August 24, 1944 and the beginning of May 1945, while fighting on the Allied side, its casualties mounted to 169,591, including 10,000 officers.

In 1945, soon after the communist-dominated Groza government had been installed in Rumania, the communists began to carry out a "democratization" of the country's armed forces. The blueprints, drawn up in the Kremlin long before, had been brought in by the victorious Red armies, together with the handful of people who had been selected to put them into effect. The task was no less than the political and ideological integration of the armed forces with the Communist party. Some years later, Gheorghe Gheorghiu-Dej, then secretary general of the central committee of the Communist party of Rumania, aptly described the official view. Speaking before the assembled central committee, he stated: "We must direct our entire care toward the army, which belongs to us all, and put at its disposal our entire support. For the army, no sacrifice will be too great." The key phrase is "which belongs to us all." The communist leader was addressing the party's central committee, not the country at large. The army, in other words, while it is officially described as "a powerful shield for the defense of the people," must also be—in the familiar words of communist manuals—"an army conscious of its historical mission in the struggle for the installation of proletarian dictatorship throughout the world," that is, a weapon and a tool of the Communist party.

In a country like Rumania, all traditional institutions, including the Church, the Monarchy, the system of justice, and the army, had necessarily to be destroyed before a communist regime could hope to secure itself in power. This the communists knew full well. They knew, too, that the Rumanian army—both the officer corps and the troops—was strongly imbued with patriotism, religious spirit, and monarchist feelings. All these things had to be subverted and ultimately done away with. Three elements favored the communists in this seemingly impossible task. In the first place, during the initial phase, the bulk of the Rumanian army was actively engaged in fighting a war beyond the country's borders. In the second place, the War Ministry was virtually in the hands of the all-powerful Soviet-dominated Allied Control Commission. In the third place, considerable bodies of Soviet troops were in the country, and could at all times be called upon to intervene.

The first step was to set up within the War Ministry a so-called Directorate for Education, Culture, and Propaganda. Organized on the model of the existing Soviet institution, this Directorate was staffed entirely with officers and noncommissioned officers of the Tudor Vladimirescu Division, which had been organized on Soviet soil from carefully indoctrinated and screened Rumanian prisoners of war. It subsequently became standard official practice in the R.P.R. to refer to the Tudor Vladimirescu Division as the "first units of the R.P.R. people's army."

After a period devoted mainly to feeling out the terrain for favorable infiltration points in each individual army unit, and especially within the War Ministry and the various commands, the real offensive was launched. Almost immediately after the Groza government was installed in power, the Directorate was transformed into "the General Inspectorate for Education, Culture, and Propaganda," outranking the existing bureau of the Ministry, and situated close to the very highest command. The two generals successively placed in command of this novel organization were selected with a view of misleading the officer corps into believing that the King and the Rumanian high command were in agreement with, or at least indifferent to, the activities of this chosen instrument of subversion. But by the summer of 1947 such subterfuge was no longer considered necessary, and a noted communist, "General" Dumitru Petrescu, who had never been an officer in the Rumanian army, but who had been most active in the creation of the Tudor Vladimirescu Division as a refugee in the Soviet Union, was appointed to head the General Inspectorate.

The first moves planned by the communists for the "democratization" of Rumania's armed forces were:

a) To reshuffle the units of the existing army.

b) To destroy the traditional spirit of the army, supplanting it with the political and military ideology of the Soviet army, involving the creation of new "suitable" cadres.

c) To propagandize the troops in favor of the then impending communist-patterned agrarian reforms.

d) To organize a "democratic army" as an intermediate phase of the ultimate creation of a true "people's army."

e) To propagandize officers and troops in view of the then forthcoming elections.

An entire apparatus of political organs was set up within every unit of the army, down to company level, known as E.C.P. (education, culture, and propaganda). The personnel of the E.C.P. bodies was presently augmented with officers and noncommissioned officers of the second division of former war prisoners formed on Soviet soil, the "Horia, Closhca, Crishan Division." By fighting units on the front, the E.C.P. operatives were generally ill-received. In many instances, commanding officers in the field simply sent them packing back to the rear; not a few suffered physical violence at the hands of the outraged soldiery; their activities were everywhere sabotaged. Notwithstanding the widespread hostility, the communists were able to carry through their program, with the powerful backing of the Soviet occupation authorities.

The cessation of hostilities against Nazi Germany found the entire operative army of Rumania on Czechoslovak soil. Two months were to go by before the troops were brought home—on foot, and with deliberate delays on the way. During that time the political propagandists worked hard inside every unit. Not only was every effort made to provoke anarchy and dissatisfaction in the ranks, but a preliminary survey of officers and non-commissioned officers was carried out, identifying those liable to prove "adaptable" and those to be discarded as "reactionaries."

One outstanding issue was the agrarian reform. In principle, the historic democratic parties favored such a reform, but they asked that it be carried through after the return from the front of the 15 divisions participating in the war against the Axis. The communists on the other hand pressed for an immediate "reform"—not, of course, that the peasants might gain possession of individual small plots of land as soon as possible, but for their own propaganda purposes. As for the soldiers, the overwhelming majority of whom were peasants whose interests were at stake, they felt very strongly that nothing should be done until they themselves had returned to their homes and were able to participate directly in whatever sharing out of land might take place. In all units, both at the front and in the rear, there were heated discussions, with the E.C.P. instructors as often as not ending up with bandaged heads. Barely was the Groza government installed in power than all such discussions and debates ended as though by magic; without any further ado, the communist-planned land reform was enacted on March 20, 1945.

The fears of the peasant-soldiery proved to have been fully justified. It was almost exclusively the "advanced elements of the working class" who benefited from the handouts, those who had been carefully kept out of battle, once they had joined either the Communist party or some approved front organization. Indeed, one of the most iniquitous provisions of the land reform law simply excluded from the benefits of the reform all who had taken part in the campaign against the Soviet Union (1941–1944). It is hardly necessary to point out that the survivors of that campaign were precisely those who formed the bulk of the forces that subsequently fought against the Nazis alongside the Allies. And it is even more obvious that the measure amounted to a gross injustice, for what can a soldier do in wartime but obey orders in the line of duty? On the part of the communists, this was a deliberately planned move that served a double purpose: it stressed the official attitude of unquestioning and servile reverence toward the "liberator," while fostering in advance a favorable atmosphere for the land collectivization that still lay ahead.

When the hostilities came to a close, on May 9, 1945 (which the communists were subsequently to make a national holiday, substituting it for May 10, traditional in pre-communist Rumania), and the troops returned and were demobilized, a new period began. Units and commands were reorganized, merged, and deactivated. This period lasted up to the time of the forced abdication of King Mihai, December 30, 1947. The communist E.C.P. apparatus was particularly active throughout this time of transition that preceded the formal enactment of the so-called People's Republic. In daily lectures, the E.C.P. workers increasingly stressed the notion that only the communists could rehabilitate Rumania. They also vilified the Western Allies at every turn, and stepped up the anti-monarchist and anti-bourgeois propaganda.

While military training went on as usual in accordance with the existing regulations, the position of all unit commanders was gradually infringed by the political officers. Disciplinary measures had to be taken "by common agreement," and it became the deliberate policy for the "politicals" to display the utmost leniency toward offenses that involved infringements of regulations, thus posing as the benefactors of the common soldier at the expense of discipline. At the same time, intense undercover activity went on. Nuclei of future communist cells were set up wherever the "educators" could recruit sympathizers among the naïve and the disgruntled. Cadres for future political organizations were prepared in stealth. The "reactionaries" among the officers and noncommissioned officers were carefully noted for early liquidation. Officers and troops were subjected to regular indoctrination sessions, to systematic subversion. Interestingly enough, the subversive organizations worked separately on the officer corps, the noncommissioned cadres, the enlisted men, and the civilian personnel.

When, in compliance with the armistice convention, the time came, in August 1946, to reduce the cadres of the regular standing army, 9,000 career officers were discharged. Soon thereafter, 5,000 career noncommissioned officers were similarly relieved of active duty. Thus, with the backbone of the army suitably softened, the E.C.P. could proceed with its work unhampered. That work was now to prepare for the forthcoming elections. In conditioning the voter-troops, no effort was spared. Opposition papers favorable to the country's traditional democratic parties were banned from all barracks. In exchange, the "governmental coalition"—Communist party control was studiously played down, the very mention of its name being avoided—was played up in every imaginable way. The only electoral mark that was mentioned was the "sun" of the coalition; the other symbols on the voting tickets might as well have not existed.

But the communists had underestimated the understanding of the Rumanian peasant-soldier. Soon after the election, it became generally known that the vote had gone heavily against the government. But the result of the election, as announced by the Government, was a "smashing victory" for the communist-dominated regime.

As one incidental result, almost the entire command of the E.C.P. Inspectorate General was ignominiously fired. Thereafter, the purges of officers and noncommissioned officers were stepped up. The armed forces as a whole were allowed to dwindle down to below the level permitted by the Paris peace treaty, that had been signed in the meantime, the provisions of which replaced those of the armistice. This was deliberate tactics. The communists were not going to repeat the mistake of underestimating the mettle of the regular army. The period of "democratization" was drawing to a close.

It can be truly said that the program to set up a sole command for Soviet and satellite armed forces, made public in December 1954, was effectively initiated about the time—six years earlier—that the Rumanian People's Republic came into being. By the beginning of 1948, the creation of a "people's army" started in real earnest.

The change was not effected under the E.C.P. Inspectorate General. Instead, a new organ was set up, the "High Political Directorate of the Army," known thereafter by its initials: D.S.P.A. The officers and non-commissioned officers belonging to it became known as "political educators." The former E.C.P. bureaus that functioned at each unit command were titled "political apparatuses." The importance attributed to this new organization may be gauged by the fact that in 1950, the man selected to head the D.S.P.A., a civilian who was designated Lieutenant General, Niculae Ceaushescu, was also appointed to be First Lieutenant Minister of the Armed Forces. The D.S.P.A., introduced on March 28, 1948, was designed to become a veritable state within the state.

The current organization of the D.S.P.A. is as follows:

1) The Organizational Directorate, with bureaus for planning, organization, and registry, handles directly all political apparatuses throughout the country's military installations.
2) The Administrative Directorate, with administration and accounting sections of its own, both locally and at the central offices, separate from those of the armed forces as such.
3) The Directorate for Education, which handles all military schools and colleges, special courses, instruction centers, schools for illiterates, etc.
4) The Army Central Club—heading all sports organizations and activities of the armed forces.
5) The Military Institute.

6) The Military Center for Physical Education which provides trainers and instructors for sports, not only for the army but also for the troops of the Ministry of Domestic Affairs, and for all paramilitary organizations.

7) The Directorate for Agitation and Propaganda, the most important section of the D.S.P.A. Superior Directorate.

8) The Cadres Directorate commands all personnel, including party cadres, military courts, investigation units, information services, and so forth. No promotion or decoration, no transfer or discharge is made without its prior approval and advice. It has the Personnel Service of the Ministry of the Armed Forces under its command.

9) The so-called *Casa Centrala a Armatei* which heads and directs all officers' clubs, clubs for noncommissioned officers and for the troops, reading rooms, libraries, army hostels, theatres and entertainment units—all that comes under the general title of arts and culture. Recent information indicates that the Army Central Club has been merged with this Directorate which now outranks it.

10) "Revista Armatei," the editorial offices for all military and specialty publications.

11) The General Editorial Offices for all dailies issued for the armed forces, notably *Apararea Patriei*.

12) The Registration and Communications Service.

Thus organized, the D.S.P.A. reaches down through its ramifications to the individual commands throughout the country. The "political commander" of each unit, though from the hierarchical point of view under the local commanding officer, outranks the latter from every practical point of view, since no measure may be taken without his consent. Below company level, the political officer is normally a noncommissioned officer, and so-called elite privates are appointed to each squad. All must be party members, and each successive echelon is responsible to the one immediately above.

With the overwhelming majority of cadres now belonging to the communist-trained younger generation, with most career officers and non-commissioned officers relegated to technical office jobs, the D.S.P.A. has a free hand. The slogan proclaimed by the current Minister of the Armed Forces, Emil Bodnarash, as far back as December 23, 1947, was "Correct political thinking is the base of correct military thinking," an obvious emanation of the Kremlin, provides the clue to its current preoccupations. The aim is to achieve an army in which thoroughly indoctrinated troops are commanded exclusively by officers and noncommissioned officers belonging to the party.

Reciprocal spying from top to bottom of the military hierarchy is strongly encouraged under the heading of "revolutionary vigilance." Denunciations, effected either through the available medium of the S.I.A. (Army Information Service) network, or through the multiple networks of party organizations, have become an integral part of military duty. No occasion is lost to belittle all that was formerly held in honor: everything pertaining to the "bourgeois capitalist regime," to the Church, to the Monarchy, to the old concept of honor, comradeship, and patriotic duty, is systematically eradicated by the "new" military education. As in all other sectors of activity, the notion of "collective leadership" is fostered throughout the armed forces. The system has the obvious advantage that any commendable achievement can be—and is—attributed to the merits of the collective command, while failures are blamed, not on the flaws of the prescribed doctrine, but on faulty execution.

In carrying out this program, the role of the U.T.M. (Union of Working Youth) organizations within the armed forces must be underscored. Members of this R.P.R. equivalent of the Soviet Union's Komsomol enjoy special privileges. They are the ones designated "elite privates"; they organize the political meetings and indoctrinate recruits; they check and report on the "attitude" of troops and cadres within their units; their recommendations carry weight with the party. The watchdog activities of the U.T.M. are further assisted by the so-called wall newspapers, now introduced everywhere in the armed forces, whose pitiless criticism is feared by officers and troops alike.

As one final result, promotions are now made exclusively on political merits, gauged by communist party standards. Indeed, such legal texts as Laws Nos. 67 and 69, of March 13, 1948, published in the *Official Gazette* No. 62/1948, expressly prescribe proficiency in Marxism-Leninism as the basic requirement for promotion. As one concrete instance of the overwhelming importance officially given to the acquisition of such knowledge, here is the curriculum prescribed for the first-year students of the R.P.R. School for Noncommissioned Medical Personnel (of the regular army), as published in the *Official Gazette* No. 58, of March 10, 1948:

Geography (of Rumania)	40 hours
Rumanian language	40 hours
Russian language	40 hours
Military hygiene	80 hours
Military regulations	30 hours
Topography (map reading)	25 hours
Elements of military law	20 hours
Armaments and munitions	25 hours
The study of the various services	30 hours
Physiology and therapeutics of gases	40 hours
Political education	100 hours

But certainly the most peremptory evidence is to be found in the prescribed oath of allegiance, which was introduced for the R.P.R. armed forces in December, 1949, following the discovery of a resistance organization within the General Staff itself. The text of this oath is as follows:

I, (name), a citizen of the Rumanian People's Republic, upon entering the army, swear to be devoted to working people, to my fatherland, and to the R.P.R. government. I swear to acquire thoroughly all military skills, in order to become a good soldier of the R.P.R. army. I swear to be a stubborn, honest, bold, disciplined, and vigilant fighter; to keep military and state secrets strictly; to have every care for the military and public property; and to carry out without hesitation the military regulations and the orders of my superiors and chiefs. I swear to hate from the depths of my being the enemies of the fatherland and of the working people. I swear to stand ready at all times, on order of the government, to fight in the defense of my fatherland, the Rumanian People's Republic, and, as a soldier of the R.P.R. army, to fight with the utmost determination and skill, at the unreserved cost of my blood and life, for full victory over the enemy. If I should break my oath, may the heavy penalty of the R.P.R. law strike me, and may I bring upon me the hatred and contempt of the working people. I pledge myself to carry out to the letter my oath, for the liberty and happiness of the fatherland and of the working people.

The terms of this fearsome pledge seem incredible in this day and age. Yet they are to be found printed as part of Decree No. 454, of December 28, 1949, issued by the Grand National Assembly's Presidium.

It remains to be reported that currently the "enemy" in all tactical drill exercises is officially designated as "the Western imperialist," "the barbarous American soldier," and "the British colonialist invader," and, for a time, "the lackey of the capitalist trusts, the Titoist enemy." These terms are prescribed also in individual drill exercises; for instance, when the sights are set at target practice, the position is explained to the trainees in a long tirade, by which they are put in the proper mood, in which the supposed invading enemy facing them is reviled and denounced. The targets themselves represent American and British soldiers in uniform.

This kind of "mental conditioning" is supplemented in various ways. Not only is the correspondence of soldiers strictly censored, but heart-to-heart talks between comrades-in-arms are discouraged by every imaginable means. The day's schedule leaves the private no leisure at all, military instruction and drill alternate with political talks, with "agitation" to the fore.

The soldier, while systematically isolated from his fellows in the most intimate spiritual sense, is at all times forced into an artificial and all-exclusive sort of ant-hill community existence. With thinking and exchange of thought studiously eliminated, he is subjected to the most rigorous regimentation imaginable. Wherever he turns, he finds himself hedged about by the jealous solicitude of the totalitarian dispensation. Relatively well fed and clothed, housed and cared for, he is denied in exchange the dignity of individuality. If he is permitted to leave his barracks otherwise than in a military formation, he may not roam at will and enjoy a brief respite of freedom. He must go out in company of one or two of his fellow-soldiers, not "buddies" of his own choosing, but "comrades" approved for him by the political educator of his unit. His very entertainment, usually provided free of charge, is of a compulsory nature. He is marched in formation to approved plays, moving pictures, lectures, and exhibitions, where the *bourrage de crâne* process that is his daily ration is simply forced into him in another guise. Indistinguishable from the soldier of the Soviet army as to uniform, equipment, and training, such is the enlisted man of the R.P.R. today.

Under the terms of the peace treaty signed with the Allies in Paris on February 10, 1947, the communist-dominated government then in power had undertaken to limit Rumania's armed forces to the following figures:

Land army	120,000 officers and troops		
Anti-aircraft forces	5,000	" " "
Naval forces	5,000	" " "
Military aviation	8,000	" " "

The gendarmerie, corps of frontier guards, and fire brigade troops, which from the operative point of view belonged at the time of the treaty to the Ministry of Domestic Affairs, but which organizationally were part of the Ministry of National Defense (the former War Ministry), were effectively merged with the land army. In other words, to the total of 138,000 officers and troops listed above, which was meant to include the forces at the disposal of the Ministry of Domestic Affairs, only the approximately 12,000 officers and men of the corps of public guards (that is, the police) ought to have been added, thus setting the permitted total of Rumania's armed forces at an absolute maximum of 150,000. Now this figure, it must be stressed, was accepted and subscribed to, like the rest of the treaty povisions, not by a government representing the will of the Rumanian people, but by a communist-dominated regime imposed by the Kremlin. Furthermore, it was also accepted and subscribed to by the sponsor and protector of that unelected regime, the government of the Soviet Union. Let us now see to what extent the communists have respected this treaty provision.

The most reliable estimates available date back to the end of the year 1953. They show the following figures:

Land army, naval forces, military aviation, and anti-aircraft troops (all under the Ministry of the Armed Forces)	240,000
Frontier Guards (Ministry of Domestic Affairs)	35,000
Security Troops (Ministry of Domestic Affairs)	55,000
Militia (Ministry of Domestic Affairs)	40,000
Guards detailed to watch roads, railroads, bridges, and so forth (Ministry of Domestic Affairs), the equivalent of the police	30,000
Corps of Fire Brigades (Ministry of Domestic Affairs)	12,000
Corps of Forest Guards (Ministry of Domestic Affairs)	7,000
TOTAL:	419,000

In addition, there are the labor units of the Ministry of Constructions, which, though they cannot be described as combat troops, represent an impressive pool of labor constantly available for military construction work of all kinds. Their total was estimated (end of 1953) at somewhat in excess of 10,000 men.

The reader will bear in mind, of course, that all data even remotely connected with military matters, in Rumania as in all communist-dominated countries, are officially considered as "top secret." Hence it is quite impossible to give precise and up-to-date figures. The figures given above do, however, provide at least the basis for gauging the approximate current size of the R.P.R. standing military forces.

We must further mention the presence in Rumania of a body of espionage and counterespionage agents, operating under the General Directorate of the People's Security, which is part of the Ministry of Domestic Affairs. This must not be confused with the Security Troops proper, enumerated above. Though its existence has been ascertained for some time, and its units are known to be operating throughout the country, the effectives of this special command cannot be estimated even tentatively at this time.

In considering Rumania's military potential, the so-called sports organization known as G.M.A. (*Gata pentru Munca si Aparare*, or "Ready for Work and Defense"), cannot be overlooked. All sports clubs in the country belong to the G.M.A. and all would-be athletes must compete for its insignia, in a test that includes such obviously paramilitary performances as long-distance cross-country marching with a full pack, target shooting, and the like. In a similar connection, the physical education provided by the Pioneer organization for young children should not be overlooked. Here too there is more than a hint of pre-military training to be clearly discerned.

The entire military strength of the R.P.R., actual and potential, is wholly subordinated to the Soviet war machine, as in the case of all other satellite regimes. The Unified Command of the communist bloc, formally set up in Warsaw in the early summer of 1955 was presented to the world at large as a defensive countermove, designed to meet the "threat" of the NATO organization. However the communist military bloc has existed in effect since about the middle of 1947, the initial steps antedating NATO by some two years. Currently under the supreme command of Soviet Marshal Koniev, the "satellite" operative forces are estimated as follows: Poland 25 divisions, Rumania 17, Czechoslovakia 8, Hungary 5, and Bulgaria 7.

Rumania had more than 400,0000 men under arms as far back as the end of 1953, exceeding the provisions of the peace treaty by over a quarter of a million. It may of course be argued that only slightly more than half of the effectives were actually under the Ministry of the Armed Forces. But, as we have already pointed out, the 1947 peace treaty provided a total figure that was meant to include the units subsequently transferred to the Ministry of Domestic Affairs. The role played by Security Troops in the launching of the North Korean aggression should be borne in mind. Furthermore, the role of Security Troops in people's democracies is well known to be that of shock troops. This was eloquently demonstrated during the years 1949–1951, when the crisis between the Cominform bloc and Yugoslavia saw the R.P.R. massing armed forces along the country's western border: the troops thus deployed were almost exclusively Security and Frontier Guard units of the Ministry of Domestic Affairs.

It should be noted further that a close study of the files of the *Official Gazette* shows that the drafting of annual contingents is carried out in two series, in the spring and in the fall. We have here an obvious subterfuge designed to camouflage true figures. From the same official source we find further that reservists are called in for maneuvers and training from time to time. This is formally prohibited by the peace treaty provisions. The fact remains that, from 1948 to the present time, reservists belonging to the contingents of 1933 through 1946 have thus been called up for temporary military duty. Such operations are carried out throughout the entire territory, as witness innumerable cases of sentences handed down by the various regional military courts for "failure to comply with concentration orders," to be found in many successive issues of the *Official Gazette*.

The R.P.R. Ministry of the Armed Forces is organized as follows:

a) The separate Commands for Infantry, Cavalry, Artillery, Tanks, Military Aviation, Navy, Corps of Engineers, Signal Corps, Anti-Aircraft Artillery, and of the Rear.

b) The High Political Directorate. As of August 27, 1954, when the "Future Statute of the Rumanian Workers' Party" was put into effect, the DSPA, though apparently still part of the Ministry of Armed Forces, in reality passed under the direct orders of the party's Central Committee.

c) The Directorates, Cadres, Administration, Military Justice, Medicine, Veterinary Medicine, Training and Education, Armament and Munitions, and Materials.

d) The General Staff, formerly independent in the Rumanian army, it passed, on December 23, 1947, under the direct orders of the Ministry of the Armed Forces. It has the following sections, Organization, Operations, Espionage and Counter-Espionage, Training, Communications, and Territorial Organization.

From the administrative and operational point of view, the R.P.R. armed forces are composed of the following so-called Military Regions:

I. Headquarters at Timishoara, covering the territories of Oltenia and the Banat (the most powerful sector of the Soviet-Rumanian strategic commands).

II. Headquarters in Bucarest, comprises Wallachia, Dobrodja, and the region of Stalin (Brashov) of Southern Transylvania (as it includes the lower reaches of the Danube and the Black Sea coast, it ranks second in importance).

III. Headquarters at Cluj, and covering Northern Transylvania (altogether secondary importance from the strategic point of view).

IV. Headquarters in Iashi, and covering Moldavia and Southern Bucovina (purely administrative importance). It is in this territorial command that the logistic potential of the Soviet occupation troops is primarily located.

Outwardly these military regions fulfil the functions of what were formerly the territorial corps, or operations involving recruiting and mobilization, military organization and equipping, provisioning, and logistic organization and so forth. In reality they simply camouflage the Army Commands, as is the case in the Soviet Union itself.

Army Corps Commands have been suppressed during peace time. They are intended to be set up in times of mobilization, becoming mobile commands, as their equivalents are in the Soviet Union.

According to the most reliable reports available, the R.P.R. armed forces—as of the year 1953—comprised the following main units:

a) Six infantry divisions, stationed respectively at Lugoj, Timishoara, Cluj, Sibiu, Craiova, and Turnu-Severin, each composed of four infantry regiments; one artillery brigade (three regiments) equipped with 76.2 mm guns, 122 mm howitzers, and 105 mm longrange guns; one regiment of assault artillery; one regiment of engineers (signal corps); one regiment of anti-tank artillery; one regiment of anti-aircraft artillery; one regiment of reconnaissance (including one tank battalion and one motorized battalion); and one aviation regiment (reconnaissance and observation).

b) Two armored divisions (Bucarest and Ploieshti), each with two brigades of 100 tanks each. The armored force command is in Bucarest.

c) Two motorized divisions (units stationed at Timishoara, Bucarest, and Sibiu), composed of two four-battalion regiments each.

d) One independent artillery division (units stationed at Tecuci, Giurgiu, and Caransebesh), composed of three brigades, each of which has two four-battery regiments (122 mm howitzers and 105 long-range guns).

e) Two alpine divisions (Targu-Muresh and Campulung, Muscel), each having eight mountain battalions and one mountain artillery regiment (76.2 guns). The command of the alpine corps is at Targu-Muresh.

f) Three cavalry divisions (Dorohoi, Iash, and Alba Iulia), each having three cavalry regiments and one artillery regiment.

g) One naval division (Constantza) composed of three marine brigades, each having two regiments of marines and two regiments of coast artillery. One brigade is titled the River Brigade and its headquarters is at Galatzi.

h) The Aviation Command (Bucarest) has three mixed divisions of three regiments each (stationed in Bucarest, Craiova, and Brashov respectively). The divisional regiments are as follows: bombers, reconnaissance planes, and pursuit planes. In addition each has approximately 500 training planes, the majority of which are propeller driven. The proportion of jet planes (Mig 15's) is estimated at one squadron to each division.

i) As of 1953, there were four Soviet jet-plane air divisions stationed on Rumanian soil (at Buzau, Ianca, Craiova, and Arad). Particular attention has been given to the construction of modern airdromes, notably in Southern Moldavia, Oltenia, and Wallachia. No less than 86 airdromes have been identified, of which 42 are very well constructed. In the course of the year 1954 a powerful force of night fighters was reported to be in operation in the country, and radar stations have been identified in a number of places, particularly in the Banat, along the Danube, and in Southern Transylvania.

j) There are fourteen anti-aircraft regiments reported, each made up of four five-battery groups, all provided with magnetic radar detection equipment. The majority are stationed near the industrial centers (Reshitza and Brashov) and in the oil-producing regions.

Reliable reports point to a recent increase in mine-throwing units (set up as independent units, but most of them attached to various infantry, cavalry, and mountain regiments). The materiel consists of 60 mm, 81 mm, and 120 mm weapons.

As in all people's republics, the Ministry of Domestic Affairs is, in the R.P.R., a key department. It is concerned with the organization, administration, and inner defense of the regime. Hence the troops at the disposal of this department must necessarily bear more than a superficial resemblance to true military formations. It will be recalled that, adopting the pattern set by the Soviet Union, the R.P.R. constitution of 1952 set up a Ministry of State Security, separate from that of Domestic Affairs. A little over a year later, in October 1953, these two Ministries were merged. At the present time, therefore, it is the Ministry of Domestic Affairs that commands the military forces on which the communist regime counts most directly for its own maintenance in power.

The R.P.R. Ministry of Domestic Affairs is currently organized as follows:

1) The General Directorate of the People's Militia, which replaces the former police and gendarmerie. In addition to the Militia Command for the Capital (that is, Bucarest), it has 17 regional commands, corresponding to the existing administrative regions. Aside from its police services and units, the Militia has four divisions organized along purely military lines.

2) The General Directorate of the People's Security. This, too, is organized into 17 regional commands and one command for the capital, but its units are not military formations. It somewhat resembles the F.B.I. of the United States.

3) The General Administrative Directorate, which heads the local people's councils (regional, raional, city, and communal).

4) The General Directorate of Prisons and Camps, which is self-explanatory.

5) The General Political Directorate, which has the same function within the Ministry of Domestic Affairs as the D.S.P.A. in the Ministry of the Armed Forces. Like the latter, it was originally an independent organ, but there is no indication available that (as is the

case with the D.S.P.A.) it is currently under the direct control of the party's Central Committee.

6) The Frontier Guard Command consisting of four border guard brigades set up along military lines, with commands located respectively in Bucarest, Oradea, Iashi, and Timishoara. It has in addition at least one special division, located in Caransebesh, and a force of "border guard vessels" operating out of Braila.

7) The Fire Brigade Command, self-explanatory in view of the known fact that all local fire brigades are organized as military units.

8) The Command of the Rear (the over-all Command of the M.A.I. Troops was abolished in 1951).

The General Directorate for Labor Service, currently under the Ministry of Constructions and Construction Materials, has cadres made up partly of former regular army officers and partly of trusted party members, with the latter, of course, in the key posts. Its forces consist of "rejects" from the regular armed forces, and of such youngsters of "bourgeois capitalist" and "kulak" origin, considered by the communists to be "unreliable" or "unadaptable." Subjected to intensive political and military training, these troops are mainly employed in the building of strategic military installations. They number approximately 100,000, and are assigned to one or another of the six Regional Directorates—Bucarest, Constantza, Bacau, Brashov (now called Stalin City), Sebesh-Alba, and Petroshani. These regional commands are in their turn made up of labor detachments, sections, and groups.

Two quasi-military formations mentioned earlier in this chapter, the so-called Guard Corps and the Corps of Foresters, are in effect well organized bodies of trusted partisans, specially trained in guerilla action and in the handling of appropriate weapons. They must certainly be included under the present general heading.

We must recall, too, the paramilitary sports organization known as the G.M.A. Sports Complex, and numbering at least one million members. As we have already shown, this reservoir of trained athletes should not be overlooked in considering the current build-up of military strength of the R.P.R.

The Pioneer organization, under the direct control of the U.T.M. (Union of Working Youth), closely follows the Soviet model. Numbering in Rumania almost 750,000 members, both boys and girls, ranging in age from 7 to 14 (*Scanteia* of July 30, 1954, set the number at 747,913), this organization provides training in various military skills, as well as political indoctrination. The red kerchief that is its special badge confers a number of privileges; it is much coveted among communist-educated children; and is the sign of the future communist militant.

Lastly, there remains to be mentioned an organization known by its initials AVSAP, *Asociatia Voluntara pentru Sprijinirea Apararii Patriei*, Voluntary Association for the Support of the Defense of the Fatherland. It is not known exactly when this country-wide organization was set up initially; the first record appeared in the R.P.R. press in 1954. Beyond the fact that its members take part in various competitions, including skiing, agricultural shows, and model airplane building, little is yet known with certainty about it. All indications point to characteristics that may fittingly be described as paramilitary. The fact that the R.P.R. propaganda machine seems reluctant to give full information about this organization is of itself suggestive.

Returning now to the actual armed forces of the R.P.R., let us consider, in the light of available evidence, what can be said of them as a fighting military body. We have seen that by the end of 1947, reorganized from top to bottom, with its cadres of officers and noncommissioned officers repeatedly purged, the emergent "people's army" already had most of the basic characteristics of its model, the Soviet army. By the spring of 1952, less than 5 per cent of the cadres were of the "old school." By the spring of 1948, units of the Rumanian army began to be equipped with Soviet and Czechoslovak war materiel (later East German equipment was added), military training was being carried out according to Soviet manuals, and Soviet army officers were assigned to units down to independent battalion level as "counselors."

Up to the present time only a small number of modern jet planes of Soviet model have been given the R.P.R. air force. But the artillery is now entirely equipped with Soviet and Czechoslovak guns, and the armored and mechanized units have Soviet tanks and medium and light assault guns exclusively. Only the navy is far behind, but there seems to be no obvious need for anything more than a small naval force under existing conditions. The armed forces of the Ministry of Domestic Affairs have likewise been armed and equipped with adequate materiel, mostly of German World War II origin. The Security Forces, of course, are at least on a par with the regular army from the point of view of armament and equipment. All uniforms are now of the models prescribed for the Soviet army.

We have already seen how the enlisted men are currently trained and indoctrinated. The officer corps, we may be sure, is even more stringently subjected to communist schooling. The most desirable type, of course, is the man of "poor peasant" or "working class" origin, a former Pioneer and then a member of the U.T.M., politically and militarily brought up in one of the many existing special schools of the armed forces, and a member of the Communist party.

The R.P.R. Military Academy, of Bucarest, provides specialized training for the various services, and each year turns out impressive numbers of well-trained and, of course, thoroughly indoctrinated officers.

All things considered, the R.P.R. army appears to be quite an impressive fighting force potentially. As such, however, it has not yet been tried. The R.P.R. enlisted man is certainly as well trained and equipped as was the soldier of 1941–1945. His commanding officers may safely be presumed to have acquired, in addition to all the political claptrap, at least the theoretical skills of war. Their instructors, able to draw on actual battle experience acquired throughout the Far East, must be assumed to have drilled much useful military knowledge into them. There can be no doubt that the communist dispensation does indeed show great solicitude for both men and officers of the "people's army." True enough, in exchange for a relative material benefit conferred an absolute, all-embracing obedience is exacted from them.

Under the specific circumstances described in this chapter, and under the general conditions described throughout this book, what can be said of the morale of the R.P.R. armed forces? What can its resultant fighting spirit be expected to be, should it be tested? Such questions, of course, are relevant, on the hypothesis of an armed conflict between East and West, but they dwindle to insignificance in the hypothesis of an indefinitely prolonged "cold war." And they may reasonably be expected to answer themselves in the event of a break-up of the Soviet empire from within. It is impossible to give a simple answer, for it is obvious that the questions themselves must be considered in the light of the passage of time.

We know that at the present time morale is far from high among

Rumanian officers and men. Lip service must be paid at all turns, the motions gone through with scrupulous care, but even under a totalitarian regime, a man's a man for all that. There can be no true *esprit de corps* where reciprocal "revolutionary vigilance" is prescribed. Fear there can be—and there is, but what loyalty can flourish in such a climate? Isolated and indoctrinated though they be from morning till night, the men and officers cannot help but be poignantly aware that things are going from bad to worse in the cities and villages, that their own kith and kin suffer increasing hardships both on the land and in the factories. They are only too well aware that they themselves as individuals are powerless to change things, that they have no chance to band together with their fellows to force a change. Can this make for high morale?

At this time, ten years after the communist regime was forcibly installed in power, if we consider the average age of the enlisted men to be twenty-two, and that of their officers nearer thirty, is it not clear that the individual Rumanian soldier has memories of better days? He can make comparisons from his own personal experience, not merely from hearsay. The traditional notions of right and wrong, of seemliness, of conduct and aspirations, instilled into the Rumanian peasant as a child, cannot be eradicated or smothered even by ten years of constant and deliberate perversion undertaken by a ruthless totalitarian regime. Conformist hopelessness assuredly is not the equivalent of "revolutionary zeal." But it no less certainly falls far short of anything more than latent discontent.

It may be assumed that a certain leveling off operates with every successive contingent that is put into uniform. Personal memories shrink as the child comes earlier under the impact of communist education. Finally the time must come when such influences of the past need no longer concern the "educators." Possibly then the "people's army" of the R.P.R. will be made up entirely of contented and compliant robots who, though still sentient and not unintelligent, will know nothing but what has been taught them from the very cradle. Of course, for the event of war, there remain to be considered the contingents of reservists, made up of those who today form the standing army. In an East-West armed conflict, how may such an army be expected to comport itself? How far can the Soviet war machine count on its cooperation?

Though at the present time, we feel safe in asserting that the R.P.R. army is still wholly unreliable from the Kremlin's point of view, its hopes and aspirations overwhelmingly directed toward the West and notably toward the United States, we can not say that this is a permanent condition. If, under the circumstances of a continuing cold war, the balance continues to incline in favor of the communist bloc, it becomes increasingly unlikely that the West will find anything like the present favorable climate in Rumania. With regard to a "conventional war" much the same can be said as for an indefinitely prolonged "cold war": time is on the side of the enemy.

labor

Though a predominantly agricultural country with a numerically insignificant industrial labor class, Rumania began enacting labor legislation as early as 1894. A set of government regulations issued on September 24th of that year aimed at the suppression or control of insanitary and hazardous working conditions in industrial establishments, was followed by the law of March 6, 1897, instituting compulsory Sunday rest. This was amended and elaborated by the law of April 14, 1910. In the meantime, a law of February 22, 1906, provided protection for mine-workers and for women employed in industries. Introduced on February 12, 1910, the extensive provisions of the Health Law afforded a more thorough protection for industrial workers, primarily through control of sanitary working conditions and safety regulations. Finally, on January 17, 1912, a law on social security came to round off what may be considered to be the initial stage of labor legislation in Rumania. It should be stressed that at the close of this period there were in the entire country only 625 industrial enterprises, employing an approximate total of 37,000 men, 7,000 women, and 3,000 apprentices.

The territorial and population increase that resulted from World War I, brought an increase in the number of industrial workers and it became necessary to provide more systematic labor organization and legislation. A Ministry of Labor was established on April 30, 1920, and the first law for the settlement of labor disputes was enacted on September 5th of the same year. A number of laws and regulations followed, with the result that by the mid-thirties it could be said that Rumania had adequate, modern labor legislation.

The principle of the freedom of labor was formally enunciated in the law of September 5, 1920; it was confirmed in Article 21 of the Constitution of March 29, 1923. Labor contracts, originally provided for in Articles 1470–1472 of the Civil Code, were regulated by the law of April 5, 1929, which covered individual, collective and apprenticeship contracts. Conciliation procedures for the solution of labor disputes were provided by the law of September 5, 1920, compulsory prior to any strike or lockout. A law of April 13, 1928, enacted as a consequence of the Washington Convention of 1919, instituted the eight-hour working day, and prohibited the employment of women and of workers under 18 years of age either underground or in night work. It also provided maternity leaves ranging from six weeks to three months. By then, work on Sundays and legal holidays had been regulated anew by a law of June 18, 1925. A law of April 5, 1929 provided guarantees for the remuneration of labor, and a law of April 2, 1931, instituted arbitration courts specifically for the settlement of labor disputes.

In addition to the above, a number of complementary laws were introduced—on June 24, 1921, July 4, 1924, May 3, 1927, and April 25, 1928 —to deal with the various aspects of sanitary and safety conditions in industries.

From the point of view of job security, the law of April 5, 1929, marked an important forward step. It provided, among other things, that individual labor contracts could not be rescinded except for reasons specified in the law itself, and with a minimal notice ranging from 14 days to one year, depending on the nature of the job and on the employee's length of service therein. Any illegal breach of contract entailed not only adequate compensation in lieu of notice, proportionate to the established wages, but also the payment of damages. All matters relating to individual labor contracts could be brought before the special labor courts.

Social security had, as we have already shown above, been started as early as 1912. The law passed on January 27 of that year provided for the payment of damages and disability pensions in cases of labor accidents, as well as for hospitalization and care in cases of sickness. It also provided for compulsory insurance, covering both disability and old-age retirement, with both employees and management contributing thereto, under the supervision of the appropriate state authorities. These provisions were amended and extended by the law of July 4, 1924. They were complemented by the law of April 8, 1933, which set up central offices of social

security, and by the law of December 22, 1938, which unified and im-•
proved the entire system of social security organization.

The right of free association, which was confirmed by article 5 of the
1923 Constitution, had long been recognized. The law of May 26, 1921,
for instance, had already formally established the right of workers to organize freely in trade unions, requiring merely the existence of a group
of at least ten persons—either private or public employees—to take such
decision. The position of the labor unions, which could be legally incorporated under the terms of that law, was further strengthened by the law
of February 6, 1924, which provided that a prior authorization or licens-
ing was no longer required for their creation. A notable feature of the
latter law was provided by Article 2, which stated that "no worker might
be compelled either to join or to abstain from joining" a labor union.
This in effect, by explicitly favoring the "open shop" system, provided
the individual worker with protection from unwonted dominance by the
unions.

As was the case elsewhere throughout Europe, Rumania's labor regime
suffered a marked setback during the period immediately preceding
World War II, as well as during the actual hostilities. Measures of exception, involving the freezing of workers at their jobs and even job
mobilization, wage control, and other restrictions, came into effect. It
should be noted, however, that, even under what was certainly an
authoritarian administration, operating under particularly adverse conditions, the personal rights of workers remained by and large unimpaired.
Industrial wages indeed rose considerably above the pre-war level. There
was no special cause for general dissatisfaction in the rank and file of labor,
aside from the disgruntlement it shared with all other categories of citizens,
and which hinged on the nature of the government, the alliance with Hitler's Germany, and the progress of the war.

Prior to the Soviet occupation which began in the summer of 1944,
the Communist party of Rumania had less than one thousand members.
At first, therefore, even while enjoying the fullest support of the Soviet
occupation authorities, and notwithstanding the numerous special agents
brought into the country, this minute and generally despised group could
not hope to carry much weight among Rumania's workers in its own name.
The forces of communist Russia had, indeed, routed the hated Nazis, so
far as the average industrial worker could see at the time of the armistice

of August 23, 1944. But the Russian liberators and allies, seen at close
quarters, could hardly be said to contribute anything toward building up
prestige for communism. And who were all these loud-mouthed agitators
who had come as camp followers of the conquerors? Where had they been
all the time? We know by now who our enemies are, but do these people
look like our friends? Thus reasoned the average Rumanian worker.

It was an unpromising outlook. The Communist party resorted to in-
filtrating the existing labor organizations and to setting up fictitious new
ones. Where persuasion did not avail and where open violence was not
yet opportune, guile had to be resorted to. The main objective was to make
it appear that the workers, acting in their capacity as true proletarians,
were behind the party's efforts.

The workers however showed greater awareness than the communists
had anticipated. They resisted communist intrusions into their unions,
and it was not long before naked force intervened. The early stages of
the communist seizure of power were marked with violence and blood-
shed.

The first communist move was to take over the existing Confederation
of Labor and to impose the creation of the so-called factory committees,
each headed by a party member or sympathizer from among the "converted socialists." The legal basis for these organizations came in the form
of Law No. 52, published in the *Official Gazette* No. 17 of January 21,
1945. This in fact was a decree imposed by the Soviet occupation authorities on the provisional government, through the intervention of the local
communists. Article 7 provided that, in order to be incorporated, a trade
union must first obtain a favorable "recommendation" from the Ministry
of Labor—one of the key departments dominated by the communists by
that time. Once incorporated, a trade union had the legal right to set up
factory committees. These factory committees in turn would "represent
the professional interests of all employees in regard to labor conditions,
wages, and moral and cultural conditions," in the terms of article 28.
These organizations, the localized equivalent of the "plant soviet," exercised full control and direction over the activities of individual workers.
The latter were legally defenseless in the face of decisions taken by these
bodies, in the election and operation of which they had no hand. According to Article 46 of the new law, trade unions could be grouped into more
general professional unions, and further form confederations of unions.

The latter, in the terms of article 48, could appoint delegates to speak and act in the name of the member unions. With the enactment of the 1945 law, the old liberal Trade Union Law of 1921 was repealed.

From every point of view, Law No. 52 proved a milestone in the forcible regimentation of Rumania's workers. Needless to say, only trade unions thoroughly dominated by trusted communists obtained the requisite "recommendation" for incorporation. Once incorporated, they fell under the strict authority and control of the so-called General Confederation of Labor, which was organized as a veritable field command of the Communist party. By way of the descending echelons of labor organizations outlined above, the factory committees became simple organs of the communist authorities within the respective enterprises. In this role, and operating with the cooperation of the communist police and of special party "shock units"—which in the United States would be described as "goon squads"—the factory committees proceeded to terrorize the workers. Beatings and arrests on trumped-up charges became the rule. Many were held by the police without any charges whatsoever; still others simply disappeared without a trace or were found dead under mysterious circumstances. Yet the workers continued to resist in every way they could —covertly if not openly.

But the factory committees had another telling weapon: they controlled the so-called *economate*, that is the plant food distribution unit or commissary, as well as the actual allocation of food cards to the employees. Any worker considered to be uncooperative by the factory committee would find himself deprived of food. It is difficult to stand up to this kind of argument.

Thus by fair means (in the form of iniquitous legislation), but mostly by foul, the communists succeeded step by step in gaining control over the entire range of what had come to be referred to as the "field of labor" —all regular gainful employment. Soon the Communist party could maneuver the "working masses" almost at will. It could stage impressive street demonstrations, monster rallies, collective protests and demands, and so forth. It made the fullest use of this hard-won supremacy when the general election of 1946, described elsewhere in this book, was finally carried out. This development was made possible only with the support— and, indeed, at the instigation—of the Soviet occupation authorities.

It is evident that the manner in which the communists organized trade unions in Rumania was in full accordance with the principle enunciated as early as 1920 by the ninth congress of the Soviet Union's own Communist party. It is appropriate to quote here that now familiar principle, if only to show how faithfully the pattern was reproduced: "The tasks of trade unions lie primarily in the field of economic organization and education. The trade unions must perform these tasks, not in the capacity of an independent, separately organized force, but in that of one of the main branches of governmental machinery, *guided by the Communist party.*" (Italics supplied.)

The trade unions are designed to be "schools of communism," as prescribed by Lenin in 1921, and are organizations intended to build up the Communist party, as prescribed in the resolutions of the fifteenth party congress of the U.S.S.R. in 1925. This role of the trade unions may, indeed, be found confirmed in Soviet textbooks on administrative law as late as 1940: "The trade unions are not party organizations, but in fact they carry out the decisions and directives of the party. All leadership organs of the trade unions consist primarily of communists who execute the party line in all work of the unions." This fine—and, to the non-communist reader, somewhat meaningless—distinction was made still more elusive by 1949, when the U.S.S.R. tenth congress of trade unions decided that "Soviet trade unions conduct their entire work under the directives of the Communist party, the organizing and directing force of the Soviet Union."

Under the circumstances, the R.P.R. trade unions of today are a far cry indeed from the non-communist conception of what a trade union should be, and from the pre-communist labor organizations of Rumania. They are no longer organs of protection for their members, either individually or collectively. Instead, they are organs of control, meant solely to carry out government—that is, Communist party—orders at the expense of everything else. This perverted role may be clearly seen in the text of joint Decision of the R.P.R. government and the central committee of Rumanian Workers' Party, which was published in the *Official Gazette* No. 16 of February 3, 1951, and which criticized the lack of activity of local party agencies, accusing the latter of "not having sufficiently directed the party's organizations, the labor unions, and the Union of Working Youth." "Union committees," the Decision went on, "have not sufficiently instructed . . . and have not taken efficient and systematic measures to enforce discipline in the field of labor. They have not cooperated sufficiently with management (of state enterprises) . . . to control unruly and undisciplined elements." It can hardly be more clearly put: the main purpose of a trade union is to "enforce discipline" and to "control" the workers.

The first constitution of the R.P.R., that of 1948, established the familiar principle already adopted in the Soviet Union: "labor is a duty." Article 12 reads: "Labor is the basic factor of the State's economic life. It is a duty for every citizen. The State supports all workers in defending them against exploitation and in raising their living standards." Article 19 further states that "citizens have the right to work." But, since this basic "right" may be exercised merely in "the organization and planned development of the national economy," it amounts in effect to a forcible regimentation of labor in "planned" work. These constitutional principles, which in fact provide the legal basis for the administration's intervention in all labor problems, and its strict control of the workers, were patterned after the Soviet constitution.

The second R.P.R. constitution, that of 1952, is even more specific and thoroughgoing. Article 15 proclaims that, "In the Rumanian People's Republic, work is a duty and a question of honor for all citizens able to work." It is in this charter that—on the model of the Soviet constitution—we find the notions of "working people" and "working class" officially proclaimed as generic entities and identified as the social categories in whose behalf the communist party ostensibly exercises the state power. It will be noted, incidentally, that the R.P.R. Communist party, though constantly referring to its own ideology as *communist*, is still coyly clinging to its original official label—the Rumanian Workers' Party, *Partidul Muncitoresc Roman*. The "working people" who have the right to vote and the right to be elected are assured, according to article 81 of the 1952 constitution, of "an absolute equality of rights . . . in all fields of economic, political, and cultural life."

This privilege is a dubious one at best. Though it is the "working people" alone who are admitted to the "field of labor"—regular gainful employment—and to membership in the various trade unions, the privilege entails admission to a system of close supervision, control, and direction by the Communist party organizations. Yet even this is a comparatively advantageous status, since exclusion from the "field of labor" means in effect deprivation of constitutional rights. In other words, we find in the constitution itself the formal basis for discrimination between social categories—a discrimination, moreover, that is arbitrary in that it is left to the communist-controlled organizations to decide at all times who has and who has not the basic citizenship rights.

The 1952 constitution actually equates the ideas of "working people" and "working class" with the Communist party. Article 86 reads in part, ". . . The most active and conscious citizens in the ranks of the working class and of the other strata of workers unite in the Rumanian Workers' Party, the vanguard of the working people in their struggle for strengthening and developing the regime of popular democracy and for the construction of the socialist society." As for the Rumanian Workers' Party, the same Article goes on to describe it as "the directing force of all workers' organizations *as well as of the state organs and institutions.* Around it are grouped *all* workers' organizations of the Rumanian People's Republic." (Italics supplied.)

It is not difficult to understand from the above what it means to be a "worker" in today's Rumania. Put in the simplest terms, it means to be forcibly regimented in a veritable labor army, under the most stringent control and direction of the officials of a regime that is itself appointed and manipulated at will by the Kremlin.

The R.P.R. *Official Gazette* of June 8, 1950 made public the text of Law No. 3, titled *Codul Muncii,* The Labor Code. Patterned on the existing labor laws of the Soviet Union, this charter laid down rules covering all aspects of labor conditions and relations. In it we meet such terms as "labor unions," "collective agreements," and "labor jurisdiction," that have a familiar sound to the non-communist student. But, as we have already seen in the case of the labor unions, these terms have a different connotation in R.P.R. official parlance.

Take, for instance, the notion of the collective labor contracts. Article 3 of the Labor Code reads: "The collective labor contract is an agreement between the trade union committee of an enterprise or institution, representing the plant or office workers on the one hand, and the party employing their work on the other hand. The collective labor contract sets forth the commitments of both parties with regard to: a) the output of production implementing the State Plan, and b) the improvement of working and living conditions of the workers." This means simply that the agreement is concluded between two government agencies, since the employee is in every case but an economic administrative unit, while the trade union committee is, as we have already seen, but an instrument of the same administration, both parties being under the complete control of the Communist party. It is as though the right hand were to sign an agreement with the left hand. From the point of view of the workers involved, it is a mere formality, the imposition of an administration-approved charter in which they have no say whatsoever, nothing but a set of orders that have to be carried out.

To make doubly sure that no "deviation" or mistake creeps in, article 7 provides that collective labor contracts must be registered with both the competent Ministry and the respective trade union, both of which agencies have to determine "a) whether the stipulations of the collective labor contract will indeed assure the implementation of the State Plan, and b) whether they do not create a situation contrary to the provisions of the (Labor) Code." Should such be the case, the same Article rules that ". . . the contract . . . shall be annulled and replaced by appropriate regulations as provided in the present Code." Furthermore, in accordance with Article 11, the authorities already mentioned have the duty "to supervise the implementation of collective labor agreements." A collective labor contract once concluded in the manner prescribed becomes, in the terms of article 5, "mandatory for all employees," that is, including those who are not union members.

The Labor Code allows individual (or simple) employment contracts to subsist, since at the time it was enacted the need for such agreements was still felt in certain enterprises. But they are stringently circumscribed. Article 20 provides a series of legal grounds for the unilateral repudiation of contract by the employer—the employer is, in the final analysis, none other than the State. The individual worker may be dismissed for such vague reasons as "unsatisfactory fulfilment of duties." He is to be dismissed if he is convicted for a crime (including, of course, such offenses as "economic sabotage" and other "political" charges), and, indeed, if he is merely arrested. Such dismissals, coming under the jurisdiction of the Labor Dispute Boards, whose main concern is to support the view of the authorities, leave the individual worker virtually without means of redress.

As for internal shop or plant regulations, which in the terms of article 24 are designed "to establish the organization of working discipline within the respective unit," Article 25 states that the models for such regulations are to be drawn up by the competent Ministries in agreement with the respective trade unions. That is, once again, we find two administration agencies legally substituted for an actual acceptance by the "workers" themselves.

The legally established eight-hour working day is itself subject to change. Article 49 provides that, "by a decision issued by the competent Ministries in agreement with the respective trade unions, categories may be established of wage- and salary-earners performing responsible technical or administrative functions, whose work is not limited to eight hours a day." Overtime is similarly left up to the arbitrary decision of "the competent Ministry in agreement with the trade union involved," according to article 57, which further provides that, "in cases considered as emergencies, overtime work may be ordered," even without outside intervention and approval. "Emergencies" being defined in the vaguest terms, an infinite range of interpretation is possible. This is in fact the dominant feature of the 1950 Labor Code in general: it is ostensibly enacted to protect the "workers," but the numerous exceptions and arbitrary interpretations it provides for on all key issues, leaves the workers, individually and collectively, in the power of the communist authorities.

Another idea introduced by the Labor Code is the "norm," or basic required output, the well-known Soviet device for speeding up production. "The competent Ministries," says article 27, "in agreement with the respective trade unions, will establish working norms for all production branches, functions, and specialties, fixing the quality and quantity of products or operations that wage-earners must furnish in a specified unit of time under normal working conditions." Meeting the norm thus becomes the condition for earning the basic wage, and workers who fail to measure up are paid, in the terms of Article 28, only "for work performed in relation to the quantity actually turned out."

Piece-work pay is calculated in relation to the norm. Article 36 is peremptory: the piece-work rate is determined by dividing the time-rate by the standard output set in the norm. It is not difficult to understand how, in this way, the worker's pay can be rigidly controlled simply by setting higher and higher norms. And, indeed, following the example set in the Soviet Union, the R.P.R. authorities have not scrupled to squeeze a maximum of production at a minimum pay-rate, out of the workers by this convenient device.

There is even a "legal" basis for this in the Labor Code itself. Article 27 states unambiguously that norms may be readjusted if and as "new measures of work rationalization or improvements of technological processes are introduced." The ultimate outcome of this is the notorious system of "Stakhanovism"—yet another Soviet gift to the workers of the people's democracies. Higher and higher production, by teams or by individuals, is assiduously fostered through propaganda, prizes, awards, publicized honors. Exceptionally high results, achieved at the cost of immense efforts, are then hailed as "improvements" and form the basis for increased norms for the entire field in which they are achieved. The outcome is that the individual worker cannot hope to earn even the average subsistence wage without seriously endangering his health.

The "workers" themselves have no say in the setting of norms. They are set and revised "by the Ministries concerned, in agreement with the respective trade unions," and require only the "approval of the Council of Ministers" to bring them into effect. Small wonder that, under these circumstances, the workers of Rumania hate the very name of Stakhanovism and quake at the mention of the word "norm."

According to articles 29 and 30, the workers must submit to pay cuts if the plant as a whole fails to meet the norm set for it, or if there are too many rejects of its products on delivery. This compulsory joint responsibility of the individual worker and the plant or enterprise as a whole, extends even to the financial aspect of production—to a field, that is, where his responsibility cannot be involved by the wildest stretch of the imagination. Decision No. 1424 of the R.P.R. Council of Ministers, published in the *Official Gazette* No. 1 of January 4, 1951, prescribes that the bank disbursing office, where the accounts of enterprises are kept, must refuse payments from funds allocated to wages if the enterprise concerned fails to fulfil the requirements of the State Plan. Funds requested in such cases must be reduced proportionally with the deficit of the enterprise in regard to the Plan.

Furthermore, article 67 of the Labor Code makes the workers responsible "for losses occasioned to the respective units in connection with their work," while article 68 extends responsibility even to cases of losses occasioned unintentionally. Should a worker's product be rejected, for instance, on grounds involving some criminal aspect (as set forth in the loosely-worded Criminal Code), his financial liability may amount to double the value of the damaged goods—*estimated at the free market price*. This brings up the general issue of the workers' insecurity, since the innumerable criminal provisions, ordinances, and other legal enactments are left vague and open to the most adverse interpretations when it comes to defining offenses. A charge of criminal negligence can be as effective as one of outright sabotage—and as difficult to disprove by the accused —in jeopardizing not merely the individual worker's wages, but also his very safety and liberty.

As for the labor unions, whose character has already been discussed, the Labor Code confirms their status as a mere branch of the administration. The agreements they sign are binding on all workers in the enterprise concerned, both members and non-members (article 7). They also have the power to dismiss workers, through the labor dispute boards (article 21), in addition to cooperating with the "competent Ministries" in drawing up internal regulations (article 25), norms (article 25), and working hours (article 49). The labor dispute boards mentioned above, which sit in judgment within each individual enterprise, are also organs of the labor unions (articles 114 and 115).

The General Confederation of Labor likewise plays an important part. It manages, directs, and controls matters pertaining to social security and insurance (articles 103–107). Article 108 further provides that, "The conditions required for granting material assistance and pensions, and the amounts thereof, as well as the procedures for establishing them, shall be determined by Decisions of the General Confederation of Labor, approved by the Council of Ministers." And, on the other hand, safety regulations and regulations regarding specific labor conditions are also of the exclusive competence of these administrative authorities. In other words, rules entailing the protection of workers' rights, which previously had been specifically provided for by laws, statutes, and regulations, are now left to the discretionary decision of the trade unions, the General Confederation of Labor, and the normal administrative authorities, the Ministries involved, all of which are but arms of the state authority that is under the strict control of the Communist party.

Turning once more to the matter of labor courts, which is treated in Chapter XVI of the Labor Code (articles 114 through 128), we find that, in addition to the labor dispute boards functioning within each separate enterprise, there are two other echelons provided. The first are the so-called "higher administrative authorities" mentioned in articles 114 and 116. Like the labor dispute boards, they consist of representatives of management and personnel; like them, they stand in fact for political authority and have little in common with the interests of the workers themselves. There are, finally, the law courts. Article 116 assigns to the ordinary law courts the competence to deal with such disputes as are not specifically given to the labor dispute boards, those in which the latter are unable to reach an agreement, matters involving criminal acts, and disputes arising in the "private sector" of industry.

The common courts are, of course, in no way specialized in labor problems. Nor have they the procedures to follow formerly prescribed by Rumania's pre-communist labor legislation. Whether they are hearing labor disputes or any other kind of cases, the present courts, having no powers separate from or independent of the administration, apply political standards in their findings, and are less concerned with texts of law than with what the communists describe as "social justice." These courts, composed of a majority of people's assessors, the political appointees of the various communist organizations, stand indeed in the same relation to the workers as does the Rumanian Workers' Party itself. In other words, the whole system of labor courts is but an elaborate front for the discretionary manipulation of labor by the Communist party.

The Labor Code provides means to legalize compulsory labor conscription. Article 111 is a case in point. It concerns not only the "working class" as such but all citizens. It reads: "The citizens of the Rumanian People's Republic may, in exceptional cases, in order to avert or combat calamities, *and to cope with a dearth of manpower,* be called upon to carry out important works of a public character or to perform certain temporary obligations of labor. The call to such temporary obligations of labor shall be made for a definite period of time through a Decision of the Council of Ministers." We have here in effect a legal provision authorizing the conscription of labor, left to the discretion of the government, in which the sole element of restriction—as loosely defined as the rest—consists of the clause requiring that such decisions shall initially set a time limit for the draft involved. But, since this too may be extended by a subsequent Decision, this is a somewhat academic point.

In addition to this legalized system of forced labor, Article 130 permits the Council of Ministers to establish "special working conditions" for workers engaged in certain categories of "temporary work," such as seasonal work in the field of construction, forestry, and agriculture, which categories are excepted from the general provisions of the Labor Code. This legalized regime of exceptions nullifies to all intents and purposes the rest of the Code's general provisions. Specifically, it provides, together with the afore-mentioned article 111, the legal basis for the establishment and exploitation of forced labor camps.

The rest of the labor legislation of the R.P.R. confirms these gloomy conclusions.

A decree, numbered 86 and published in the R.P.R. *Official Gazette* of March 7, 1949, established the so-called Offices for the Allocation of Labor Reserves, and made provisions for distributing manpower to various enterprises and works projects, in accordance with the administration's requirements. The business of these bureaus is to keep records of all employment vacancies, and of "all people available for placement in the field of labor," as well as to make allocations of available manpower. Local People's Councils are likewise required to maintain offices for the local distribution of labor reserves.

Another decree, number 68, published in the *Official Gazette* of May 18, 1951, provides for the annual drafting and training of 45,000 to 55,000 "young workers." The training of these youngsters lasts two or three years and is given in special vocational schools. Or else the "young workers" may take special six-months' training courses at their regular places of employment. The actual drafting is entrusted to the local people's councils. After training and graduation, the "young workers" become available for "distribution and assignment" to such work as may be called for by the plans approved by the Council of Ministers. Once allocated, according to article 6 of the decree, they must spend "at least four years" in whatever enterprise they are placed.

Obviously meant to enforce the above, Decree No. 511 of December 14, 1951 amended the Penal Code. It added to the existing article 244 a new paragraph which read: "Failure by graduates of technical, pedagogical, or qualification courses, of secondary schools, and of institutes of higher education to report for work shall be punished by imprisonment for terms ranging from three months to one year, if their graduation is connected with the obligation to do so, and the offenders have been appointed without delay."

A General Directorate of Labor Reserves was set up by Decision No. 399 of the Council of Ministers, published in the *Official Gazette* No. 56 of May 18, 1951. The Directorate supervises the drafting and training mentioned above, and "distributes any available skilled or non-skilled labor reserves in rural and urban areas, in accordance with the requirements of the national economy." Its role is self-explanatory.

Decision No. 4454 of the Council of Ministers, issued on January 9, 1954, provides: "Technical and administrative personnel and skilled workers shall be appointed to the units of the socialist sector, either directly by the respective units, or through allocation by the agencies of the General Directorate of Labor Reserves (which is), attached to the Council of Ministers." The Directorate may also—"in exceptional cases"—allocate personnel not subject to such drafting normally, like medical personnel, teachers, engineers, architects, and so forth.

The inference is inescapable: the communist regime of Rumania has made forced labor a statutory institution. With the translation of attempted evasion into a criminal offense, the official recognition of this iniquitous feature of "popular democracy" becomes manifest. Clinching the point, article 1 of Decree No. 207, published in the *Official Gazette* No. 113 of November 21, 1951, unambiguously proclaims: "Manual workers, clerical employees, engineers, and technicians of state enterprises and agencies, construction projects, and mass organizations shall not leave their employment without prior consent from the head of the respective unit." The punitive consequence is provided in Article 6: "No person may be given employment unless legally released from the previous employment." Other provisions make it compulsory for the "workers" so exhaustively enumerated in Article 1 to accept whatever jobs they may be assigned, and that they may be transferred from one job to another—and from one locality to another—whether they agree or not to such changes.

A more recent decree (No. 265 of August 3, 1954), aimed specifically at railroad workers, amended and supplemented the Penal Cole to fit a situation that developed subsequently to the passing of that criminal statute. The decree altered article 242-2) of the Penal Code to read as follows: "Departure from the place of work, or failure to report for work without justification by railroad exploitation personnel shall be punished with correctional imprisonment ranging from three months to one year." It also changed article 242-3) to read: "Unjustified failure to report for work for over three days—even with interruptions—in the course of any one month by railroad exploitation employees shall be punished with correctional imprisonment ranging from one month to six months."

Providing a general means of control over the comings and goings of all "workers", Decree No. 243, published in the *Official Gazette* No. 101 of November 6, 1950, requires all workers to register with local police authorities in order to obtain identity and work cards. This provides the additional advantage to the police authorities that workers expelled or barred from the "field of labor" can easily be identified and thus made available for internment in labor camps. Article 22 of this decree is peremptory and suffers no exceptions: "No person may change residence without previously obtaining an official moving permit from the Militia."

Finally, we may cite certain orders by individual departments, designed further to restrict and control the workers. The *Official Gazette* No. 41 of May 13, 1950, and No. 63 of July 27, 1950, make the possession of labor cards mandatory for all workers. These documents must record all pertinent facts relating to the individual concerned, in the form of periodical entries specifying qualifications, jobs held, penalties incurred, and so forth.

Let us note further that the possession of such labor and identity cards governs the obtaining of ration cards. Distributed solely to persons belonging to the "field of labor," labor and ration cards entitle the possessor to the privilege of buying certain quantities of food and clothing at special rates (which are considerably lower than those obtaining on the so-called free market). Specifically, one must belong to one or another of the so-called labor unions to rate such privileges. Ordinance No. 1720 of the Ministry of Domestic Trade, published in the *Official Gazette* No. 113 of December 11, 1950, prohibits the distribution of food and clothing cards to persons that do not belong to a trade union. Similar orders are issued reiteratively each successive year.

The situation of the workers—those very workers ostensibly favored and, indeed, represented by the present "popular democratic" regime of Rumania—is clear. Strictly regimented, coerced at every turn into compliance, brutally overworked, spied upon at all times, harassed and terrorized, blackmailed by the fear of losing even this bare subsistence privilege, they have become mere manpower, to be manipulated at will by the communist regime. Perhaps worst of all, the workers do not even have the compensation of feeling that the fruits of their labors enrich their own land and people. They know full well that they are exploited for the ultimate benefit of the Kremlin.

13

the pattern of power

The administration of Rumania has undergone a number of significant changes since the "liberation". Following the introduction of the people's councils (soviets), and the entrenchment in power of the single totalitarian party, the Rumanian Workers' Party, the "dictatorship of the proletariat" was formally set up. Rumania thus became almost indistinguishable from the other European satellite administrations called "people's democracies."

It was the 1923 constitution that was formally reinstated in Rumania following the coup d'état of August 23, 1944. Under that charter, the executive was but one of the three branches of state power. While the 1923 constitution was first in effect—from the time of its original introduction until 1938—two fundamental laws, passed in 1929 and subsequently amended and elaborated several times, provided the bases for Rumania's central and local administrative organization. The aim of this legislation was, on the one hand, an increasing decentralization and, on the other, the gradual elimination of political interference and corruption from the state-administration. The administrative structure, notwithstanding the impact of intervening rightist dictatorships, may be considered to have remained virtually stable and unchanged from 1929 at least until 1948, when the Soviet-type administration was put into operation. The government—the cabinet with its various departments—was, up to 1938, under the control of the bicameral parliament; the judiciary functioned independently, and its highest court, the Court of Cassation, controlled the constitutionality of legislative enactments; and the legislature, comprising several rival parties, operated under the normal system of elections. The central administration was represented locally by the prefects of the individual departments (*judetze*) and by the mayors of the urban and rural communes, much as was the case in other European countries governed by constitutions of similar type. The municipal and communal councils, which assured local administration in cities and villages were elective. Elections, in the years of democratic rule in Rumania, were free.

THE TERROR

This state structure the communists set about destroying the moment they set foot in the stirrup, with the help of the occupying Red armies. Conditions favored the camp followers of the Soviet invaders. The country was disrupted by years of war: whole provinces had been torn from its body; the democratic political parties had not wholly recovered from the effects of the previous dictatorial regimes; the bulk of the armed forces were fighting the retreating Reichswehr beyond the borders. But even when they were firmly in the saddle, the communists found it expedient to maintain the state structure outwardly during the initial period. It was necessary to raise and train their own cadres for the intended new set-up. It was also necessary thoroughly to undermine the existing framework.

The first move was to seek control of the key Ministry of the Interior. With the assistance and direct supervision of the MVD, the hastily organized "shock brigades" proceeded to wield the political weapon of terror against the administration—the administration to which the Communist party itself belonged as part of the "coalition." Following Vishinsky's ultimatum of March 6, 1945, the communists gained the coveted Ministry of the Interior and thereby effectively seized the reins. The key department became an annex of the Soviet command, notably of the MVD. Purges, mass arrests, naked terror soon sapped the state apparatus. But purges, mass arrests and naked terror continued to mark every succeeding phase of entrenchment in the saddle of totalitarian power. Two groups provided the necessary levers for this permanent policy: the militia and the Soviet "counselors."

The state militia was simply a legally organized version of the original communist strong-arm squads, the extra-legal "shock brigades". Operating from the very beginning with unlimited powers as local organs of the Ministry of the Interior, the militia was later to assume a "popular" function, with wide-ranging control over every sector of the nation's existence. It recruited labor for public works, created and maintained labor camps, organized economic mobilization, expropriations, agricultural collectiviza- tion, collection of farm products and so forth. With the introduction of the "procuratura," the Soviet-type state prosecution organ, as part of the reform of the judiciary carried out in January 1948, the militia also be- came an arm of the Ministry of Justice.

The second institution, that of the Soviet "counselors," permeates to this day every department, particularly the Ministry of Domestic Affairs (formerly of the Interior), and all affairs of an economic nature. Though little is known of the manner in which this vast body of Soviet advisers actually operates, it *is* known that the activities of its members were until recently coordinated and ultimately controlled from the Ministry of Do- mestic Affairs. There were in this department Russian-staffed sections corresponding to every main sector of state activity, and the head of the entire organization was (at least up to the time of Beria's downfall) the head of the MVD in Rumania, who dealt directly with the Kremlin without the intermediation of the Soviet embassy in Bucarest. In other words, the entire apparatus of the "dictatorship of the proletariat" in Rumania was in reality, as in the rest of the "people's democracies," but the form through which the plans and orders of Moscow were carried out.

It was in late December 1948 that the R.P.R. government formally announced in the Grand National Assembly that the country would soon know the blessings of a "People's Democracy which fulfils the functions of a dictatorship of the proletariat." And indeed soon after the law for the introduction of the people's councils was passed. The beginning of the year 1949 saw the quasi-Soviet state set up as a "people's democracy." By March of that year a resolution of the central committee of the Rumanian Workers' Party marked the inception of land collectivization and the transformation of the two trial one-year economic plans (1949–51) into a five-year state plan, based on the idea of speeding up the country's in- dustrialization.

THE TERRORIST STATE AND ITS RULERS

The Rumanian People's Democracy belongs, according to the official communist doctrine, to a sub-division of the socialist states called popular republics, or popular democracies. These differ from the Soviet State, of which the only example is the U.S.S.R. Within the category, communist doctrine distinguishes between the Chinese Popular Republic, and the rest of the Popular Republics: those of Eastern Europe and Outer Mongolia.

The functions of such a state are, according to official doctrine (see L. Rautu in *Scanteia*, December 29, 1951), "to crush the classes overthrown at home, to defend the country against aggression from outside, and economic-organizational and cultural-educational construction. These are functions characteristic of the dictatorship of the proletariat in the first stage of its existence; from the conquest of power until the liquidation of the exploiting classes.

"In the present stage the repression of the classes overthrown from power is of special significance. This function of the State is very important because in Rumania there are still remnants of the crushed exploiting classes, particularly the most numerous capitalist class, the kulaks. It is also important because the chief organizers of conspiracies against the Rumanian People's Republic are abroad, in the capitals of the imperialist states, especially in the United States of America. Because of this, the class war in a people's democracy cannot be considered separate from the struggle of the two systems in the international sphere.

"The second function of the State of people's democracy, the defense of the country against aggression from outside is of enormous importance. Although the peoples, by taking their fate into their own hands, are better prepared than ever to avoid war, this is no reason for negligence or bourgeois-pacifist illusions. Maximum vigilance is required."

It is clear that these particular tasks of the state are, in the Rumanian People's Republic, fulfilled only with the massive help of the Soviet Army. Full recognition is given up to the present by Rumanian Communist leaders (see Miron Constantinescu in *For a lasting peace*, March 9, 1956) to the help of the Soviet might. This is, of course, the great difference between those states and the Chinese Popular Republic, on the one hand, and Yugoslavia, on the other.

But the state has also a third function. This is defined by Rautu as "economic-organizational and cultural-educational construction." "This function can develop fully only in the second stage of the State of people's democracy, when the exploiting classes have been abolished for good and the State is able to extend its planning and organizing activities over the whole of the economy. For the present the existence of a wide non-socialist sector in agriculture and of a still considerable capitalist sector in trade, limits the power of the State to exercise this function, which nevertheless is developing in step with the growth of the Socialist sector in national economy.

"As in the other people's democracies, this function is exercised in various ways. In spite of the existence of a considerable non-socialist sector, economic life in its essence is directed by the State economic plan. Economy does not develop haphazardly, but in accordance with the policy of the party and the government, with the plans worked out by them.

"State activities are of enormous importance in the mobilization of the workers for the fulfilment and overfulfilment of the State Plan. With the help of agencies of the dictatorship of the proletariat, such as the trade unions, the youth organizations, etc. the State encourages the creative initiative of the masses.

"It has to be said that the State of people's democracies has the duty to make use of coercive measures against those who disorganize production willfully. Measures against breaches of discipline in work, and against people whom their desire to earn easy money induces to change their job all the time, serve the vital interests of those who work."

This provides a fair description of the totalitarian state. All communist states, of any category, are indeed enormous machines which control, direct and make use of all individuals for their totalitarian ends.

But in order to do so, the totalitarian people's republics need a very strong administration. From this point of view it is better to look at the situation in Rumania from two angles. The first is that of the Central Administration and its personnel; the second of the local administration and its personnel.

The role of the State, as defined by the Communists "makes it imperative for the Party to consolidate the State. The Party is the vital basis of the regime of people's democracy."

The cryptically worded paragraph 4 of article 86 of the 1952 R.P.R. constitution is the sole text in that basic charter dealing with the Rumanian Worker's Party. It amounts in effect to setting up that party as the sole political party permitted to operate in the country and to giving it the final word in the state administration.

This would lead to the conclusion that the mechanism of the "party leadership" is an extremely simple one. The Rumanian Workers' Party delegates its trusted members to fill all the important posts in the central administration, to the exclusion of anyone else. Government thus becomes one with the work of political and social transformation that forms the main objective of the party. The Central Committee and the Politbureau are the government of the government. The same persons are encountered in different capacities and with different powers, but with identical aims, in one and in the other. Ana Pauker, for instance, was at the same time Minister of Foreign Affairs and responsible for matters of agricultural production, as a member both of the government and the Central Committee.

However, there are two fundamental considerations that alter this simple relationship between party and government in the R.P.R.

The first hinges on the fact that the regime functions in a country under virtual occupation. Unlike what happens in the Soviet Union, the government has a greater importance and a capacity for swifter decision, precisely because the alien power's occupation organs work with the various departments directly, without control at every step from the party's ideological authorities.

The second difference arises from the fact that—as is the case in the Soviet Union and in the other satellite administrations—a formal, but highly significant, separation has been made between party and government, between the function of Prime Minister and that of First Secretary of the Central Committee, following Stalin's death. In the R.P.R., after a characteristic delay, this separation was put into effect in April 1954, and it is not unlikely that this may result in the setting up of two teams, two mentalities and two objectives. The statutory control of the party over the government may very well become a cause of conflict or at least antagonism.

The Statutes of the R.P.R. Communist party draw a distinction between control over central administration and over local. Article 37, paragraph 2, states that "the Central Committee of the Rumanian Workers' Party conducts the activities of the central agencies of State power, and of the public organizations through the party groups within these agencies and organizations." In view of the fact that the political powers of the Central Committee are, during the intervals between plenary sessions, taken over by the Politbureau the latter is the significant body.

Article 61 reads: "In view of increasing the importance of the party's base organizations in production and trade enterprises, including tractor and machine stations, state farms and collective farms, and in order to increase their responsibility for the quality of work accomplished by these units, base organizations are conferred the right of control over the activity of the administration (of such units). Party organizations within the Ministries, which are precluded by specific working conditions of State institutions from carrying out functions of control, have the duty of discovering shortcomings in the work of such Ministries and institutions and of their employees, and draw attention to them by forwarding their observations and suggestions to the Central Committee of the Rumanian Workers' Party and to the head of the respective Ministry or institution. All party members who work in the central administration of a Ministry or institution belong to the single party organization of that Ministry or organization as a whole. Secretaries of base organizations in Ministries and other central institutions must be confirmed by the Central Committee of the party".

These two texts together show that, while the Central Committee and the Politbureau conduct the activities of all departments of the central administration, and likewise maintain a constant and detailed check upon their execution of the party's directives, the base organizations check the activities of all organs of local administration—regional, raional, municipal and rural—within which they function. This mechanism and the manner of its operation have been repeatedly confirmed in published reports on regional conferences. We find, too, that base organizations frequently come under fire from higher organs for failing to control and stimulate the activities of the various administrative and economic organisms to which they belong. The tendency to increase this control is becoming increasingly evident. An intermediary organ, titled the "active," not yet clearly defined, appears to provide the meeting place for all those holding posts of responsibility in the administration, and for the secretaries, organizers, agitators, and activists of local party organizations. These "actives" are constantly being urged by the R.P.R. press and higher communist authorities to discuss all problems, both practical and ideological, and to provide information to the party representatives concerning all activities of the state organs.

It is of the greatest interest to see what develops, under the circumstances outlined above, in the case of Bucarest. Here we have the City party organization comprising the base organizations of the Bucarest raion, within whose province lie all the Ministries and the central institutions of the government. The fact that the Statutes deal quite exhaustively with this problem is not surprising. During recent years the Bucarest organizations have been through one crisis after another, precisely on account of the confusion of authority between them and the various departments and government agencies. The first major crisis developed in 1952 when Vasile Luca, then Minister of Finance and Vijoli, the head of the State Bank, were ousted, for allegedly sabotaging the monetary reform. The official view was then that, together with the two institutions involved, the raional committees of the Tudor Vladimirescu and Stalin wards, where the respective buildings as well as the bureau of the Bucarest City People's Council stood, bore part of the blame, for having failed in their vigilance. Of course, the party organizations within the Ministry of Finance and the State Bank were likewise held responsible together with everyone else involved.

A second major crisis occurred in June 1953, when the Plenary of the Bucarest City Committee sharply criticized the leadership of that Committee for failing to control the central institutions in charge of education, higher education and culture. At a stormy meeting, speaker after speaker denounced the grave errors found in the manner in which the courses were taught at the various Institutes and University Schools and within the Union of Composers and the Writers' Union. Even the R.P.R. Academy and the competent Ministries came under fire. The defense offered by the First Secretary of the Committee was that, in existing circumstances, the base organizations had no means of effectively controlling the central departments. This was rejected and he was replaced, together with the majority of the members of the bureau.

The Council of Ministers is ostensibly the supreme executive organ of the R.P.R. It coordinates and conducts the various departments, or Ministries, which at the present moment number twenty-four, as well as several commissions and committees that work directly with the Prime Minister. The Council of Ministers is currently composed of the Prime Minister, three First Vice Presidents, three Vice Presidents and the rest of the cabinet which comprises titular Ministers, First Lieutenant Ministers, and simple Lieutenant Ministers. (It should be remarked that the institution of multiple vice presidents is of Soviet importation; and that the number of separate ministerial departments is disproportionately large for the needs of a small country like Rumania.) The two First Vice Presidents, whose powers of control are most far-reaching, are those who are also at the head of the military-police apparatus and of the Central Planning Commission respectively.

The latter institution is the state agency which coordinates the activities of all departments involved in the State Plan. On the international plane, it operates in conjunction with the Council for Mutual Economic Assistance, the organization set up in 1949 to assure thorough Soviet control over the economies of the Eastern European satellites. The current regional economic plan for 1955–1960, based on the closest possible integration of the individual satellite economies with that of the Soviet Union, was the joint work of each of these countries' planning commissions, under the control of that of the Soviet Union. On the domestic plane, the technical personnel of the R.P.R. Planning Commission, ramified throughout the country's economy, form a team of supervisors for all economic departments. The ousting of Vasile Luca in 1952 marked the first "success" of these planners. The dissolution of most of the "Sovroms" in 1954 was another notable achievement. On the other hand, these technicians are the representatives within the R.P.R. administration of the social-professional group known as the "technical intelligentsia." The group is influential throughout the Soviet orbit. It is indeed highly probable that all the qualified technical personnel that the various schools, institutes and universities of the R.P.R. turn out is immediately put at the disposal of the Planning Commission, which then directs its distribution through the sectors of production. It is this category of trained technical-administrative personnel that forms the special stratum of "responsibles" in the R.P.R. state apparatus. From all points of view, the State Planning Commission may be considered a veritable "inner circle". However, the actual influence exercised upon the central administration by the large body of technicians working under that Commission remains obscure at the present time.

Finally it must be mentioned that the R.P.R. central administration is subject to control by the State Control Commission for financial and disciplinary matters and by the "procuratura" in legal and juridical matters. These are controls of a constitutional character, as shown in our chapter on the R.P.R. Constitution.

The control exercised upon the central administration by the Politbureau of the Rumanian Workers' Party is absolute and unconditional. It is in this relationship between the government and the party that the main locale of power under a communist regime must be sought.

In the ambience of intricate confusion which prevails in the R.P.R.

and subject, of course, to the ultimate authority of the Kremlin, power remains discernibly concentrated in the hands of the eleven persons that make up the Politbureau. One of these is the Prime Minister, six are also Vice Presidents of the Council of Ministers, one is the First Secretary of the party, and yet another is the President of the party's Control Commission. In every known state of Soviet type the Politbureau is in the last analysis, always the supreme organ of political decision. And in the R.P.R., even more than in the other people's democracies, it seems likely that the Politbureau has had its power and influence increased as the result of the statutory division recently defined between the party secretariat and the cabinet.

In addition to becoming the top organ of political direction, the Politbureau now provides the sole statutory common meeting ground for the First Secretary and the Prime Minister. Hence it is the only conceivable arbiter in case of conflict between these two, or between the bodies they represent. From the point of view of practical politics, this means that whatever group of members is able to constitute a majority within the eleven, must be taken to be the effective head of the administration. It should be noted that this group of members need not necessarily include the Prime Minister or the First Secretary. And it is no less interesting to note that each of the members enumerated above—all of whom are possible candidates for the top place—also represents one of the "inner circles" we have encountered in the course of this analysis, or an important segment thereof.

The *dramatis personae* that confront one another within the Politbureau, each with his retinue behind him, are the following: The Prime Minister, with the bulk of the administration, representing the anonymous mass of the "bureaucracy"; the First Secretary with part of the party, and probably, a large part of the workers' unions; the chief of the Section of Propaganda and Agitation, backed probably by part of the cadres of party janissaries and leaders recently trained in the special schools; the President of the Control Commission, presumably backed by many of the older party cadres; the head of the Organization and Cadres Section, with a probable following of cadres and unions (the current occupant is in addition the representative of the powerful Magyar section of the R.P.R. Communist party); the President of the State Planning Commission, backed presumably by the teams of younger "responsible" technicians and by the "intelligentsia"; and, last but assuredly not least, the Minister

of the Armed Forces, backed by the military-police apparatus and with
the team of political generals within the administration and the party
(one of the latter is currently the only person to be at the same time a
member of the Secretariat, of the Orgbureau, and of the administration,
concentrating thus within his own competence a number of concentric
powers).

It may be taken for granted that, operating in the atmosphere of reciprocal jealousy and hatred that is so characteristic of Communist parties
everywhere, all the above, either singly or in coalition, are vying for the
top position. An attempt to forecast the outcome of this covert struggle
for power lies beyond the sphere of the present study. The reader will
note that we have not even listed the names of most of the *dramatis
personae* currently to be presumed in reciprocal competition. This is accounted for by our own belief that it is the groups forming the inner
circles that are significant, and not the persons that may be heading them
at any given moment. It is within these groups and in their interaction,
that the social-political authority of the R.P.R. must be sought. Together,
these inner circles form what may be defined as the ruling clique. It is
they that form, under the domination of the occupying power to which
they owe their very existence, the precarious levers of authority. It is they,
sharing complicity—and well deserved public opprobrium—that form the
ruling class of the R.P.R. and not the proletariat or the "workers."

THE TERRORIST STATE AND ITS SERVANTS

The few who rule the Rumanian People's Republic need a colossal apparatus of local agents to execute their orders and to fulfil their assign-
ments. The problem of local administration in such a state can best be
seen under two main angles. One is that of the institution of the people's
councils (Soviets); the other is that of the administrative personnel
needed by both central and local administrations for the carrying out of
duties.

The current constitution of the R.P.R. discloses certain apparent contradictions with regard to the location of state power. Article 2 describes the
people's councils as "the political base of the R.P.R." Article 22, on the
other hand, refers to the Grand National Assembly as "the supreme executive and administrative organ of the state power," while article 51 proclaims the people's councils to be the "organs of state power in the regions,
raions, cities and rural agglomerations." Behind this confusing verbiage

at least one thing is clear: there is a central administration (the government) and a series of local administrations (the people's councils), and the true political power belongs to the first.

There is every evidence that the local administration is altogether inferior, *per se* powerless, and wholly subordinate to the central. The tendency is manifestly to make the local people's councils the persecuted strata of the "people's democracies." It is they that must bear the blame for all the mistakes, blunders and inefficiencies of the regime's planners. Overburdened with impossible and often contradictory tasks, the executive committees of the local people's councils must bear the consequences of failure, the accusations of "bureaucracy," and the brunt of the criticism that may not be directed at the regime itself, at the system and the conception, but only at the manner of execution. And the trend is to add constantly to the responsibilities of these alleged repositories of the people's authority, though the theory of "democratic centralism" must be increasingly strained to justify the obvious fact that the power is not in the people's councils but in the central administration.

The law on the people's councils, passed on January 15, 1949, already laid down in article 18 the powers of these bodies as being: "to apply locally the principles of the socialist order; to assure the participation of the masses in public concerns; to carry out the local plan; to strengthen the friendship among the workers, without distinction of race, language and religion; to raise the cultural and political level of the masses; to protect public health; to organize the provisioning of the workers and to put down sabotage and speculation; to strengthen the equality of rights between men and women by setting up maternity wards and schools; to control the citizens in carrying out their legal obligations." Article 19 provides that these multiple duties, left purposely vague in their wording, must be carried out by conducting and controlling the "social, cultural and economic activities of the institutions . . . within the jurisdiction of the people's councils." Furthermore, according to the same article, the people's councils must "set up and carry out the local plan and budget; examine problems of a general nature" and so forth. This tall order was later increased by the various decrees and special laws that heaped additional duties on the shoulders of the people's councils. Such special tasks as setting up "architectural sections," fostering cotton cultivation, tending the crops, taking emergency fire-prevention measures in times of drought, taking a census of children between the ages of 1 and

14, transporting lumber products, keeping communal agricultural registers, organizing sales cooperatives and agricultural associations (of the TOZ type), taking steps to put down porcine pest, organizing the public guard, administering markets and fairs, securing the payment of state and local taxes, and many others, both temporary and permanent, have been assigned to the people's councils. Aside from all these, the people's councils are expected to carry out whatever urgent and imperative tasks may be given to them in connection with every drive or campaign of a nation-wide character, no matter what the objective.

People's councils are regional, raional, urban and rural. There are 16 regional people's councils, including the city of Bucharest considered administratively of regional rank. They are: Bacau, Baia Mare, Bucarest (regional), Cluj, Constantza, Craiova, Galatzi, Hunedoara, Iash, Oradea, Piteshti, Ploesti, Stalin (Brashov), Suceava, Timishoara, and the "Magyar Autonomous Region." The raional people's councils vary in number, as additional ones are set up by splitting up one or more of the existing ones; currently they number 192. Regional and raional people's councils are headed by their executive committee, with a membership varying between three and eleven, by a chairman (president), one to three vice presidents, and a secretary. The latter is usually the trusted local representative of the Communist (Rumanian Workers') party. Members of the people's councils are called deputies, and they are "elected" by the "people." (In 1956, 137,508 such deputies were elected.) In turn, they elect the members of their executive committee from among themselves. Apart from the fact that Decree No. 391 of 1953, introduced a number of restrictions of a political and social character on eligibility for election to the people's councils, all lists of candidates must have prior approval by the Ministry of Domestic Affairs. In other words, no one is in principle elected to any people's council without endorsement from the security agency. Indeed, it may be taken for granted that the lists themselves are drawn up by the party organizations in the first place.

Relations between the local administration and the central are set down in the Law for the People's Councils, in Articles 66 and 67. The Grand National Assembly, its Presidium and the regional people's councils control the activities of the lower echelons, while the cabinet (the Council of Ministers), the agencies of the central administration, and the executive committees of the regional people's councils control the executive committees of the rest. The Grand National Assembly and its Presidium may suspend and even dissolve any of the people's councils and order the holdings of new "elections." Such phrases as "democratic centralism means the subordination of the lower organs to the higher ones," and the "consequence of centralism is that all people's councils are directed by a single centre: the government" indicate sufficiently how insignificant the power of the local administrative organs is in reality.

It is also interesting to note that, although the people's councils must cope with many and varied responsibilities, and therefore may be expected to require an immense personnel, the entire 1954 budget allocation for "local agencies of State power," that is, for the people's councils, was barely 5,061,000 lei, while that for central administration totalled 32,-694,000 lei. Under the circumstances, it would be difficult to maintain that the local administration, as embodied in the people's councils, has any true powers or competence. This is hardly surprising since, patterned after the Soviet model which has now been in operation for forty years, the people's councils of the R.P.R. could not be reasonably expected to differ materially from the original.

The conception of administration under a communist regime is fundamentally different from, and far more complex than, that in a democratic state. In the latter, the main function of the administration is management, conduct of affairs and stewardship, aimed at securing the smoothest possible relationship between the citizens and the state, between private and public interests. In the communist state, however, the state administration not only controls, but creates, conducts and carries out all major activities of a political, cultural, social and economic nature.

Now, though it is not too difficult to visualize an entire country transformed into a vast prison and labor camp, it is hard to see how the communist regimes of the people's democracies manage to assure the general economic, cultural and administrative functioning of the societies they rule. How, in other words, does the "party and government" find the necessary technical and political personnel to fill the framework of such an enormous and complex organism? The answer is twofold. On the one hand there is what the communists call "the creation of cadres." On the other there is what is known in the R.P.R. and the Soviet Union, but not in the rest of the people's democracies, as "posts of responsibility."

An interesting study published by I. Lorincz, in the R.P.R. law periodical *Justitia Noua,* states that the most difficult problem of a new state apparatus is that of cadres. "Cadres", writes the author, "are essential for the executive agencies of State power, both local and central, for the judiciary and the procuratura, and for the complex system of public and mass organizations that work together with the State agencies." The people's democracy in Rumania, he points out, solves the problem by: a) giving the workers a direct participation in the conduct of the State; b) transforming workers through education into intellectuals; and c) using and re-educating the specialists taken over from the bourgeois-landowning regimes of the past.

Yet, unlike what happened in the Soviet Union immediately following the revolution, and even in Eastern Germany and Czechoslovakia, where the communist workers were given the hope at first that they and their unions would have a hand in the conduct of the state, in Rumania the regime of quasi-occupation has from the very first kept the workers in check. In Rumania, of course, the industrial proletariat is numerically small. And so, initially, the communists recruited their administrative personnel from the most diverse elements, both socially and nationally. In certain provinces, the heads of the administrative apparatus were appointed—and, in many cases even brought in—by the Soviet army command, during the first few months that followed the armistice. These appointees then made up their own teams with people of all kinds. Much the same situation prevailed in the various plants, institutions and other enterprises. The key positions were held in the first years by trustees of the regime, while the technical and administrative personnel was mostly made up of what are described as "inimical social elements," and even in some cases "war criminals," who had been released from prison or labor camps after a longer or shorter sojourn for "re-education."

But this of course was not enough. In order to remedy this difficult situation the Communist party has had to set up its own special schools and courses for the training of party cadres. The lack of success encountered in the numerous "short-order" courses and schools has been often admitted, notwithstanding the no less frequently proclaimed help received from the Soviet Union in this as in other fields of endeavor. At this time, with the available experts and specialists of top level still largely drawn from "re-educated" elements trained under the pre-communist regimes, the regime seeks to provide its future technical cadres with a semblance of a rounded general education once more. From

Gheorghiu-Dej's speech on August 23, 1953, we know that this education fell short of its aims and targets. Yet with trusted communists in control of every school, and with the teaching personnel overwhelmingly recruited from the cowed and compliant, but at heart still non-communist, intellectuals (admitted or not to the party), a hybrid situation has resulted.

What now are the "posts of responsibility"? They are all those positions through which the party and government must conduct the action called for by the economic plan for each individual sector and unit of every kind and at all levels. It is certainly significant to find that the problem of these "posts of responsibility" is treated and provided for in the Labor Code of June 8, 1950. It means that such posts are distributed throughout all sectors of activity, and not only in the state administration. A Decision (No. 139 of January 17, 1953) issued long after the introduction of the Labor Code includes the list of these posts. This exhaustive list shows clearly enough that they form a complete network covering every echelon of each field of activity. Here it is in its entirety.*

"The following functions exercised by employees of State agencies and institutions, State economic enterprises and organizations and cooperative and public organizations are considered posts in the sense of the Labor Code:

a) The posts of heads of institutions and of State and cooperative economic organizations and enterprises.

b) Those of directors-general, directors, and heads of independent departments of Ministries, institutions and enterprises, of co-operative and public organizations, and functions similar to them.

c) Those of technical managers and chief engineers.

d) Those of chief and principal accountants, if they head the respective accounting department.

e) Those of chiefs of working sites or production sections.

f) Those of judges, prosecutors, and State arbiters.

g) Those of leaders and of responsible heads of administration in scientific, educational, literary and artistic institutions.

* In the Soviet Union such "posts of responsibility" have certainly existed in the past, for both the Administrative and Criminal Codes refer to them under the name *dolzhonostnoye litso*; they probably still exist at this time. Although a number of Western writers on Soviet state structure (notably the American scholar J. Barrington Moore) have dealt at length with this institution, so far no list of such key positions in the Soviet Union has ever come to light. It is not at all unlikely that the R.P.R. list we give is either a translation or an adaptation of the hitherto unpublished Soviet original.

h) Those of inspectors of republic-wide and regional competence attached to the units specified under par. a above.

i) Those of regional delegates of the State Committee for the Collection of Agricultural Products.

j) Those of heads of departments attached to the Executive Committees of regional, city and raional People's Councils.

k) Those of legal advisers of ministries and other central agencies of the State administration, and heads of legal departments.

l) Those of chief editors, deputy chief editors, and chief departmental editors.

m) Those of secretary general of newspaper offices.

n) Those of heads of health units.

o) Those of administrators of pharmacies.

p) Those of elected employees who exercise functions paid by the organizations that elected them.

q) Those of secretaries of the offices of Ministers and Lieutenant Ministers.

r) Those of station master of the principal railroad stations.

s) Those of commandants of vessels of the merchant navy.

t) Those of heads, administrators, and leaders of economic sections, departments, and similar units, of canteens, workshops, and all other sub-units organized on the principle of independent management, even if they are not actually corporate bodies.

u) Those of heads of State stores and of cooperative commercial enterprises.

v) Those of heads of security and fire brigade sections.

w) Those of deputies or legal alternates of the functions listed above in the present Decision."

In order to realize just how exhaustive this long list is, each of the posts enumerated must be multiplied by the thousands of analogous positions there are at all the specified levels throughout the complex administrative-economic structure of the present planned society. Indeed, the significance of this will become still more obvious when it is borne in mind that the list was drawn up precisely at a time when the R.P.R. communists were drafting, and preparing for the execution of, their first five-year plan.

This leads us to conclude that under a communist regime control is not exercised solely by the recognized official representatives of the party, such as the secretary, the "activist," the party member, in accordance with the familiar theory that "where the party member is, power is too," which makes of power a subjective personal factor that the party representative carries with him. The list shows, to a certain extent, that power may also reside in certain objective impersonal posts—posts for which the requisite and trusted personnel must be found.

bibliography

1 GENERAL

a) Books and Articles

BARRINGTON-MOORE, JR. Soviet Politics. The Dilemma of Power. Harvard, 1950.

BAUMONT, M. La Faillite de la Paix (1918-1939), Paris, 1951.

BISHOP, ROBERT and CRAYFIELD, E. S. Russia Astride the Balkans (Robert M. McBride, New York, 1948).

BRANNEN, BARRY. "The Soviet Conquest of Rumania" in *Foreign Affairs*. New York, April, 1952.

BRATIANU, GHEORGHE. La Bessarabie. Droits Nationaux et Historiques. Bucarest, 1943.

BYRNES, JAMES. Speaking Frankly. Harper. New York, 1947.

CAMPBELL, JOHN C. and THE RESEARCH STAFF OF THE COUNCIL ON FOREIGN RELATIONS. The United States in World Affairs, 1945-1947. Introd. by J. Foster Dulles. New York. Harper, 1947.

CAMPBELL, JOHN C. "The European Territorial Settlement" in *Foreign Affairs*. October, 1947.

—————— "Diplomacy on the Danube" in *Foreign Affairs*. January, 1949.

CATROUX (GENERAL). J'ai vu tomber le Rideau de Fer, Moscou, 1945-1948. Hachette, Paris, 1952.

CHURCHILL, SIR WINSTON. The Second World War. Vol. I-VI. Houghton Mifflin, Boston, 1948-1953.

CIUREA, EMILE C. Le Traité de Paix avec la Roumanie du 10 Février 1947. Paris, 1954.

COUR INTERNATIONALE DE JUSTICE. Recueil des arrêts, avis consultatifs et ordonnances. Interprétation des Traités de paix conclus avec la Bulgarie, la Hongrie et la Roumanie. Avis consultatifs du 30 mars 1950. Leyde, A. W. Sijthoff (1950).

────── Mémoires, plaidoiries et documents. Interprétation des Traités de paix conclus avec la Bulgarie, la Hongrie et la Roumanie. Avis consultatifs des 30 mars et 18 juillet 1950. Leyde, A. W. Sijthoff. 1950.

CRETZIANU, ALEXANDRE.   La Politique de la Paix de la Roumanie à l'égard de l'Union Soviétique. Institut Universitaire Roumain Charles I-er, Paris, 1954.

────── "The Offensive against the Soul" in *The New Leader*. New York, January, 1949.

────── "The Soviet Ultimatum to Rumania" in the *Journal of Central European Affairs*. Boulder, January, 1950.

────── "Rumanian Armistice Negotiations" in the *Journal of Central European Affairs*. Boulder, October, 1951.

────── "Rumania's Robot State" in *The New Leader*. New York, October, 1950.

────── The Regime of Forced Labor in Rumania. Rumanian National Committee, Washington, 1952.

DENNETT, RAYMOND and JOHNSON, JOSEPH.   Negotiating with the Russians. World Peace Foundation, Boston, 1951.

DEPARTMENT OF STATE.   Postwar Foreign Policy Preparations. 1939-1945, Washington, D. C., 1949.

────── Treaties of Peace with Italy, Bulgaria, Hungary, Rumania and Finland (English version)—European Series 21, Washington, D. C.

────── Violations of Peace Treaty Guarantees of Human Rights. Vol. Rumania. Expression, Press and Publications, Washington, 1951.

────── Evidence of Violations of Human Rights. Provisions of the Treaties of Peace by Rumania, Bulgaria and Hungary. Submitted by the United States to the Secretary General of the United Nations Pursuant to the Resolution of the General Assembly of November 3, 1950, vol. I, Violations by the Rumanian Government. Freedoms of Expression and of Press and Publication. Washington, D. C. 4376. 1951.

DEWAR, MARGARET.   Soviet Trade with Eastern Europe. 1945-1949. London, 1951.

ETHRIDGE, MARK.   "The Blacking out of News in Eastern Europe" in *The New York Times Magazine*. April 14, 1946.

GAFENCO, GREGOIRE.   Preliminaires de la Guerre à l'Est, Fribourg. Egloff. 1944.

GIURESCU, CONSTANTIN.   Istoria Românilor. I-III. Bucarest. 1935-1942.

GLUCKSTEIN, YGAEL.   Stalin's Satellites in Europe. Allen and Unwin, London, 1952.

HILLGRUBER, ANDREAS.   Hitler, Konig Carol und Marshall Antonescu. Franz Steiner, Wiesbaden, 1954.

HOUSE, E. and SEYMOUR, CH.   What really happened at Paris: The story of the Peace Conference. 1918-1919. New York, 1921.

IONESCU, G.   "The evolution of the Cominform" in *The World Today*. London, May, 1950.

────── "The governing personnel in the Popular Democracies." Paper read at Soviet Affairs Seminar, School of Slavonic Studies. London, 1955.

——— "The Peasant in Eastern Europe's Economic Planning" in *World Today*. London, August, 1949.

——— "Rumania in 1952" in *World Today*. London, July, 1952.

——— "Changes in Eastern Europe's Economic Planning" in *World Today*. London, December, 1953.

——— Social Legislation in Rumanian agriculture. Mid-European Studies Center. New York, 1954.

IORDAN, CONSTANTIN. The Rumanian Oil Industry. New York University Press, 1955.

IORGA, NICOLAE. A History of Rumania: Land, People, Civilization. London, 1925.

——— La Place des Roumains dans l'Histoire Universelle. Bucarest, 1935.

——— Byzance après Byzance. Bucarest, 1935.

KING, WILLIAM B. and O'BRIEN, FRANK. The Balkans, Frontier of Two Worlds. Knopf, New York, 1947.

KONRAD, G. I. Die Wirtschaft Rumaniens, 1945-1952. Berlin, 1953.

LEE, AIR VICE-MARSHAL, ARTHUR GOULD. Crown Against Sickle. Hutchinson, London, 1949.

LUKACS, JOHN A. The Great Powers and Eastern Europe. Henry Regnery, Chicago, 1953.

MADGEARU, VIRGIL. Evoluția Economiei Românești dupa Razboiul Mondial. Bucarest, 1940.

MANUILA S. and GEORGESCU, D. C. Populatia Romaniei. Bucarest, 1938.

MANUILA S. The Vienna Award and its demographical consequences. The National Institute of Bucharest, Bucharest, 1945.

MARKHAM, REUBEN. Rumania under the Soviet Yoke. Meador, Boston, 1949.

MITRANY, DAVID. The Land and the Peasant in Rumania. Cambridge University Press. 1924.

MOORAD, GEORGE. Behind the Iron Curtain. Latimer House, London, 1947.

MOORE, WILBERT. Economic Demography of Eastern and Southern Europe. Geneva, 1945.

MOSELY, PHILIP E. "Is Bessarabia next?" in *Foreign Affairs*. April, 1940.

NANO, FREDERIC. The First Soviet Double Cross in the *Journal of Central European Affairs*. Boulder, 1952.

NEMOURS, L. Roumanie: 1946 in *Etudes*. Paris, July-August, 1946.

PROST, H. Destin de la Roumanie. (1918-1945). Paris, 1954.

ROBERTS, HENRY L. Rumania: Political Problems of an Agrarian State. Yale, 1951.

ROYAL RUMANIAN FOREIGN OFFICE. Conventie de Armistitiu intre Guvernul Roman pe de o parte si Guvernele Uniunii Sovietice, Regatului Unit și Statelor Unite ale Americei pe de altă parte, în limbile Română, Rusă și Engleză. București, 1944.

——— Mémoire sur l'Effort Militaire et Economique de la Roumanie dans la Guerre contre l'Allemagne et la Hongrie (Bucarest, Imprimerie de l'Etat, 1946).

RUMANIAN NATIONAL COMMITTEE.   Suppression of Human Rights in Rumania.
Washington, 1949.
———— Persecution of Religion in Rumania. Washington, September, 1949.
———— The Perversion of Education in Rumania. Washington, July, 1950.
SELECT COMMITTEE ON COMMUNIST AGGRESSION.   House of Representatives.
83rd Congress.   Tenth Interim Report. U. S. Government Printing Office,
Washington, D. C., 1954.
SETON-WATSON, HUGH.   The East European Revolution. London, 1950, Praeger,
New York, 1951.
———— The Pattern of Communist Revolution. London, 1953.
SETON-WATSON, R. W.   A History of the Rumanians from Roman Times to the
completion of Unity. Cambridge. 1934.
TRUMAN, HARRY S.   Years of Decision. Doubleday, New York, 1955.
UNITED NATIONS. International Labor Office.   Report of the Adhoc Committee
on Forced Labor. Geneva, 1953.
UNITED STATES GOVERNMENT PRINTING OFFICE.   Paris Peace Conference 1946
selected Documents. Washington, D. C., 1948.
ZAGOROFF, S. D. and others.   The Agricultural Economy of the Danubian coun-
tries, 1935-1945. Stanford, 1955.
ZISSU, IANCU.   The Regime of Forced Labor in Rumania (II). Rumanian
National Committee. Washington, 1952.

La Roumanie devant la Conference de la Paix, Paris, 1946.
La Roumanie devant la Conference de la Paix, II, Observations sur le projet
de Traité de paix avec la Roumanie, Paris, October, 1946.
La Roumanie et la reconstruction économique européenne, Paris, August, 1947.

b) Periodicals

American Slavic & East European Review (Columbia, New York).
Journal of Central European Affairs (Colorado)
Ost-Europa (Münich)
Slavonic Review (London)
Wissenschaftlicherdienst Südost-Europa (Münich)
World Today (London)

Free Europe Committee Publications
(110 West 57th Street, New York 19, N. Y.)

Buletinul de Stiri din România și Comentarii. Weekly. (1953-   )
Cronica Românească. Monthly. (1950-   )
News from behind the Iron Curtain. Monthly. (January 1951-   )

Rumanian Exile Publications

Information Bulletin. Rumanian National Committee. 2810 Cathedral Ave.
N.W. Washington, D. C. Monthly (March, 1950-December, 1954).
La Nation Roumaine. Monthly. 33, Rue de Lubeck. Paris. (August, 1948-   )

2 R.P.R. PUBLICATIONS

a) Books and articles

Abecedar, Bucarest, 1954.
AFANASIEF, A. C.   Bazele întocmirii bilantului, Bucarest, 1954.
Aspects du commerce extérieur de la République Populaire Roumaine, Bucarest,
   1954.
Bibliografia pe teme pentru "Planificarea economiei naționale." Bucarest, 1955.
Bugetul de Stat al R.P.R., vol. 2, Bucarest, 1955.
Cercetări filozofice, vol. 2, Bucarest, 1954.
COMAN ALEXANDRU și alții.   Economiile bănești ale populației,si rolul Casei
   de Economii și Consemnatiuni, Bucarest, 1954.
Comsomolul. ajutor credincios si rezervă de luptă a Partidului Comunist al
   Uniunii Sovietice, Bucarest, 1954.
Construirea și dezvoltarea industriei în țara noastră. Lupta partidului pentru
   întărirea alianței clasei muncitoare cu țărănimea muncitoare, pentru dezvol-
   tarea producției agricole și transformarea socialistă a agriculturii, Bucarest,
   1955.
Despre cointeresarea materială a oamenilor muncii din agricultură în sporirea
   producției agricole, Bucarest, 1955.
Despre contractări și achiziții, Bucarest, 1955.
Despre cultura grîului și a porumbului în R.P.R., Bucarest, 1955.
Documente din Istoria Partidului Comunist, Bucarest, 1953.
Editura Academiei R.P.R., Catalog 1948-1954, Bucarest, 1954.
Exportlemn. Empresa de estade para el comercio exterior. (Exportlemn. Intre-
   prindere de stat pentru comerțul exterior). Bucarest, 1955.
Finanțarea și decontarea investițiilor, Bucarest, 1954.
GHEORGHIU-DEJ, GH.   30 de ani de luptă a partidului sub steagul lui Lenin și
   Stalin, Bucarest, 1955.
HOSSU, GH.   Construcțiile social-culturale realizate de regimul democrat-popular,
   Bucarest, 1954.
Hotărîri ale Consiliului de Miniștri, Bucarest, 1955.
Hotărîrea Comitetului Central al Partidului Muncitoresc Român și a Consiliului
   de Miniștri al Republicii Populare Române cu privire la desființarea sistemu-
   lui de aprovizionare pe bază de cartele și rații, Bucarest, 1954.

Hotărîrea Consiliului de Miniștri al R.P.R. și a Comitetului Central al P.M.R. cu privire la îmbunătățirea sistemului de contractare și achiziție de animale, păsări și produse animale, Bucarest, 1955.

Indreptar cu privire la controlul financiar în industrie și în întreprinderile comunale și de gospodărie locativă. Bucarest, 1955.

Indrumări pentru constituirea cooperativelor de credit si economie și începutul funcționării lor, Deva, 1955.

Indrumătorul pentru Invățământul Mediu, Bucarest, 1948.

Industria grea—baza dezvoltării întregii economii naționale. Bucarest, 1955.

Industria locală de stat și cooperatia meșteșugărească în R.P.R. Bucarest, 1955.

Istoria Evului Mediu, Bucarest, 1952.

Istoria Literaturii Romîne pentru clasa a VIII-a, Bucarest, 1955.

Istoria R.P.R., Bucarest, 1952.

Literatura Romînă. Culegere de texte pentru clasa a IX-a, Vol. 2, Bucarest, 1955.

Lupta partidului pentru dezvoltarea producției agricole și pentru transformarea socialistă a agriculturii, Bucarest, 1954.

Lupta P.M.R. pentru înfăptuirea revoluției culturale în țara noastră. Datoria utemiștilor de a-și însuși știința, tehnica și cultura înaintată, Bucarest, 1955.

MIHAI, ION. Amortizarea fondurilor fixe si reparațiile capitale în R.P.R., Bucarest, 1955.

MIHALE, AUREL. Facem și noi o întovărășire, Bucarest, 1955.

NESTOR, GEORGE. Manual de calculații economice agricole, Bucarest, 1954.

Normarea tehnică a muncii și salarizarea în industria socialistă, Bucarest, 1955.

ONIGA, N. ȘI APOSTOLATU I. Munca politică pentru crearea de noi întovărășiri agricole, Bucarest, 1955.

Organizarea conducerii industriei socialiste în R.P.R., Bucarest, 1955.

Pământul aparține celor ce-l muncesc. 10 ani dela înfăptuirea reformei agrare, Bucarest, 1955.

Partidul Muncitoresc Român—partid de tip nou—forța conducătoare și îndrumătoare a poporului nostru, Bucarest, 1955.

POPOVICI, V. V. Organizarea muncii în gospodăriile agricole colective. Bucarest, 1954.

Prețul de cost al producției industriale și căile reducerii lui, Bucarest, 1955.

Probleme ale Literaturei Noi în R.P.R., Bucarest, 1952.

Procès du groupe de traitres à la solde de la clique fasciste de Tito, Bucarest, 1950.

RAITA, GH. și MARIN, A. Pentru continua creștere a productivității muncii, Bucarest, 1955.

Regulamentul organizației de pionieri din Republica Populară Română. Bucarest, 1955.

Rezolvarea problemei naționale în Republica Populară Romînă de către Partidul Muncitoresc Romîn, Bucarest, 1955.

Sarcinile organizațiilor de bază U.T.M. din S.M.T. și G.A.S. în efectuarea la timp și în bune condițiuni a lucrărilor agricole. Dezvoltarea atitudinii socialiste față de muncă și de bunul obștesc—sarcina centrală a acestor organizații, Bucarest, 1955.

Sistemul financiar al Republicei Populare Romîne, Bucarest, 1955.

Statutul model al gospodăriei agricole colective, Bucarest, 1954.

TISMANEANU, L. Legătura cu masele—izvorul forței și invincibilității partidului, Bucarest, 1955.

TAVANET, P. V. Judecata și felurile ei, Bucarest, 1955.

Trial of the former National Peasant Party Leaders Maniu, Mihalache, Penescu, Niculescu-Buzesti and others, Bucarest, 1947.

b) Periodicals and newspapers

Buletinul Oficial, Daily. (March, 1949-January, 1952)

Colecție de Legi, Hotărîri și Decizii ale Consiliului de Miniștri. Monthly, (January, 1948-   )

Contemporanul. Weekly (October, 1946-   )

Gazeta Invătământului. Weekly (March, 1949-   )

Gazeta Literară. Weekly (March, 1954-   )

Informația Bucureștiului. Daily. (August, 1953-   )

Justiția Nouă. Published at irregular intervals (1954-   )

Monitorul Oficial. Daily. Name changed to Buletinul Oficial in March, 1949.

România Liberă. Daily. (September, 1944-   )

Scânteia. Daily. (September, 1944-   )

(The above publications are available at the Library of Congress. Washington, D. C.)

index

Date Due

PRINTED IN U. S. A.